Praise fo

"Unappreciated during her lifetime for her wit and her camp, and with her own bisexuality effaced yet kept as an open secret, Susann is well worth rediscovery today, especially through the lenses of queer theory and mass culture studies, as Feil convincingly proves. This is a learned and substantive book."

—Steven Cohan, author of *Incongruous Entertainment: Camp, Cultural Value, and the MGM Musical* and *Hollywood by Hollywood: The Backstudio Picture and the Mystique of Making Movies*

"In *Fearless Vulgarity*, Ken Feil embarks on a detailed, fascinating, and illuminating study of Jacqueline Susann's work. Eschewing camp as a reception practice, Feil argues that Susann encoded her work with camp sensibilities such that it could be read by her legions of readers as camp. *Fearless Vulgarity* is a vital contribution to studies of stardom, production, media, and camp."

—Alfred L. Martin Jr., author of *The Generic Closet: Black Gayness and the Black-Cast Sitcom*

"Proving that 'once is not enough,' Ken Feil applies established expertise on genre and camp humor to the case of roman á clef author Jacqueline Susann. In *Fearless Vulgarity: Jacqueline Susann's Queer Comedy and Camp Authorship*, Feil positions Susann's relentless self-promotion and 'bad manners' novels about celebrity and sexual identity as central to the circulation of camp, feminism, and queer politics in popular culture since the 1960s. A critical work as fearless as its subject!"

—Mary Desjardins, author of *Recycled Stars: Female Film Stardom in the Age of Television and Video*

"Camp is lit within, and Jacqueline Susann, a writer stigmatized as trans by Truman Capote, will flicker further thanks to *Fearless Vulgarity*—and Feil's unparalleled knack for the mass love machine."

—Quinlan Miller, author of *Camp TV: Trans Gender Queer Sitcom History*

Fearless Vulgarity

Contemporary Approaches to Film and Media Series

A complete listing of the books in this series can
be found online at wsupress.wayne.edu.

GENERAL EDITOR

Barry Keith Grant
Brock University

Fearless Vulgarity

Jacqueline Susann's Queer Comedy and Camp Authorship

Ken Feil

W

WAYNE STATE UNIVERSITY PRESS
DETROIT

Library of Congress Control Number: 2022945062

ISBN 978-0-8143-4604-4 (paperback)
ISBN 978-0-8143-4603-7 (hardback)
ISBN 978-0-8143-4605-1 (e-book)

Wayne State University Press rests on Waawiyaataanong, also referred to as
Detroit, the ancestral and contemporary homeland of the Three Fires Confederacy.
These sovereign lands were granted by the Ojibwe, Odawa, Potawatomi, and
Wyandot Nations, in 1807, through the Treaty of Detroit. Wayne State University
Press affirms Indigenous sovereignty and honors all tribes with a connection to
Detroit. With our Native neighbors, the press works to advance educational equity
and promote a better future for the earth and all people.

Wayne State University Press
Leonard N. Simons Building
4809 Woodward Avenue
Detroit, Michigan 48201-1309

Visit us online at wsupress.wayne.edu.

In memory of

Barbara Seaman
(1935–2008),

Patty Duke
(1946–2016), and

Edward Feil Sr.
(1924–2021)

Dedicated to

Naomi and Ed Feil
(who put a little *Valley of the Dolls* into
The Inner World of Aphasia) and

Michael S. Keane
(my doll and love machine,
twenty-five years are not enough)

Contents

Acknowledgments

Numerous kind people played a part in creating this book, and to express the depth of gratitude that I feel, the penultimate scene in the movie *Valley of the Dolls* comes to mind: Neely O'Hara (Patty Duke) taking stock of her fabulously tattered life by uttering the names of the main characters of the film, sometimes screaming them, each a sort of revelation. In my transposed version, sacrificing the abjection but not the running mascara, let me belt appreciation to everyone who contributed to this years-long project.

First, Annie Martin and Marie Sweetman at Wayne State University Press have been nothing but inspiring and supportive influences—as Jacqueline Susann would have said, "my people"—who got the enormity of "the other Jackie" and whose insight and determination made this project prevail even when I was doubtful.

I am very fortunate to have had such consistent support from staff, faculty, and administrators at Emerson College in Boston, beginning with Robert Sabal, dean of the School of the Arts, and chairs of Visual and Media Arts, Brooke Knight and Cristina Kotz Cornejo. The wisdom and kindness imparted by Sofie Belenky, Bob Colby, Maria Corrigan, Jim Delaney, Peter Flynn, Hassan Ildari, Cher Krause Knight, Eva Jansen Morales, John Albert Mosely, Maria San Filippo, Michael Selig, Rae Shaw, Shujen Wang, Sarah Zaidan, and so many more folks proved stabilizing in the past few years of this project, especially when work and life could be, like the streets of New York in *Valley of the Dolls*, "an angry concrete animal."

So much of this project took shape through conference participation, at Console-ing Passions and especially the Society for Cinema and Media Studies (SCMS). Thanks go to Michael DeAngelis, Mary

Desjardins, Jon Lewis, David Lugowski, Al Martin, Ernest Mathijs, Linda Mizejewski, Tamao Nakahara, Gary Needham, Diane Negra, Wyatt Phillips, Isabel Pinedo, Janet Staiger, Polly Thompson, and Tanya Zuk for your cherished collegiality as well as generous, insightful feedback on emerging ideas and chapters. Dating back to the early 1990s (before the "M" was added to SCS), I will always be grateful to Matthew Tinkcom for screening sequences from *Valley of the Dolls* and demonstrating the film's historical significance and fabulous absurdity. Jeffrey Hitt at the University of Texas at Austin also deserves credit along these lines, for an answering machine message of Jennifer's phone conversation with her mother that left an impression for decades.

Many kind folks contributed richly to this book's research: the generous and warm staff of the Emerson Iwasaki Library, namely, Tina Dent, Bob Fleming, Cheryl McGrath, Sydney Orason, Cate Schneiderman, Maureen Tripp, and many more folks; Alonso Duralde, who graciously gave time for an interview and a copy of the *Valley of the Dolls* miniseries; Brendan Lucas and Jessica Broutt at OutFest, in addition to Susan Tenenbaum at the UCLA Media Lab and Leslie Singer, who helped me track down and screen *Taking Back the Dolls*; Robert Silman at Tambar, playwright Paul Minx, and actress Debora Weston, who amiably furnished a copy of Mr. Minx's play *See How Beautiful I Am*, a video excerpt of Ms. Weston's performance, production stills, and permissions to implement these; John Epperson, for his kind permission to use photos; Louis Wyman at the US Copyright office; Sara M. Hutcheon and staff at the Radcliffe Institute's Schlesinger Library (the Barbara Seaman Collection); Charlotte V. I. Priddle, Marvin J. Taylor, and Nicholas Joseph Martin at the Fales Library, NYU (Ira Silverberg Collection); John Calhoun at the Billy Rose Theatre Collection (John Epperson Collection), NYPL; Tim Wilson at the San Francisco History Center (SFPL); Mark Ekman, Martin Gostanian, Teresa Sadowska, and many more folks at the Paley Center for Media in New York and Beverly Hills; Annie Watanabe-Rocco, Molly Haigh, and the staff at the Charles E. Young Research Library (UCLA); Louise Hilton at the Margaret Herrick Library; Kathleen and the staff at Hotel Wolcott; Christian Kneedler at Dan Tana's; and dear friends Bonnie Datt and Jonathan Goldman, whose conversations about Jackie Susann amid New York research inspired both fun and invention.

A plethora of anonymous readers greatly affected this book in numerous stages, beginning with Palgrave Macmillan (for Pamela Demory and Chris Pullen's collection *Queer Love*) and then at *Celebrity Studies* (for Mary Desjardins and Michael DeAngelis's special issue on star biography). I remain indebted to the anonymous readers enlisted at WSUP, whose feedback—honest and rigorous, wise and meticulous—inspired me to write a better book than I thought was possible.

Finally, my undying, adoring, loving thanks go to Michael Keane, whose backbreaking assistance with archival research, brilliant artwork, good humor, and unending support made this project possible. I must also commemorate Stuckie and Stoughtie, our feline Josephines, now romping in the Valley of the Paws after leaving their pawprints (and teeth marks) on every step of this project.

Introduction

On December 29, 1969, American network television's top-rated program *Rowan & Martin's Laugh-In* paid a musical salute to "the sexy sixties." Led by guest star Nancy Sinatra, ensemble members of the comedy-variety show Goldie Hawn and Ruth Buzzi let loose a stream of references to cultural works both popular and controversial for their sexually provocative content. The miniskirt-clad trio referenced *Hair* and *Oh, Calcutta!*, New York shows notorious for nudity and orgy scenes, in addition to the popular Swedish art film *I Am Curious (Yellow)* (1967) and current causes célèbres of popular fiction, *Portnoy's Complaint* and *Myra Breckinridge*. The lyrics deviated from citing titillating titles, though, when Buzzi encapsulated the Dionysian decade in a name: "the Jackie Susann sixties!" Jacqueline "Jackie" Susann had skyrocketed to international celebrity in 1966 through the fabulously successful, notoriously "dirty" bestseller *Valley of the Dolls*, followed by the blockbusters *The Love Machine* (1969) and *Once Is Not Enough* (1973). Prior to her publishing juggernaut, Susann had penned *Every Night, Josephine!*, a popular comic memoir about Susann's career as a TV performer, her show business marriage to publicist and TV producer Irving Mansfield, and the upbringing of their poodle, the titular Josephine. Her last work *Dolores*, scribed as Susann struggled with breast cancer, initially appeared in *Ladies' Home Journal* in 1974 and was published posthumously in hardback in 1976.

The first author to achieve three number-one bestsellers in a row, Susann's strategy of relentless self-promotion made her an omnipresent mass culture personality, and as Susann's publicist Abby Hirsch testified in 1976, "the Jacqueline Susann novel together with its hardsell campaign became a 1960's pop phenomenon" (1976, 6). Wrapped in glitzy haute couture, often Pucci, flashing an enigmatic smile, and topped by a glossy black hairpiece, Susann's brand combined glitzy pizzazz with what *Time* magazine reviewer Jay Cocks (1975) called "fearless vulgarity." Typically uttering outrageous opinions, often in the face of hostile cultural watch-dogs, Susann had "a thick skin and the reflexes of a mongoose," according to Hirsch, packaged in the image of an "old-time Broadway glamour girl, often resembling those fantasy-star cardboard cut-outs in front of movie theaters" (1976, 6). Susann had indeed been a "Broadway glamour girl," filling incidental roles since the 1930s when she ventured to New York from her native Philadelphia, taking notes along the way on women in show business, their celebrity and backstage lives.

Jacqueline Susann's scandalous opuses fit into the "sub-category of popularly-written *romans à clef*," as Nora Ephron explained to *New York Times* readers in 1969 (Ephron 1969, 12). The "novel with a key," this disreputable literary genre enticed readers with gossipy stories about historical figures and events, names changed and details rearranged.[1] The roman à clef achieved renewed popularity in the 1960s thorough an outpouring of popular fiction about celebrities and show business authored by Harold Robbins, Alvah Bessie, Morton Cooper, and Henry Sutton (a.k.a. David Slavitt), among others. Susann stood out from her male counterparts, though, by implicating herself in her stories: alluding to details made public knowledge; and divulging secrets, carefully encrypted, about her bisexuality and nonmonogamous marriage, being Jewish, having an autistic son, managing addictions, and living with breast cancer. Susann delivered an amalgam of clues in her omnipresent promotional campaigns and her novels, which swerved imperceptibly from gossip to confession and boldly embraced taboo topics such as female sexual desire, nonmonogamy, homosexuality, transsexuality, abortion, drug use, and mental illness. As biographer Barbara Seaman averred in 1996, precipitating a revival of interest in Susann and her work, "what her books lacked in literary value and graceful prose they made up in raw reader appeal. Critics sneered, yet those books entertained millions, and continue to do so today. Dismissed when they were published as 'fairy tales for adults,' they now seem in some respects prophetic. Jackie explored the emerging themes of the 1960s—the drug culture, the acceptance of homosexuality, the changing aspirations of women" (Seaman 1996c, 459).[2]

Jacqueline Susann's trilogy of transgression—*Valley of the Dolls*, *The Love Machine*, and *Once Is Not Enough*—positioned her in the forefront of the "permissive" and profitable sexual revolution, and as I argue,

Publicist Abby Hirsch testified that "the Jacqueline Susann novel together with its hardsell campaign became a 1960's pop phenomenon," and popularized the image of Susann as an "old-time Broadway glamour girl . . . resembling those fantasy-star cardboard cut-outs in front of movie theaters."

humor provides the "key" to comprehending Susann's literary maneu-vers, the impact of her promotional performances, and the various cul-tural events of her reception, in addition to the manner in which her life has been dramatized in biopics and bioplays. The "Jackie Susann Sixties," to begin with, brimmed with a comedic, "camp" response to sexuality, both a mechanism for managing the shocks and manufacturing them. In this dynamic, Jacqueline Susann and her popular creations served as ridiculous objects for readers and critics as well as subversive agents, during Susann's heyday from the late 1960s to the late 1970s, and in the decades to follow, for an expanding feminist and queer fan community who continue to value the novel *Valley of the Dolls* and venerate the 1967 film adaptation as the "cornerstone of camp cinema," in the words of gay film critic Alonso Duralde (2005, 217). Since the author's brief revival in the late 1990s, a handful of feminist and queer literary critics have reclaimed *Valley of the Dolls*, but within consistent limits. In addition to overlooking Susann's other writing, no one has yet to identify and exam-ine her force and uniqueness as a funny woman, despite an abundance of evidence. A veteran of performing and writing comedy for stage, radio, and television, Susann's books demonstrate her perception of humor's power, and so do the author's appearances promoting them. The per-sistence of Susann's funny reception, moreover, has defined biographical portrayals of her and illuminates varied, often conflicting social and cul-tural positions about gender, sexuality, and aesthetic value.

Susann generates humor through a writing formula that I call *sleazy realism*, which combines with the components of the roman à clef to sub-vert any number of popular genres, particularly Hollywood, and the star biographies associated with them. Sleazy realism undermines the sani-tized wholesomeness of Hollywood heterosexual romance with stories of celebrity scandal featuring women in show business, their journeys of gender impropriety, and the patriarchal intrusions as well as heteronor-mative dysfunction that beset them. Susann famously drew her signa-ture motifs from personal experience and insider knowledge of star secrets culled from years in show business. Staging in her gossipy novels shocking disclosures of celebrity misbehavior and the machinations of the culture industry, Susann devised variations on what theater historian David L. Hirst terms the "comedy of bad manners" (1979, 60–61). In this case, the culture clashes Susann spun involved characters based on real celebrities whose spectacular outbursts of vulgarity clashed with their "official" personas and the popular genres they were famous for, all hewn according to narrow, normative constructions of identity and reality.

Susann orchestrates numerous potent bursts of "bad manners comedy" in *Valley of the Dolls*, for instance, through encounters among protagonists who vividly conjure up actual women stars: the proper, blond protagonist Anne Welles, who Susann hinted she based on Grace Kelly and herself, both of them famous Philadelphians; Neely O'Hara, the showbiz wunderkind with peerless pipes, drawn from Judy Garland; and the brassy Broadway veteran Helen Lawson, inspired by Ethel Merman.[3] Sleazy realism and manners comedy run rampant in Neely and Helen's blithe use of obscenities, frank discussion of sexuality, and garish tastes, particularly in their encounters with the demure, white-bread Anne. And through the devices of the roman à clef, Susann enables readers to imagine overhearing the popular voices of Garland and Merman proclaiming oaths and sharing earthy confidences that shatter their wholesome star images simultaneous to scandalizing Anne/Kelly. When Neely gleefully announces that her fiancé Mel "went down on me," Anne conveys outright shock and disgust, pushing Neely to reply, "Now Anne, stop being so prissy." Revisiting the topic later in their conversation, Neely speculates, "I bet coming the other way won't be half as great," leading to the punchline, "Anne choked with embarrassment" (Susann 1997c, 110). Susann understood the depths of pleasure tapped by enabling readers to "overhear" Judy Garland discuss cunnilingus, or listen to Ethel Merman commenting during a rehearsal that her musical number is "a piece of shit!" (Susann 1997c, 77). The climactic, iconic powder room confrontation between Neely and Helen shatters any pretenses of bourgeois propriety, when Helen/Merman taunts Neely/Garland about her failed marriage to Ted Casablanca, an obvious stand-in for Garland's ex-spouse Vincent Minnelli. "Christ, you couldn't even hold your faggot," goads Helen, "not even with twins as a bargaining point"; after Helen queries, "Hey—are they faggots too," Neely rips off Helen's wig and flushes it down the toilet (Susann 1997c, 299–300). Such shocking revelations of celebrity unseemliness might appear homophobic, but the characters also trumpet matter-of-fact acceptance of homosexuality with similar vocabulary, such as Neely/Garland's observation that Dickie, a "fag" dancer in her show, "is having a ball with all those chorus boys—it's like smorgasbord"

(Susann 1997c, 71). The comedy of bad manners abounds through the intrusion of sleazy realism, springing from the incongruous fit between a star's chaste public persona and the private shenanigans Susann portrays, compounded by the echoes of Hollywood tropes. Helen's voice, for instance, rings with explicit banter evoking the hardened dames of pulp fiction and film noir rather than musical comedy clichés, while Neely delivers her sexual confessions and observations about gay men with the innocent, cheerful spunk of a musical comedy ingenue.

Susann's promotional appearances composed another comedy of bad manners, this one populated with critics horrified by an upstart female vulgarian barging into the male literary firmament. When Susann appeared on *The David Frost Show* (Syndicated, 1969–1972) to plug *The Love Machine* in 1969, for one infamous example, highbrow critic John Simon locked horns with Susann in a battle of wits and shtick.[4] With Simon seated in the audience, Susann perched on the dais next to Frost, the critic hurled his condemnation at the author like a heckler slinging putrid tomatoes, calling Susann's bestseller "trash," "rotten stew" that made him "puke," and cynically written to "get rich quick, get famous quick." Susann inaugurated her counterattack, not by defending the novel's literary merits but with a stream of Nazi jokes. Like a seasoned vaudevillian, Susann kidded, "What did you say your name was? Goebbels, Göring or Simon? . . . You know you sound like a stormtrooper." And affecting a cartoon-German accent, Susann reposted, as if under interrogation, "And how dare l write *zese* books, right?" Replying to Simon's question about "what kind of story" she wrote, Susann first dove to her knees, a move that recalled the musicals she appeared in as well as the 1946 comedy *Between the Covers*, in which she played a stripper modeled on Gypsy Rose Lee: "Too sophisticated a story for you to understand," Susann blurts, "because it's '*dirty!*'" (*David Frost*, July 16, 1969). Usurping male privilege professionally and sexually, Susann and her characters cracked one-liners, at turns humorous or menacing and, for a woman, "dirty." Radiating what her journalist friend Carol Bjorkman called "female awareness and vitality" as she defended herself against Simon's elitist, male gaze, Susann took the stage through her humorous choreography and literalized her "fallen" status: first by kneeling, and then by identifying with "dirty," the imputed failure of artistry and femininity.

Like a seasoned vaudevillian, Jackie Susann deflects critic John Simon's slurs with schtick on *The David Frost Show*, July 16, 1969.

Nearly three decades later in 1997, after the author's premature death in 1974 and fall into cult obscurity, the *New York Times*'s Doreen Carvajal heralded a "new Jacqueline Susann Zeitgeist" (1997, 24). The Susann revival extolled the novelist's kitsch, paraded the queer, feminist meanings of her work, and characterized Susann's coup of cultural and gender norms as a hilarious victory over repressive tastefulness. This newly minted star persona accompanied new editions of Susann's novels as well as a reprint of Seaman's tell-all biography *Lovely Me: The Life of Jacqueline Susann*, first published in 1987. The laughter of Susann's queer, feminist champions, once underground, now rang out, through participatory screenings of *Valley of the Dolls* hosted by drag queens and often attended by the film's cast, the American Movie Classics documentary *Hollywood Backstories: Valley of the Dolls* (Farinola, 2001), and eventually, a DVD edition of the film containing special features laden with praise by gay and feminist fans. Biographical depictions of Susann correspondingly reimagined her life and personality through varying degrees of camp comedy fueled by feminist, queer awareness: the made-for-TV movie *Scandalous Me* (McDonald, 1998), the feature film *Isn't She Great* (Bergman, 2000), and the theatrical comedies *See How Beautiful I Am* (Paul Minx, 2001) and *Paper Doll* (Mark Hampton and Barbara J. Zitwer, 2001).

Although Susann's comeback never quite reached the peaks that the culture industry had planned for it, the novel *Valley of the Dolls* remains in print and the film version endures as a camp-cult favorite that, whenever popular culture references it, serves as a comedic reference point as well as an immediate signal of camp taste. "Sparkle, Neely, sparkle" rings out on *RuPaul's Drag Race* (Logo TV, 2009–16; VH1, 2017–present) as an affirmation and a directive and solidifies the place of *Valley of the Dolls* in North American drag history. Lee Daniels introduced his Fox TV drama *Star* (Fox, 2016–19) during the fiftieth anniversary of the novel as an unofficial adaptation of *Valley of the Dolls*. Implanting blatant visual and verbal quotations from *Valley*, including "Sparkle, Neely, sparkle," Daniels trumpeted to mainstream viewers the film's significance for Black gay and genderqueer fans. That same year, Laverne Cox recorded the audio book for *Valley of the Dolls* accompanied by publicity interviews in which the actress and trans icon commented on the novel and film's camp history as well as expressed interest in acting in a film or TV adaptation. Most recently, Steven Canals's television drama *Pose* (FX, 2018–21) featured Billy Porter as Pray Tell, elder figure of New York drag balls and living with HIV, watching *Valley of the Dolls* on television and educating his younger lover about gay camp icon Judy Garland (August 6, 2019). These contemporary citations signify the persisting meaningfulness of

Valley of the Dolls and the camp comedy surrounding it at the same time as interrupting the implicitly white, gay, male proprietorship of canonized camp such as *Valley of the Dolls*.

Feminist and queer literary critics consistently underestimate Susann, most evidently by focusing on *Valley of the Dolls* to the exception of her other novels, and more subtly, by not acknowledging the author's comedic agency or her feminist and queer legacy. Taking Susann seriously as an author accompanies an underlying trepidation to acknowledge her pervasive funniness.[5] Imelda Whelehan, for example, vitally commends *Valley of the Dolls* in the evolution of the "feminist bestseller" as a novel that attracted women readers, otherwise expecting gossipy stories modeled on actual celebrity scandals, to tales of "women [who] suffered just because they were women" (Whelehan 2005, 40). Whelehan also unearths elements of Susann's humor, albeit, without identifying them as such or exploring their importance as feminist comedy. Whelehan detects, for instance, the subversion of classical Hollywood romance with "sleaze" in *Valley of the Dolls*, provides anecdotes about Susann's "garish" fashions and show business brassiness, identifies Susann's manipulation of the "fictionalized exposé of Hollywood" combined with the form of "confessional," and moreover, notes the critical reception of *Valley* reverberating with charges of "vulgarity" by the champions of "great literature" (Whelehan 2005, 2, 36–38, 40, 41). Claire Knowles furthermore asserts that *Valley of the Dolls* exposes "female suffering at the hands of men and patriarchal institutions" as well as alludes to Susann's innovation of the show business roman à clef by locating "the logic of gossip and scandal" that drives the novel (Knowles 2016, 63–64, 77). Through the parodic treatment of stars and popular genres, however, Susann consistently and oftentimes shockingly introduces humor that coincides with women fighting back as well as suffering, and in both cases, humor that discombobulates gender performance. And by darting from outwardly directed gossip to self-reflexive confession, Susann's identity begins to merge with the unruliness of her characters in the eyes of critics and fans, as violations of cultural decorum and feminine propriety.

Ken Gelder assembles a feminist defense of *Valley of the Dolls* as an "anti-romance celebrity novel" abundant with camp vulgarity, but this only serves as a platform to appreciate the feminist camp agency of Susann's literary successor, Jackie Collins (Gelder 2004, 133–34). Susann's camp novel remains in this case an unselfconscious reflection of her alienated role as author and "brand," "the toll that the entertainment industry takes" on women (Gelder 2004, 132–33). Gelder's displacement of agency from Susann to Collins implicitly coincides with the distinction between intentional camp and naive camp and results from two missteps in the terrain of camp history and theory. First, Gelder implies Susann's ignorance of camp, and therefore her lack of camp agency, when mistakenly observing that the publication of *Valley of the Dolls* in 1966 coincided with the debut of Susan Sontag's "Notes on 'Camp,'" the catalyst for popularizing camp sensibility in mass culture (Sontag 1966, 133). Susann's own use of the term "camp" demonstrates the author's awareness of the concept, though, dropped once in *Valley of the Dolls* and discussed twice among characters in *The Love Machine* to denote a sensibility of "failed seriousness" and "so-bad-it's-good" (Susann 1997c, 393; Susann 1997a, 439, 484; Sontag 287).[6] Camp entered into mass culture parlance, moreover, after *Partisan Review* first published Sontag's essay in late 1964. As Fabio Cleto explains, Sontag's "Notes" rapidly inspired numerous popular newspaper and magazine critics to pen pieces, and Cleto includes *Valley of the Dolls* in an extensive genealogy of camp criticism and literature (Cleto 1999, 302–4, 464).

Implementing feminist and queer theory, Michael Trask situates Susann's *Valley of the Dolls* and the work of a number of other postwar women writers in the context of "the alibi-ridden, impression-managed social space of a pre-Stonewall world," in which camp sensibility "absorbs not only gay men but all comers in the logic of a closet culture" (Trask 2013, 14). While highlighting the signs of intentional camp wit in such literary heavyweights as Patricia Highsmith, Mary McCarthy, and Susan Sontag—their "camp archness," "bitchy putdowns," and "camp slyness"—Trask positions Susann as unintentional camp, someone with "the unlucky tendency to run afoul of gender ascription, presenting her femininity in ways liable to call the wrong kind of attention to its owner" (13–14, 181, 186). Trask unquestioningly denies the author's agency by situating Susann as an accidental drag queen: "outed" in 1969 by Truman Capote, who mocked her as a closeted drag queen on the *Tonight Show*, and by *Harper's* magazine, which revived the imagery of drag performance to depict the author's perverse artificiality (Trask 2013, 182). This gossipy exposure of Susann's gender performance,

Trask contends, coincides with the experiences of Susann's characters in *Valley* and reflects women entrapped by the patriarchal gazes defining successful female performance (181–85; 186–89). Susann and *Valley of the Dolls* therefore materialize the patriarchal "limits" reigning in women's advancement and empowerment, the conflict between female success and performing for the male gaze, made all the more anxious by postwar-era suspicions of professional women as queer, nymphomaniacal, or frigid (181–82, 190). Without disputing Trask's feminist critique of Susann's detractors, their camp ferocity and misogyny, or contesting the camp "closet culture" operating in both Susann's reception and her *Valley of the Dolls*, Trask nevertheless redoubles the negation of Susann's agency by inhabiting the position of so many elite critics who configured Susann as a naively camp figure, as an author who unwittingly recorded her own experiences, and as a woman who failed at pulling off her femininity. A wealth of evidence complicates Trask's conclusions, from the queer narratives of *The Love Machine* and *Once Is Not Enough* to numerous signs of Susann's deliberate camp humor and the author's queer reception.

Fearless Vulgarity: Jacqueline Susann's Queer Comedy and Camp Authorship dissects the humor that traverses Susann's variety of performances, her publishing trifecta and other writing, as well as her book promotion in print, on the radio, and on TV. Susann's sleazy realism produced a comedy of bad manners bound up with a complex of closets, all the result of maneuvering the ambiguously fictional roman à clef to gossip and confess. Susann's deployment of the camp closet emerges with special power in *The Love Machine*, whose narrative is structured around closet plotlines about sexual secrets. Susann's protagonist, network television executive Robin Stone, remains an enigma whose bold display of heterosexual promiscuity masks childhood sexual trauma and renders him "a machine who passes for a man" (1997a, 9). Susann furthermore surrounds Robin with queer and camp characters, such as Sergio, Robin's gay confidant, and Sergio's lover Alfie, both movie stars concealing their relationship due to the "morals clause" in their studio contracts. Ethel Evans, a brassy, promiscuous network publicist, becomes the "beard" and soulmate to Sergio and Alfie, and they become her platonic saviors from a loveless marriage to a loathsome TV comedy star. Susann also implements a passing plotline indicative of the racialized closet and redolent of *Imitation of Life*, involving the blond model Amanda and her African American foster mother Rose. Susann likewise fuels *Once Is Not Enough* with literal and figurative closet plotlines: married millionaire socialite Dee Granger and her years-long affair with the mysterious, elusive and bisexual Hollywood star Karla, clearly modeled after Greta Garbo; Karla's clandestinely cared-for daughter, intellectually disabled and born out of wedlock; and Tom Colt, the Norman Mailer–inspired author whose ostentatious man's-man bravado compensates for the closely guarded secret of diminutive endowment and impotence.

Focusing on *Valley of the Dolls* to the exclusion of Susann's subsequent bestsellers further nullifies the queer-feminist alliances represented in her novels and promotional performances, notwithstanding a recurrent allegiance to closet logic, along with Susann's fan followings. If, as Trask opines, "there are no drag queens in *Valley of the Dolls*, strictly speaking," there are several in *The Love Machine*—in addition to transsexuals and closet cases—which appeared in bookstores just a little more than a month before the Stonewall riots. That *Once Is Not Enough* provides Susann's most extensive, sympathetic, and appreciative representation of lesbian characters also goes overlooked in all these scholarly discussions, as does the book's historical significance to lesbian readers and its publication the same year that the American Psychiatric Association eliminated homosexuality as a psychological disorder. Susann claimed that the bisexual Karla ranked as her fans' favorite character, and both *The Love Machine* and *Once Is Not Enough* prompted journalists and readers to note Susann's support of homosexuality.

Queer and feminist laughter also greeted Susann. Where the normative ridicule of critics positioned the author as unintentional camp due to a "failure" to "pass" as both a literary force and a woman, queer journalists such as Carol Bjorkman, Rex Reed, Liz Smith, and John Alfred Avant generated adoring camp endorsements. They cited similar signs of cultural and gender failure as Susann's detractors, yet by identifying with Susann through a camp gaze, transformed her theatricality, sexual aggressiveness, and excess into forces of success, glamor, charm, and creativity. Their camp accounts of Susann, furthermore, present glimpses into the historical operation of camp sensibility and the entrenched role of the comedy of the closet, the revealing wit of suggestion and innuendo.

Overlooking the comedy of Jacqueline Susann, even more, belies the fact that Susann factored comedy into her authorial agency. As the novelist remarked in the 1967 promotional documentary *Jacqueline Susann and the Valley of the Dolls*, "I'm going to write the way I want to write. And I want to show I can go both sides of the street. I can write funny, and I can write serious, and I have this to say." Prior to her literary superstardom, Susann's acting career recurrently included performing "funny": in her first Broadway acting gig, Claire Booth Luce's *The Women* (1936); musicals such as the Eddie Cantor star vehicle *Banjo Eyes* (1941); and on TV, in *The Morey Amsterdam Show* (Seaman 1996c, 109–11, 201–3; Mansfield 1983, 71).[7] When Susann turned to writing, amid a dead-end acting career and personal turmoil, she wrote two theatrical comedies and a radio sitcom, all coauthored with her friend Bea Cole (Seaman 1996c, 109–11; Collins 2000; Mansfield 1983, 53–55, 68–69).

Their plays *The Temporary Mrs. Smith* (a.k.a. *Lovely Me*, 1946) and *Cock of the Walk* (1952) anticipated the comedy of gossip in Susann's novels with showbiz characters based on actual celebrities, redolent of the hit Broadway comedies *The Royal Family* (Ferber and Kaufman, 1927), a parody of the Barrymore acting dynasty, as well as *The Man Who Came to Dinner* (Kaufman and Hart, 1939) and its parodies of Alexander Woollcott, Noël Coward, Gertrude Lawrence, and Harpo Marx.[8] According to biographer Barbara Seaman, journalist Amy Fine Collins, and Susann's spouse Irving Mansfield, Susann and Cole based the titular *Mrs. Smith* on a fading actress Susann knew as a neighbor at the Navarro Hotel. *Cock of the Walk* took its basic story from Susann's clandestine affair with married comedian Eddie Cantor during the production of *Banjo Eyes*. In addition to satirical parodies of show business figures, their tastes and pretensions, descriptions of each play suggest how Susann and Cole infuse the comic character type of the screwball heroine with a sophisticated treatment of sexuality.[9]

Comedy also played a role when, after playwrighting failed, Susann returned to TV in 1955. As the spokesperson for Schiffli Lace alongside her poodle Josephine, "I'd write funny commercials and I'd have Josephine on with me. We'd do mother and dog collars, or mother and dog hats."[10] One of Susann's colleagues described these routines as "high camp before the days of Andy Warhol" (as told to Seaman 1996c, 242), and they led to Susann's first published book, *Every Night, Josephine!* (1963). A memoir

After cowriting two theatrical comedies and a radio sitcom with friend Bea Cole, Susann returned to TV. As the spokesperson for Schiffli Lace, alongside her poodle Josephine, their "funny" and "high camp" commercials inspired *Every Night, Josephine!* (1963).

about her beloved eponymous poodle, Susann devised a Runyonesque, showbiz-inflected comedy of manners orbiting around the urban, nocturnal, "kooky" Broadway lifestyle of Jackie the TV performer, her TV producer spouse Irving, and their sophisticated puppy, soon to be a TV star. Far from the suburban, WASP propriety of the American Kennel Club, Josephine cavorts among Susann's circles of girlfriends and glitterati in a screwball parody of domesticity. *Every Night, Josephine!* brimmed with implications of messy behavior, including casual references to canine homosexuality and human barbiturate use, but as a nonfiction memoir, required heavy self-censorship. Susann could abandon restraint in *Valley of the Dolls*, protected by the facade of fiction, and steer her sleazy realism from outrageous comedy to tragic melodrama and grim irony.

The roman à clef afforded Jacqueline Susann the principal tool in her creative arsenal and set the foundation for both her comedic appeal and polarized reception.[11] The genre hinged on revealing and concealing scandal in what Barbara Judson calls a "masquerade," a dance of open secrecy around numerous closet doors (Latham 2009, 56–58; Judson 2000, 158, 159–60). Sean Latham explains how this masquerade "could abruptly congeal in sometimes comic, sometimes tragic, and sometimes dangerous ways as historical fact," and amid the inception of "celebrity culture" in the late nineteenth century, "sold millions of copies to readers eager to savor its genuine comic appeal while also seeking out its latent, gossipy secrets" (Latham 2009, 18, 45). The "scandalous and infectious" genre furnished further opportunities for parodying and satirizing public figures under the duplicitous alibi of fiction (McCoy 2014, 128–33; Latham 2009, 12–13, 29, 53). The duplicity fundamental to the roman à clef corresponded with a "trashy" historical reputation that made it even funnier. The roman à clef first and foremost thwarts one of high art's cardinal rules by collapsing life with art, and to do so, implements the low genres of gossip and confession. Viewing the genre as just "gossip" or "merely recycling one's experience" consigned it to "the garbage bin of literary history," because it defied the separation of "art" from mundane, common, everyday life, or as Latham puts it, the "demand that fiction's autonomy be preserved from fact's crude intrusions" (Latham 2009, 4, 5, 9; Huyssen 1986, 7–8).

Besides the examples of scandalous, duplicitous star-gazing in *Valley of the Dolls*, masquerade and parody flourish in Susann's second best-selling showbiz saga *The Love Machine*, in which the author based the protagonist on former CBS president James Aubrey, a friend and mentor who embraced association with the novel. Susann's maverick network executive bounds from the boardroom to boudoir and the occasional orgy. He also cries "Mother" on orgasm with his lover Maggie, identifies with the androgynous woman heroine of the Broadway musical *Lady in the Dark*, cultivates close camaraderie with a gay man, makes love with a trans woman, and remains subject to gossipy speculation about his "AC/DC" and "queersville" sexual proclivities. Susann also devised a central character based on her late friend, early champion, and rumored lover, *Women's Wear Daily* writer and former fashion model Carol Bjorkman, to whom Susann dedicated the book. Garland returns in a cameo, too, here an aging musical star attempting a TV comeback whose tryst with Robin inspires one of the book's melodramatic and comedic highpoints, Maggie's attempt to burn down Robin's love nest. In *Once Is Not Enough*, besides the detailed and pointed reconstructions of bisexual Garbo and impotent Mailer, Susann morphed Gloria Steinem and Helen Gurley Brown into the swinging, wisecracking women's magazine editor Linda Riggs who, among other things, saves her sex partners' semen to use as face cream.

Susann indeed emphasized the *fun* of speculating about the novelist's celebrity models and parodies when promoting her work, a strategy that captured the irresistible inducement for readers to dig for the "*clef*," the key to the identities of the characters. As Winzola McLendon confirmed in a 1966 *Washington Post* piece, "Show business has a new guessing game. It's 'Who are the main characters in Jacqueline Susann's just-out novel, Valley of the Dolls?'" (McLendon 1966, B5). Similar "guessing games" transpired in the promotion and reception of *The Love Machine* and *Once Is Not Enough* as well as the posthumously published *Dolores* (1976), all of which drew on what Latham calls, with respect to Oscar Wilde's *The Picture of Dorian Gray*, the "tantalizing anonymity" regarding celebrity figures and their scandalous activities, the "confusion of fact and fiction" entangled in "a confusing configuration of secrecy and disclosure" (Latham 2009, 48, 53).

Susann coaxed readers further to speculate about the degree to which her own experiences informed the transgressive antics. Regarding *Valley of the Dolls*, the actress manqué admitted to modeling characters on herself and, besides the usual celebrity roundup, dear friends and fellow show people Bea Cole, Joyce Matthews, and Carole Landis. Landis had also been Jackie's lover, and if Susann left that last detail unmentioned in promotional statements, she dramatized their affair in *Valley of the Dolls* with such sexual and romantic fervor that it might have left queer readers both wondering and smiling with knowing recognition. Susann's friendship with Garbo was well known by the time *Once Is Not Enough* went into print, with headlines such as "Jackie Susann Huddling with Garbo" making it possible to imagine Susann as the rich, married woman having the affair with the Garbo-inspired Karla character (Haber 1971, F12). Susann launched the same book with a resoundingly perverse autobiographical tease that routinely surfaced in publicity. Having dedicated *Once Is Not Enough* to "Robert Susann, my father, who would understand," Susann fabricates a young, female protagonist driven by a powerful and much discussed "Electra Complex" for her overbearingly virile dad. As critic and ally Rex Reed humorously pondered at the time, entirely in the spirit of the guessing game, "Raised eyebrows?" (1974, 248).

Equipped with a flamboyant, irreverent persona and a literary genre that veered between comedy and tragedy in its duplicitous realism along with prompting a playful guessing game, Jacqueline Susann joined an abundance of commercial culture during the sexual revolution perceived as funny through camp sensibility. Camp's iconoclastic attitude toward bourgeois taste codes and penchant for theatricality and ambiguously queer connotations offered an almost self-evident means to appreciate such literary scandals of the late 1960s as *Myra Breckinridge*, *Candy*, and *The Magic Christian* as well as popular personalities such as Phyllis Diller, Mae West, Tiny Tim, and Truman Capote.[12] Susann and her gossipy, over-the-top potboilers would appear to have been fabulous fellow travelers. Similar to her eventual rival Capote, Susann embraced the mantle of bawdy raconteur when promoting her sexy showbiz exposés, capable of one-liners aimed at herself and badinage about other celebrities. Amid promoting *The Love Machine*, for instance, Susann commented on author Philip Roth, whose competing bestseller *Portnoy's Complaint* boasted a comic hero obsessed with masturbation: "He's a great writer but I wouldn't want to shake hands with him" (Kelly 1969, A20).

The perception of Susann as a naive camp figure unaware of her own vulgarity nevertheless persisted, in league with the construction of her as an artless recorder of her seamy showbiz exploits. *Laugh-In*'s

"Sexy Sixties" number alluded to this construction and numerous critics or literati explicated it, most infamously and influentially Capote. "All of our writers going pornographic / Have really been / Stopping traffic," belted the *Laugh-In* ensemble, who offered as evidence "the *Portnoy* sixties! Jackie Susann sixties! *Myra Breckinridge* sixties!" (December 29, 1969). Susann emerges here as an avatar for all her "pornographic" work, synonymous with two *fictional* figureheads of the sexual revolution, Portnoy and Myra, all three of them uproarious for their outrageousness and excess. Collapsing Susann with her scandalous novels discredited her as someone who wrote confessional gossip drawn from her perverse experiences, novels devoid of the requisite distance or imagination to legitimate her authorship. By this logic, Susann simply *was* a funny character, or as Susan Sontag had put it just a few years earlier: "The pure examples of Camp are unintentional; they are dead serious. . . . Genuine Camp . . . does not mean to be funny" (1966, 282).

Gloria Steinem first labeled Susann as unintentional camp in a *New York Herald Tribune* review of *Valley of the Dolls*, but Capote launched Susann's loudest moment of camp reception in summer 1969 on the *Tonight Show*. Employing camp vocabulary and sensibility but not the word "camp," Capote's admitted "bitchiness" reigned when knocking Susann's fashion and hair as "sleazy" and her writing as "rotten." Capote also alluded to the gay, trans, and drag queen characters in Susann's recently published, chart-busting *The Love Machine* when he sarcastically recommended casting her as Myra Breckinridge in the upcoming film adaptation, characterized Susann as a "born transvestite," and most enduringly, called her "a truckdriver in drag" (Anon. 1969c, B23; Nizer 1980, 27–31). When threatened the following day with a libel suit for his quips, Capote added, "She doesn't have a sense of humor, either" (Anon. 1969c, B23). Capote contrived an interpretive frame containing Susann within camp ridicule that, rationalized by restrictive taste codes and gender norms, collapsed the novelist with her characters and voided any trace of self-conscious wit or authorial credibility. Numerous cultural custodians followed Capote's example. Susann's "vulgar," sexualized, formulaic, and confessional romans à clef, as well as her acting the role of "Jacqueline Susann," provided the evidence of unwitting comedy and reasons for mocking Susann's work as "junk" by way of ridiculing her gender performance.

Reducing Susann to naive camp coincided with an understanding of the roman à clef as a low cultural, feminine genre mired in gossip, yet this also concealed the genre's subversive functions for women and queer authors. Lauren McCoy's account of the nineteenth-century roman à clef substantiates how the "blending of the novel and gossip" led to controversy over content, confusion over form, and suspicions about readerships (McCoy 2014, 131). Such diminished cultural status, however, also camouflaged the "discounted voices" dishing the dirt: dissident women novelists such as Lady Caroline Lamb, McCoy's subject, whose 1816 roman à clef *Glenarvon* disputed the "more established narratives" of lofty male figures such as Lord Byron (McCoy 2014, 129, 148). Latham points to later examples of romans à clef that revealed the "illicit pleasures" of disenfranchised queer milieus, unveiled by Oscar Wilde, Radclyff Hall, and Compton Mackenzie (Latham 2009, 7–8, 11). Susann indeed asserted the discounted voices of show business women in *Valley of the Dolls*, *The Love Machine*, and *Once Is Not Enough*, or as Knowles observes of *Valley*, the "deployment of the logic of gossip and scandal to make visible the sufferings of women in the patriarchal culture of the post-war United States" (Knowles 2016, 63–64).

Alongside the melodrama of female suffering, however, Susann maneuvered the machinery of the roman à clef to concoct comedies of women's bad manners. As gossip converged with confessional in Susann's novels, and when Susann invited her readers to play that notorious "guessing game," the delights of her romps around truth and fiction multiplied in proportion to the author's transgressions of "tasteful" gender and genre norms. For most critics, Susann's showbiz stories signified as "social melodramas," as genre historian John Cawelti called them, or in Hirsch's description, "part soap opera, part B-film": morality lessons in which heroines paid for their trespasses against chastity, monogamy, and marriage (Hirsch 1976, 6; Cawelti 1991, 44–47). What appeared as simplistic cautionary tales and voyeuristic gossip to some readers, however, elicited laughter and smiles from others, the opportunity for ironic identification with stars whose formerly sanitized stories were iconoclastically rewritten, and the chance to view Hollywood tropes irreverently revised, now bursting with female and queer misbehavior and revelatory in their litany of men's mendacity and manipulations.

Jacqueline Susann's Comedic Cocktail: Gossip and the Comedy of Bad Manners

Jacqueline Susann staged a comedy of manners in her tales of women in show business, and she participated in one as a celebrity author. By testing codes related to taste, sex, and propriety, in her literary work and promotional performances, Susann invoked typical features of the comedy of manners, a theatrical genre that, as dissected by Hirst, explores "the way people behave, the manners they employ in a social context," driven by class-conscious preoccupations with "sex and money . . . marriage, adultery and divorce" (Hirst 1979, 1, 116). Hirst additionally alludes to similar mechanisms as the roman à clef when commenting on how the comedy of manners historically functioned for closeted gay playwrights. As "the province of homosexual writers," Oscar Wilde, Noël Coward, and Joe Orton "translated their life-style [*sic*] into their plays," and by wielding style, triumphed as "arbiter[s] of good taste" and "powerful critic[s] of conventional values" (Hirst 1979, 3–4). The queer commandeering of manners comedy especially jibes with what Hirst distinguishes as the comedy of *bad* manners (60). Hirst links this variation to Coward's plays *Hay Fever, Private Lives*, and *Design for Living*, in which "Bohemian," ill-mannered behavior by "selfish," "overbearing," "artistic" characters clashes with "mundane behavior," outsmarts convention, and finally wins the audience over to the protagonists' deviant "design for living" (60–61, 64–66). The comedy of bad manners furnished a closet through which the assertion of unconventional tastes and behaviors normally deemed vulgar and immoral could be recoded and legitimized as stylish.[13] Columnist Rex Reed tellingly likened Susann to "somebody in a Noel Coward play" in a feature article promoting *Once Is Not Enough*, a characteristic that frames his subsequent intimations of Susann's misbehavior as a Cowardian comedy of bad manners, including the blatantly personal theme of paternal incest in her novel and her polyamorous marriage to Irving Mansfield (Reed 1974, 245).

The gossipy, confessional dimension of the roman à clef only magnified Susann's manners comedy. As Patricia Meyer Spacks argues with respect to Richard Brinsley Sheridan's *The School for Scandal* (1777), a comedy of manners about acid-tongued aristocrats consumed by sexual desire, class pretension, and tittle-tattle, "Gossip's purpose . . . is to generate comedy, finding in observed trivia material from which to manufacture entertainment" (Spacks 1985, 136). Contemporary comedies such as Kaufman and Hart's *The Man Who Came to Dinner* (1939) also flood their banter with gossip, made funnier when a character based on Noël Coward recounts the sexual affairs of another character implied to be Gertrude Lawrence. The same can be said of Coward's own *Design for Living*, in which the gossipy repartee coincides with a narrative about a ménage à trois involving a woman and two men, one of whom is a writer originally played on Broadway by Coward.[14]

Spacks specifies the comedic dimension of gossip alongside its normative, repressive role as "*meta*-sex, a mode of control, a way of containing contradictory feelings" through "extravagant" and "witty" language that "may yet partake of the spirit of play, the delight in human possibility that inform comedy" (Spacks 1985, 136–37, 144). Although Sheridan satirizes the manners of his gossipers as hypocritical and misbehaved, their "verbal extravagance" nonetheless nourishes spectatorial pleasure and provides a performative replacement for physical sexual activity (Spacks 1985, 144–46). Henri Bergson also alludes to this "artificial" and "refined" form of comedic compensation in manners comedy, building on his concept of comedic "transposition": "To express in reputable language some disreputable idea, to take some scandalous situation, some low-class calling or disgraceful behaviour, and describe them in terms of the utmost '*respectability*,' is generally comic" (Bergson 1928, 123, 125–26). This "transposition upwards from below" only works when "it gives us a glimpse of an entire system of transposition accepted in certain social circles and reveals, as it were, a moral organisation of immorality" (125–26). Bergson concludes, similar to Spacks, that this comically ornate inversion of virtue and goodness leaves "the moral value of things" undisturbed, that "*transposing the natural expression of an idea into another key*" generated corrective laughter, the kind that Spacks traces in Sheridan's satire (Bergson 1928, 123). As Bergson puts it early on in his essay, "laughter 'corrects men's manners.' It makes us at once endeavour to appear what we ought to be, what some day we shall perhaps end in being" (17).

Coward's comedies of *bad* manners present a challenge, however, to "the moral value of things" as well as the normative functions of manners comedies such as *School for Scandal*: the possibility for wit to "correct" the constrictions of "good" manners, and to propose, by extension, an alternative moral vision that was funny because of the possibilities it unearthed, not for being incorrect. As Coward established himself an arbiter of both alternative taste and morality, the gossip unfurled in his plays was also confessional and self-directed, most famously and daringly displayed in *Design for Living*. Anticipating what Penny Farfan calls Coward's "sexual modernism," Hirst observes that "wit was not an affectation [for Coward] but the natural expression of a complete lifestyle," in addition to serving as an implement of critique (Hirst 1979, 4, 65; Farfan 2005, 680). Farfan similarly explores how Coward's comedies challenge conventional sexual morality at the same time as providing a protective closet. In plays that could "'pass' as light entertainment within the theatrical mainstream," Coward could spurn "neat binaries of desire in favour of a triangular relationship involving two men and a woman" as well as trumpet "the impossibility of marriage" and "the vain attempt to conform to sexual convention" (Hirst 1979, 4, 60, 65; Farfan 2005, 678, 680, 683).

Susann likewise enlisted the comedy of bad manners to accomplish a variation on the "transposition upwards from below," both in her novels and public persona, but quite differently from Coward, she rejected the aristocratic flourishes of literary modernism through the style of sleazy realism. Susann persistently transposed taste codes intersecting with gender codes by, as she sums up the character Ethel Evans in *The Love Machine*, "playing a man's game, with a man's rules" (Susann 1997a, 204). Susann's overarching comedic gesture, the transposition of values and norms related to gender and taste, transforms the "natural expression" of female propriety as well as aesthetic refinement. Susann's transpositions further extended to blending "feminine" and "masculine" voices and genres, involving a pastiche of styles and vulgar intrusions into gendered genre conventions that coincided with confounding and mocking normative, bourgeois notions of "good taste." Recall Anne and Neely's conversations about sex from *Valley of the Dolls* and the powder room altercation between Neely and Helen. Ethel Evans in *The Love Machine* and Linda Riggs in *Once Is Not Enough* likewise appropriate masculine privilege through stylized, vulgar wisecracking that flaunts both their sexual and career aspirations. Like Neely and Helen, Ethel and Linda's agile command of profanity serves as a compensation, not for any immorality as Bergson might have it, but to counterbalance what they and all women are subjected to: the regime of femininity and the surveillance of the male gaze.

In the same gesture as challenging the conventions of gender, Susann persistently, brazenly, and hilariously transposes *outré* taste into "good taste," bolstered by the soaring popularity of her novels. As Susann informed *Harper's* magazine in 1969, "When I saw people reading *Valley*, I would think, they have very good taste" (Davidson 1969, 71). Comments like that galled critics, appalled by the virtual coup of the literary establishment that Susann committed: turning celebrity gossip and personal confession full of foul-talking women and their sexual shenanigans into an unprecedented three consecutive number one bestsellers. Charged by her stunning popularity and armed with her "dirty" yet glamorous sensibility, Susann shamelessly flaunted the appeal of her self-labeled "storytelling" over high modernist authors she called "boring," with a hit list including Henry James, Vladimir Nabokov, and James Joyce, along with their champions, "cerebral," "double-domed" literary critics, as she liked to brand them (Meehan 1967, 22; Howard 1966, 69; Anon. 1969b; Davidson 1969, 70; Kelly 1969, A20). Alongside boldly rejecting literary modernism, Susann brazenly inscribed her place in postmodernity. Just a few months before *Laugh-In* jokingly proclaimed her the perverse patroness of the decade, Susann opined to the *Boston Globe*, "Will Jacqueline Susann be remembered in 50 or 100 years? Yeh, I think I will, I think I will! I think I'll be 'The voice of the 60's'!" (Kelly 1969, A23).

Susann's performance as subversive tastemaker and vulgar wisecracker flowered through the comedy of the closet. Ambiguity about the identities of her characters amplified the draw of Susann's novels, according to the comedy of bad manners in addition to the comedic scenarios of masquerade and mistaken identity as well as the devices of suggestion, innuendo, and double entendre. Susann indeed played off what Lynne Joyrich articulates as "the keen and artful presence of a certain absence in the texts—and the accompanying logic of undecidability, incongruity, and allusion—that seems most to mark them as somehow queer" (Joyrich 2001, 453). As the proctor for an elaborate guessing game regarding the real-world models for her characters that implicated her among the suspects, Susann was notoriously generous in feeding clues and frustratingly cagey when it came to pinpointing the truth. Numerous columnists at the time documented Susann denying connections between her novels and real people yet dropping hints that could only encourage readers to imagine the author, along with a host of her celebrity friends, adversaries, and acquaintances, engaging in the taboo horseplay of the novels' characters.[15] This open secrecy occasioned Susann's flamboyant wit, her "chutzpah" as *Women's Wear Daily* put it, an ironic, theatricalized female persona that particularly appealed to fashion writer Carol Bjorkman (Anon. 1969e, 5). Bjorkman celebrated Susann's closet comedy in the pages of *Women's Wear*, which in turn engendered the novelist's comic transpositions of taste and gender decorum, her dance between glamorous sophistication and sleazy vulgarity enlivened by associations with the characters and events in *Valley of the Dolls*. In this dynamic, Bjorkman proved a variation on the "knowing viewer" that Joyrich traces in the context of commercial television comedy's closet (Joyrich 2001, 453), here a *knowing interviewer* reveling in Susann's "artful presence of a certain absence," and gleefully welcomed by Susann to read as well as laugh between the lines.

Bjorkman inaugurated her most extensive *Women's Wear* piece about Susann with a playful encapsulation of the novelist's closet comedy, which in turn illuminated Susann's comedy of bad manners. Bjorkman begins, "Jacqueline Susann was hiding behind the cover of one of the hottest books going today—HER book—'Valley of the Dolls.'" Having established Susann's mischievous *style* of concealment, the telling scene of Susann using the cover of her roman à clef as a mask, Bjorkman quotes the novelist: "When I wrote my first book, 'Every Night, Josephine,' I received letters from dog lovers. When I wrote 'Valley' I thought: 'Now I will move in a literary circle with Norman Mailer, Mary McCarthy and Victor Lasky,' but I keep getting letters from junkies and they want to know which hotel I wrote about on 45th Street—or something" (Bjorkman 1966a, 8). Bjorkman launches her adoring piece by illustrating Susann's ironic self-awareness of her positioning, on the threshold of vulgar and glamorous femininity, by divulging that people perceived her, not among the literary giants, but as a connoisseur of sleazy Times Square landmarks. These ambiguous gestures altogether trumpet the transpositions of Susann's comedy of bad manners and style of sleazy realism, in addition to the closet of the roman à clef that enabled her to nourish this strategy. By extending the play of authenticity and fiction from her novels to her promotional performances, Susann

In Carol Bjorkman's *Women's Wear Daily* column, the journalist cheered Jacqueline Susann's comedy of bad manners, an ironic camp game with pretty and funny, tasteful and vulgar, closeted and out, as well as success and failure.

could revel in the hilarious obviousness of what remained unstated and only partially visible.

Bjorkman's adoring, humorous gaze complements Susann's, whose play at the closet door of vulgar, failed femininity inspired a range of pleasures and successful outcomes. Jack Halberstam's meditations on the "queer art of failure" speak to Susann's comedy of bad manners, which stages heteronormative failure through gossip manifested in spectacles of vulgarity as well as Bjorkman's expressed delight. Halberstam locates "the crucial link between failure and style" entrenched in "gender trouble, gender deviance, gender variance" (2011, 96), an equation that ties to Hirst's submission that the victory of "style" in the comedy of bad manners "is all-important . . . not merely a superficial manner of expression but a definition of behavior. The winners are always those with the most style" (Hirst 1979, 2). The victory of style, furthermore, supplants the priorities of bourgeois morality and heteronormativity, society's usual measures of failure and success, which explains "the repeated charge," Hirst points out, "that the comedy of manners is immoral and unpleasant. It is undoubtedly the most anti-romantic form of comedy, for in plays of this type the conventional moral standards are superseded by the criterion of taste, of what constitutes 'good' form" (Hirst 1979, 2). Transgressive deeds can triumph through "the way in which they are performed," but only by maintaining the closet, "the style with which they are concealed" (2). Transposing the failure of "conventional" taste and morality into the victory of style, the comedy of bad manners turns the failure to conform to heteronormative gender into a triumph of taste-making.

Amid a patriarchal minefield that offers women an impossible route to safe, functional femininity, manners comedy enabled Susann and co-conspirators such as Bjorkman to furtively explode sanctified gender ideals and make each other laugh in the process. Bjorkman—a close pal of Susann's, possible lover, and inspiration for Amanda in *The Love Machine*—immediately validates the novelist with a female gaze that, authenticated by *Women's Wear Daily*, transitions from homosocial to homoerotic in concert with their conspiratorial laughter.[16] Following the juicy insinuations of sleaze in the outrageous opening quotation, Bjorkman declares Susann's glamour, modernity, and desirability. "Jacqueline's vitality and female awareness charged through her modern apartment facing Central Park South," observes Bjorkman, who commences to survey the author's "good looking legs," "Mondrian black striped white jersey dress," and "dark brown eyes. . . . Every time Jacqueline shuts those dark brown eyes one of her books checks out—now it is about 112,000 in six weeks" (Bjorkman 1966a, 8). Bjorkman condenses praise for Susann's face, figure and fashion with admiration for her literary success, and correlates the novelist's theatrical eye flutters with the accelerating rate of her book sales. Bjorkman turns this image into a running gag that also involves Susann's guessing game: "Isn't it true a lot of people are comparing Neely to Garland? Jacqueline closed down those big brown eyes and I could see another 50,000 books checking out" (1966a, 8). Susann first dispels connections to herself and real celebrities, then drops names to Bjorkman of probable models for the characters in *Valley of the Dolls*, from Merman to Garland as well as her friend Joyce Matthews, finally imparting juicy tales about unnamed "monsters" of show business while professing her "love" for them and spotlighting their struggles. Susann emerges in Bjorkman's estimation as an avatar of "vitality and female awareness," as stylish and "modern," precisely due to her dance along the border of tastelessness and at the threshold of the closet. Bjorkman and other allies confirm Susann's perception of the "very good taste" of her readers with queered cultural criteria that communicate ironic recognition of the author's agency.

Susann effectively staked a queer space for readerly pleasure, protected by the closets of manners comedy and the roman à clef, in which gossip blurred with confession in stories of "nonconformity" and "nonreproductive life styles," morality tales that depicted the failure of "heteronormative common sense" and its constructions of "family, ethical conduct, and hope" (Halberstam 2011, 89). Journalist Sarah Davidson appears to perceive all of these queer signals of failure in her 1969 feature on Susann for *Harper's*, absent any of the identification that Bjorkman and other allies affirm: "Jackie is one of those women, like the late Judy Garland, Bette Davis, Edith Piaf, and critic Judith Crist, who are beloved by homosexuals. In Jackie's case, it is due not only to her strident personality but to the fact that she treats homosexuals with dignity in her books" (Davidson 1969, 66). Following this portrait of queer camaraderie, Davidson assesses a perverse agenda in Susann's novels, where "there are no children . . . no families living and growing up together. She creates a dream world of stardom, money, and power where personal ambition and lust are the only forces"; consequently, "Susann's characters experience no guilt about sex or anything that might be considered 'sin' in the Judeo-Christian tradition" (Davidson 1969, 69, 70). Susann's failure to conform to heteronormative common sense charges much critical vitriol, yet it also fuels the comedy of bad manners that Susann unspools, in particular, the transposition of taste and gender, by appropriating "masculine" vulgarity amid the masquerade of femininity.

Camp and Camping: Jacqueline Susann's Comedic Agency

Despite Susann's cues of camp awareness, from dialogue in *Valley of the Dolls* and *The Love Machine* to her flamboyant personality and reputation for attracting gay fans, critics routinely mocked the novelist as a cynical kitsch-producer and vulgar lowbrow barely capable of forming a sentence, let alone orchestrating a camp comedy of manners. Jonathan Baumbach of *The Nation* minced no words, for example, in his review titled "The Stupid Machine": "Despite her pretense to sophistication, Miss Susann is, in effect, a primitive" (Baumbach 1969, 188). Calling *The Love Machine* "a novel of manners without nuance," Baumbach notices "no discernible vision in the novel outside of popular culture's vision of itself" (190). *Time* magazine made a similar case for the novelist's bogus urbanity when alluding to Susann's sleazy realism, which "unwittingly gravitates toward a caricature of naturalism" and consists of "seminal spillage," "leaving nothing behind but a bad taste" (Anon. 1969b). Without redeeming Susann's agency or artistry, other critics perceived accidental humor, or what Sontag classifies as "naïve," "pure," "unintentional" camp (Sontag 1966, 282–83): the fabulous failure of an unabashedly commercial writer who ridiculously misunderstood her own taste as "good." Ephron affirmed Susann's distinction, for instance, after considering "all the sloppy imitators of Miss Susann's style": "Good kitschy writers are born, not made. And when Jacqueline Susann sits down at her typewriter on Central Park South, what spills out is first-rate kitsch" (Ephron 1969, 3). Sontag explains this perceptual distinction using one of *Valley of the Dolls'* blockbuster predecessors as an example: "Camp taste nourishes itself on the love that has gone into certain objects and personal styles. The absence of this love is the reason why such kitsch items as *Peyton Place* (the book) and the Tishman Building aren't Camp" (Sontag 1966, 292). As "naïve camp," Susann was "born" to create "kitsch" and radiated the "love" in her labor, her "failed seriousness," "passionate failure," and appreciation for "vulgarity," qualities of her novels that also collapsed with perceptions of her androgyny, her similarity to camp icons such as Bette Davis, and ties to gay readers.[17] Whether deeming Susann charming or cynical, these critical positions functioned to disregard her as a "machine" of consumerist reproduction, devoid of agency and unconsciously vulgar, attitudes that echoed elitist, implicitly misogynistic perceptions of Susann's genre. In this mindset, Susann's writing—a sensationalistic mishmash of Hollywood and pulp genre tropes, gossip columns, and personal confession—merely reflected her "feminine" priorities as a consumer of mass culture mired in the mundane details of everyday life.

As restrictive taste codes collapse with the normative terms of gender, ridiculing Susann as a "passionate failure" generated from a variation of the male gaze that Linda Mizejewski identifies as "the dynamic of pretty versus funny," a patriarchal running gag that deems "failed" femininity "funny" and implicates all women as the potential butt (Mizejewski 2014, 3). Mizejewski helps elucidate the rationale for demeaning Susann as well as appreciating her, in both cases as the gossipy author of romans à clef whose sleazy realism centralized failed femininity in comedies of bad manners. Perusing the work of several contemporary women comedians, Mizejewski reveals how they variously transform the tyranny of "pretty versus funny" into "a transgressive comedy grounded in the female body—its looks, its race and sexuality, and its relationships to ideal versions of femininity. In this strand of comedy, 'pretty' is the topic and target, the ideal that is exposed as funny" (5). Mizejewski's model for "transgressive" women's comedy likewise compares to what Pamela Robertson Wojcik identifies as "feminist camp," "a female form of aestheticism, related to masquerade and rooted in burlesque, that articulates and subverts the 'image- and culture-making processes' to which women have been given access" (Wojcik 1996, 9). Susann's supporters such as Bjorkman, Reed, and Smith discerned a dazzling performer whose comedy of bad manners comprised an ironic camp game with pretty and funny, tasteful and vulgar, closeted and out as well as success and failure. Promoting a style that nourishes queer pleasure and foments community corresponds with Halberstam's idea that "Failure loves company" (2011, 120–21). Camping also loves company, as Sontag relates about people "singled out by the Camp vision" and who "respond to their audiences," all who happen to be women in Sontag's ensuing list: "Mae West, Bea Lillie, La Lupe, Tallulah Bankhead in *Lifeboat*, Bette Davis in *All About Eve*" (Sontag 1966, 283). Susann fomented queer company with her fans by exposing "pretty" as "funny," such as when she dished to Bjorkman about her seedy reputation. Bjorkman, whom Ephron lauded for penning a "column that left its readers charmed and chuckling," crystallized the rapprochements of pretty and funny in her own work and Susann's, to reconcile female success and failure in the process of establishing Susann's agency (Ephron 2007, 71).

Susann's camp nevertheless also involved what Wojcik calls "camp's guilty pleasure, its two-sidedness," the mixed messages and closet logic that coexist with camp's "oppositional modes of performance and reception" (Wojcik 1996, 9, 17). Jane Howard vividly portrayed this comedic dynamic of camp duplicity in her 1966 *Life* magazine story on Susann and the phenomenon of *Valley of the Dolls*: "Critics who maintain that the activities and argot of show business folk might have been chronicled more tastefully and less anatomically in *Valley* get the back of Jackie's hand. It is not, she insists, a dirty book—'I'm just writing about what I know. If I knew about a farm in Maine I'd write about that; what I know about happens to be show business. It so happens that people in show business don't talk like schoolteachers in Philadelphia'" (Howard 1966, 77). Susann's ironic assertions bridge the comedy of bad manners directly to the mockery of "pretty," crowned by the fact that Susann *was* from Philadelphia, her mother Rose a "retired schoolteacher" (71). The adventurous showbiz "single girl" who fled Philadelphia pursuing her Broadway dreams, however, alternated with Susann's pose as the housewife-turned-TV-personality, winner of Best Dressed Actress on Television from 1953 to 1957 (71). Howard finally solidifies Susann's "two-sidedness" at the conclusion of the article. After quoting Susann's defense of homosexuality and a wife's right to "cheat," in addition to criticizing the gendered "double standard" that brands promiscuous women "weirdoes," Howard closes with a romantic photo of Jackie kissing her husband on the beach: "'Irving,' she says, 'is divine'" (Howard 1966, 77, 78). Susann's slippage between rebellious "weirdo" and conventional wife in her publicity appearances mimicked the duplicity of her novels, seemingly generic, moralistic social melodramas on the surface that, from a queer view, imploded through their parade of subversive perspectives. Susann's play with pretty/funny and success/failure likewise urges the comic collision of incongruous social and cultural contexts that correspond to her ambiguous masquerade of femininity: "dirty," urban Broadway and Hollywood versus purportedly proper Philadelphia and rural Maine; sexual revolutionary versus devoted wife and fashion plate.

Journeying with *Jacqueline Susann*

Valley of the Dolls bursts with sensational salaciousness. This feature appeared to many critics as the author's device both for attracting prurient readers and driving a morality tale cautioning women to keep in their place. Sleazy realism exceeds the services of social melodrama, though, as chapter 1 explores, through the queer comedy of bad manners that Jacqueline Susann produces. Susann's project reveals the influences of

Hollywood movies, popular women's literature, lesbian pulp novels, and her own prior comedic writing, as well as illustrating the author's innovations of the roman à clef. Susann's first book, *Every Night, Josephine!* (1963), exhibits the author's fondness for manners comedy and sick humor, founded in the perspective of a female veteran of showbiz. Rona Jaffe's novel *The Best of Everything* (1958) also proves a vital predecessor to *Valley*, an ambiguously confessional novel whose plotline linked "single girl" adventures with scandal and gossip. In *Valley of the Dolls*, Susann cultivates Jaffe's single girl subjectivity; magnifies the gossip, confession, and scandal; and expands the spaces for the single girl's sexuality that Helen Gurley Brown ambivalently concedes in the 1962 lifestyle manual *Sex and the Single Girl*: to be a "playboy" as well as bisexual. Susann further subverts the pronounced male gaze that Harold Robbins enlisted in his best-selling show-business roman à clef *The Carpetbaggers* (1961) by confusing the boundary between outwardly directed, voyeuristic, punishing gossip and self-directed, reflexive, forgiving confessional. Such ambivalence and vacillation yield the multilayered portrayals of Neely O'Hara and Helen Lawson, "monstrous" divas humanized by Susann's identification with them and the comedic agency with which Susann endows them.

Susann's sleazy realism dismantles the star personas inspiring her characters and barges into any number of Hollywood genre tropes with shocking hilarity, melodrama, and tragicomedy. Sleazy realism persistently and ironically disputes heterosexual romance and marriage, especially personified in the novel's ironic, dispiriting conclusion—Anne Welles downing dolls to maintain the fantasy of her "beautiful" marriage—and the plotline of character Jennifer North. Bisexual and erotically knowing, a celebrity of the scandal sheets turned showgirl and art movie star, Jennifer's sexual agency evokes both the "gold digger" and innocently sexual character types from Hollywood sex comedies, in addition to the melodramatic fallen woman and its variations in art cinema and lesbian pulp fiction. Ironic to the end, though, Jennifer inscribes her witty sensibility into her suicide notes. The chapter concludes by exploring the conspicuous negation of both comedy and queer themes in the sanitized film adaptation of *Valley of the Dolls*, a dynamic that correlates with the film's camp reception as well as feeds the perception of Susann as unintentional camp.

Jacqueline Susann fuels *The Love Machine*, the subject of chapter 2, with a sleazy realism shaped by queer irony: heterosexual romance with a happy ending—the only one in Susann's novels—driven by the comedy of the closet. Susann inhabited an ironic position, the product of numerous closets and productive of subversive authorship: hiding her bisexuality and polyamorous marriage in plain sight as well as her Jewishness, and working within a culture industry that enforced such furtiveness.[18] *The Love Machine* stands out among all of Susann's novels for the relative success of heterosexual romance plotlines, but these happy endings rely, ironically, on their intersection with a gay closet plotline. Queer causality yields hetero happy endings, and at the same time exposes how the closet operates for all of the characters. Susann flagged her awareness of Black readers and encoded her sense of Jewish otherness in the same novel through a racialized closet plotline with obvious ties to *Imitation of Life* (Sirk, 1959). The tragic outcome of the racial closet, however, correlates with the plotline's marginalization in the overall novel. Deprived of the comedic pleasures accorded the queered closet plotlines as well as their upbeat conclusions, the racialized closet of *The Love Machine* reinstates the norm of whiteness rather than challenging it. The chapter closes by analyzing the movie adaptation of *The Love Machine* (Haley, 1971) and its reception. The film produces a different kind of queer irony than the novel, in which Susann furnishes the opportunity for queer identification as well as the pleasures of a happy ending. The film's irony, by contrast, emerges in its failure to convey a moralistic critique of the sexual revolution, and in the film's camp reception, which revolves around "hip homophobia" (borrowing Andrew Sarris's expression) and ridicule of Susann and her novel.

Chapter 3 explores how the concatenation of taste and gender norms turned Susann and her gossipy novels into camp, a quality that critics routinely declared in the form of gossip meant to exert laughter. Susann and her work embodied for numerous cultural custodians feminized mass culture as a vulgar menace, only redeemable and controllable through mockery. The secrets Susann's books and interviews insinuated, in particular the portrayals of gays and gender nonconformity in *The Love Machine*, provided cultural ammunition to devalue both her writing and gender performance as "camp," "pop," and following Capote's kidding, "drag." Although some critics objectified Susann as naive camp or cynical kitsch, others instead unearthed the novelist's camp subjectivity, her agency as wit, parodist, and performer. Susann also cultivated the perception of this agency by making fun out of her work and persona in television comedy appearances and, coming full circle, by enlisting her romans à clef to parody her critics. In *Once Is Not Enough*, for instance, Susann's travesties of Capote, Gloria Steinem, and Norman Mailer produce a protofeminist parody of gender constructs and taste as well as communicate appreciation for single women, but they also reveal Susann's ambivalence toward the women's movement along with her homophobia and deep investment in the logic, ethics, and taste codes of the closet.

Gossip and camp adorned and fueled the Jackie cult of the 1980s and the Susann revival of the late 1990s, the subject of chapter 4. Susann had long since passed away and her novels aged into out-of-print, cult collectibles, despite the publications of Irving Mansfield's 1983 memoir *Life with Jackie* and Barbara Seaman's 1987 biography *Lovely Me: The Life of Jacqueline Susann*. During the era of Reagan-Bush backlash, in the context of a burgeoning queer politics, AIDS activism, and outing, the equation of artistic failure with heteronormative failure served as the overt terms for Susann's resurrection, the conception of Jackie as "drag queen" finally empowering and exalting her. John Epperson, better known as Lypsinka, gloried in Susann and *Valley of the Dolls* for East Village audiences. For the backstage parody musical *Ballet of the Dolls*, Epperson played the Anne Welles character in 1985 at the Pyramid Club, portrayed Susann for the 1988 revival at La MaMa, and, as Lypsinka, led a 1987 "Tribute to the World of Jacqueline Susann" at the Pyramid.[19] AIDS activists Liz Tracey and Sydney Pokorny parlayed low-tech aesthetics toward transgressive taste-making in their self-labeled "dyke" zine *Dead Jackie Susann Quarterly* (1992–96), which received several mentions in the *New York Times*. And amid the peak of the New Queer Cinema movement, Leslie Singer's video short *Taking Back the Dolls* (1994) circulated queer inflections of Susann and *Valley of the Dolls* throughout the film festival circuit. Seaman fomented this wave of affection in her 1987 Susann biography, reissued in 1996: painstakingly researched, abundantly gossipy, and abounding with alternately hilarious, tragic, and outrageous accounts of Susann's theatrical personality, androgyny, Jewish background, bisexuality and open marriage as well as struggles with addiction, breast cancer, and her son Guy's autism. For the Grove Press 1997 editions of Susann's trifecta of bestsellers, editor in chief Ira Silverberg concocted a marketing campaign that revolved around *Valley of the Dolls* and provided a gay camp key for all readers to appreciate the author and her most famous work.

As renewed interest in Jacqueline Susann passed from low-tech subculture to mainstream, the commercialized camp discourse foment- ing the Susann revival largely squeezed out the taste-making efforts of Susann's "dyke" fans. The book promotion campaign, defined in large part by the visibility of Susann's white gay male fans, featured male drag queens as avatars for Susann and centralized the film *Valley of the Dolls*. Besides the dearth of lesbian voices hailing Susann's comeback, this strategy largely sidelined lesbian fan pleasures, considering that the movie version of *Valley* excised the novel's lesbian plotline, and taking into account that *Once Is Not Enough*, Susann's most elaborate lesbian love story, barely had a presence in the promotional campaign. Regard- less of the lesbian content in her work, Susann's lesbian fans, and the biographical gossip about Susann's infatuation with Ethel Merman and passionate affair with Carole Landis, the Susann revival consistently underplayed the author's lesbian stories, readers, and bisexual backstory.

Inspired by the 1990s revival, dramatizations of Jacqueline Susann's life appeared first on cable television, then in theater and film, the focus of chapter 5. Every version of Susann's life employs a variety of approaches to hone in on Susann's reflexive camp persona, her perfor- mance as a "woman" and literary figure. All four star biographies must also grapple with the challenges posed by Susann, a "bad" subject for the typically normative star biography, from her association with low culture to her "failed" female body fallen by disease and sullied by scandalous misbehavior. The USA network's *Scandalous Me: The Jacqueline Susann Story* (McDonald, December 9, 1998), a labor of love from producer-star Michele Lee and adapted from Seaman's biography by Michele Gallery, imbues serious scenes and made-for-TV narrative norms with camp irony and queer significance. The Universal Studios biopic *Isn't She Great* (2000), starring Bette Midler and Nathan Lane with a screenplay by Paul Rudnick, fashions a slickly sanitized comic gloss on talentless Jackie's rise to fabulous celebrity. Playwright Paul Minx's one-woman tragicomedy *See How Beautiful I Am* (2001) presents an outrageously bawdy, often ago- nizing confession from Jackie on her last night alive, acting out everyone in her life from Ethel Merman to Johnny Carson and God, as well as herself. The play *Paper Doll* (2001) by Mark Hampton and Barbara J. Zitwer concentrates on Jackie's final years and her charming tasteless-ness, swinging back and forth in time to extol her flamboyant personality and reveal her unconventional relationship with Irving Mansfield. *Isn't She Great* and *Paper Doll* cushion the cruel ironies of sleazy realism with pop shine. Fashioning Jackie as an updated Auntie Mame in a Runyon-esque comedy of manners, both bios cleanse Susann's queer vulgarity and bisexuality by relegating them to comedic innuendo as well as ease the anguish underlying Susann's masquerade as healthy in the face of impending death from breast cancer. *Scandalous Me* and *See How Beau-tiful I Am*, on the other hand, each incorporates camp and sleazy realism to tease out the deep contradictions, significance, and corresponding pleasures of Jacqueline Susann's life and work.

The conclusion of *Fearless Vulgarity* engages two applications of the "Susann sensibility" that challenge the normative, commercialized con-struction of Susann and her work since the 1990s revival, defined by white gay male fan history. Carrie Fisher obliquely claims Susann's *Valley* as her inspiration for *Postcards from the Edge* (Nichols, 1990); Fisher's adaptation of her roman à clef features a drug-addicted celebrity protag-onist named Suzanne Vale, a pun on Susann and *Valley*, whose repartee includes a reference to the film *Valley of the Dolls* and whose mother Doris evokes Debbie Reynolds, Fisher's mother. Fisher's made-for-TV movie *These Old Broads* (ABC, February 12, 2001) appropriates Susann's strategies and camp tropes for feminist camp and, building on *Postcards*, revises the camp figure of the aging diva. Fisher thrives in the contexts of *bad* manners comedy as well as the roman à clef, and in *Broads* scores laughs through a narrative about elder Hollywood divas playing versions of themselves: Debbie Reynolds, Fisher's mother; Elizabeth Taylor, her godmother and mother's former romantic rival; and her mother's friend Shirley MacLaine, who had played a fictionalized version of Debbie Reynolds in *Postcards from the Edge*. As the fourth "old broad," Joan Col-lins compounds the camp by resuscitating her persona as Alexis on the 1980s TV drama *Dynasty*. Reviving imagery from *Valley of the Dolls* such as the notorious brawl between Neely O'Hara and Helen Lawson, Fisher also flags her awareness of the film's gay following by staging a grand musical number in a gay dance club meant to reconcile one of the stars with her estranged, recently outed son (Fisher's stand-in for herself, an adult child of a celebrity).

Amid celebrations for the fiftieth anniversary of *Valley of the Dolls*, Lee Daniels announced that his drama series *Star* (Fox, 2016–19) grew out of the producer-director's affection for *Valley of the Dolls*. Daniels's presence in the conversation commemorating *Valley's* first half century proved a vital disruption of the whiteness reflected among the voices celebrating Susann and her novel, and more generally, canonized gay male camp culture. Introducing a hitherto hidden reception history, *Valley of the Dolls* resonates for Daniels in the history of musical girl-groups such as The Supremes, Destiny's Child, and TLC in addition to an array of camp works including *Dreamgirls*, *Paris Is Burning*, *Sweet Charity*, and *Female Trouble*. Daniels also demonstrates a renewed sense of political urgency for camp and, in particular, the camp value of *Valley of the Dolls* and its tropes. *Star* unfolds the dramas of aspiring girl group performers Star Davis (Jude Demorest), Star's half sister Simone Davis Rivera (Brittany O'Grady), Star's friend Alexandra Crane Jones (Ryan Destiny), and their manager Carlotta Brown (Queen Latifah), a music business veteran now running an Atlanta hair salon with her trans daughter Cotton (Amiyah Scott) and gender-nonconforming stylist Miss Bruce (Miss Lawrence). Quoting famous lines from *Valley* such as "Sparkle, Neely, Sparkle" and dialogue from the Helen/Neely confrontation scene, and replicating the iconic publicity shot for the film *Valley of the Dolls*, Daniels also infuses plotlines with Black Lives Matter and the movement for trans and nonbinary inclusion, in addition to exploring poverty, religion, and drug abuse. Daniels's camp references to *Valley of the Dolls* on *Star* confer bursts of both parodic escapism and tragicomic irony simultaneous to redefining the camp meanings, functions, and appeal of *Valley of the Dolls*.

1

Sleazy Realism and the Single Girl

Valley of the Dolls, the Roman à Clef,
and the Comedy of Bad Manners

Resuscitating and innovating the roman à clef proved a creatively fruitful, commercially perceptive choice by Jacqueline Susann. To delight readers and spur sales of *Valley of the Dolls*, Susann promised a page-by-page guessing game whose revelations of scandal mingled the voyeuristic gossip of a showbiz insider with the self-reflexive confessional of a participant. The author presented her fiction narrative as the disguise readers sought to see through. Susann also steered an emotional roller-coaster of a story assembled from diverse genre influences, from Hollywood comedy to melodrama, film noir, and backstage musical in addition to lesbian pulp fiction, art cinema, memoir, star biography, and cultural history. Susann's sleazy realism became her signature and turned genres inside out through the way the author combined them as well as dosed them with gossip and confession. Abrupt and intrusive, sleazy realism disrupted the norms of narrative unity, along with the decorum of literature and the typical heterosexual romance narrative.[1]

The roman à clef provided Susann with a crucial device for creating *Valley of the Dolls* as well as promoting it, the element that incited Susann's guessing game, framed her sleazy realism, and set the stage for a comedy of bad manners about celebrity misbehavior and literary merit. Susann's 1963 memoir *Every Night, Josephine!*, about her showbiz lifestyle with TV producer husband Irving Mansfield and their titular poodle, anticipated some of these strategies by fashioning an outright comedy of manners with a show business setting, but sleazy realism emerges only by suggestion, inhibited by the transparency of memoir. When Susann's girlfriend Last-One Hershkovitz blames Jackie's nocturnal, showbiz lifestyle for "ruining" Josephine, Last-One reasons, "You're an actress and statistics prove most actresses are a little crazy" (Susann 2004, 162). In the roman à clef, beneath the cover of "conditional fictionality" (Latham 2009, 58), Susann could now immerse herself in the "crazy" of both her life and her friends in addition to the showbiz legends whose paths she had crossed. The roman à clef offered an enabling veil of fiction, and, combined with the comedy of bad manners, also equipped Susann with "a set of oppositional tools," as Jack Halberstam terms it (2011, 88), to ironize heterosexual romance and the male gaze that drives it.

Valley of the Dolls opens in 1945 with the arrival of young Anne Welles in "dirty" New York City amid a heat wave "and a convulsive end-of-the-war excitement," having fled her repressive New England hometown Lawrenceville, the expectation to get married, along with "emotions stifled beneath the creaky iron armor called 'manners'" (Susann 1997c, 7, 9). Anne soon finds a room in a brownstone and secures a job at the Bellamy and Bellows theatrical agency, the vehicles for introducing most of the novel's key characters: Neely O'Hara, a sixteen-year-old vaudeville entertainer living in a neighboring room; Henry Bellamy, the avuncular entertainment lawyer, Anne's employer and mentor; the playboy theatrical agent Lyon Burke, Anne's eventual lover and husband; and the agency's biggest client Helen Lawson, a Broadway legend, Henry's former lover, and currently in rehearsals for the musical *Hit the Sky*. Anne convinces Helen to cast Neely in *Hit the Sky* and then befriends another cast member, the compassionate, deceptively sharp, dazzlingly attractive showgirl Jennifer North. Jennifer, whose family went broke before the war, had lived in Spain with her wealthy boarding school lover Maria until marrying an abusive aristocrat, then divorcing him in a storm of scandal and arriving in New York a celebrity of the gossip columns.

Anne, Jennifer, and Neely find an apartment to share, but each woman's "climb to the top of Mount Everest to reach the Valley of the Dolls" soon separates them. Jennifer elopes, again seeking financial security, with sex-hungry star crooner Tony Polar; Anne rejects Lyon's first marriage proposal and ascends to TV stardom as a model; Neely conquers nightclubs, recording, and then Hollywood. Pill addictions ensue—to sleep, stay svelte, and keep peppy—along with divorces. Jennifer leaves Tony after suffering his sexual abusiveness, topped by his diagnosis with a degenerative mental disorder, and Neely leaves her stolid publicist husband Mel for glamourous Hollywood dress designer Ted Casablanca, rumored to be queer. Jennifer has an abortion then migrates to France to find stardom in art films, while Neely advances into full diva mode after winning an Oscar. Reliant on dolls and booze, Neely is fired from her latest film and attempts suicide, then loses her studio contract, spars with Helen in the powder room of the Persian Room, fails in an attempted comeback on television, and is eventually institutionalized, followed by another comeback. Jennifer, meanwhile, thinks she has met a man who genuinely loves her for more than her body, but after being diagnosed with breast cancer, recognizes his duplicity, loses hope, and takes a suicidal overdose of Seconal. Anne marries Lyon but, as he philanders with Neely and a stream of women clients, enters her forties in 1965 reliant on dolls to cope with her "beautiful"-looking marriage.

Mainstream commentators typically perceived *Valley of the Dolls* as a morality tale about women suffering for their ambition and independence, an assumption that Susann ambiguously encouraged when promoting the book. Gloria Steinem's scathing review summed up the melodramatic plot and message "that nobody can be successful and happy at the same time: that's the moral," adding to this its appeal to women readers, as "Hollywood's 'it's-somehow-more-American-to-fail' formula, bound to comfort, if not surprise, dime-store salesgirls across the country" (Steinem 1966, 11). Nora Ephron also put forth this position in a delighted assessment of the novel, its "standard female fantasy—of going to the big city, striking it rich, meeting fabulous men," a scenario that "went on to show every reader that she was far better off than the heroines in the book—who took pills, killed themselves and made general messes of their lives. It was, essentially, a morality tale" (Ephron 1969, 3). John Cawelti gave scholarly legitimacy to this interpretive frame in 1976 by placing the novels of Susann, in addition to best-selling contemporaries Harold Robbins, Arthur Hailey, and Irving Wallace, "in the tradition of social melodrama," a moralistic mode that punishes any form of sexuality outside of heterosexual romance, monogamy and the goal of "regeneration": "But those who exploit sexuality as a means to power . . . or who fail to understand the necessary relationship between sex and love are doomed to failure . . . on their way to 'The Valley of the Dolls'" (Cawelti 1991, 44–46).[2] This interpretation overlooks a glaring—and to some readers, funny—irony: the absence of any real heterosexual "success" stories in *Valley of the Dolls*, the fact that everyone in the novel is a "failure" in heteronormative terms.[3]

Ephron avows her pleasure in *Valley of the Dolls* as an ironic woman fan. Perching herself ambivalently among the book's "readers (most of whom were women and a large number of whom were teen-agers)," Ephron compares her experience with *Valley of the Dolls* to "reading a very very long, absolutely delicious gossip column full of nothing but blind items; the fact that the names were changed and the characters disguised just made it more fun" (Ephron 1969, 3). Ephron finally puts her camp cards on the table—flagged by the illustration adjoining her *New York Times* article of Roy Lichtenstein's definitive pop art work *Crying Girl*—to characterize her appreciation of Susann as a "kitschy writer" and her pleasure in Susann's "sincere" novel as "first-rate kitsch" (Ephron 1969, 3). When Ephron proceeds to review Susann's second novel, *The Love Machine*, the same ironic criteria apply: "It is still, to be sure, not exactly a literary work. But in its own little sub-category of popularly-written roman à clef, it shines like a rhinestone in a trash can. . . . With the possible exception of *Cosmopolitan Magazine*, no one writes about sadism in modern man and masochism in modern woman quite as horribly and accurately as Jacqueline Susann" (Ephron 1969, 12).

As Ephron unpacks the delights of reading Susann, the function of the "morality tale" grows ambiguous, an excuse for the "fun" content, a device that functions parallel to the "delicious" "gossip column" and guessing game without necessarily obstructing their pleasures, and a feature that confirms the book's status as "first-rate kitsch" for women readers such as Ephron. If "'Valley' had a message that had a magnetic appeal for women readers" as Ephron (1969) proffered, its melodramatic moralizing appealed to this woman reader as a predictable element in the kitsch formula, not as the verification of domestic ideology. Cawelti (1991) assumes that melodramatic narrative causality dictates moral closure for readers, but Ephron's ambivalence defies a one-dimensional vision of audience reception. Her reading experience is "funny" in both senses of the word, strange as well as humorous, one that seems to see through any monotonal moralizing and affirms the fun of reading about heterosexual power dynamics dramatized through the scandalous behavior of celebrities.

Ephron alludes to but never quite locates Susann's sleazy realism, how the author implements the "kitsch" formula of the roman à clef to charge the gossipy guessing game as well as infiltrate and recombine popular genres. In *Valley of the Dolls*, the palimpsests of Judy Garland, Ethel Merman, Marilyn Monroe, Jayne Mansfield, Grace Kelly, and other celebrities alternately pop with bursts of vulgarity and sexuality to produce incongruity, often humorous, that upsets the Hollywood genres, films, and star personas confining women: as practitioners, representations, and readers. Imelda Whelehan helps identify the operation of sleazy realism in *Valley of the Dolls*, "moments which are strikingly reminiscent of key Hollywood films of the 1930s, 1940s, and 1950s, such as *The Women* (1939), *The Razor's Edge* (1946), *All About Eve* (1950), and *A Star Is Born* (1954), but the glossier dominance of the romantic storylines in the films is replaced by sleaze, observed with a harsh naturalistic eye for detail" (Whelehan 2005, 38).

The rich pertinence of these particular film references goes unnoted, though: two comedies of manners dominated by women and rooted in camp culture, *The Women* and *All About Eve*; and two melodramas, beginning with *A Star Is Born*, Judy Garland's comeback film after her 1950 suicide attempt; and the epic-scale *The Razor's Edge*, which although led by a male protagonist features the tragically drug-addicted "fallen woman," Sophie. The "backstudio" melodrama *A Star Is Born* and the backstage manners comedy *All About Eve* are also significant for their show business settings and the timing of their production. Popular perceptions of a "monstrous Hollywood" began to emerge in 1950, Steven Cohan illuminates, in concert with Garland's widely reported, harrowing near-death experience, known to be fueled by her contract suspension at MGM, a perception of Hollywood eventually compounded by the tragic end of Marilyn Monroe (Cohan 2019, 116). Susann surely depicts Hollywood as monstrous in *Valley of the Dolls*, emblematized in her portrayal of the studio chief "The Head" and his treatment of the Garland-inspired Neely O'Hara—who attempts suicide after he fires her from a film—as well as Jennifer North, a supposed composite of Monroe and Mansfield, whom The Head demeans as a sex object even as he relies on her box-office draw. Susann nevertheless also adheres, at least superficially, to the pattern of backstudio narratives focused on "narcissistic, self-destructive older women" (Cohan 2019, 116). Neely uses the word "monster," for instance, to describe Helen Lawson, the Merman character, her bloated ego and manipulative behavior, and several years later, an ambiguously fatherly Hollywood director refers to Neely as a "monster" for disrupting the production of his picture (Susann 1997c, 87, 267).

That *Valley of the Dolls* evokes both comedic and tragic examples of "monstrous" behavior in show business speaks to Ephron's sense of "fun" in reading *Valley of the Dolls*. The pleasure is not just from reading an extended gossip column about celebrity scandals, but from Susann's combination of gossip about the entertainment industry with tropes from Hollywood films redolent of *All About Eve* and *A Star Is Born*, films that are thematically synchronous in their jaundiced view of show business yet emotionally mismatched, sophisticated comedy and tragic melodrama. An otherwise excoriating comment about the book by *Time* magazine nevertheless located at least part of Susann's project: "The cliche [*sic*] of show business as a dream world may have been wide-eyed and saccharine. But Novelist Susann's view of Hollywood as nightmare Valley merely adds up to the old naivete in reverse" (Anon. 1967f). Blemishing the sanitized gloss of Production Code–approved Hollywood romantic fantasy and star personas, Susann finally mines humor and melodrama in *Valley of the Dolls* from depicting "the old naivete in reverse."

As Susann blurs gossip directed at others with the self-directed disclosures of the confessional, the author privileges the gazes of "single girls" confessing their exploits and gossiping about others, all elements that situated *Valley of the Dolls* in the landscape of popular reading for women.[4] These features differentiated *Valley of the Dolls* from the purely voyeuristic story of female star exploitation in *The Carpetbaggers* (1961), the best-selling roman à clef by Harold Robbins, and they tied *Valley* to Rona Jaffe's *The Best of Everything* (1958), a bestseller about single women in publishing and theater. Susann credited Jaffe's novel as her primary influence due to its structure of alternating perspectives among the women characters (Seaman 1996c, 351).[5] Jaffe further established the conditions for both confession and gossip by forging a personal connection to her scandalous characters, and in her protagonist's plotline, pronounced the analogy between scandal and the "single girl" lifestyle that Susann magnified in *Valley of the Dolls*. *Cosmopolitan* editor Helen

Gurley Brown's *Sex and the Single Girl* (1962) codified and popularized the expression "single girl" and provided a combination instruction manual and "manifesto" for the same women whose stories Jaffe had told in *The Best of Everything* and Susann would make legendary. Similar to Susann and Jaffe, Brown spoke from personal experience, and in her jubilant rupture of preconceptions about gender roles Brown performs a kind of comedy of manners comparable to Susann's.

Valley of the Dolls captures how women suffer subjected to the male gaze, but Susann's aesthetic of sleazy realism and comedy of bad manners also locate the pleasure that her "single girls" take in exploding constructions of femininity. Susann dramatizes women's delight in vulgarity, their own and others, women using "profanity" to teach and entertain each other as well as a tool for survival in a patriarchal world. If Anne desires a flight from "the creaky iron armor called 'manners,'" Neely nevertheless warns early on, presciently, "Those fancy manners are gonna stand in your way, Anne" (Susann 1997c, 7, 21–22). Neely, Helen, and Jennifer all deploy "bad" manners openly and strategically in their masquerades of femininity, and Susann often dares the reader to laugh when sleaze erupts. This alternates with more bitter outbursts of (paraphrasing Whelehan) "harsh naturalism" by men compensating for their fears and inadequacies with absurd double standards, outright misogyny, and sexual abuse. Although patriarchal control strikes back cruelly—and in Jennifer's case tragically—the comedy of bad manners nevertheless rewards women's stylized vulgarity, as they commandeer conventionally male manners in their work lives and sex lives.

Jennifer's bisexual sophistication furthermore fortifies her comedy of bad manners and sense of wit, in sharp contrast to the abject tragedy that finally befalls her in the search for heterosexual, domestic conformity. Susann's collision of Hollywood tropes and redefinition of the melodramatic "fallen woman" surely apply to all of her women characters in *Valley of the Dolls*, but these textual operations congeal most abundantly, humorously, and bracingly through Jennifer, whose bisexuality materializes as, according to Maria San Filippo's formulation, "bitextuality" (San Filippo 2013, 40–41). Bisexuality might leave Jennifer's story relatively early but it informs her ensuing plotlines, attests to her complexity, nourishes her sense of antiromantic irony, and helps redirect a normative moral interpretation of her storyline.[6] Susann employs

Rona Jaffe implicated herself in the "single girl" narrative of *The Best of Everything*, as did Helen Gurley Brown in the *Cosmopolitan* editor's lifestyle book *Sex and the Single Girl*. *Valley of the Dolls* incorporates as well as modifies elements from these predecessors, whose authors lauded Susann's publishing triumph.

Jennifer to finally equalize homo and hetero relationships in an expression of witty, queer ennui that gains even more radical traction next to the stream of rancid heterosexual romances littering the Valley. That Jennifer's bisexuality and wit are excised from the film adaptation speaks volumes for the textual trouble that her fluidity engenders as much as the challenges that Susann's novel presented for a Hollywood adaptation.

"Sex and the Single Dog": *Every Night, Josephine!* (1963) and the Comedy of Bad Manners

As Jacqueline Susann related to *Cosmopolitan* magazine in 1967, amid the hoopla of *Valley of the Dolls* (soon to be a major motion picture), typecasting by producers had impeded her acting career, "so I locked myself up and wrote something funny": *Every Night, Josephine!*. "When I wrote

Valley it was a big departure. They wanted to typecast me again—as a funny writer. So I broke out and wrote *Valley*—some people say a hard-hitting, savage novel" (Manville 1967, 78). Resisting the confinement of typecasting, Susann turned from "something funny" to "hard-hitting" and "savage," although such product differentiation vastly underestimated her agility with blending genres and modes in both of these books. *Josephine!* remains undeniably a comedy, although read retroactively through the prism of her subsequent work, the "savage" lurks within the comedy of bad manners, including interludes of sick humor and references to drug use, homosexuality, abortion, divorce, and polyamory. Susann likewise interwove "funny" events and dialogue into the drama of *Valley of the Dolls*, but even more, enlisted "savage" sleazy realism to achieve a comedy of bad manners that upended the norms of taste, gender roles, and sexuality.

The manners comedy of *Every Night, Josephine!* stems from Susann humanizing her poodle throughout thirty-three vignettes chronicling Josephine's adoption, burgeoning TV career, sexual liaisons, diet regimes, and health scares; in turn, Susann redefines "human" through the perspective of a showbiz woman as well as glorifies her own Broadway persona. The centrality of Broadway manners and a showbiz sense of reality reveals the influence of Susann's friend and mentor Damon Runyon in addition to her reshaping of Runyon's male gaze.[7] Susann would eventually incorporate a narrational style in *Valley of the Dolls* proximate to Runyon's, to render the Broadway milieus, seamy street cant, and often darkly comic predicaments of her single girls and elder dames, but in *Josephine!*, retains a decidedly more Hollywood rendition of Runyon's style immortalized in *Guys and Dolls* (Mankiewicz, 1955) and *Pocketful of Miracles* (Capra, 1961). Among Runyon's signature characters and motifs, Guy Szuberla communicates an assumed gendered division of "fluff-headed Broadway dolls" on the one hand, and on the other, "lovable mugs" such as the first-person male narrator: "a knowledgeable 'citizen' of Broadway . . . a 'wise boob.' He is a 'nod-guy' who says yes to 'propositions' of which he silently disapproves or questions" (Szuberla 1993, 71, 73).[8]

Susann revises Runyon's gendered division of characters and perspectives in *Josephine!* by embodying the role of "nod-guy" in her first-person narration and portraying herself as both a "fluff-headed Broadway doll" and "a knowledgeable 'citizen' of Broadway." Susann materializes as a seasoned Broadway denizen, a "Truewit," the character in the comedy of manners who acts as "the play's certified pragmatic philosopher," David Pierson explains, and as Alexis Greene adds, someone who wields "a sophisticate's perception of the rules," "a creative, or inventive, faculty" as well as "understands and accepts his egoism, his need to satisfy both his aversions and his desires" (Pierson 2005, 39; Greene 1992, 79, 81, 83).[9] Susann inculcates both Josephine and her readers with the philosophy of showbiz and the rule of her comedy of bad manners, that "show business is the great equalizer" (Susann 2004, 127). Susann's stance reinstates Josephine's human charms as much as it normalizes showbiz people such as Jackie and Irving.[10] In vignettes about Josephine's television career and celebrity, for instance, Susann observes how "Josephine just naturally fell into the business," with a vocabulary that surpassed the "smart dogs" lexicon to include "Nielsons, shares, prime time, tape, summer replacement, and pilot film. . . . She knew the word 'thirteen' was not just a number, but a television cycle. Twenty-six meant a good television cycle, and thirty meant, 'Throw away the Miltown, we're in'" (Susann 2004, 101). The view of the world through showbiz-tinted glasses included downing "Miltown" tranquilizers to cope with the anxiety, a different set of standards and priorities than civilian society that also extended to making Josephine an equal.

Satirical culture clashes accumulate throughout *Josephine!* between Susann the Broadway Truewit and the civilians she encounters, all opportunities to endorse her show-business taste, lifestyle, and worldview. When the upper crust breeder Mrs. Addison from Westchester, Connecticut, demands to screen Susann before considering a sale, the ensuing exchange pits Susann the TV performer against the Protestant work ethic. Following Mrs. Addison's inquiries about Susann's religion and feelings about Republican Senator Barry Goldwater, none of which ever go directly answered, a standoff finally erupts after Mrs. Addison asks if Susann "intended to show the poodle." Responding with showbiz tunnel vision, "I was flattered as I realized Mrs. Addison had probably seen me on television and was a fan. . . . Mrs. Addison said she was not alluding to television shows. . . . 'Mr. Addison and I wouldn't have a television set in the house. Even our children think it's a time waster and a bore'" (Susann 2004, 17).[11] Realizing what "this endearing woman" meant, Susann parades her decadent, lowbrow outlook: "I was delighted to say that the nearest I had ever gotten to a dog show was when Lassie appeared on television and that I intended to keep it that way" (Susann 2004, 17). Susann's showbiz lifestyle, taste, and worldview render her a "slob" in the eyes of another breeder (19), and when her friend Last-One Hershkowitz boards Josephine during Jackie and Irving's Hollywood junket, the poodle-sitter welcomes them back with objections to Josephine's nocturnal lifestyle and table manners, which Last-One blames on Jackie: "It's your profession that's ruining her. It's just not right for a poodle to go around acting like an actress" (Susann 2004, 161–62). What remains "not right" to Last-One ironically defines the pleasures and credo of *Every Night, Josephine!*, show business, which transforms Jackie-the-actress into an inverted role model of parenting and domesticity.

Susann's narration also swerves into grotesque and sick humor, which further pronounces her showbiz sensibility and satire of conventional taste.[12] Susann closes the chapter on Last-One's incessant nitpicking and sermonizing, for example, with a confession of homicidal desire. Having showered her neighbor with expensive gifts for her troubles, "It's only when my eyes fasten to the Italian gold wristwatch that graces her arm as she deals the cards, that I secretly toy with the idea of stabbing her!" (Susann 2004, 165–67). In addition to this murderous fantasy, Susann routinely dots *Josephine!* with Nazi jokes: referring to Josie as "a card-carrying member . . . of the new Master Race"; comparing one of Josie's austere dieting regimes to "Stalag 17" and another to "concentration-camp living"; and fearing that Josie, after a painful visit to the dentist, viewed her "as if I was the real Ilse Koch," a.k.a. the Witch of Buchenwald (Susann 2004, 3, 148, 179, 197–99, 219, 231, 237). Susann's closeted Jewishness emerges in *Josephine!* as well, insinuated through her encounter with WASPy Mrs. Addison, the Nazi jokes, in addition to Irving, their ethnically inflected friends, and more distantly by the Broadway setting.[13] Sick humor serves Susann as another expressive means in her comedy of manners, to assert her own style, taste, and truth.

As Susann drops the real names of celebrities in *Every Night, Josephine!* and avoids anything explicitly seamy or complicated, the sleazy realism of scandal lurks in the background, elements incorporated into *Valley of the Dolls*. Commonsensical remarks about downing a Miltown to relax or a Seconal to end an argument, coupled with repeated diagnoses of neurotic behavior, predict the characters' struggles in *Valley* with pill addiction and mental illness.[14] Actress friend Joyce Matthews and her theatrical impresario husband Billy Rose appear frequently, too, but their widely reported, troubled relationship remains a subtext: multiple separations and Matthews's suicide attempt, which Susann incorporated into the travails of Jennifer North in *Valley* (Seaman 1996c, 293).

Susann's voice as Runyonesque truewit further resonates in *Valley* through Neely O'Hara, the Broadway ragamuffin who calls it as she sees it in streetwise wisecracks, and when she ascends to diva, rationalizes her addictive behavior as well as her backstabbing with the earthy gibes of a perpetual survivor. During her institutionalization, Neely explains to a doctor about her Seconal abuse, "If everyone who took them was in a loony bin, you'd have half of Hollywood and all of Madison Avenue and Broadway in here" (Susann 1997c, 364–65). And soon after,

Susann's voice as Runyonesque truewit and emergence as gay icon resonate in *Valley of the Dolls* through Neely O'Hara, based on Judy Garland. Garland was originally cast as Helen Lawson for the film (seen here with Susann at a press conference). (Source: OrphanDomino.)

Neely reasons, "maybe my inkblots will show I'm some kind of a nut. . . . That's why I'm a star. . . . Why, if you threw a butterfly net over Sardi's and Chasens and gave them Rorschach tests, you wouldn't release any of them for years" (Susann 1997c, 366). Judy Garland would eventually adopt the same reasoning as her fictional alter ego; during a press conference after Garland was hired to play Helen Lawson in the film version, a reporter queried, "The book deals with pills, to some extent. . . . Have you found that prevalent around show business people?" Garland retorted, "Well, I find it prevalent around newspaper people, too" (quoted in Schmidt 2014, 375). When Susann moved to fiction and the roman à clef to confess and gossip in the style of sleazy realism, the author could draw from the "savage" details of many showbiz careers and divulge a genuine comedy of bad manners.

Gossip, Confessional, and Scandal: From *The Carpetbaggers* to *The Best of Everything*

If gossip "sells," as Patricia Meyer Spacks avers (1985, 68), Harold Robbins's roman à clef *The Carpetbaggers* (1961) offered proof. A best-selling forerunner of *Valley of the Dolls*, *The Carpetbaggers* provided sexually spectacular peeks into the fictionalized lives of Howard Hughes, Jean Harlow, and other recognizable historical figures from Hollywood, Wall Street, and Paris. Besides tapping into Hollywood history, *The Carpetbaggers* anticipated Susann's adoption of Hollywood cinematic techniques, such as recognizable genre tropes, flashbacks and flash-forwards, and privileging dialogue (Wilson 2007, 114–15, 184–86). Susann also follows Robbins in incorporating tropes from the lesbian pulp novel, a trend in popular fiction of the period (Grier 1966). Robbins strikes a distance between himself and the roman à clef scandal narrative, however, imposing an adamantly voyeuristic, masculinized gaze especially evident in *The Carpetbaggers* through the representation of queer women.[15] Spacks teases out the "voyeuristic" power relationships and "aggressive" affect of gossip by way of applying Freud's theory of jokes and wit (Spacks 1985, 49–51, 57). Approximating Spacks's definition of gossip as "conversation about the private life of another" (1985, 122), Freud's joker "adopts a humorous attitude towards others," and through ridiculing the butt of the joke, finds "an outlet for aggressive tendencies" and "acquires his superiority

by assuming the role of the grown-up" (Freud 1963, 265–66). Gossip likewise involves "the pleasure of voyeurism . . . as well as aggression," and
disguised in "moral speculation" and "sympathy," invests the gossiper
with "dominance over the hated or feared object" (Spacks 1985, 50–51).
The voyeuristic male gaze operates from the start of *The Carpetbaggers*,
and with particular force in the depiction of the Harlow character, polysexual starlet Rina Marlow, who figures as little more than a pawn in a
narrative of sexual victimization, debauchery, and tragedy.[16] Preyed on
by numerous straight men and worst of all a "mannish" lesbian and closeted gay man, Rina finally succumbs to illness, her sensational story ultimately overwhelmed by the primary plotline about Hughes's alter ego,
the megalomaniacal, womanizing businessman Jonas Cord (see Robbins
1961, 317–21). Robbins could boast "almost no risks," as *Time* magazine
illuminated in 1962, and "there is absolutely no necessity that the author
know any inside gossip. . . . Robbins merely gets rich by naming 'facts'
and implying names" (Anon. 1962, 105). Relieved of any kind of "inside"
connections to the sensational antics he recorded, Robbins writes risk-
free, his authorial autonomy preserved through detachment.[17]

   The element of authorial confession, by contrast, frames Rona
Jaffe's *The Best of Everything*. If gossip imparts the secrets of others much
like the joke mocks the failings of the butt, the woman's confessional
novel exemplifies a literary mode in which the subject and object of
gossip converge, comparable to the dynamic of self-directed humor. By
conflating joker and butt, humor defuses the threats of adult reality
by making fun out of them and forgiving the butt's failures (Freud 1963,
266).[18] The woman's confessional novel compares in this respect to self-
directed humor by striking a "narrative intimacy" through the author's
reflections on her experiences as a woman, including the unpretty and
imperfect, and investing them with a pleasure and import denied by
the patriarchal parent culture (Whelehan 2005, 1–2, 13, 63). The confessional novel offers, just the same, voyeuristic pleasures similar to
gossip-as-exposé, and like the roman à clef, "tantalized the readers
with the promise of the kind of deep dark revelations of autobiography"
(63). The voyeurism of the confessional deviates from gossip-as-exposé
by implicating the teller, and similar to humor, replaces the othering
dynamics of moralizing and pity with a space for identification, recognition, forgiving, and pleasure.[19]

New York Times columnist Gilbert Millstein insinuated Jaffe's orchestration of gossip and confession in *The Best of Everything*, about single women seeking careers in Manhattan. Millstein first informs how the author, "an attractive-looking girl of 26, obligingly, possibly eagerly, submitted to posing for the photograph on the front of the jacket," and next hints at Jaffe's inside knowledge by identifying the book's "appalling verisimilitude" (Millstein 1958, 33). The play between voyeuristic, judgmental gossip and forgiving confession in *The Best of Everything* pertains to the contradictory messages underpinning the characters' travails. As Jaffe recalled in 2005, "To this day women come up to me and say that the book changed their lives. After they read it, they decided to come to New York and work in publishing. I was a little surprised, because I thought *The Best of Everything* was a cautionary tale. But of course an exciting life, even if very difficult, is better than a dull one, even if it changes you forever" (Jaffe 2005, ix). If Jaffe's novel, Pamela Wojcik reasons, aims to "steer female readers away from careerism and the life of a spinster" and point them toward "monogamous domesticity," it accomplishes this through "a detour, a passage through bohemianism and sexual experience" (Wojcik 2010, 167). This is especially the case for the protagonist Caroline Bender, a recent Vassar graduate working in the Madison Avenue publishing industry and advancing from secretary to editor. When the abrupt, surprising conclusion introduces star scandal into Caroline's single girl experiences, Jaffe offers latitude for her character's "bohemian," "exciting" pursuits to overcome the "cautionary tale" advocating domesticity and punishing the single girl's sins.

Caroline's fate finally provides what might seem to be a confession from Jaffe, the book jacket's avatar and authenticator of "verisimilitude," and a humorous form of forgiving tendered toward Caroline's scandalous life. After Caroline spurns her "true" love Eddie—college sweetheart and former fiancé who married another woman for familial and financial reasons then offered to keep Caroline as his mistress—the ambitious editor makes an impulsive decision: to accept an invitation to Las Vegas with movie star John Cassaro. Their affair causes a scandal worthy of front-page attention, and Jaffe closes the novel by submitting Caroline to voyeuristic, moralistic gossip through the eyes of Eddie reading the newspaper during his flight home. "God, she was *sleeping* with that guy! What would make her do a thing like that?" (435). Conveniently forgetting his recent confessions to Caroline about his unsatisfying marriage and failed efforts to enlist her as his mistress, Eddie envisions his wife, baby, and their upcoming Christmas together, and gloats to himself, "You could see the future, planned, secure, getting better and better as the years went by" (435–36). Eddie's supposed happy ending of nuclear family bliss and "future" still fails to hold his attention: "He'd never be able to figure it out about Caroline. . . . She'd be famous now herself, the girl who was with John Cassaro in Las Vegas. Eddie shook his head" (436). Eddie reacts to the gossip about Caroline's sex scandal with the moral superiority of domestic ideology, but his hypocrisy as well as envy creep through to render this moralizing unconvincing. Jaffe might close the novel with Eddie's self-satisfied meditation, "Sometimes life *is* simple—sometimes, just when you think it will never be simple again" (437), but Jaffe destabilizes Eddie's "simple" domestic ideology with the thrill of her ostensible alter ego's "exciting life," concretized at the con-clusion with the celebrity sex scandal.

Inspired by Jaffe's confessional narrative filtered through women's gazes and topped by scandal, as well as the humor and tolerance that results, Susann heightens the risks Robbins deflected by impressing her personal involvement in the scandal plotlines of *Valley of the Dolls*. "I'm just writing about what I know," Susann informed *Life* magazine in 1966 (Howard 77), and her veiled confessions, often humorous, proved instru-mental in orchestrating the guessing game. Susann equivocated about renditions of real people's experiences and her own but gave readers ample reason to see through her hedging, such as when she addressed rumors that Ethel Merman disapproved of *Valley of the Dolls*: "She didn't speak to me before I wrote the book. Now she's not speaking to me, only louder" (Adams 1966, 21; Adams 1967, 32; Bjorkman 1966a: 8; Bjorkman 1966c: 8). Susann ambiguously encouraged readers, furthermore, to con-flate her with the "single girl" experiences and attitudes of her characters. It "made her laugh," according to *Cosmopolitan*'s W.H. Manville, when he asked Susann how "autobiographical" *Valley of the Dolls* was, but her ensuing comments hilariously inject ambiguity: "If it were . . . I'd be in a jar at Harvard. If you went through all the things I wrote about, you'd have no time to write. And yet, there's a bit of you in every character" (1967, 79). Susann had already alluded to *Life* magazine which "bits" of her might inform the *Valley* characters when pondering, "It shouldn't be so wrong for a woman to cheat on her husband, either, if he was away and she was left in New York when, say, she met a man who was a big game hunter and her own husband was terribly cerebral" (Howard 1966, 77). Susann's humorous shilly-shallying pertains directly to the merging of gossip and confessional, and in her playfulness as well as absurdity reveals tolerance toward the rejection of monogamy as well as an embrace of women's promiscuity. Entangling herself in the scandalous spectacle, Susann in turn complicates the readers' pleasures, combining the possibilities for identification with the delights of voyeuristic speculation about the characters's actual identities.

Sex, Dolls, and the Single Girl: Anne Welles's Antiromantic Comedy

Playing at the border of fiction and reality, Jacqueline Susann promoted *Valley of the Dolls* through the shifting ideology of the "single girl" popularized in her friend Helen Gurley Brown's best-selling lifestyle book, *Sex and the Single Girl*: normalizing love and marriage yet upholding the options of nonmonogamy and career. A press release for *Sex and the Single Girl* by publicist and future feminist publisher Letty Cottin Pogrebin, who later designed the publicity campaign for *Valley of the Dolls*, enlisted revolutionary rhetoric to both humorously defuse and pointedly illuminate the implications of Brown's design for living: "Single women of the world unite! Here is your manifesto!" (Reed 1966, 99).[20] If Brown provided the single girl's "manifesto," Susann presented single girl readers with creative and practical applications, in addition to capturing Brown's humorous attitude, the sensation of fun in freely disputing double standards. Brown counsels women readers to pursue a career, cultivate taste and sophistication, in addition to enjoying sex, all as a vehicle toward landing a husband. "Theoretically," Brown ponders, "a 'nice' single woman has no sex life. What nonsense! She has a better sex life than most of her married friends. She need never be bored with one man per lifetime.... Her married friends refer to her pursuers as wolves, but actually many of them turn out to be lambs—to be shorn and worn by her" (Brown 2003, 7).[21] Brown's quip produces numerous comedic revelations evocative of "fallen women" in early 1930s Hollywood comedies released prior to the strict enforcement of the Production Code: characters who,

Janet Staiger unpacks, "may seek economic independence and use men's gullibility about sex and women to succeed"; and women like Gilda in the movie adaptation of Noël Coward's *Design for Living* (Lubitsch 1933), whose "agency of desire for two men (not a monogamous choice) creates the comedic conflict . . . without needing to kill off Gilda" (Staiger 2010, 46, 52). The "Single Girl" indeed prevails, Hilary Radner reasons, to pursue "other avenues that lead to other feminine identities outside of marriage," and as Wojcik notes, "presents a challenge to domesticity not only in championing the single state, but in its indifferent attitude toward marriage" (Radner 1999, 16; Wojcik 2010, 156).

Susann challenges the heterosexual romance and its destination of marriage just a few pages into *Valley of the Dolls*, when the reader learns that Anne Welles "hadn't just left Lawrenceville—she had escaped. Escaped from marriage to some solid Lawrenceville boy, from the solid, orderly life of Lawrenceville. The same orderly life her mother had lived. And her mother's mother" (Susann 1997c, 6–7). Anne's final embrace of marital propriety, in turn, proves a terrible liability as she downs dolls for a distraction from her husband Lyon's philandering. After Anne witnesses Lyon's womanizing firsthand at their New Year's party, Susann brings *Valley of the Dolls* to its close: "She brushed her hair and freshened her make-up. She looked fine. She had Lyon, the beautiful apartment, the beautiful child, the nice career of her own, New York. . . . She could always keep busy during the day, and at night—the lonely ones—there were always the beautiful dolls for company. She'd take two of them tonight. Why not? After all, it was New Year's Eve!" (Susann 1997c, 441–42). A grimly ironic exclamation point closes the novel and punctuates the joylessness of Anne's "beautiful" existence, preceded by a scene that could be transplanted from sex farce: Anne lying down in her and Lyon's darkened bedroom, overlooked by the furtive adulterers who discretely leave the lights off. Susann held fast to this dispiriting conclusion conveying the bleak prospects of marriage, and bristled at the film adaptation's hokey inspirational ending (Duke and Turan 1987, 180; Seaman 1985; Seaman 1996c, 348–49). In *Valley of the Dolls* domesticity yields tattered lives, safer than the alternately thrilling and terrifying experiences of single life, but deadening.

The contradiction at the heart of single girl narratives provides the material for drama and soul-searching in *Valley of the Dolls*, although it also occasions humor and irony. Well before the unhappy ending, Anne sarcastically contests the wish-dream of marriage in the unapologetic voice of, as Lyon calls her, "a fallen woman." When Lyon visits Anne in Lawrenceville as she settles her deceased mother's estate, his proposal that they marry and live there meets with Anne's flat refusal. After months of sleeping with Lyon and fantasies of marrying him, she adamantly sacrifices bourgeois respectability to validate her own desire for independence, urban sophistication, and working in show business. Echoing the "cynical" and "wisecracking" women protagonists from 1930s Columbia comedies discussed by Joy Gould Boyum (2015), Anne counters each of the elusive playboy's enthusiastic affirmations of an agrarian Eden with a humorously laconic retort. "He smiled. . . . 'Say, this is beautiful country.' 'The snow helps,' she said without enthusiasm" (Susann 1997c, 214). Prefacing his marriage proposal, Lyon kids with Anne, "'You're a fallen woman. . . . Looks like I'll have to marry you quickly. Restore your honor in this town.' 'I don't care what this town thinks of me'" (Susann 1997c, 215). Each of Anne's ripostes defy the Hollywood mandate encapsulated by Kathrina Glitre, that a woman's "virginal status functions to signify her 'worth' and the rate of sexual exchange is marriage" (Glitre 2006, 35), much as Brown's "single girl" disputes the condition of premarital chastity as a criterion for assessing a woman's value.

Susann further revises the gendered associations of romantic comedy, in which the desire for love and domesticity appears to emerge naturally for women, even proto-single girls. When Lyon urges Anne to marry him and live in Lawrenceville as a housewife while he writes a novel, Anne responds: "But what would I do? Join the women's club? Play bingo once a week? Renew my so-called friendships with the dreary girls I grew up with?" (Susann 1997c, 217). Anne's protests against stultifying rural domesticity echo lines from Kaufman and Hart's *The Man Who Came to Dinner* (on Broadway in 1939, film in 1942), when the effete Manhattan sophisticate Sheridan Whiteside disputes his secretary Maggie Cutler's desire to quit her glamorous New York career and marry a small-town newspaper editor: "It's completely unbelievable. Can you see yourself, the wife of the editor of the *Mesalia Journal*, having an evening at home for Mr. and Mrs. Stanley, Mr. and Mrs. Poop-Face, and the members of the Book-of-the-Month Club?"[22] The vital, obvious difference between Susann's version of this dialogue and Kaufman and Hart's is that the "single girl" in Susann's story is voicing these objections to marriage. Although Anne's irony soon turns to disheartenment as Lyon's proposal turns into an ultimatum, her words continue to cut toward the comedic by brazenly celebrating her independence, "fallen" or not: "Lyon, don't you understand? Just as you have certain principals—you couldn't let me support you in New York—well, I have my blind spots too. Not many—in fact, just one. Lawrenceville! I hate it! I love New York. Before I came to New York I lived here, in this mausoleum. I was nothing. I was dead. When I came to New York it was like a veil lifting. For the first time I felt I was alive, breathing" (Susann 1997c, 217). Anne's expression of loathing toward Lawrenceville is funny, with a joke-styled set-up—"I have my blind spots too. Not many—in fact, just one."—followed by a pithy punchline: "Lawrenceville! I hate it!" Anne's declaration furthermore reverses the expectations of romantic-minded heroines such as Maggie in *The Man Who Came to Dinner*. Maggie counters her employer Sheridan's admonition of a boring connubial country life with affirmations of true love and the seemingly natural step toward marriage: "Sherry, I've had ten years of the great figures of our time, and don't think I'm not grateful to you for it. . . . I don't think anyone has ever had the fun we've had. But a girl can't laugh all the time, Sherry. There comes a time when she wants—Bert Jefferson. . . . I love him, that's all." Such dialogue encapsulates an inevitable path to marriage for the single girl, but Anne affirms, by contrast, that if she married Lyon and moved back to the "mausoleum" of Lawrenceville, "A part of me would die" (Susann 1997c, 217), a prediction that Anne ultimately fulfills in her "beautiful," picture-perfect marriage to Lyon, and a harbinger for her friend Jennifer, whose ultimate yearning for heterosexual marriage leads to her death.

Sex and the Single Diva: Humoring Helen Lawson

In the wake of *Valley of the Dolls'* sensational success, it was no secret that Susann based Helen Lawson on Ethel Merman, confirmed by friend Carol Bjorkman in one of her *Women's Wear Daily* columns describing the guests at a swanky Manhattan Christmas party: "Jacqueline Susann in covered-up gold smock dress with gold stockings and gold shoes—Ethel Merman sheathed up in black lace over pink satin. (No, Jacqueline and Ethel certainly did not sit down and chat.)" (Bjorkman

1966c, 8). Susann's depiction of Helen/Merman as a flamboyantly vulgar celebrity "monster" surely reflects the power of the voyeuristic gossiper, but as Susann attested on the late-night radio talk program *The Long John Nebel Show*, superior distance from Helen/Merman fluctuated wildly with identification:

> The terrible thing that happens to a star as they get older . . . they emasculate men without meaning to . . . because to get to the top— It is a man's world—they've fought for story properties, they've fought with directors, they learned to get tough. And then the only way they prove they're a woman is sexually. . . . I tried to show that with Helen Lawson, who came on like a steam engine in her approach for a man with all the finesse of a stevedore grabbing a dancehall girl, in reverse. Because this woman had fought and clawed her way to the top . . . she lost every bit of reliance upon a man as someone that was stronger than she was. And no man would want to be around her. (December 18, 1966)

Susann leaps from sympathy to pity, irony and mockery, at turns diminishing distance and seeming to court it. It was clear, however, that Susann knew Helen, not only as Merman but also by drawing on her own experiences as an aging woman performer. If she was taking revenge on Merman, with whom she admittedly had "an old score to settle" (Seaman 1996c, 289), Susann nevertheless gave permission and rationale for her readers to locate the author in Helen. As she averred to Bjorkman, "I wrote every character out of love and I had access to the system that makes people become this way"; Susann continues with a gendered analogy for women stars and their audience that renders the fan a "male lover" who "makes you king" then "drops you cold" (Bjorkman 1966a, 8). Susann further aligns with Helen as a middle-aged woman unafraid to pursue sex, and very aware of the stigma attached to such women, "the double standard" as she put it to *Life* magazine: "The great thing is that men can disconnect physical prowess from emotion. . . . Women who do that, of course, are weirdoes" (Howard 1966, 77). Susann's observations about women's struggles in show business and her revelations of active female sexuality both resonate in Helen, in addition to Susann's reputation for flamboyance and profanity, as well as her vulnerability as a middle-aged woman.

Through the interplay of gossip and confession, Susann solicits derision toward Helen as well as sympathy, or in Umberto Eco's terminology, replaces a "comic" depiction of an aging woman with a "humorous"
one: "A case of comic is a decrepit old woman who smears her face with
make-up and dresses like a young girl; facing such a picture one notices
that this woman is the opposite of what a respectable old woman should
be. In a case of humor, one understands why the old woman masks herself, to regain her lost youth. The character is still animal-like, but in
some way one sympathizes with it. One finds oneself halfway between
tragedy and comedy" (Eco 2018, 32). Susann articulates such ambivalent
compassion when the narration describes Anne, now turning forty and
approached by a young fan who recalls Anne's glory days as a fashion
model: "Anne smiled. Suddenly she knew how Helen Lawson had felt"
(Susann 1997c, 437). Similar to Freud's conception of the joke, Eco's
notion of "the comic" rests on "animalization" and "ridiculization" to the
exception of sympathy or identification; "the comic" reinforces the "rule"
or "social frame" violated by the "animal-like" butt, and in the process,
bolsters the "superiority" of the spectator (Eco 2018, 26–27). Humor, by
contrast, mingles comedy and tragedy, distance and identification, in
order to consider, "Maybe the frame is wrong" (32).

Analogous to Eco's humorous challenge to the social frame, Susann
recruits Helen to scrutinize "the system that makes people become this
way" through the diva's alternately humorous, sad, and outrageous
struggle with the male gaze. The author illuminates the patriarchal social
frame that animalizes and diminishes Helen due to her age, body, and
active sexual desire as well as generates the "double standard" that renders Helen a "weirdo" for abandoning passivity and seeking sex. When
Helen pursues Gino Cooper, a middle-aged millionaire who Anne introduced her to, Gino disparages Helen to Anne in broadsides that echo
Susann's ambivalence: her sympathetic analogy of the fan-as-lover who
"makes you king" then "drops you cold," and her derisive comparison of
Helen to "a stevedore grabbing a dancehall girl." Begging Anne to "call
her off my back," Gino blurts, "that old bat practically touched my—my
privates . . . and begged me to come up for a nightcap. I pretended not
to understand, Boy, I ran for my life. . . . I just want a girl who's pretty,
who has a good body. She doesn't have to have brains or be a legend. . . .
What do I want with Helen Lawson? She's like a bull in heat" (Susann

1997c, 102–3). A normative gaze of taste, desirability, and feminine decorum besets Helen, first positioning her as a deviant for acting on her sexual impulses then animalizing and masculinizing her as "a bull in heat." In light of the "love" that Susann signals for Helen's comedy of bad manners, however, Gino's mocking insults also appear as misguided reasoning. While Helen nurses her desire for Gino after two nights of clubbing with him, for instance, she wonders to Anne about Gino's lack of erotic reciprocation. Anne speculates that "he has respect for you," but Helen ripostes, "Who wants respect? I want to get laid!" The subsequent line, "Anne's gasp was audible," serves as the punchline in this round of Helen's comedy of bad manners (Susann 1997c, 96).

If Helen's brazen "masculine" agency threatens to make her ridiculous, the diva's command of oaths, profanity, and epithets nevertheless empower Helen and encourage admiration. During Anne's nightclubbing with Helen and Gino, for example, "Anne quickly caught the mood of hilarity and even found herself laughing at some of Helen's off-color jokes. It was impossible not to like Helen" (Susann 1997c, 83). After Helen's director Gil resists the star's advice to recast the gorgeous ingenue in *Hit the Sky* with the unglamorous but talented Neely O'Hara, Susann's description and dialogue depict another shocking and liberating instance of Helen's disruption of feminine decorum: "Helen's eyes narrowed. 'And what should an ingenue look like? A fucked-out redhead with big tits?'" (Susann 1997c, 121). Helen transgresses the "polite" rules of female discourse in the very act of criticizing, as Knowles puts it, "the callous reality of a patriarchal industry that has a vested interest in promoting one (rather damaging) version of femininity" (Knowles 2016, 75). Helen's duplicity further speaks to these patriarchal pressures; neither a genuine champion for Neely nor an advocate for unconventional female casting, Helen acts out of self-preservation, her fears of competing with Terry, the younger, more conventionally attractive woman initially cast as the ingenue. The male gaze endures as a fundamental condition of public life for Susann, her single girls and celebrity divas, patrolling appearances and policing any scandalous, unwomanly behavior (Trask 2013, 181–83). And where most of Susann's male characters exercise their power by wielding the gaze and framing its objects through vulgar sexual language, Helen resists and vandalizes its frame through the humorous transposition of gendered norms.

Single Girls Queering the Valley: Friends of Neely, and, Jennifer's Jocularity

Amid the skyrocketing sales of *Valley of the Dolls* throughout 1966 and 1967, apropos a writer of romans à clef, Susann made sure to tie the "single girl" attitudes of her characters to her own, presumably heterosexual, life experience. The author also dropped queer hints in her promotion of *Valley*. She insisted to radio host John Nebel, for instance, "Any sex—any love between two people is very natural," and maintained in *Life* magazine, "If two adults fall in love who happen to be of the same sex . . . then I don't see what's the harm in anything they do" (*Jacqueline Susann*; Howard 1966, 77). Susann's position aligned with the logic of the single girl, wherein taking the scenic single route could also extend to bypassing heteronormative regulations (see Radner 1999, 31–32). Brown extolls gay men in *Sex and the Single Girl*, for example, as "wonderful friends" for single women: loyal, tasteful, attractive, and insightful about men (Brown 2003, 31). Gay male readers of *Valley of the Dolls* indeed proved steadfast fans, recalls writer and artist Gary Indiana, as "author and book became vastly popular as homosexual kitsch. . . . *Valley*'s downfall portraits of fag-hag divas Judy Garland and Ethel Merman won fans among the then-clandestine gay community; for the first time in pop fiction characters openly referred to 'queers' and 'fags' in the entertainment industry" (Indiana 2008, 216). Susann consistently links showbiz gay men with the Garland and Merman characters, and in Neely O'Hara's ascent to stardom, pairs the aspiring performer with gay musical director Zeke Whyte; "He said I'm a cross between Judy Garland and Mary Martin," Neely gushes to Jennifer (Susann 1997c, 181). Susann might have tapped Garland's "downfall" reputation with Neely, but Indiana forgets that this version of Garland, flawed, troubled, and talented as she is, remains a survivor, the spirit of which Susann stressed in promoting her novel in 1967: "I think Judy will always come back. She kids about making a lot of comebacks. But I think Judy has a kind of a thing where she has to get to the bottom of the rope. And things have to get very very rough for her. And then with amazing inner strength that only comes of a certain genius, she comes back bigger than ever" (*Jacqueline Susann*).[23] Neely's comeback concert following rehab captures this camp paradox after Susann describes the audience's "audible gasp" on seeing the singer, having gained considerable weight: "Neely heard it and grinned. 'I'm real fat,' she said heartily. 'But so are a lot of opera singers. . . . I'm just here to sing my heart out for you—and my heart is big and fat, too, so if you like, I'll do a lot of singing.' The applause was deafening" (Susann 1997c, 403). As gay men forged a camp bond with Susann through her abundant epithets and stereotypes, they could also appreciate how Susann sculpted a camp Garland, paraphrasing Cohan on *A Star Is Born*, "that theatricalizes transparency and then naturalizes the theatricality" (Cohan 2005, 25).

Brown also validated a Sapphic route for the single girl, something Susann briefly affirms in *Valley*. Toward the end of Brown's treatise, the fleeting, ambivalent section "Suppose You Like Girls" includes the compassionate concession, "I think it's a shame you have to be so surreptitious about your choice of a way of life," but Brown retrenches her heterosexuality when explaining, "I could contribute no helpful advice" and "I don't know about your pleasures" (234). Lesbian relationships nevertheless offer one "choice of a way of life" for a single girl, and even if wrongly defining homosexual desire as a matter of volition and lifestyle, Brown values the single's agency by conferring possibility and validity on this alternative. Just a few pages later Brown iterates these mixed messages. "Put Your Guilt Away," Brown calms concerned readers, in the face of "your most wicked and base thoughts—secret fantasies—even leanings to homosexuality," however, the price of this peace of mind is not acting on one's desires (257).

Although Susann's promotional statements defended homosexuality in gender-neutral terms such as "any love between two people" and "two adults . . . who happen to be of the same sex," these sentiments nonetheless present a frame for the brief backstory about Jennifer's passionate relationship with her schoolmate Maria. They also provide a key for queer readers to decode *Valley of the Dolls* as a queer social melodrama and a confession from Susann.[24] Unlike her friends Anne and Neely, Jennifer cannot escape the Victorian melodramatic legacy that dictated the "narrative outcome for the fallen woman who was not rescued by her family or society": "death, either by her own hand or the hand of the trade in which she worked" (Staiger 2010, 35–36).[25] Considering the traditionalism that critics attributed to Susann's morality tale, *Valley of the Dolls* appears to punish Jennifer, like so many queer characters, for being driven by deviant, unprocreative desires. From the vantage point of the single girl, though, Jennifer's queer desire corresponds to a vitality and freedom that the pressures of heteronormativity finally crush. If the necessity for heterosexual romance motivates Jennifer's suicide, what Halberstam dubs "heteronormative common sense" (2011, 89) remains impossible and fatal. Ephron (1969) detects this duplicity in *Valley of Dolls* but stops short of locating the queer pleasures and wisdom it affords: the bogusness of heterosexual romance and the cruelty of men, which result in Jennifer's masochistic self-destruction; and the conflict between, on the one hand, the scandalous fun of women's misbehavior and celebrity gossip, and on the other, the formulaic and punishing morality tale. A queer moral perspective materializes in *Valley* that exalts Jennifer, the bisexual divorcée-turned-showgirl and art movie star, as the fallen hero of the Dolls.

Valley of the Dolls bifurcates Jennifer's narrative consistent with Maria San Filippo's definition of "bi-textuality," a variant of "double plot structure" that "operates to formulate and convey . . . a metaphor between bisexuality and an analogous identity construct that also resists containment within a binary taxonomy" (2013, 41). Bisexual logic explodes the "seemingly natural progression toward sexual partnership with opposite-gendered individuals for the purpose of heterosexual procreation and propagation of heteronormativity," and in conjunction, complicates the facade of feminine ideality (San Filippo 2013, 12, 53). Bisexual logic indeed powers Jennifer's agency as a bohemian single girl who appropriates the male playboy's privileged sexual agency and wit. Jennifer's recognition of active sexual desire, the power of masquerade, and the nourishment of irony all trace back to her passionate affair with Maria. Jennifer's heterosexual romance plotline, by contrast, involves her ultimate attempt to believe in the unification of true love and domesticity and results in tragic self-destruction. *Valley of the Dolls* generates a queer moral outlook from recognizing that Jennifer and Maria's sincere, mutual passion never recurs, for Jennifer or any of the principal characters, and, that Jennifer's sophistication and insight into heterosexual relationships stem from her bisexual experiences. All of this dissolves, though, when Jennifer avows to Anne, "I want a man to love me . . . I want a child" (Susann 1997c, 317).

Taking hints from the lesbian pulp novel, whose "golden age" was just coming to a conclusion in the mid-1960s, Susann's tender and passionate rendering of Jennifer's relationship with Maria plunders and revises some of the genre's homophobic, voyeuristic tendencies (Grier 1966; Keller 1999, 2–3). Jennifer's gaze of passion flourishes from the moment she espies "the most beautiful girl in school," with whom—just a few pages hence—"Jennifer found herself responding with equal ardor and reaching peaks of exaltation she never dreamed of" (Susann 1997c, 171, 175). Even so, Maria attests at the dawn of their relationship, "We are not Lesbians like those awful freaks who cut their hair and wear mannish clothes," and their affair goes the way of many a 1960s lesbian pulp novel by ending in breakup when Maria's possessiveness increases in proportion to Jennifer's economic reliance on her (Susann 1997c, 174, 176). Susann nevertheless alters what Yvonne Keller refers to as lesbian pulp fiction's "homophobic looking relationships," and the related trope of "the man who always gets the girl—at least the most feminine girl—in the end" (Keller 1999, 3–4). Susann also lifts strategies from "pro-lesbian pulps," published from 1955 to 1965 and written by lesbian authors, both "against the genre's norms" and adhering to a heteronormative "moral code": "Their authors' tactics often resulted in obvious contradictions within the texts, such as perfectly content lesbians who suddenly commit suicide or marry men at the end of the book" (Keller 1999, 5). Susann first affirms lesbian desire with the condition of maintaining a femme facade, and at last, qualifies Jennifer's narrative tragedy and challenges the stigma of her bisexuality. Susann shores up the pragmatic contradictions of being a queer single girl and deploys them against the normative reading that would fault Jennifer.

Susann's presence in *Valley of the Dolls* conveys to queer women readers the possibility that she, unlike Brown, *does* "know about your pleasures" and *is eager* to share her "most wicked and base thoughts—secret fantasies—even leanings to homosexuality," and perhaps not just fantasies. As Barbara Seaman informs in her biography, Susann based Jennifer and Maria's affair on her relationship with actress Carole Landis in 1945: "The depth of Jackie's feelings for Carole, and the nature of their physical relationship, can be surmised from the tender lesbian affair described in *Valley of the Dolls*. In it, Jennifer North, the blond beauty based at least in part on Landis, has the only truly satisfying love of her life with a woman—a brunette like Jackie" (Seaman 1996c, 154). Seaman cites Susann's editor Don Preston for corroboration; Preston wondered if the author "hadn't come to terms with sexuality yet," then opined, "She

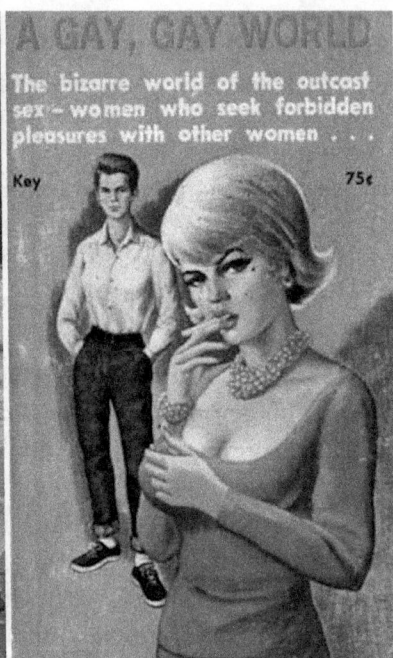

Susann draws from the personal and the pulp to render Jennifer's relationship with Maria: her affair with Carole Landis and tropes of lesbian pulp novels like *69 Barrow Street* by Sheldon Lord (a.k.a. Lawrence Block, cover illustration by Paul Rader, 1959) and *A Gay, Gay World* (1963) by Ronnie Edmunds.

couldn't write a romantic sex scene between a woman and a man. . . . Her lesbian scenes were more tender. She was more free to romanticize and idealize" (quoted in Seaman 1996c, 296). Preston alludes to the absence of a voyeuristic, distanced, objectifying male gaze in Jennifer and Maria's love scenes and a confirmation of Susann's confessional gossip, a variation of Keller's characterization of lesbian pulp novelist Randy Salem as "simultaneously voyeuristic and antivoyeuristic" (Keller 1999, 6–7). Robbing the male gaze of erotic power, Susann in turn invests the gazes shared between Jennifer and Maria with greater force than any of the novel's women experience in heterosexual couplings.

Jennifer embodies the bohemian single girl throughout most of the novel, and when she ascends to stardom in sexual French art films, approximates what San Filippo terms the "bisexual-bohemian" character type, introduced into film culture through art cinema and drawn from 1950s lesbian pulp fiction (San Filippo 2013, 53–55). Usually a white woman, one variation of this narrative positions her between "safely gender-conforming and heteronormative" American customs and "'third world' exoticism" or "'European-style' eroticism," with the goal of "decontaminating and domesticating her body, agency, and desire as safely gender-conforming and heteronormative" (53). Susann renders Jennifer's bi-textuality, however, in a plotline where decontamination and domestication kill her, and which depicts Europe and the United States as equally sexually exploitative, demonstrated through the institutional norms of art cinema and Hollywood. Jennifer's bi-textuality, finally, coincides with Susann's sleazy realism, in particular, the recombination of classical Hollywood melodrama and comedy in jarring, sometimes shocking pairings.

Jennifer's expression of sexual agency as well as her witty urbanity and the contorted sexual scenarios she navigates recall several comedic variations of the fallen woman: "the burlesque showgirl" who could "lead silly men to ruin," such as the "blonde diamond digger" Lorelei Lee in Anita Loos's 1925 novel *Gentlemen Prefer Blondes*, eventually immortalized by Monroe in Howard Hawks's 1953 movie adaptation; and in early 1930s comedies, sexually savvy, successful, and witty women such as Mae West's Lou in *She Done Him Wrong* (Sherman, 1933) and Miriam Hopkins's Gilda in *Design for Living* (Staiger 2010, 46–48; 51–52). Many of Jennifer's male partners furthermore materialize an array of "silly," "fallen men" from early 1930s pictures (46–47). Jennifer's practical view of sex-for-marriage does not preclude her own desire for sexual satisfaction, and when these manifest through comedy "are treated as circumstances, but not as moral problems, for the narrative to resolve" (51). Glitre identifies a dynamic of antiromance in 1950s sex comedies parallel to these early 1930s comedies and indicative of Jennifer's wisdom, wherein "romance is associated with the artifice of seduction, in opposition to the 'naturalness' of 'true' love. Seduction and romance are revealed to be based upon manipulation and commodification" (Glitre 2006, 35). These generic features translate to Jennifer's embodiment of "the permanent single" girl whose sexuality "becomes a lifestyle, much like that of the playboy" (Wojcik 2010, 156), and by extension, male playboy characters of postwar Hollywood sex comedies such as Rock Hudson in *Pillow Talk* (Gordon 1959) and Tony Curtis in *Sex and the Single Girl* (Quine 1964).

When Jennifer usurps the playboy privilege of seduction and manipulation assumed to be men's property, sleazy realism intrudes into the careful "clockwork arrangement" (in Bergson's [1928] expression) of Hollywood romantic genres. Susann first introduces Jennifer through Anne's competitive gaze, a dazzling beauty across a crowded nightclub seated with Anne's crush, theatrical agent Lyon Burke. When Susann takes Jennifer's perspective, the reader discovers someone with an impoverished past and needy mother who uses her sexuality for advancement as well as enjoys sex with women and men. Jennifer's date with Lyon bears a practical motive, "to keep publicity going" after her front-page divorce from Prince Mirallo, but Jennifer also "had felt a surge of excitement in meeting a man she knew she wanted, a man she wanted for nothing beyond her own pleasure. She had intended to have him that night; then Tony Polar materialized. . . . As a man Tony could not compare to Lyon. . . . But Lyon Burke was only an agent; Tony was a star. That had made her decision. . . . It was that simple" (1997c, 165–66). Susann employs the comedic motifs of animated cartoons next when identifying Jennifer's acumen as a single woman and a survivor, the "mechanism [that] seemed to click within [Jennifer's] mind, automatically eliminating the impractical with the precision of an IBM machine" (1997c, 166), an image evoking cartoon gags in which dollar signs flash in characters' eyes or cash registers replace their heads.[26]

The tragicomedy of manners that ensues between Jennifer and crooner Tony Polar demystifies any semblance of romance, exploded by the pathetically funny, grotesque, and abusive side of male playboy privilege. After sex-obsessed Tony repeatedly postpones marriage, Jennifer transforms into a variation of the "professional virgin," another type from 1950s sex comedy: a single girl fully aware of her body as "capital," carefully negotiating men's sexual aggressiveness and vowing to abstain until marriage (Radner 1999, 11, 16, 22; Glitre 2006, 144–47). The contorted scenario Susann concocts veers between comedy and melodrama, from Jennifer's active desire to Tony's sexual abusiveness, yet concludes with an ironic victory for Jennifer. Resisting Tony at her apartment while roommate Anne is at work—"Not now. Not until you marry me"— Jennifer receives a telegram about the death of Anne's mother, then calls her friend to impart the sad news (Susann 1997c, 195). Distracted, "She felt Tony enter her, roughly, pounding into her. She clenched her teeth and kept her voice even. 'Yes, Anne . . . I'm terribly sorry.' She hung up. Tony had fallen across her, panting in satisfied exhaustion" (Susann 1997c, 197). Repartee follows redolent of sex comedy, at Jennifer's expense: "'Tony, that wasn't fair. That was taking advantage of me.' . . . 'Baby, you were born with the advantages—a pair of them'" (Susann 1997, 197). Tony vamooses, then Jennifer ponders, "What timing. . . . Damn all mothers! Even in death they reached out and loused you up," then she retrenches her plans (198). In a gesture of seeming camaraderie with Anne, Jennifer offers to drive her roommate back to Lawrenceville for the funeral, but this serves Jennifer's project to hook Tony by making her body unattainable.

Susann's ironic and disturbing scene invokes typical tropes from sex comedy, as well as women's fiction and Hollywood melodrama, then revises them as a range of violations that undercut anything closely resembling true love and romantic altruism. The scene invokes characteristic sex comedy imagery that, viewed from Jennifer's perspective, becomes grotesquely unfunny: seduction during phone calls, which forces one party to masquerade as if all is normal; the persistent playboy's seduction and the female protagonist determined to get married; the playboy's smooth-talking objectification of women and dismissal of their protests; and occasional plotlines involving camaraderie among women to push the playboy toward marriage. These generic motifs twist into violence through Tony's shocking sexual assault and Jennifer's pose of calm on the phone, followed by the crooner's ridiculously sleazy dialogue, Jennifer's dispassionate duplicity, and her ambiguous motivations for seeking community with Anne.[27] Jennifer's condemnation of "all mothers" furthermore injects a kind of sick comic redirection that reassigns blame for Tony's violation at the same time as blending genre patterns. In sex comedy, cynically sex-driven men despoil the ideal of motherhood, which proves an obstacle in their coital pursuits, and in the melodramatic woman's picture, "fallen" daughters such as Veda in *Mildred Pierce* (Curtiz, 1945) and Sarah Jane in *Imitation of Life* (Sirk, 1959) spurn their mothers. Inasmuch as Tony embodies an extreme version of the sex comedy playboy, he also personifies a melodramatic villain through his brutal behavior and salacious joking as well as a fallen man with a simpleminded, helpless obsession for Jennifer's body. Susann finally frees Jennifer from Tony's tyranny with a spectacular revelation that operates as moral punishment and smacks of melodramatic excess, that Tony has a terminal, degenerative intellectual disability.

Although Susann explains Tony's sexual obsession and abusiveness as a matter of bodily malfunction rather than patriarchal trespass,[28] his disposition nevertheless jibes with numerous men in *Valley of the Dolls*. These events also generate further antiromantic activity brimming with single girl incongruity: Jennifer's abortion in New Jersey, divorce from Tony in Mexico, and in the same paragraph, Jennifer's New York homecoming, whereupon she "entered into the excitement of the new fall openings and went on a shopping spree for new clothes" (Susann 1997c, 241–42). With an assertion of style worthy of a comedy of bad manners, Jennifer returns to New York a fallen woman rejuvenated, her single girl freedoms restored. Now primed to perform in French "sex pictures"—"Artistic—but semi-nude"—Jennifer wittily disabuses Anne and the reader of their worst assumptions while calling out the prurient male gaze of art cinema: "Oh, I don't mean dirty pictures—I mean movies with a real plot. Only when you take a bath in a scene, they photograph it" (Susann 1997c, 244). Determined to remake her career in Paris, Jennifer flippantly proclaims both her awareness of director-producer Claude Chardot's artificiality and exploitative motives—"I know Claude is a phony. . . . He expects to make money with me"—and her fatalistic sense of adventure: "What have I got to lose?" (Susann 1997c, 244).

Susann's trajectory for Jennifer demonstrates how the "exciting life" of a single woman regularly requires negotiating the male gaze and a range of its brutal tolls, the greatest one in believing in it. After a life and career of masquerade, Jennifer thinks she has found a man who genuinely loves her and can provide financial stability, a widowed millionaire senator, but his reaction to Jennifer's breast cancer diagnosis reveals the extent to which he fetishizes her: "He caressed her breasts. 'These are my babies,' he said softly. . . . But as long as they never harm my babies . . .' He caressed her breasts again" (Susann 1997c, 334). Despair over her need for a mastectomy in light of the senator's sleazy disclosure motivates Jennifer's suicidal overdose of Seconal. Susann nevertheless invests Jennifer with the agency of ironist in her suicide note to the senator, which subtly calls him out as a fallen man: "I had to leave—to save your babies.

Thanks for making it all almost come true" (Susann 1997c, 336). Jennifer's "Thanks" and rationale for suicide could be easily interpreted as a masochistic acknowledgment of her failure to reconcile sexuality, love, and domesticity; however, her graciousness and humility harbors a sarcasm critical of heterosexual romance founded in the male gaze.[29]

For queer women readers, though, Jennifer's tragic ending might have seemed a throwback. Notwithstanding the "happy endings" that some lesbian pulp novels offered, such as Ann Bannon's Beebo Brinker books, popular fiction of the 1960s also began supplanting lesbian pulp.[30] Jennifer's tragedy in this case might have echoed the fate of Rina Marlow in Robbins's *The Carpetbaggers*, the culmination of lifelong sexual victimization meted out most cruelly by a lesbian and a closeted gay man, even though the causality surrounding Jennifer's suicide is drastically dissimilar from Rina's demise. Mainstream bestsellers, Keller adds, sometimes delivered queer women characters who prevailed, such as the unapologetic, heroic Lakey in Mary McCarthy's 1963 novel *The Group* (Keller 1999, 19–20). Keller makes no mention of *Valley of the Dolls*, but Jane Howard of *Life* magazine commented in 1966 that Susann's "heroines constitute a sort of chorus girls version of Mary McCarthy's *The Group*" (69). Although Lakey differs considerably from Jennifer, the two share stunning beauty and a form of sophistication related to their queerness that eludes their straight friends. Jennifer nevertheless requires the kind of "ambivalent" reading strategies all too familiar to Eisenhower-Kennedy-era lesbian readers, practiced in shifting perspectives based on "irreconcilable" points of identification: with the novel's lesbian couple; the voyeuristic white male character who challenges as well as objectifies them; the "pseudonymous author"; and finally, readers identifying "only with their desire" (Keller 1999, 17).[31]

Susann was not pseudonymous, and although certainly closeted about her bisexuality, delivered vague clues through the play of gossip and confession in both the novel and her public statements that, for ambivalent readers, could cluster around Jennifer. Susann defended homosexuality when promoting *Valley of the Dolls* and encouraged the assumption that this roman à clef was peppered with "a bit of" herself "in every character." Such closeted play might have eluded straight readers such as Ephron, but queer readers were used to discerning what Andrea Weiss refers to in lesbian film spectatorship as "fleeting gestures and coded language" (1991, 286). If the full promise of queering the Valley is fore-shortened by Jennifer's fleeting lesbian experiences, tragic demise, and narrative exit, compounded by Susann's unwillingness to come out as bisexual, the author's "coded language" encourages a queer reconsider-ation of the morality tale. Following brief bliss with her brunette lover Maria, one of Susann's stand-ins, heteronormative pressure conditions Jennifer's melodramatic victimhood. While the pleasure of gay male fans in Indiana's (2008) account orbited around the iconic camp divas Hellen/ Merman and Neely/Garland, their vocabulary of gay euphemisms, and the gays of showbiz swirling within the novel's sidelines, Jennifer's bisex-ual wit prevails throughout coping with abuse and facing mortality, which is enough to make her a camp hero.

"... a brutal climb ...": Twentieth Century-Fox's *Valley of the Dolls*

When Hollywood adapted the "single girl" bestsellers *The Best of Every-thing* and *Sex and the Single Girl*, the primacy of romantic love, chastity, and domesticity replaced what Jaffe (2005) and Brown (2003) had deter-minedly demystified. Warner Bros.' *Sex and the Single Girl* (Quine, 1964) turns into a typical sex comedy narrative, determined to render mar-riageable its mismatched single protagonists, repressed psychoanalyst and pop-psychology author Helen Brown (Natalie Wood) and playboy journalist Bob Weston (Tony Curtis), as well as reconcile a married cou-ple (Lauren Bacall and Henry Fonda) whose relationship is on the rocks.[32] Twentieth Century-Fox's *The Best of Everything* (Negulesco, 1959), mean-while, ends with the promise of marriage for a virginal Caroline (Hope Lange), not singledom, sexual experience, and scandal as in the novel.

The same studio's adaptation of *Valley of the Dolls* (1967), directed by Mark Robson and adapted first by Helen Deutsch and then Dorothy Kingsley, might have advantaged from adjustments to the Production Code in 1965. The film could employ an expanded vocabulary ("boobies," "bitchy," "queer," "s.o.b.," and "fag," among others), more suggestive cos-tuming, even partial nudity, although the Production Code Administra-tion required that the film "carry the designation 'Suggested for Mature Audiences' in all advertising" (Ferguson 1967; Shurlock 1967a; Shurlock 1967b; Bart 1965, 37).[33] The film nevertheless simplifies both Susann's fallen women and the epic plotline.[34] Neely (Patty Duke) and Helen (Susan Hayward) never get to charm with their lexicon of vulgarisms, earthy sense of humor, or their most extreme egoistic excesses, nor does the narrative contextualize their misdoings with an exposé of "the system that makes people become this way," as Susann put it to Bjorkman. Neely's passage from sweet, talented naïf to showbiz monster is clarified in broad strokes by making her much nastier than in the novel, demonstrated in the changes to Neely and Helen's powder room showdown for the film. Susann casts Helen the aggressor; Neely, fresh from being fired by the studio, experiencing a weight gain, and extremely vulnerable, joins Anne in the powder room of the Persian Room nightclub and when Helen arrives, just wants to leave, but Helen's snipes and aspersions finally provoke Neely's appalling behavior, all of which Anne witnesses. The film's Neely, by contrast, aims to get both Anne and Helen at their most vulnerable, first by making it clear to Anne (Barbara Parkins) that she is carrying on an affair with Lyon (Paul Burke), and immediately after, crashing the theater party celebrating Helen's new show, making an entrance that overshadows Helen, and finally following Helen into the powder room intent on confrontation. Jennifer (Sharon Tate) in the film still commits suicide after being diagnosed with breast cancer, but the adaptation painstakingly assures the audience of her heterosexuality and her innocence. Now a purely passive victim of circumstance, Jennifer's relationship with Tony (Tony Scotti) transforms into true love, not sexual exploitation, and she selflessly sacrifices herself to the indignities of disrobing in art films just to support Tony's hospitalization.

Anne receives a similar scrubbing, no longer the determined single girl detesting her hometown and delighting in New York living, resisting bourgeois convention yet finally falling prey to the fantasy of connubial bliss and using dolls to suspend her disbelief. The film's Anne flees back to Lawrenceville at the end, away from nursing a doll addiction and living in sin in sunny Tinseltown with the determined bachelor Lyon, to restore her innocence in the safe, wintery landscapes of her New England hometown and the embrace of her Aunt Amy (Judith Lowry). Lyon follows, now a sullen, pathetic fallen man desperate to get hitched, but Anne politely spurns his marriage proposal, then leaves him behind in her own home to stroll triumphantly through the snowy woods. Susann's bracing denunciation of marriage turns into, for the film, Anne's triumphant female redemption, sans marriage, the resuscitation of her purity and the affirmation of bourgeois values.

The film version of *Valley of the Dolls* reduces Susann's sleazy realism
and virtually erases her deliberate humor and guessing game, the women's misbehavior now orchestrated like clockwork according to a melodramatic scale. Force-fitting the epic, twenty-year timespan of the source
novel into the narrow contours of a two-hour backstage/backstudio picture, the film whittles the novel down to a morality tale about show business in which the "monstrous" behavior of women celebrities indicates
the threat of "unruly female stars" and their "uncontrollable agency"
(Cohan 2019, 123). This restrictive format unsurprisingly squeezed out
the novel's ingredients that "made it more fun" for readers like Ephron
in addition to the novel's queer fans: the roman à clef gossip column;
aggressive female sexual desire, bisexuality, and homosexuality; and
flamboyantly vulgar, poetically profane dialogue. The morality tale that
remains forms the spine of the film and affords little opportunity for the
kind of comedy of bad manners that comments on class, gender, and
sexual norms, or the queer outlook that Susann furnishes in the novel,
however ambiguously. The dampening of Susann's sleazy realism enables
the film to sustain the genre tropes that the novel upended and carries
over to the loss of comedic agency for the women characters.[35] A tepid
romantic comedy meet-cute transpires, then, between Anne and Lyon
to establish the playboy/virgin dynamic; Tony's romantic crooning to
Jennifer the night they meet gushes with the spontaneity and unity of
love and desire; and the humble origins of Neely, prior to her fall into the
Valley, bespeak the PCA-approved wholesomeness of a musical comedy
like *Babes in Arms* (1939).

Preproduction publicity for *Valley of the Dolls* almost immediately
presented harbingers of the film's timid treatment of Susann's "dirty"
source. Promises from the adapters to remain "tasteful" accompanied
assurances of retaining a degree of the novel's crudities for the purposes
of characterization and serious social commentary, a kind of tasteful
vulgarity. As the *Film Daily* reported after a fall 1966 press conference
with director Mark Robson, producer David Weisbart, and screenwriter
Helen Deutsch, "although the scenario will be in 'good taste,' it will not be
laundered rinso white" (Anon. 1966b, 1). Covering the same press conference, *Variety* revealed that "scripter Helen Deutsch said she is 'struggling'

with the lingo of Jacqueline Susann's novel in order to 'stay within the bounds of good taste,'" although as *Film Daily* informed, Deutsch's promise of "'good taste' . . . was quickly followed by assertions from Robson and Weisbart, with an affirmation from her, that earthy language appropriate to characterization would not be expunged in the process" (Anon. 1966c, 5; Anon. 1966b, 1, 8). Pledges that profanity would have the proper narrative motivation stretched to Weisbart's goal of reaching general audiences, especially "younger people," a strategy that bore prosocial, moralistic motivations because "the subject of the novel 'is very valuable for a broad cross-section of people to see. . . . It shows the pitfalls of certain ambitions'" (Anon. 1966a, 8).

The impact of "good taste" on the narrative, in which moral and educational value justified the seamy situations and "four letter" dialogue (Anon. 1966b, 1), coincided with reducing the characters to simplified types as well as the virtual erasure of the comedy of bad manners, such as Anne's encounters with the salty speech and sexual attitudes of Neely and Helen, in addition to Jennifer's sophisticated, wry outlook and the tragicomic dimensions of her experiences. Queer characters and content virtually disappear, beginning with the ambient gay men of show business and the bisexuality of Neely's husband Ted Casablanca (Alexander Davion). Although the word "fag" occasionally flies out of characters' mouths, the film lacks Neely's affectionate uses of the word in her associations with gay men throughout her career, to say the least of such shocking excesses as Helen's paroxysm of "faggot" in her confrontation scene with Neely.

Jennifer's lesbian affair inevitably disappears in the film, a negation of the novel's tenderest, most erotically charged representation of sexuality that coincides with the erasure of Jennifer's wit and sophistication. A conversation between Jennifer and Anne in the novel at the height of Jennifer's movie stardom and shortly before she meets the senator concretizes her bisexual wit:

"They love my face and body. Not me! There's such a difference, Anne." Then she shrugged. "Maybe I'm just not very lovable."

"I love you, Jen—really."

Jennifer smiled. "I know you do. It's a pity we're not queer—we'd make a marvelous team."

Anne laughed. "If we were, maybe it wouldn't work out this way. As you said, one loves and the other is loved. Or maybe it's different with Lesbians."

Jennifer had a far-off look. "No . . . even with queers, one loves and the other is loved." (Susann 1997c, 317)

Deutsch's show of "good taste" in the first draft of the screenplay includes Jennifer as the helpless heterosexual victim of unwanted lesbian advances, a melodramatic plot turn worlds away from the bisexual sophistication exhibited in the dialogue above. Having established the true love between Jennifer and Tony, Deutsch turns Miriam Polar, Tony's sister and manager, into a predatory lesbian. Miriam heinously launches her advances on Jennifer just as Tony's illness worsens, a violation that Jennifer repels with moralistic fury—"Go away! Get out! You filthy—Go away, get out! Get out!"—but that nonetheless catalyzes Jennifer's suicide. Downing a suicidal handful of dolls afterward, recollections flash through Jennifer's head of her sexual exploitation as an actress, along with memories of (in Deutsch's expression) "Miriam's lesbian pass" (1966, 149–52). Kingsley's rewrite adheres to the "strictly heterosexual" (as *Variety*'s reviewer put it) and limits dialogue referencing "fags" in the entertainment industry to a few scenes (Anon. 1967j, 6).

Despite the backstage and backstudio plotlines, the filmmakers also erased what *Variety* called "the Hollywood expose [*sic*]"; as the *Washington Post* had announced, "David Weisbart will thank you please to keep your cotton pickin' pickings of Judy Garland, Ethel Merman and Grace Kelley 'types' out of his daily mail," followed by Weisbart's robotic recitation disclaiming any of the characters' resemblances to "persons living or dead" (Anon. 1966c, 5; Manners 1966, C10). This strategy to offset libel suits nevertheless failed to silence the "guessing game," which persisted in journalistic reports during production, no doubt encouraged by the expanding readership as the paperback edition hit the market.[36] The film discouraged the deeper pleasures of the roman à clef fostered by Susann, though, particularly the celebrity comedy of bad manners involving evocations of Merman and Garland. The original stunt casting of Judy Garland as Helen Lawson might have enabled some of the novel's parodic and satirical temptations to endure in the film, even if one journalist observed, "When Judy signed the Fox contract gossipers were temporarily stymied" (Adams 1967, 32). A full-page ad in the *New York Times* announcing that the film started shooting, not two weeks after Garland's signing, seemed to encourage speculation, though, by dispelling Hollywood illusion. The ad clamored, "No Amber Lights, Please. No Gauze on the Cameras. Just the Hot, White Light of Truth." The text below filled in what the heading teased: "'Valley of the Dolls' boldly breaks into the playground of Broadway and Hollywood—where the games are rough, but open to all aspirants who want to play" (Anon. 1967a, 38). Garland's casting most likely impressed the roaring promise of "TRUTH," given her widely reported inspiration for the novel's Neely, Garland's years as a musical comedy star in MGM's Freed Unit, her well-reported struggles with substance abuse and comebacks, even Garland's performances with Merman on her television variety show. Recasting Helen with Susan Hayward removed the instantaneous unity of the film and novel's frame of reference that casting Garland had materialized.

Deflecting the guessing game and framing the film through the general social problem of pill addiction also dodged the social problems harbored within the entertainment industry. Susann dissects the tyrannical, abusive and seductive male gaze that drives show business and frames its stars through a controlling Hollywood studio chief whose melodramatic villainy oozes through devious scheming and vulgar, misogynistic dialogue. Aptly nicknamed "The Head," and clearly inspired by Louis B. Mayer and Darryl F. Zanuck, the malignant paterfamilias of Century Studios lives up to the punning implications of penis and pissoir conjured by his nickname: cultivating Neely's pill addiction to keep his starlet svelte as well as requiring Neely to stay unhappily married to "double-gaited" clothing designer Ted Casablanca, "for her public image" as "the girl next door" (Susann 1997c, 263). When the Hollywood studios later grow desperate in their losing competition with television, The Head plots to recruit Jennifer, now an international star in sexy, high-grossing French art films.[37] Resentful of his reliance on Jennifer, The Head launches into a rant bemoaning the decline of decency in the movies: "Something's happening to this country. We're going to go immoral. And television is doing it. I've always stood for clean American pictures, but now we have to fight television with everything we can get—tits, asses, French whores" (Susann 1997c, 278). With a flurry of self-righteous, ridiculously hypocritical slut-shaming, in dialogue that anticipates David Rabe's

Hollywood exposé *Hurlyburly* (1984), The Head blames Jennifer for Holly-wood's exploitation of her. Removing The Head from the film adaptation not only concealed the studio system's role in fomenting the drug addictions of contract players such as Garland but also the patriarchal double standards reflective of both male control and the exploitation of women performers represented by Neely and Jennifer.[38]

Such extensive alterations of Susann's novel did not seem to concern the movie industry trade paper *Independent Film Journal*, which hailed *Valley of the Dolls* a "pre-sold property," one that "should give a brand new meaning to the word, 'money,'" and that "doesn't really need any selling," primarily due to its "slick job of translating an enormously popular book into cinematic terms" (Anon. 1967c).[39] Confident in the film's "pre-sold" status, Twentieth Century-Fox released *Valley* at Christmastime, wrapped with salient signs that it imported the novel's adult content: advertising that teased, "Have you got 'The Dolls' for Christmas?" along with the warning, "Suggested for Mature Audiences"; and the "B" rating of "morally objectionable" assigned by the National Catholic Office for Motion Pictures (NCOMP), formerly the Catholic Legion of Decency (Ferguson 1967; Anon. 1967b, 4). A full-page ad in *Variety* boasted the film's lucrative New York debuts at the Criterion and Festival theaters: "V.O.D. Wow! . . . The Biggest Pre-Christmas Business in History of Both Theatres!" (Anon. 1967h, 19).

The huge success of *Valley of the Dolls* flagged the passage into the "permissive" era of "New Hollywood," although the film remained disqualified from the ranks of "new" pictures such as *Bonnie and Clyde* or *The Graduate*, financial successes marked by similarly "shocking" content yet met with plaudits for their artistic, cinematic innovations (Anon. 1967e). *The Graduate*, a box office hit released within a week of *Valley*, would garner the kind of artistic praise for its subversive and sophisticated sexual comedy never tendered to the vulgar, melodramatic *Valley*.[40] Even NCOMP preferred *The Graduate*, *Variety* reported, ranked by the Catholic organization among its "Best of the New Films" (Anon. 1968). NCOMP panned *Valley*, *Variety* also reported, as "a filmic failure on almost every level," "a screen adaptation of a shoddy novel (which) appears to have no purpose in telling its story except to wallow in it," an assessment that was "much stronger than that for most films which have recently been 'condemned'" (Anon. 1967b, 4).

The *Independent Film Review* forecasted the box office success of *Valley of the Dolls* as well as its camp reception, echoing what Steinem had identified in her review of Susann's book the year before as "moments of the sort once deplored as embarrassing or inadvertently funny, and now exalted as Unconscious Low Camp," such as the "television-bad" dialogue by a "former TV actress" (Steinem 1966, 11). The *Independent Film Review* pinned a similar assessment to screenwriters Deutsch and Kingsley for their "unintentionally funny and foolish" dialogue, which "adds to the film's entertainment values" (Anon. 1967c, 24). The artistic failure of the film related to this comedic dimension of "inadvertent" or "unintentional" humor, although this form of camp reception also contributed to erasing Susann's authorial agency. As Bosley Crowther opened his *New York Times* review, for instance, "Bad as Jacqueline Susann's 'Valley of the Dolls' is as a book, the movie Mark Robson has made from it is that bad or worse," a backhanded compliment that the reviewer follows with a jab at "Miss Susann's penny-dreadful plot" (Crowther 1967, 51). Crowther proceeds to find *Valley* "every bit as phony and old-fashioned as anything Lana Turner ever did," and funny by accident: "all a fairly respectful admirer of movies can do is laugh at it and turn away" (5). The success of *Valley of the Dolls* did not compensate for Susann's resentment toward the hokey ending and the general mangling of her personal epic, her bildungsroman à clef, and it certainly failed to win her any more respect among critics, who equated the slickly cheesy film with her novel and considered all of them naive camp at best. If Susann had once confessed to *Cosmopolitan* her resistance to being pegged "as a funny writer," culture critics nevertheless continued to "typecast" Jacqueline Susann as a "bad" writer of purportedly serious, moralistic fiction, sometimes laughably so as "pop" and "camp."

Although the adapters defused Susann's sleazy realism and comedy of bad manners to restore some semblance of classical Hollywood wholesomeness, the hallmarks of *Valley of the Dolls'* comically camp undoing nevertheless contributed to the collapse of heterosexual narrative logic: absurd causality, contrived genre motifs, hollow moralizing, overwrought scenes of drug abuse, contrived titillation, hyperbolic performances, brief and surprising bursts of Susann's vulgar dialogue, and expensive yet tacky production numbers.[41] Generated by a laughable adherence to the conventions of Victorian melodrama and "fallen

The Carol Burnett Show recognized the camp appeal of *Valley of the Dolls* in the 1968 parody sketch "Valley of the Dollars," featuring Burnett as Anne/Barbara Parkins, Gloria Loring as Jennifer/Sharon Tate, and Vicki Lawrence as Neely/Patty Duke.

woman" narratives, heterosexual romance paradoxically withers in the film's happy ending: Anne's flight back to wintry Lawrenceville following a near overdose on dolls in Hollywood, then rejecting Lyon's proposal in her family home and leaving him behind in the foyer to take a triumphant walk along a snowy-white, tree-lined thoroughfare.[42] If producer Weisbart and director Robson had promised that Susann's novel would "not be laundered rinso white," as the *Film Daily* confirmed, the ending managed this in every way, from the mise-en-scène to Anne's restoration of her virtue. Anne's destination in *Valley of the Dolls* materializes a subversive contradiction perfectly encapsulated by Lisa M. Dresner about 1980s teen sex comedies: "Oddly, then, the removal of the woman from the realm of satisfied sexual subjecthood appears also to remove her from the dangerous, distracting realm of sexual objecthood" (Dresner 2010, 185). Sanitized but not sane, the film's "odd" conclusion especially exhibits what *Variety* had reported as the adapters "struggling" with Susann's source material. Despite deleting the novel's lesbian sexuality and dropping the ironically depressing portrait of a marriage that closes Susann's epic, the film provides something of a lesbian happy ending engendered by the crumbling of heterosexual romance: Anne's freedom from men, marriage, and domesticity. If "good taste" muted Jacqueline Susann's subversive spin on the single girl, it also upended narrative coherence and spawned absurdities whose final illogic queer audiences could relish.

2

The Roman à Closet

Queer Irony, Closet Plotlines, and *The Love Machine*

Jacqueline Susann's *The Love Machine* raced into bookstores in May 1969 during a busy period for publishing controversies. Stoked by best-selling authors such as Gore Vidal, John Updike, and Philip Roth perceived as unable or unwilling to "resist the urge to flaunt their knowledge of sexual perversity," literary scandals "provoked 'rallies for decency' around the country" (Bisbort 2008, 80). Vidal's *Myra Breckinridge* continued to leave an impression a year after publication, with its "swinging" transgender protagonist and window into the polysexual revolution; and Roth's novel *Portnoy's Complaint*, boasting a protagonist obsessed with masturbation, remained the current *succès de scandale* before *The Love Machine* usurped its place atop the bestseller list (Eisner 1999, 255–60; Gunn and Harker 2013, 4–5). It came as no surprise, then, when Susann's editor Michael Korda at Simon and Schuster promoted *The Love Machine* against *Portnoy's* competition. Speaking with Nora Ephron for a *New York Times* story, Korda's pitch for product differentiation nevertheless appeared particularly defensive. "You have these two giant books out at the same time," Korda mused, "and their merits aside, one of them is about masturbation and the other is about successful heterosexual love. If there's any justice in the world, 'The Love Machine' ought to knock 'Portnoy' off the top simply because it's a step in the right direction" (Ephron 1969, 12). Korda's case for "heterosexual" "justice" met with an abundance of contravening evidence, however, within Susann's novel and its reception. Susann powered her *Love Machine* with queer themes and characters to such an extent, indeed, that this began to shape her authorial persona.

Sarah Davidson at *Harper's*, for instance, proclaimed amid the promotion of the book that Susann was "beloved by homosexuals . . . due not only to her strident personality but to the fact that she treats homosexuals with dignity in her books," a perception later verified by the *New York Times* and especially attributed to *The Love Machine* (Davidson 1969, 66; Kasindorf 1973, 86). Competing novelist Gwen Davis also disputed Korda's position when touting her new book *The Pretenders*, which she wrote to throw a monkey wrench into Susann's best-selling *Machine*, because "my husband was demanding equal time for heterosexuals," and since *The Love Machine* "isn't that well written and is too full of . . . joyful titillation" (Warga 1969, C1, C11).

Susann commits to queer "titillation" in *The Love Machine* from the start, beginning with the male protagonist Robin Stone, modeled after CBS president James T. Aubrey (with a little Edward R. Murrow thrown in). A TV news reporter whose unfaltering climb to president of the IBC TV network is joined by an equally endless show of dauntless masculinity, connotations of the closet and passing burst forth in Susann's prologue: "A machine who passes for a man often rules societies—a dictator is a power machine in his country. A dedicated artist can become a talent machine. Sometimes this evolution occurs without the man realizing it. . . . Robin Stone was a handsome man. He could smile with his lips. He could think without emotion. He could make love to her with his body. Robin Stone was The Love Machine" (Susann 1997a, 9). Steven Cohan helps illuminate Susann's coded, Cold War–era logic by explaining, "The closet does not hide homosexuality but instead actively pivots around an axis of symmetrically paired gender values (virile/sissy, dominant/ submissive, visible/invisible, normal/deviant, authentic/fake, disclosure/ secrecy) that keeps queering masculinity so that it cannot possibly be read as 'straight'" (Cohan 1997, 274). Robin might "make love to her with his body," but the playboy's heterosexuality and masculinity beg scrutiny, as a closet case, a "fake" man in Cohan's parlance, and in Susann's, a "machine who passes for a man . . . without the man realizing it." The same reasoning also makes Robin's masculinity questionable due to the feminized, domestic "Love Machine" most closely associated with him, television.[1] Susann proceeds to depict Robin through feminine gazes and tropes. Women both idealize and objectify Robin, and his psychological disorder aligns him early in the novel with the female protagonist

Jacqueline Susann promotes *The Love Machine*. Susann's cameo in the movie adaptation reinforces the centrality of TV, in the novel and in Susann's promotion of it.

of *Lady in the Dark*, a 1941 Broadway musical about a woman magazine editor in psychoanalysis.[2] (As Ephron observed in 1969, Robin's psycho-sexual plotline also closely resembles that of Marnie [Tippi Hedren] in the eponymous 1964 Hitchcock film, aligning Robin yet again with a woman protagonist.) Although Robin's psychic disorientation poises him for a final sacrificial grand gesture that signifies his recovery and redeems him for heterosexual romance, for the bulk of the novel Robin can only perform as a spectacle of masculinity, a "Love Machine" without genuine agency.

The Love Machine traces Robin's career at the IBC television network, where he first crosses paths with Amanda the fashion model, his hopelessly devoted, tall, blond, and "boyish" lover and eventual cast member of IBC's hit comedy-variety series headed by comedian Christie Lane. Amanda personifies a white ideal of glamorous beauty while she keeps secret her African American foster mother, Rose Jones, as well as the reason for her extreme anxiety over money, funding the infirmed Rose's hospitalization. When Christie proposes to Amanda, she considers marrying the grotesque TV comedian for financial security to care for Rose, but Amanda ultimately rejects Christie due to his racist reaction to Rose as well as Amanda's lingering love for Robin. Heartbroken by Rose's death, Amanda flees from Robin into the arms of the exploitative director Ike Ryan, and, eventually, dies of leukemia. Amanda's rejection of Christie sends him into the arms of IBC publicist Ethel Evans, nicknamed "celebrity-fucker" by her colleagues for flagrantly sleeping with numerous stars and rating their prowess. Robin's rise to network president also brings him into the sphere of Judith Austin—a middle-aged socialite and wife of the network's CEO Gregory Austin—who pursues an affair with Robin. Maggie Stewart comes into Robin's orbit, too, a brunette journalist from Philadelphia who has a few one-night stands with a drunken Robin before ascending to stardom in Hollywood. After meeting again their affair intensifies, but Robin's emotional equivocating and philandering finally drive Maggie to light his bed on fire.

When Robin ventures to Rome to visit his ailing dowager mother, he meets and befriends her gay majordomo, Sergio. Robin discovers with Sergio's aid that he was adopted from a German sex worker, and after returning to New York, sinks to the point of brutally beating a sex worker, sees an analyst, and finally recalls under hypnosis his childhood

trauma of witnessing his birth-mother's murder. Sergio eventually relo-
cates to Hollywood for a movie career, where he meets and become lovers with closeted movie star Alfie Knight. It turns out that Alfie knows
Ethel, a close friend who acts as his "beard" at celebrity fetes much as
he (and eventually Sergio) help Ethel through her loveless marriage to
Christie. Alfie also knows Maggie, from working together in the movies
and sleeping together in a ménage à trois.

In the climactic party sequence at Alfie's home, Robin rejects a desperately randy Judith, who then bitterly threatens to out Alfie and Sergio,
make it appear Robin is involved with them, and imperil the "morals
clause" in all three of their job contracts. A row explodes that brings in
the police, nosy reporters, and launches a full-blown sex scandal. Robin
coolly contrives a story, however, making it appear that he and Alfie were
fighting over Judith. The sex scandal restores Judith to social promi-
nence, the alibi contrived by Robin sustains Alfie's and Sergio's closet and
their careers, and Ethel basks in her camaraderie with Sergio and Alfie
as well as her newborn baby. Robin quits his job at IBC, writes a novel,
and finally confesses to Maggie that he pines for her, whereupon Maggie
quits her film (costarring Alfie) to reunite with Robin.

Susann crams queer signals and supporters into Robin's course
toward heterosexual mental health and happily ever after, the foundation
for the queer irony that pervades the entire novel. Robin ponders to his
psychoanalyst Archie, for instance, in the classic terms of the closet case,
"Everyone is *not* heterosexual or homosexual. There are people who are
just plain sexual" (Susann 1997a, 284). The unapologetically gay Sergio
helps Robin confront his oedipal crises and his homophobia and finally
inspires Robin's confirmation that gay men make ideal intimates: "But
then, many girls had fags as confidants and close friends. Amanda even
said a model friend of hers lived with a fag. And look at him with Sergio"
(Susann 1997a, 409). When searching for his birth mother in Hamburg,
Robin has sex with a cabaret performer, Brazillia, whom he discovers
afterward is transgender; the narration clarifies Robin's reaction of silent
disgust and condescending detachment by establishing his fear of being
a failed man, a "loser" (Susann 1997a, 397–402, 412–14; Anon. 1969a). The
queer events and insights accumulate further, including rumors about
Robin's relationship with close male associate Dip Nelson (modeled after
Aubrey's minion Keefe Brasselle), and the climactic, queer-tinged sex

scandal, all of which lead Robin to happy heterosexuality: sacrificing his career as president of the IBC television network, resolving his psychic barriers to vulnerability as well as curvy brunette women, and finally uniting with Maggie.

The Love Machine hardly qualified as radical gay fiction, but the timing of its release poised it for queer attention. In addition to the aforementioned publishing controversies, *The Love Machine* also arrived just a little more than a month before the Stonewall riots, which fomented the gay liberation movement, and amid what Michael Bronski describes as the "attack on traditional gender and sexual expectations" by incipient mainstream gay literature (Bronski 1984, 157; Bronski 1998, 96). Truman Capote reflected Bronski's assessment in his own "attack" on Susann and contributed to the queering of both Susann and *The Love Machine*, a camp reception explored more closely in the next chapter. Quipping to Johnny Carson on *The Tonight Show* in July during the reign of *The Love Machine* atop the *New York Times* Best Seller list, Capote likened Susann to Vidal's transgender hero Myra Breckinridge, a character that Douglas Eisner asserts bears "deific power" as well as fuses "the leftist critique of power and the camp aesthetic" (1999, 256, 260). Elitist insult notwithstanding, Capote's badinage underscored Susann's queer reputation and her novel's.

Susann telegraphs her sympathies with gay men, drag queens, and trans women in *The Love Machine* and, furthermore, integrates queer causality into the novel's scandal narrative that revolves around the closet and enables the fulfillment of heterosexual romance, a comedic happy ending. The plotline of closeted gay lovers Sergio and Alfie especially affects the heterosexual success stories in unexpected ways that trumpet what Jerry Palmer identifies as comedy's "logic of the absurd." Having established Ethel's role as confidant and "beard" to Alfie and Sergio, whose Hollywood contracts require them to pass for straight, the sex scandal that erupts initially pits Judith in hostile competition with the gay couple and furnishes opportunities for her homophobic epithets as well as their misogyny. The disastrous threats to everyone's reputations and relationships the scandal posed are resolved, though, victoriously and humorously: reinstating the gay men's heterosexual facades, which their acting careers depend on, and assuring their continued alliance with Ethel, which her welfare depends on; elevating the middle-aged, fallen socialite Judith to the top of the society columns, rechristened a "glamorous" woman after a plunge in popularity that correlated with her age and desirability; and motivating both Robin's resignation from IBC and his final union with Maggie.

Susann also devises a closet plotline for Amanda and Rose that stands apart from the rest for its theme of racial passing and fixity in melodrama. Similar to her first novel, the author recycles and revises tropes and situations from Hollywood films such as *Pinky* (Kazan 1949) and the musical *Showboat* (Sidney 1951), but the Rose-Amanda plotline especially replicates the subplot involving Annie Johnson and her mixed-race daughter Sarah Jane in Douglas Sirk's popular 1959 remake of *Imitation of Life*: the white-passing daughter in show business secreting her mother; the melodramatic irony and agony when the daughter refuses to identify her mother in the presence of white people; the stereotypical tropes of victimhood, tragedy, and maternal sacrifice that litter their story, in addition to the spectacle of martyrdom; and the narrative marginalization of their subplot (Heung 1987, 26, Floreani 2013, 109).[3] Rose and Amanda's storyline might reflect Susann's attempt to address the sizable Black readership for *Valley of the Dolls* that Mel Watkins had reported the prior year in the *New York Times* (Watkins 1968, A24), but it renders both characters tragic, suffering social victims, and the fact that they disappear from the novel little more than halfway through only quiets their plotline further and reinstates the norm of whiteness. After broaching the intersection of race, gender, and class through Amanda—her childhood in a working-class Black neighborhood of Miami, Rose's devoted care for her as a default mother and namesake (Amanda's given name is Rose), and Amanda's celebrity persona of wealth and whiteness—the death of Rose ceases these themes, trumped by the announcement of Amanda's illness and forgotten in Amanda's prolonged suffering. The only "comedic" cues arise in Christie Lane's reaction to Amanda's confession, after he proposes to her. Christie's vulgarity bursts in a stream of racist and misogynistic one-liners and, in a nod to *Imitation of Life*, his suggestion that Rose masquerade as their maid. Similar to The Head's misogynistic vulgarity in *Valley of the Dolls*, Christie's grotesquery here renders the character ridiculous for his racism and sexism. Amanda and Rose never get the opportunities for comedic agency, though, accorded to other characters involved in closet plotlines, such as Ethel, Maggie, Judith, and Alfie.

Susann's empathy with Amanda and Rose nonetheless surfaces through the racial closet narrative, considering that Susann concealed her Jewish heritage until the end of her life, unmentioned in articles about her until 1973, having even converted to Catholicism at one point (Kasindorf 1973, 11; Seaman 1996c, 232). Susann also confirms her sympathies for Amanda by basing her on friend Carol Bjorkman, a *Women's Wear Daily* columnist and former fashion model who succumbed to leukemia while Susann worked on *The Love Machine* and to whom the author dedicated her novel. Susann's biographer Barbara Seaman also probed the possibility during research that Bjorkman was a lesbian and that she and Susann were lovers, as evidenced in Seaman's archived interview transcripts, although no such discussion reached the finished biography (Seaman 1984; Seaman 1996c, 213–14).

Where queers and Jewish people round out many of the secondary characters, and closet plotlines prevail in the context of gender and sexuality, the limits of metaphorical representation and closeted identification become clearer with Rose, the sole Black character in the novel.[4] Susann's "off-white" passing finally seems more apparent through the way race in *The Love Machine* is separated from the masquerades associated with gender and sexuality, bereft of any of the fun of the other storylines. Melodramatic "impossibility" and "unfulfillment" coalesce with a position of narrative marginalization that together stem consideration of the social issues associated with the racialized closet plotline, by contrast to the queer closet plotline central to the happy endings of the novel's primary heterosexual romances. Queerness might also remain marginalized within the narrative hierarchy, a kind of closet, but its endurance in the hetero characters' stories at least extends queer visibility and prolongs the message humanizing gays.[5] Rendering Blackness melodramatic contains the racial themes to stale tropes in a plotline separated from the novel's comedy as well as the happy ending. Susann's novel, structured around closet narratives and driven by irony, renders queerness pervasive and axial while depicting race as well as racism as fixed, concrete, and compartmentalized.

Columbia Pictures' *Jacqueline Susann's The Love Machine* (Haley Jr., 1971) intertwines queerness and heterosexual promiscuity as comparable signs of the sexual revolution, similar to the novel, yet their values plummet in the adaptation, while Black characters and storylines about racism sink out of sight entirely. As the film interprets the novel as a morality tale about the perils of the sexual revolution, the excesses of this object lesson, according to reviewers, undermine the melodramatic messaging and make it "failed seriousness," naive camp. Critics roundly attributed the film's failings to faithfully adapting Susann's source novel and, combined with the movie's campy gay characters in addition to the visual spectacle of gorgeous leading man John Phillip Law as Robin Stone, perceived *The Love Machine* as advocating the sexual revolution it was ostensibly condemning. Similar to the incongruity that pervades Susann's novel, the film appears simultaneously both queer and straight, yet the novel invests queerness with value through sympathetic gay and trans characters, the play of closet plotlines, and a happy ending that extends to the gay characters. The film's melodramatic narrative and melancholic conclusion clearly condemn both heterosexual promiscuity and homosexuality as corrosive social threats, and if the movie's failed seriousness produces irony, this also rationalizes movie reviewers' sense of moral superiority to Susann the sexual revolutionary as much as it motivates their critical dismissal of the novel.

Jacqueline Susann's Queer Irony

Piloting a *Love Machine* that runs both straight *and* queer, Susann devises an "invariably comic" situation, according to one of Henri Bergson's axioms, because *Love Machine* "is capable of being interpreted in two entirely different meanings at the same time" (Bergson 1928, 96), as a novel that validates "successful heterosexual love" while also appearing to require "equal time for heterosexuals." Judith Mayne locates a similar quality in the films of Hollywood director Dorothy Arzner, a "lesbian irony" that communicates queer female desire also legible as heterosexual. Arzner's drama *Christopher Strong* (1933) exhibits, for example, an "ironic inflection of heterosexual norms" that manifests the "irony of equally compelling and incompatible discourses" (Mayne 1991, 120, 123). Arzner's backstage musical comedy *Dance, Girl, Dance* (1940) likewise "functions in two radically different ways, both of which are 'true,' as it were, and totally incompatible" (Mayne 1991, 117).[6] Susann cultivates queer irony in all her romans à clef, exemplified in chapter 1 through *Valley of the Dolls*, how the novel's heteronormative social melodrama harbors a queer morality tale. *The Love Machine* stands out within Susann's trifecta by combining the incongruity of heterosexual/queer with a conventional happy ending, arrived at through an improbable chain of events and reversals best characterized by Bergson's concepts of "comic absurdity" and the "inversion of common sense," or what Jerry Palmer has called "the logic of the absurd" (Bergson 1928, 185–86; Palmer 2018, 54; Palmer 1994, 96). "Inversion" fuels *The Love Machine*, both in its themes and plots, as "the absurd" reversal of social and aesthetic norms transpires.

Susann's "inversion of common sense" stems from plundering the tropes of classical Hollywood romantic melodrama and romantic comedy, which include the way gender and sexuality are typically represented. The "impossibility" of fulfilling female desire in the form of romantic love characterizes melodrama: narratives structured around an individual woman with an unattainable love object, destined for an unhappy ending in plotlines generated by misunderstanding, separation, and longing (Neal and Krutnik 1990, 133–36). The repeated frustration of desire nevertheless also applies to comedy, in "circular" plotlines pinpointed by Bergson that repeatedly return characters "back to the same spot" (Bergson 1928, 83). Recurrent failure in comedy narratives transforms into a successful outcome through the culmination of the "snowball," when an activity that persistently meets defeat systematically intensifies into an outcome "as important as it is unexpected," or what in Aristotelian terms constitutes a peripeteia, the "reversal of fortune" (Bergson 1928, 81; Neale and Krutnik 1990, 28; Palmer 2018, 51–52). In romantic comedy, the "unexpected" volte-face arises in the fulfillment of romantic love despite the initial incompatibility of the central romantic couple (Neale and Krutnik 1990, 139). Characters in comedy, consequently, must also exhibit absurd reversals, but only after their "automatic" quirks and eccentricities have repeatedly snowballed into mounting disappointment (Bergson 1928, 146, 148).

If the generic norms of comedy function to rationalize and naturalize absurd reversals that yield happy endings, when this occurs in melodrama, Steve Neale notes, "the fulfillment is precisely implausible, incredible, extraordinary" (1986, 21). Merging comedy and melodrama in *The Love Machine* sets such improbability in relief. This is especially potent when the absurd narrative outcomes reverse the predominant social norms also embedded in these genres, for instance, a heteromasculine hero defined by queer eccentricities, and whose hetero happy ending results from queer interventions.

Susann foments further irony through the "duplicitous structures" of the roman à clef: the "open secrets" the genre houses, as Sean Latham uncovers, analogous to "the homosexual closet" and popping with "genuine comic appeal" (Latham 2009, 45, 57, 63). Eve Sedgwick pinpoints the comic attraction for queer authors who can engage in the "playful and seductive version of the Glass Closet" to underscore the comedy of their duplicity as well as their characters' (Sedgwick 1990, 164–65). Bergson helps dissect the humor of the "Glass Closet" in authorial performance when referring to, in comic literature and theater, the "character playing a double part," "the dual personality," whose "external" performance generates from "the altogether inner comedy of which this scene is no more than the outer refraction" (Bergson 1928, 75). The "inner comedy" of Susann's Glass Closet solicits a form of funny speculation similar to what Lynne Joyrich traces in the closet of television comedy, when "a program . . . cheerfully permits viewers to prick at its ostensibly heterosexual surface," coaxing a comedic and camp response from a "knowing" audience (Joyrich 2001, 453). The savvy TV audience in Joyrich's discussion compares closely to the reader of the roman à clef detected by Latham, who delights in "identifying those seemingly innocuous textual details that can abruptly turn fiction into gossip" (Latham 2009, 57–58). Fiction slips into gossip and confession in the queer romans à clef, where the Glass Closet reflects the inner comedy of the author and of her characters. By flaunting her duality as both straight and queer, Susann could "pluralize sexual definition," in Cohan's expression (1997, 274), to intensify the inner comedy of the closet. This dynamic applied as a strategy for promotional statements in which Susann defended homosexuality, polyamory, and promiscuity as well as flaunted her knowledge about orgies and drag queens, all while showcasing her husband Irving Mansfield and emphasizing the joys of marriage. Susann could assure the *Los Angeles Times* that marriage "has always been more important to me than career" and yet testify, as *Time* magazine quoted her in its review of *The Love Machine*, "It's not a question of 'I'm going to have an orgy tonight.' You have your choice to do it or not. In certain groups it goes on frequently" (Vils 1967, 10; Anon. 1969b). Susann planted contradictory clues about her personal life that speak to the events of her roman à clef; posing as straight commentator of the sexual revolution *and* perverse participant—as wife *and* "weirdo"—the author "cheerfully permits" speculation that she might be a member of "certain groups."

The logic of the closet furthermore guides Susann's organization of *The Love Machine* and the construction of all her characters. Similar to Cohan's assessment of the sex comedy *Pillow Talk* (1959), whose narrative "turns around the masquerade required of the closet" (Cohan 1997, 289), Susann's narrative culminates through the inner comedy of closeted characters. The concealing of secrets and managing of gossip, scandal, and fame snowballs into an absurd, queer peripeteia that preserves the closet while satisfying the characters' desires. Susann heals her hardened heterosexual hero by queering him, orchestrates her melodramatic plotlines toward an improbable comedic resolution, and by merging melodrama and romantic comedy and toying with their outcomes, transforms Hollywood and Broadway tropes that restrict the range of gender performance and sexual desire.

Susann's oscillations between gossip and confession in *The Love Machine* produced further irony, moreover, to inaugurate the roman à clef guessing game the author again plays with her readers. Designing her male protagonist and three of her principal women characters—Maggie Stuart, Ethel Evans, and Judith Austin—with qualities that flagged numerous noisy clues to Susann's "bad" behavior and painful struggles, the author mediated her confessions with obvious gossip about other celebrities, as she had done in *Valley of the Dolls*.[7] Susann replays the role of gossipy voyeur with her women characters, but in the context of the novel's queer humor, to the say the least of several characters' positive outcomes, underscores her identification. Unlike all her other novels, Susann gives *The Love Machine* a happy ending, a romantic comedy conclusion that revolves around gossip and sex scandal, only reached by queering the heterosexual male hero, endorsing homosexuality, and accepting nonbinary gender.

"Laddy in the Dark"

Susann alluded to the gender trouble of her protagonist in *The Love Machine* when explaining the origins of his name to the *Literary Guild*

Newsletter: "Robin is not a particularly strong name. It's an elegant name. It's a neuter name, like it could be a boy or a girl. But nothing is stronger than stone" (Susann 1969d). Susann chooses a likewise androgynous intertextual corelative for Robin's dramatic and psychological journey: the 1941 Broadway musical comedy *Lady in the Dark* (adapted to film in 1944), about a career woman in psychoanalysis experiencing "cross-gender identification" (McClung 2007, 268). The prevailing psycho-analytic wisdom that "homosexuality manifested itself in gender-role inversion" surfaced in *Lady in the Dark* and, with echoes of the roman à clef, also bore whispered autobiographical significance to the show's librettist, Moss Hart, furtively nicknamed by Broadway producer Billy Rose as "poor little Laddy in the Dark" (McClung 2007, 271). Alluding to Hart's rumored homosexuality by way of associating him with the musical's heroine, Rose's gossipy sobriquet might have been familiar to Susann through her close friendship with Rose and his wife, Joyce Matthews. Susann presents in *The Love Machine* another "Laddy in the Dark," Robin Stone, whose epicene name belies his hypermasculine performance as much as does his affinity for Moss Hart's heroine.

As Robin racks his brain to recall the name of the woman he slept with the night before, later revealed as Maggie Stewart, he cites *Lady in the Dark*, whose heroine Liza Elliot experiences a mental block to recalling the song "My Ship," due to its associations with her father; by the end of the novel, Robin and Liza's likeness comes to fruition, as childhood oedipal trauma explains each character's memory loss and gender-role confusion. Clues to Robin's cross-gender identification and what it symptomatizes accumulate early on, through his selective recollections of Maggie: "her breasts were magnificent. He didn't usually pay much attention to breasts—there was something childish to him about sucking a full breast. . . . It was a longing for Mama. There was something *weak* about a man who wanted to lay his head against a woman with big breasts. Robin dug blondes, clean and bright, slim and hard. There was a symmetry to their bodies that he found exciting. But the girl last night had been a brunette, with beautiful full breasts" (Susann 1997a, 22). Where Liza Elliot dressed in masculine styles and dated a passive man while unconsciously desiring a dominant father figure, so Robin's conscious desires for gamine blonds such as Amanda remain at cross-gendered purposes with his unconscious desires for buxom brunettes, "feminine" women

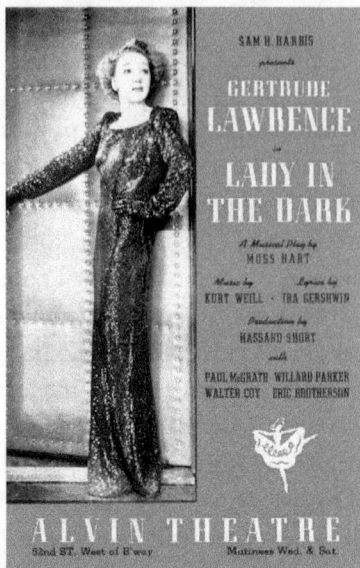

Susann incorporates the Broadway musical *Lady in the Dark* in Robin Stone's "Laddy in the Dark" plotline, and in Amanda and Rose's story, alludes to the popular Hollywood melodrama *Imitation of Life* (Juanita Moore and Susan Kohner pictured).

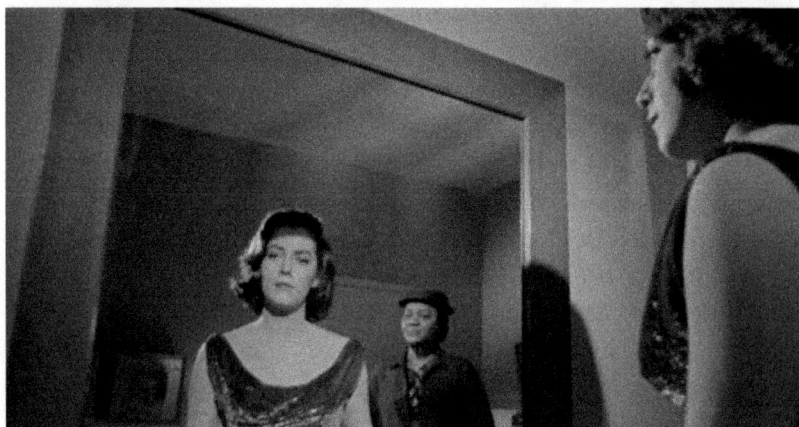

who remind him of "Mama," such as Maggie (Susann 1997a, 14). Both Liza and Robin undergo analysis to relocate a lost memory whose oedipal significance has affected their sexual desire and ability to love, and they also suffer from nightmares that evoke these memories. In *Lady in the Dark* Liza's nightmares take the form of surreal musical numbers in which she performs as "feminine," something she unconsciously desires and associates with her father. And in *Love Machine*, Robin's nightmares alternate with episodes in which he boozes excessively to perform sexually with buxom brunettes who remind him of his birth mother.[8] The similarities between Robin Stone and Liza Elliot compound further. Both of them work in the entertainment business, she the founding editor of a fashion magazine and he the head of a TV network, each surrounded by homosexual men and glamorous, sexualized women.

The Love Machine notably departs from *Lady in the Dark*, though, particularly in terms of how the narrative values gender trouble and queer desire. By turning Liza into Robin, to begin with, Susann inverts the gendered power dynamic of *Lady*, in which Liza's competitive male ad director ridicules her unfeminine behavior until she finally bows to him romantically and professionally, in perfect symmetry with her therapeutic epiphany about desiring a strong father figure (Glitre 2006, 30–31). Susann subjects Robin, in similar fashion, to gossipy suspicions by the network brass that he is "AC/DC" and "queersville," based on his participation in orgies, close association with actor-producer Dip Nelson, and finally, his friendship with gay lovers Sergio and Alfie (Susann 1997a, 438, 445, 462, 484). When the "scandal sheet" *Undercover* makes Robin the cover story, Maggie informs him, the rag assigns a nickname to Robin's private plane, "the Flying Couch": "And according to *Undercover* you don't care *what's* on that Flying Couch with you, man or woman, just as long as you can hump!" (Susann 1997a, 492). Robin follows Liza's lead and, after recalling his birth mother in addition to protecting his gay comrades from scandal, signifies his newfound mental health to Maggie by sacrificing his high-power job and acknowledging he needs her. The stigma attributed to cross-gender identification and homosexuality in *Lady in the Dark* grows steadily ambiguous in *The Love Machine*, where any sense of correcting cross-gender identification dissolves in proportion to Robin's increasing ease with both queer people and the homophobic gossip about him.

Just a little more than halfway through the tome, Sergio enters to set an example, influence Robin's perspective, and negate the idea that gender nonconformity and queer desire require a cure, a process that ironically helps render Robin a suitable romantic partner for Maggie.[9] Sergio cares for Robin's wealthy widowed mother Kitty in Rome, where he first meets Robin, although Robin's attraction to the young man first surfaces on a long-distance call arranging his visit. Despite Robin's wariness of "these gigolo types," Sergio "was getting to him right through the phone" (Susann 1997a, 269). Soon after Robin's arrival in Rome, the narration heaps praise on Sergio through Robin's point of view for his stunning looks and demeanor: "The boy was exceptionally handsome, better-looking than any movie star. Definitely light on his feet but he didn't swish. . . . His manner was right—eager and enthusiastic, yet not subservient" (Susann 1997a, 270). Although Robin initially "wondered what made a boy who had everything turn queer," Sergio increasingly disabuses Robin—and the reader—of a stream of homophobic assumptions, to the point that the narration comments, "The boy was giving homosexuality a crazy kind of dignity" (Susann 1997a, 271, 277). Sergio also calls out Robin on his homophobic presumptions, such as when Robin warns Sergio to stop gazing at him desirously. Sergio replies, "I cannot help it, any more than a girl could help it if she saw you. Yet if a girl stared at you this way, you would not hate her. I stare at you from the heart. I cannot help the way my emotions go. But do not worry" (Susann 1997a, 275). Sergio allies himself with a heterosexual woman's desiring gaze, which naturalizes the stereotypical equation of homosexuality with cross-gender identification as much as it normalizes the erotic gazes of cisgender straight women and woman-identified gay men. Robin later reverts back to his old prejudices, following his sister's denunciation of Sergio as a "fairy" fortune hunter and suspects that the young man took advantage of him during one of Robin's drunken stupors. Sergio, hurt and insulted, first indicates "the trouble with people" who believe that "a homosexual will go for just any man"; he then poses the confrontational question, "You hate what I am, don't you Robin?"; and finishes by affirming his basic humanity, that "I am what she calls a fairy. It is true. But I am also a person" (Susann 1997a, 400–401).

Susann introduces additional characters who inform readers on the realities of being queer, such as the German trans cabaret performer

Brazillia, with whom Robin has a tryst, and gay English actor Alfie Knight, who eventually partners with Sergio. Joyrich illuminates the "enlightening" function of "gay sidekicks," whose secondary status in the narrative hierarchy closets them in plain sight, yet, whose narrative marginality conditions visibility, knowability, and the soothing of homophobic fears, devoid of "mystery" or "scandal" (Joyrich 2001, 454). Such gay sidekicks can offset demonizing stereotypes in addition to providing coherence for readers to grasp the narrative and the larger social context reflected in it (456). Knowledge about homosexuality and trans experience delivered through peripheral characters in *The Love Machine* might not subvert the narrative dominance of Robin's hetero-male point of view, but Sergio's self-actualization stands in bold contrast to Robin's repressed sexual conflicts, which he vents most savagely on a sex worker.[10] Sergio not only advises Robin to see a headshrinker prior to this violent, misogynistic outburst, he also provides a role model of authenticity and stability after the protagonist discovers that his birth mother was a sex worker murdered by a client (Susann 1997a, 279).[11] In the midst of questioning his own mental stability, Robin addresses Sergio's accusation, "You hate what I am": "No, Sergio. At least you know what you are, who you are and what you want out of life" (Susann 1997a, 340).

In much the same way as the queer characters enlighten the heterosexual characters and support them through their conflicts, Sergio and Alfie enable the narrative snowball to finally build into the absurd reversal, their plotline unifying the others and rendering them coherent according to the "*inversion* of common sense." The stability of *The Love Machine*'s primary heterosexual romance between Robin and Maggie relies on the Alfie-Sergio plotline, as do the plotlines involving Ethel and Judith in which the appearance of marital bliss rests on the shoulders of the gay couple. The comedic happy ending that Susann orchestrates in *The Love Machine* depends on the intersection of straight and queer plotlines whose thematic and diegetic unity revolve around maintaining the closet and managing scandal.

Maggie the "Nut"

Susann toys with both the mechanics of Hollywood genre narratives and character types in *The Love Machine* to produce queer irony, compounded by her presence among the characters as narrator and participant. For Susann's women, network television and Hollywood provide "an arena of patriarchal exploitation and of female self-representation," paraphrasing Mayne (1991, 117). And through Susann's presence in the roman à clef, the author implicated herself in an adjacent arena of self-representation, most explicitly through the character Maggie Stewart. Maggie combines numerous publicly known features of the author: hailing from Philadelphia with brunette hair; spurning her proper upbringing; forging an acting career and an interest in broadcast journalism; dating Jewish men; expressing ambivalence toward both marriage and the swinging Hollywood lifestyle, having also attended an orgy or two; and demonstrating her determination "to break a lot of rules" (Susann 1997a, 258). As gossip columnist Liz Smith coyly remarked about her friend's latest novel, trying to "identify" the actual celebrities portrayed, "There is one curiously bloodless, rather tough brunette movie star who finally brings Robin to heel. I couldn't identify her for beans; maybe she is a real fictional character" (Smith 1969, 4). Smith's conjecturing hints at the closeted truth, that Susann is Maggie, by playing between ignorance and knowledge, silence and revelation, then rejoining it with a suggestive declaration: "For the most part, Jackie Susann holds an accurate mirror up to one frazzled corner of life," which includes the author's "iron butterfly approach to femininity" and "zealous attention to the seamy details of the more rancid side of show biz" (Smith 1969, 4). Smith alludes to Susann's playful guessing game and the author's intimate involvement in her narratives—Susann's role as both quizmaster and one of the answers to the quiz—in addition to authenticating the novelist's "accurate" rendering of "iron butterfly" women and "seamy," "rancid" show business. For Susann's women characters in *The Love Machine* and her intimate connections to them, the author constructs a closet of confessional and exposé in which gossip both implicates and detaches her as well as assures the novel's realism.

Maggie distinguishes herself in a plotline that begins in melodrama and develops into romantic comedy. Her privileged, WASP upbringing contributes to her initially melodramatic story involving enforced marriage to a blue-blood brute,[12] but Maggie the heiress develops into a screwball, or a "nut" as Robin calls her on several occasions, redolent of Susann's self-descriptor in *Every Night, Josephine!:* "Josephine stared at me as if I was some kind of a nut" (Susann 2004, 3). Maggie's defiance of a proper Philadelphia upbringing, furthermore, coincides with her transformation from melodramatic victim into single girl playboy and screwball heroine. Fleeing from her abusive marriage, Maggie initially seeks a broadcast journalism career, through which she first works with Robin and then breaks out in Hollywood movies. Maggie morphs into a screwball single girl, someone who "felt exhilarated" taking the initiative with Robin and who vows as a result, "she was going to break a lot of rules. . . . From now on she would sleep in the nude . . . she felt a sense of freedom she had never known" (Susann 1997a, 258). Maggie consequently makes no effort to conceal her impropriety, such as when "the gossip columnists attacked her for living openly with [film director] Adam Bergman at his beach house. . . . They condemned a 'nice' girl for flagrantly ignoring matrimony" (Susann 1997a, 346). When her agent Hy Mandel urges, "Why don't you two kids get married," Maggie determinedly rejects the public denunciations and pressure to lead a more orthodox lifestyle: "I've spent enough of my life living up to conventions and rules" (Susann 1997a, 351).

Maggie initially transgresses the role of screwball heroine by rejecting the marriage track, and she also challenges the divisions between eccentric and crazy as well as civilized and savage. Discovering that Robin has eluded her yet another time for another rendezvous, in this instance with washed-up Hollywood star Diana Williams, Maggie sneaks into his apartment and, with the naked lovers lounging in the den, showers his bed with lighter fluid and sets it afire. Spectating the burgeoning inferno across the street from Robin's building, "A slow smile crossed her face," and on viewing Robin and Diana among the evacuating tenants, "Maggie tossed her head back and laughed" (Susann 1997a, 381). Robin sends Maggie a telegram, having deduced she set the blaze, announcing "YOU'RE A NUT!," and in their first encounter afterward, Maggie affirms, "just like you said, I'm a nut" (Susann 1997a, 387, 433).

In a character reversal worthy of Hollywood and reminiscent of the turnarounds and contradictions in Susann's promotional statements, Maggie's independent spirit eventually compels her to dismiss the swinging Hollywood lifestyle as hypocritical after formerly embracing its nonconformity. Following her ménage à trois with director Adam and costar Alfie, Maggie objects to "making excuses for sexual deviations because we're artists," then tells Adam, "I want a husband, not a bright young director who smokes pot and makes it with a boy occasionally for kicks" (Susann 1997a, 352, 353). Susann depicts Maggie's rejection of "sexual deviations" as an assertion of individuality and resistance to social pressure, consistent with being a "nut" and now conducive to a conventional heterosexual romance conclusion. Maggie finally links her eccentricity to a masochistic devotion to Robin in their last liaison prior to the climactic party and ensuing sex scandal: "I'm insane. Know why? Because I *want* to see you. That means I *have* to be crazy—like asking for punishment" (486). Maggie's eccentricity initially coincides with her "crazy" desire for Robin despite knowing the painful outcome, in addition to experimenting with polyamory and other rule-breaking, even arson. In a turnaround, eccentricity now leads to both her self-discovery and independence from Robin. Spurning Robin's initial marriage proposal, Maggie tells him, "Don't call me anymore, Robin. Please. Never! . . . Not unless you can call me and say you *need* me" (493).

Despite rejecting her "crazy" self, Maggie finally fulfills the role of screwball heroine by teaching Robin that "needing" her does not make him a "loser," consequently replacing Sergio and Robin's analyst Archie as the instructor of Robin's psyche and paving the way for heterosexual romance. As Kathrina Glitre explains, "most screwball heroines acknowledge their own desire before the heroes acknowledge any desire. . . . It is the man who must learn to acknowledge the woman's desire and the education that takes place does not necessarily demand the woman's 'emergence' as an autonomous being, but the man's recognition of her (existing) autonomy" (Glitre 2006, 52). Maggie's actions furthermore reverse the patriarchal dynamics that dictate such romantic comedy narratives as *Lady in the Dark*, Robin's leitmotif, in which Liza's transformation into a "healthy," "feminine" woman is facilitated by her scornful ad director Charley Johnson, to whom she cedes her editorial control and her heart. Robin, who admits to identifying with Liza in *Lady*, turns into the "feminine" figure who sacrifices his career, kills his pride, retires his manly guardedness, and learns how to be vulnerable. Robin's association of emotional vulnerability with being a "loser" initially deludes him into thinking that he must win Maggie by playing the masculine "winner" opposite her role as feminine "nut." "The world was not made for losers," Robin thinks, having just exited from his tryst with Brazillia, now plotting his corporate tactics while remembering his desire for "that nut Maggie Stewart" and vowing to impress her as "the biggest winner of them all!" (Susann 1997a, 414). *The Love Machine* concludes with Robin quitting his powerful position at the IBC network after the sex scandal at Alfie's party, then writing the novel he had started prior to his TV career, and finally, sending the message that Maggie commanded, both against and in accordance to the conventions of romantic comedy: "I NEED YOU" (511).

Ethel and the Funny Men

Like Jennifer North in *Valley of the Dolls* and according to the strategies of the "single girl," Ethel Evans hinges her capacity for independence in a man's world on the "capital" of her body (Radner 1999, 11). A combination of the Doris Day career woman and the Mae West "gold digger," the thirty-year-old publicist at the IBC network steers her savvy saleswomanship through numerous liaisons with showbiz celebrities and eventually to marriage with star TV comedian Christie Lane. Ethel initially negotiates her self-worth through the terms of a punishing male gaze that marks her as a scheming "hooker" and aims to closet Ethel during her courtship with Christie.[13] Ethel also determinedly resists the male gaze, first by talking back to straight men with wisecracks about their piggish behavior, and finally, by privileging the adoring gay gazes of Alfie and Sergio. An accomplice to her gay friends' scandalous antics, Ethel supports their public masquerade as straight people, and, ultimately manages to succeed: *despite* landing a rich and famous husband in a picture-perfect marriage that makes her miserable, and *because* of her queer friendships and performance. Her queer masquerade with Alfie and Sergio at the center of the showbiz "in" crowd replaces heterosexual romance as a vehicle toward Ethel's happy ending. Susann hinted at her affinity for Ethel when she told Cindy Adams at *Photoplay* during the promotion of *The Love Machine*, "What really counts is a lady who *won't* do what he wants. If she says yes on the first date and he takes her out the second night and she says yes, he's not going to hang around the third night" (Adams 1969, 90).[14] Susann also implied another likeness with Ethel, her friendships with both closeted and out gay men, such as critic Rex Reed and *Boys in the Band* playwright Mart Crowley (Kelly 1969, A16; Quinn 1970, 19).

The IBC network executives deem Ethel, prior to her marriage to Christie, a threat to their star comedian's "family" image if her past is exposed, but Susann soon exposes the power and threat of Ethel's sexual gaze. Ethel's sexual conquests with TV stars and producers remain legendary, spectacularized in her witty reports with "ratings" of her encounters—in a deliberate pun on the Nielsen ratings—that she shares with her girlfriends. Usurping the role of seducer and objectifying men, Ethel is stigmatized, stamped "celebrity-fucker" by snickering, gossipy co-workers, and branded "one step removed from a hooker" by detestable TV executive Danton Miller (Susann 1997a, 44–45, 301). When ad executive Jerry Moss warns Danton of the risk Ethel poses to sponsorship for Christie's show, the perils of exposure also extend to Danton:

> "If one of those scandal magazines ever decides to do some real research on Ethel, we're dead! She's got a girl friend on the Coast who saved all her letters with ratings of the stars in the kip. She's had them mimeoed and passes them around. If those letters ever got into print! Incidentally, Dan, I hear your 'rating' is listed, too."
> Dan's smile disappeared.
> "Look Dan, I'm not a prude. That kind of publicity might help a swinging singer, but not our little minstrel man. He appeals to a family-type audience. . . . You've got a gold mine with this show—and we can't let Ethel stand in the way. It's too big a risk."
> (Susann 1997a, 198)

Money, misogyny, and mainstream family values prompt Danton's intrusion into Ethel and Christie's affair, although the executive remains ridiculously motivated by masculine pride. Susann conjures a humorous image when Jerry informs Danton of Ethel's "rating" for him— "Dan's smile disappeared"—then follows up later on Danton's distress with his comically insecure inner monologue: "Dan thought about the situation for several days. . . . Jesus, what had she said in her letter about him?" (Susann 1997a, 199). The outing of Ethel's past threatens Danton's job and masculinity, his professional capital and his gender capital. The problem remains, however, that "Christie has to have a girl," as network CEO Gregory Austin tells Danton, making clear that questions of closeted behavior also apply to the male comedian: "Personally, I'm always

suspicious of a man who is over forty and has never been married"
(Susann 1997a, 301).[15]

Power plays, gendered gazes, and sexual secrets culminate at Danton's final showdown with Ethel and Christie. Ethel's predicament as
Christie's closeted lover solidifies with a vengeance, "listening to Danton Miller evasively and politely plotting to alibi her presence in Christie's life," and seeing herself through the punishing male gaze: "she felt
as shabby as the soot-stained drapes that hung limply on the grayish
windows. She suddenly saw herself through Danton Miller's eyes, and
she wanted to run!" (Susann 1997a, 304). Surveilling herself "through
Danton Miller's eyes," Ethel loses confidence in her masquerade "to
be someone. . . . Because everything Danton said made sense" (Susann
1997a, 305). Susann designs a narrative reversal but renders Ethel's victory
temporary and pyrrhic, undermined by patriarchal patronizing. Christie
engages in a masculine cockfight with Danton and the network, which
mounts until the comedian explodes, "And neither you nor Mr. Robin
Stone is going to dictate to me what I am. I am me! Get it? *Me!* And I'm
marrying the only broad I care about—Ethel Evans" (Susann 1997a, 309).
It requires Christie's institutionalized power as a male star to release
Ethel from her single girl closet into the light of a forgiving male gaze,
as "a real broad," in Christie's words, "A great broad" (Susann 1997a, 307).
Christie's gesture appeals to Ethel's earlier fantasy that marrying him
would enable her to "tell them to all fuck off. Dan—Robin—the whole
world. *Mrs.* Christie Lane! Mrs. TV Star! Mrs. *Power!*" (Susann 1997a, 205).
Susann demystifies Ethel's association of domesticity with power and
self-fulfillment, however, when the newlywed must endure a loveless
marriage that revolves around a small stipend and requires her labor as
Christie's publicist: "Suddenly she felt as if she had been tricked—like
hitting an oil well and waking up the next morning to find it had run
dry" (316).

Ethel's survival strategy for suffering through marriage with Christie involves closeted, gay movie star Alfie Knight, a relationship that
impresses the queer moral code Susann had concretized through Sergio's
enlightenment of Robin: "Ethel had gotten into the Alfie set. Alfie confided in her, adored her—and Ethel went everywhere to act as a 'beard'
to cover whatever boy he was romancing. The threesome made all the
openings together while Christie worked on his show. . . . Hell, Ethel was

so *in* now that he [Christie] never saw her" (Susann 1997a, 444). When Christie complains to Danton about Ethel's relationship with Alfie, the comedian's homophobia is at fault rather than Ethel's duplicity: "Ethel has a great life. . . . Every night I come home and we either have a date with Alfie or we're going to a party. . . . You call it going up in the world to sit around and laugh at Alfie's jokes and watch him make calf eyes at some actor he's in love with? . . . Ethel gets mad when I call her 'doll.' I'm supposed to call everyone 'luv.' You like that? A group I'm travelling with where men call each other 'luv'?" (Susann 1997a, 445). Alfie's transparency as well as his closeted concealment offend Christie, required to witness the movie star's gayness as well as act as an accomplice in maintaining Alfie's hetero facade. If the glass closet provides a heteronormative screen for the larger public, being seen in its reflection threatens to queer anyone supporting the masquerade.

The masquerade of Ethel's "happy" marriage combines seamlessly with Sergio and Alfie's closet and blossoms into camp agency. Although Ethel's camp persona reaffirms a "fag hag" stereotype—the straight married woman replacing sex with gay friendships and high society—it nevertheless evolves into a relationship in which Ethel, Alfie, and Sergio humanize each other.[16] At the end of *The Love Machine* when Ethel, Christie, and their newborn fly from LA to New York for his new show, they provide the picture of the perfect family, although the image is actually incomplete: "Ethel smiled as she held the child. 'We're going to have a smash opening. Alfie and Sergio will fly in and so will half of Hollywood.'" As Susann closes on Ethel's story, her former single girl from Hamtramck, Michigan muses, "She had a good life—she was den mother for Alfie and Sergio, *the* hostess of Hollywood" (Susann 1997a, 509). Ethel's gleeful participation in the queer closet as a means of coping with the confinement of marriage presents an alternative to *Valley of the Dolls* in which such relationships are ridiculed as a sign of feminine failure. And by contrast to Anne Welles, mired in a doll-induced stupor and self-deception about her "beautiful" marriage, Susann suggests Ethel's ironic awareness in the final phrases of the character's story: "Of course there was no handsome leading man—there was just Christie. She had plenty of time on her hands to play around, but she didn't get any offers. She was respected. She was *Mrs.* Christie Lane. Oh well, you couldn't have everything" (Susann 1997a, 509). Ethel's masquerade as wife and the delight she takes in uniting with Alfie and Sergio to maintain their closet flag the subversive, comedic contradictions of her own closeted position: as domestic woman as well as former libertine.

Judith Austin's Farce Lift

The extended family of Alfie, Sergio, and "den mother" Ethel could have crumbled under the weight of scandal and the gay movie stars' contractual "morals clause," but a comic about-face affords them as well as Judith Austin with a happy ending. Susann sends her middle-aged stand-in Judith on a plotline worthy of sex farce and shares with her character the insecurities imposed by the male gaze on an aging woman, in addition to a fondness for appearing in *Women's Wear Daily*, approval of cosmetic surgery, and the acquisition of social advancement through scandal. Scandal underpins both the stories Susann writes and her reputation as vulgar, best-selling gossip, and scandal restores Judith's social status atop the newspaper columns and every social butterfly's guest list. Although Susann purportedly based Judith Austin on Babe Paley, socialite wife of CBS CEO William S. Paley, the character's evocation of Susann was not lost on British talk show host Elaine Grand, who commented on Susann's portrayal of "admirable artifacts," women who have "got silicone in their bosoms, they've got false hair hanging down here, they've got scars there [indicating the face] . . . and you write about them with admiration because they fought off age" (*Good Afternoon!*, 1973). Susann develops Judith in sympathetic and humorous terms regarding her position as a middle-aged woman. In pursuit of an elusive Robin, Judith tracks him down consorting with a younger woman, and echoing Susann's fantasies about "stabbing" Last-One Hershkovitz in *Every Night, Josephine!*, "Judith wanted to reach out and stab her" (Susann 1997a, 423; Susann 2004, 167). As the socialite ponders her junior competitor, the narration validates Judith's sexual desire, desirability, as well as her insights into the gendered double standards of aging: "she was old enough to be her mother! The girl was also too young for Robin, yet she was staring at him with open adoration. Oh God, it *was* a man's world. Age didn't count with a man. Ten years from now, Robin would still have a twenty-two-year-old stewardess staring at him like this" (Susann 1997a, 423). Susann provides comedic cues in Judith's theatricality, dramatic thought process, and unabashed egoism, and her revelation that "it *was* a man's world" ties the patrician Judith incongruously to the working-class Ethel, who (in Robin's words) has "been playing a man's game with man's rules" (1997a, 204). Susann establishes further commonality between the women, both who acquire agency through marriage to perform as "Mrs. *Power*" while their spouses remain oblivious to their deceptions. After Judith labors through sex with her husband, for example, the narration divulges, "Judith felt she deserved an Academy Award" (1997a, 454). Susann especially develops Judith's husband Gregory Austin as a pathetic comic cuckold in stark contrast to his public image as the big man running a TV network. Another "machine who passes for a man," Gregory's reliance on routine and appearances leaves him clueless to Judith's infidelity, let alone her needs, desires, and dissatisfaction.

With a reversal of fortune worthy of a comedy of manners, the stylish Judith emerges the winner of her closet plotline, but only after delivering vicious threats to out Alfie, Sergio, and Robin in addition to enduring physical humiliation easily interpreted as misogynistic. The climactic, scandalous incident that resurrects Judith's reputation in New York society occurs at Alfie's Hollywood home, where Robin escorts her to a party, unaware that Gregory is having Robin "tailed" by a private detective to amass dirt on his employee. Since Judith's return from Switzerland, where Gregory recuperated from a nervous breakdown and she got plastic surgery, her status as society beauty and hostess has declined—"It had been over a year since her picture had appeared on the front page of *Women's Wear*"—while her desire for Robin and frustration at being snubbed by him have only escalated (Susann 1997a, 454–60). With rising impatience at the Hollywood party, Judith demands the resistant Robin that they depart for some privacy, but Alfie retorts with queer advice: "Look, luv . . . we all can't have just what we want. Now I'd like to marry Sergio and have babies. Unfortunately, it just can't work out" (Susann 1997a, 497). Judith nonetheless aims to take control and uses heteronormative superiority as her weapon, first asking Robin, "You like being here with all these degenerates?" "I like being with my friends," Robin replies (Susann 1997a, 497). When she discovers the gold "slave bracelet" that Robin gave Sergio with a personal inscription, Judith vows to use this as incriminating proof that Sergio, Alfie, and Robin are "fairies": "I think Gregory will be delighted with this bracelet. I think all the scandal sheets will enjoy it too" (Susann 1997a, 498–99). A struggle over the bracelet ensues during which Judith clocks Sergio with an Oscar statue and Alfie slaps Judith as well as drags her by the hair. Evoking Helen Lawson's imbroglio with Neely O'Hara in which the younger star rips off the elder's wig, the narration notes Judith's "hairpiece was askew and looked oddly comical against her battered face," an ambivalent punchline considering Susann's reliance on wigs during her cancer therapies (Susann 1997a, 500; Seaman 1996c, 434). When the police arrive, Robin slugs Alfie to create the alibi of a heterosexual brawl among the men over Judith. The press, alerted by the private detective Gregory had hired, swarm the tattered celebrants at the police station and trumpet the scandal in hilariously clichéd headlines, although the repercussions work entirely in Judith's favor. Having previously lamented her loss of social standing, that "we're not invited to all the 'in' parties," the scandal puts her back into the headlines: "Greg, would you believe they all think I'm glamorous?" (Susann 1997a, 472, 504). Judith's story closes with her husband Gregory, blissfully unaware of his wife's infidelities, marveling in her picture on the cover of *Women's Wear* and how the scandal "made her a celebrity again" (Susann 1997a, 510).

Susann might have been gossiping about Babe Paley through Judith's scandalous experiences, but inscribing herself into the roman à clef also encouraged readers to ponder her proximity to Judith: both middle-aged women negotiating glamor and nursing ambivalence toward the male gaze, and both catapulted to celebrity through the medium of gossip. If Susann seems to subject Judith to "recuperative" punishment at Alfie's party, as "tantalizing spectacle" in Mayne's expression, this also amounts to what Mayne refers to as "female self-representation," guided here by a queer moral code that deems Sergio and Alfie "friends," not "degenerates" (Mayne 1991, 116, 117). Judith ultimately succeeds, though, and her victory punctuates Gregory's laughable presence, impaired by mechanical thinking about his power, his trophy wife, and their simulation of a successful marriage. Susann surely failed to locate an alternative space of women's agency, but she nevertheless fuels her *Love Machine* with irony and steers it on a collision course with marriage, monogamy, heterosexuality, and the governing male gaze. The closets and the stages Susann furnishes for Judith as well as Ethel enable them to perform and prevail, unimpaired by heterosexual romance.[17]

Amanda, Rose, and the Melodramatic Closet: Susann's Off-White Color Blindness

Amanda the supermodel dies of leukemia long before the conclusion of *The Love Machine*, when Susann confers comedic closure on her closet plotlines. Although Amanda's story remains anchored in her unrequited, masochistic love for Robin, Susann also gives her a closet plotline, melodramatic and tragic. The blond, svelte, and glamorous model might embody an Anglo ideal for her admirers, but only because she keeps secret her "white trash" origins and her African American Aunt Rose, the woman who selflessly reared Amanda. Named after Susann's schoolteacher mother and combining qualities of the author's childhood babysitter, Rose first arrives in flashbacks of Amanda's childhood as devoted, wise, and good-natured, a far better parent than the child's deceased birth mother, and who helps Amanda become a fashion model (see Seaman 1996c, 107, 380–81). Cultivating a successful modeling career requires Amanda to maintain a racialized closet that, after Rose suffers two strokes and requires hospitalization, coincides with economic anxieties related to supporting her care. Amanda's tragic melodrama stands in stark contrast to the novel's comedic queer irony and also illuminates the landscape of Susann's closet plotlines: the racist and heteronormative limits that persist and the genre tropes that pertain to those constraints, in addition to the selective presence of irony that ultimately signals a racialized hierarchy of plotlines in *The Love Machine*.

Susann's universe of 1960s showbiz glitterati subsists on the closet by averting scandal and living in partial visibility, an arrangement that only accommodates the kinds of "deviance" that can pass publicly for "normal." In this respect the reach of Susann's queer irony falls short of rethinking the racialized causality among her plotlines as well as the place of race within her closeted Jewish authorship. Mayne takes Arzner to task for a similar shortsightedness, for implementing "racist clichés" devoid of "a critical use of the racial stereotype"; "to ignore . . . the intertwining of sexual and racial codes of performance," Mayne contends, "is to claim female authorship as a white preserve" (Mayne 1991, 124, 126). Helene Meyers summarizes this idea in a manner especially pertinent to Susann's "off-white" position as a Jewish writer passing for Gentile: "Given that whiteness is not a given, off-whiteness leaves room for Jews to court whiteness and to resist it, sometimes simultaneously," an apt summation for the operations of *The Love Machine* and Susann's closet plotlines (Meyers 2011, 126). Susann might "court whiteness" as well as "resist it," but by marginalizing Rose and Amanda's racialized plotline, nevertheless misses an opportunity for, in Meyers's words, "embracing and resignifying the abjected status of not-quite white" (127). As Susann's stand-in for her "not-quite white" identity, Amanda's narrative abjection only reinforces hegemonic whiteness, as a masochistic victim with a secondary plotline in which racism itself comes second to unrequited romance.

Douglas Sirk's 1959 version of *Imitation of Life*, one of the top-grossing films of the year and released a decade before the publication of *The Love Machine*, provided a popular prototype for the racial closet narrative that Susann fashions for Amanda and Rose. *Imitation of Life* focuses on a white single mother and her daughter (Lana Turner and Sandra Dee), with a symmetrical subplot about Annie Johnson (Juanita Moore), a self-sacrificing single Black mother, and her mixed-race daughter Sarah Jane (Susan Kohner). Susann employs the traditional trope of maternal self-sacrifice to depict Rose, similar to Annie in the Sirk film, but unlike Sirk's Sarah Jane, Amanda's genuine love for Rose never wavers, nor does she signify as a "vamp," to the extent that her sexual activity never negates her maternal love and the aspiration for true love (Heung 1987, 126; Floreani 2013, 109). By contrast to Sarah Jane, whose determination to pass for white intensifies in proportion to her resentment toward Annie, Amanda venerates Rose as "the finest woman I've ever known," and she lives in guilt for allowing her desperation over Robin to detain her from Rose's deathbed. Although Amanda's preoccupation with Robin distracts her from visiting Rose the night her foster mother passes away, her emotional vulnerability and insecurity as well as Robin's cruelty are to blame, not Amanda's lack of maternal devotion. The melodramatic tensions of the racialized closet and sacrificial mother nevertheless erupt in Amanda and Rose's plotline, and the hospital visit when Amanda discovers Rose's death particularly echoes the dressing room scene toward the conclusion of *Imitation of Life*: Annie, her death imminent, visits Sarah Jane (now a Las Vegas showgirl) in her dressing room to bid her daughter goodbye, but to maintain Sarah Jane's ruse in front of her daughter's white castmate, must pretend to be Sarah Jane's "mammy" (Heung 1987, 26; Freedman 2009, 174–75). Similar to *Imita-tion of Life*, misinformation and misunderstanding generate the heart-break in *The Love Machine*. The nurse who notifies Amanda about Rose's death remains unaware that Rose was essentially Amanda's mother and Amanda her namesake. Rose had befriended Amanda's pregnant, aban-doned mother, who named her daughter after her friend, and then Rose rescued the six-year-old after the mother's death, working tirelessly to support her as a daughter (Susann 1997a, 144). The nurse thus wonders to Amanda why Rose asked, prior to passing away, "Where's little Rosie?" and why she refused to eat because, "I'm waiting for my child" (Susann 1997a, 159).

Despite rendering Amanda white, Susann's racialized closet plo-tline nonetheless "tapped into larger narrative concepts of the 'tragic mulatto,'" paraphrasing Racquel J. Gates, which include "the (always) tragic love story between the tragic mulatto and her white lover" as well as "struggles over her racial identity" (Gates 2018, 125). When Amanda "comes out" to her admirer Christie Lane about Rose, in hopes that he will agree to financially support Rose if they get married, the comedian's usual sexualized, misogynistic rants combine with a racist outburst. The scene begins with Amanda wanting to talk while Christie has other ideas: "Okay, you win. . . . For all the action I'm getting I could look at *Playboy* and jerk off" (Susann 1997a, 156). Christie's vulgarity transitions from sexist to racist when, following Amanda's confession, he refers to Rose as "a sick dinge" and refuses to pay a cent for her care: "Holy shit! . . . I've found the classiest broad in the world. And suddenly as a little dividend you spring a black relative on me—not even a healthy one we could pass off as the maid! Doll, when you say you want to talk, you sure don't fuck around!" (Susann 1997a, 156–58). Christie's vulgar outbursts, similar to The Head in *Valley of the Dolls*, leverage his assumed position of power, reflected in the comedian's perplexed response to the incongruities of class and race that Amanda now embodies: "I figured maybe you came from some fancy family . . . and you coolly tell me you're illegitimate, you were raised by a black chambermaid. . . . The next thing I know you'll want to name our kid Rastus" (Susann 1997a, 158). Although Susann employs traces of the tragic mulatto scenario to criticize Christie's racism, making Amanda white bypasses the charged scenario of interracial sexual desire as much as casting Rose as Amanda's *foster* mother reduces her to playing

Black sacrificial mother for a white child. These gestures only compound the oppressive dynamic observed by Tracy Floreani in *Imitation of Life*, "the attempts to portray the lives of African Americans . . . filtered through the lives of the white characters within the setting of their home in, presumably, all-white communities" (2013, 111).

The Love Machine consists of an "all-white community" among its principal characters, and Rose's brief spectacle of melodramatic self-sacrifice pales by contrast to the depiction of Amanda's last days in the throes of cancer; as the model's illness progresses and she finally fades, so does the memory of Rose. Amanda's suffering and transcendent death more closely evoke the "eradication and glorification" of the sacrificial mother Annie in *Imitation of Life*, her opulent funeral with Mahalia Jackson's transcendent rendition of "Trouble of the World" accompanying Annie's procession, lavishly garnered with carnations (Heung 1987, 37). As Amanda's lover Ike relates to Robin, "the goddam illness makes her even more beautiful. Makes her skin like china," a scene of suffering whiteness that negates memory of Amanda's racialized past (Susann 1997a, 222). When Amanda passes away, Ike marvels, "even that morning she looked great. . . . She was sitting in bed—all made up—in a beautiful dressing gown, addressing Christmas cards" (Susann 1997a, 264–65). Amanda's final moments of magnanimity bespeak her purity and self-sacrifice, with her request for Robin to care for her cat Slugger and her last words assuring Ike of her love for him; "That was part of the sweetness and the gallantry of Amanda," Ike tearfully affirms (Susann 1997a, 265). Susann frames Amanda's death through Ike's worshipful and repentant perspective, a sadly fitting finale to her modeling career and subjection to the male gaze. Ike's elegiac rendition of Amanda's demise furthermore forgets her racialized identity as much as Rose's marginal position in Amanda's narrative obscures what Rose sacrificed to rear a white orphan girl in 1940s Miami.

It is in distinguishing the seriousness of the Rose-Amanda plotline from the comedic ones, however, that Susann finally forecloses on both narrative equity in addition to the plotline's antiracist power and capacity for wish fulfillment. Susann mutes an opportunity that Gates identifies in the 1959 *Imitation of Life*, the potential for revealing through the passing scenario "that racial identity is itself a performance, one rendered more or less believable by the bodies that perform it" (Gates 2018,

125). Susann singles out Amanda for her emotional honesty and vulnerability, by contrast to other characters equipped with the agency to perform, Ethel, Judith, and Maggie, in addition to Alfie, all who push gender performance to the fore as both humorous and constructed. If Amanda resembles dimensions of Sarah Jane in *Imitation of Life*, Susann denies Amanda both Sarah Jane's mixed-race parentage and the character's proclivity for "subversive" performance, made manifest in a moment of flamboyantly "acting colored" for the white partygoers where her mother Annie works as housekeeper (Gates 2018, 125; Butler 2016, 9). Although the character's parody of the racist stereotype is hardly straightforwardly funny, and as Gates explains "is meant to convey Sarah Jane's ignorance and disrespect of her mother and white patron," the "subversive interpretation" of constructed racial performance it also yields offers what Gates elsewhere pinpoints as an enduring function of African American comedic traditions: "to criticize mainstream institutions and practices while operating *within* mainstream institutions and practices, a way of pointing out issues and problems while avoiding detection" (Gates 2018, 48, 125). Amanda and Rose get no such opportunity. Despite the potential for Susann to revise racialized melodramatic tropes of tragic victimhood, it is only in the closet plotlines that coalesce around gender and sexuality where characters have the agency of comedic masquerade and are rewarded with happy endings. Susann's melodramatic plotline for Amanda and Rose and her choice to keep comedy at bay might speak to the nobility of the characters as well as briefly protest racist constructs and gender norms, but at the expense of denying Amanda and Rose performative and critical ammunition, the power of masquerade to manage and negotiate their closets.

"It came a lot without a key / Pursuing freedom and never free": *Jacqueline Susann's The Love Machine*

Ruth Batchelor's theme song for *Jacqueline Susann's The Love Machine* (Haley Jr., 1971) evokes the sexual revolution as lonely, aimless, and decidedly antiromantic: "He touched you once but now he's gone / The pillow that his head was on / Is colder than the silent dawn." As for whom the lyrics refer to, as Dionne Warwick warbles, "That's Robin Stone," avatar of a sexual revolution that he televised and lost: "He's tried it all from A to Z / It came a lot without a key / Pursuing freedom and never free."[18] As the first example in the film of "transcoding" the novel's themes into different media and social-cultural contexts, the theme song performs what Linda Hutcheon refers to as "a double process of interpreting and then creating something new" (2013, 8, 16, 20). Transcoding, Hutcheon explains, is "necessarily a recoding into a new set of conventions as well as signs" (16). Batchelor's lyrics recode the novel's queer themes, Robin's in particular, through allusion. "He tried it all," the lyric states, "from A to Z," which almost rhymes with "AC/DC," one term attributed to Robin in the film when suspicions arise about his sexuality. The next line, "It came a lot without a key," directly evokes the enigmatic nature of the protagonist, his experiences, and the mysteries of the promiscuous sexual revolution that he personifies; it might also refer to the roman à clef, the novel with a key. The lyrics offer a bleak perspective of the inscrutable Robin and his sexualized quest, "Pursuing freedom and never free."

Advertised as *Jacqueline Susann's The Love Machine*, Columbia Pictures' film adaptation attributes its authorship to the novelist but markedly recodes Susann's view of the sexual revolution. Rearranging the novel's plot mechanics and redefining the queer characters from

"This is the only straight movie I've seen," cracks *Vogue*'s Muriel Resnik, "in which the camera spends more time on the pectorals of the hero (John Phillip Law) than on those of his bedmates."

enlightening to frightening, *The Love Machine* fashions a punitive social melodrama that enlists sexually desirous and deviously calculating women, merciless male libertines, and bitchy, predatory gay men to condemn promiscuity, nonmonogamy, and homosexuality. This operation comes to fruition, first by having Amanda commit suicide, next when Robin brutalizes a sex worker, and finally with the climactic party at Alfie's, which leaves Robin a fallen soldier in the sexual revolution. The melodramatic reversal of the film centers on the outcome of the sex scandal, Robin's ouster from IBC due to breaching his contractual morals clause. The film's depiction of gay men as sadistic, plotting predators, confirmations of social fears, and butts of ridicule coincides with turning Robin into a deviant deserving of his downfall due to his cruelty, heterosexual hedonism, and queer alliances. The film additionally simplifies the women characters into unambiguous character types, or deletes them entirely, such as reducing Ethel Evans to a petty opportunist comically content with a rich husband and gloating publicly about it, whittling Maggie Stewart down to an insignificant walk-on, and eliminating Rose from Amanda's storyline.

The perception of irony rings through the reception of *The Love Machine*. Reviewers identify the movie as classic naive camp, what Susan Sontag (1966) dubs "failed seriousness." Particularly evident in the film's "serious," melodramatic opprobrium of the sexual revolution, the resulting camp reception takes joy in exposing the failure of the film's sex-fueled moralizing as an inadvertent revelation of deviance. As a result, the film bursts with "inner comedy" by "playing a double part," its heteronormative morality tale failing to squash the sexual perversity that it supposedly denounces. The tension produces unintentional camp comedy, although the glee reviewers take stems from outing not just a badly made and exploitative picture but also a perverse film attempting to pass as a straight social melodrama. Reviewers furthermore conflate novel and film, and in evaluating the two works as identical, formulate uniformly terrible assessments that hold Susann responsible for the film's inept depiction of sexuality. While the movie version of *The Love Machine* endeavored to contain Susann's queer permissiveness, reviewers laughed at the film as a failure whose inability to disguise Susann's excesses with melodramatic moralizing served as an endorsement of her perversity.

Samuel Taylor's adaptation of *The Love Machine* targets the sexual revolution as a social problem, that permissiveness undermines romantic love, subverts heterosexuality, and enables gay liberation. De-queering Susann's closet plotlines, the film also deracinates them, deleting Rose entirely along with the antiracist themes. Excising the Amanda-Rose plotline might have been a reflection of its outmodedness as a tired melodramatic trope, but the film develops no equivalent to the novel's antiracist themes, limited as they are. By contrast to extracting the novel's sole African American character, the film fashions vividly repugnant gay figures in actor Alfie Knight (Clinton Greyn) and especially fashion photographer Jerry Nelson (David Hemmings).

A morally driven social melodrama, the portrayal of queer difference takes on a menacing quality that resituates the story within homophobic narrative causality. Jerry Nelson, Robin's openly gay pal, amalgamates most of the gay and homoerotic characters in Susann's novel and embodies *all* the stereotypes that Susann takes such pains to undercut through Sergio: duplicity, predatoriness, bitchiness, and misogyny. The name "Jerry Nelson" combines two characters from the novel: Jerry Moss, the TV ad executive whom Susann portrays as sexually confused (and in her next novel *Once Is Not Enough* reappears as a full-on "closet case"), and

Deviating from the novel, Alfie (Clinton Greyn) and Jerry (David Hemmings) plot their seduction of Robin after Jerry agrees to conceal Robin's brutal beating of a sex worker.

Dip Nelson, Robin's ostensibly straight fixer whose constant compan-
ionship with Robin, even at orgies, provokes rumors of a covert affair.
Not long into the film, Jerry introduces his apparent friend Amanda (Jodi
Wexler) to Robin at a photo shoot, something Jerry Moss does in the
novel, but in the film Jerry swiftly shifts from supportive matchmaker
to competitive backstabber as his designs to seduce Robin grow clearer.
Jerry gladly lets Robin use him as a buffer to evade intimacy with Amanda,
and he expresses sadistic pleasure in Robin's detached treatment of her:
"Dear-heart! I am handy, aren't I? She beginning to crowd you already?
Ah, my Robin, you do play rough." Robin subsequently commends
Jerry because "you never make a pass," but his ally replies, "I'm biding
my time." In direct contrast to Sergio, who in the novel berates Robin
(and the reader) for believing the stereotype of the predatory gay man,
every act of Jerry's friendship toward Robin contributes to his calculated
plans for seduction. When Jerry discovers that Amanda has committed
suicide, for example, he cares more about protecting Robin's reputation than Amanda's tragedy and seizes her recorded suicide message.
Jerry also helps cover up Robin's violent assault of the sex worker, as Dip
does in the novel, by offering an alibi and daintily applying makeup to
Robin's bruised knuckles.

Whereas the novel's comedic finale intersects Sergio and Alfie's
closet plotline with the heterosexual happy ending for Maggie and Robin,
the film's grim conclusion is premised on Robin's failure as a man due to
his affiliation with Jerry and Alfie. For Robin in the novel, suspicions
that he is a "fag," "AC/DC," or "queersville" make no difference to him
when he hands in his resignation, but in the film these accusations decide
his downfall. The party at Alfie's home and the ensuing struggle occur
similarly in the film: Judith's fight with the gay men over possession of
the bracelet with the suggestive inscription from Robin, the arrival of the
police, and Robin's fabrication of an alibi. The film nevertheless faults
Jerry for the altercation and ensuing scandal, due to his machinations to
seduce Robin; and in the only comedy at the film's conclusion, Jerry exits
the police station after the tussle holding Alfie's arm, who vainly schmoozes
with the reporters. Robin's subsequent removal from the TV network
for breaching his morals clause closes the film, his lonely walk away at
the end accompanied by Dionne Warwick's reprise of the title theme
"He's Moving On," the failure of Robin's heterosexuality inextricably

tied to his relationship with the deviant and duplicitous Jerry. Where the novel's Robin progressed from "Laddy in the Dark" to healthy heterosexual under the tutelage of the enlightening Sergio, the film turns Robin's "friends" back into "degenerates" whose manipulations implicate Robin.

The film's depiction of Robin and Jerry as variations of masculine deviance intersects with its corresponding treatment of Ethel, Judith, and Maggie. Casting the young Dyan Cannon as Judith Austin, the film not only undercuts the theme of aging women's sexuality but also reduces the character to a calculating, spoiled femme fatale: responsible for vindictively lighting Robin's bed on fire; humiliated at Alfie's party for her scandalous behavior yet also validated for her diminutive view of "fags"; and never rewarded with the novel's ironic plot twist. Alongside virtually eliminating Maggie (Sharon Farrell) from the narrative, the film adaptation diminishes Ethel (Maureen Arthur) to a sneaky, foul-mouthed gold digger who marries Christie Lane (Shecky Greene) and waves her new status in the faces of her former network co-workers. Although the film grants Ethel "the celebrity banger" a moment of sympathy when she tells Christie with sincerity, "When I ball a guy, it's 'cause I dig him," it all but erases the depth and dimension of Ethel's sexuality, humor, humanity, and insight into the machinations of men. For Muriel Resnik writing in *Vogue*, Ethel is reducible to the scene when she returns to IBC as Mrs. Christie Lane and, "wearing a mini chinchilla coat and matching hat" to parade her newfound prosperity to her former co-workers, "makes a vulgar gesture in general use by waiters in small pizzerie [*sic*]" (Resnik 1971, 178). Never following Ethel after her ascendance to "Mrs. *Power*," her disenchantment with marriage and compensatory relationship with Alfie and Sergio, Ethel's plotline in the film provides pat comedy closure and the only example of a successful heterosexual relationship.

The reception of *The Love Machine* diverges from the typical pattern of critics who demean a film adaptation of a literary work as the "shadow" of its source, a bastardized distortion of a beloved original (Hutcheon 2013, xxv, 3–4, 6). Reviewers instead collapse Susann's *Love Machine* with the film, the novel bearing so little authority in critics' minds that it seems doubtful that they even read it; skewering the novel runs parallel with slamming the film, holding Susann responsible, and laughing at all of them. Even when noting significant deviations from the novel, movie critics curiously confer continuity and sameness when comparing

The film's Ethel Evans (Maureen Arthur) becomes a calculating gold digger who marries Christie Lane (Shecky Greene) and embraces the role of "*Mrs. Power.*" Judith Austin (Dyan Cannon), meanwhile, is turned into a spoiled femme fatale who, among other transgressions, lights Robin's bed on fire.

the celluloid re-creation to Susann's source. *Variety*'s Murf assesses, for instance, that "Jacqueline Susann's novel . . . has been telescoped somewhat by adapter Samuel Taylor. Some will regret the omission of the book's resolution, others may miss some greater character development. However, if audiences put in as much of its own imagination to the film as they did the book, little will be missed" (Murf 1971, 18). Marvin Kitman of the *Washington Post* communicates a similar sentiment of dismissal with a more satirical spin, calling his piece "'The Love Machine' as a Documentary": "Some critics said that 'The Love Machine,' the movie based on Jacqueline Susann's novel, was the worst movie of the year. . . . The film critics were wrong. . . . It is a documentary about the television business. What does Jacqueline Susann tell us about the TV industry in her documentary?" (Kitman 1971, B9). If Murf indicates the differences between book and film while Kitman overlooks them, the assumption of continuity and consistency between the "pulp novel" and "the worst film of the decade" persists for both reviewers to trumpet their dismissal.

Mocking *The Love Machine* as a "terrible" film and attributing this to Susann's salacious sensibility coincides with perceptions of the sexual revolution as a challenge to conventional constructs of both social reality and aesthetic realism. By this reasoning, Susann's demonstrations of active female sexuality, empowered queer sexuality, and fluid masculinity defy both verisimilitude and tastefulness. Kitman's dissection of "Jackie's

helluva documentary," for instance, derisively questions the believability of Robin's ouster from IBC for violating his "morals clause": "Can you
imagine anybody being tripped up by bad morals in a Jacqueline Susann
work?" (Kitman 1971, B9). The suggestion of Susann's immoral permissiveness, moreover, provides additional laughs that negate by implication the
book's defense of sexual others, in particular, Sergio and Alfie's repeated
trepidation over being outed due to the "morals clause" in their studio contracts. Wielding what movie critic Andrew Sarris called "hip homophobia"
(Sarris 1993, ix), reviewers commandeer camp sensibility to mock the film's
queerness, which extends to Susann's influence. *Time* magazine's review
immediately cites Susann's authorship in the title "Valley of the Dregs,"
an allusion to Susann's first novel that also announces the critic's position on the film and novel *The Love Machine*. Echoing Kitman, the review
decries how every element of the movie is ridiculously sexualized, from
themes to character and plot motivation: the basic morality tale premise,
"the rise and fall of a libidinous television executive"; Judith Austin's "pel-
vic instinct for talent," which gets Robin hired; and Robin's own "insatiable and some-what kinky appetites," which "get him into a good deal of
trouble" (J. C. 1971, 60). The *Time* reviewer clarifies the depraved fluidity
imposed by such sexualized logic, transitioning from Robin's "kinky appetites" to "David Hemmings, swishing about in a limp-wristed parody of his
fashion-photographer role in *Blow Up*" (J. C. 1971, 60).

Vogue's Resnik extends this sense of "limp-wristed parody" to the
entire film and suggests that a queer gaze actually predominates despite
the seeming efforts of *The Love Machine* to be a "straight movie." Invoking the concept of naive camp, Resnik calls the film a "good-bad spectacular" and explains that it "has been produced with the care and respect one
would give the 'Book of Job'" (Resnick 1971, 178). Resnik's reasoning blurs
"good-bad" taste with the themes of the sexual revolution, beginning with
the example of the film's failure to pass. "This is the only straight movie
I've seen," cracks the critic, "in which the camera spends more time on
the pectorals of the hero (John Phillip Law) than on those of his bedmates," a brimming queerness illustrated on the next page with a sexy
photo of a shirtless Law (Resnik 1971, 178, 179). Following commendations
for the "vulgar" and "dirty" performances by Maureen Arthur as Ethel
and Dyan Cannon as Judith, Resnik mentions Jacqueline Susann's diminutive cameo and then points to "David Hemmings, the good gay guy,

[who] delivers his lines like Angela Lansbury doing Bette Davis" (Resnik 1971, 178). The critic follows this by returning to the excessively *"beautiful"* Law, blameworthy for the film's failures due partly to his position as "the new breed of *l'homme fatale*, the cold-hearted but winning victim of the liberated feminine libido" (178–79). Modifying the popular stereotype of strong women yielding effeminate men, a Momist idea revived in the wake of the women's movement, the passive and objectified Law proves an unconvincing hero. Surrounded by gay men and camp women, from the characters in the film to author Jacqueline Susann, Law remains the feminized object of a queer gaze. Although these reviewers scoff at the film's simplistic morality tale, they nevertheless reproduce similar moral disapproval toward the sexual revolution and Susann's contributions to it.

Jacqueline Susann's The Love Machine and its reception reignite the anxieties voiced when the novel hit bookstores: Susann's editor Korda recommending the novel because it "is about successful heterosexual love," and competing author Gwen Davis, who penned her novel to provide the "equal time for heterosexuals" that *Love Machine* lacked. Although the film errs from the novel by removing Maggie and Robin's romance and replacing their "successful" union with Ethel and Christie's, these distinctions matter less to movie reviewers than what the book and film share: the authorial presence of Jacqueline Susann, glued to the movie in advertising, and the imagery of the sexual revolution, such as camp gay men and sexually active women. The film appears determined to provide the "equal time" Davis calls for, and so do the reviewers. Collapsing the film with the novel and assuming its alliance with a range of queer themes, reviewers engage in the game of camp gossip that the next chapter expands on: locating the signs of "AC/DC" adorning the film and outing them, exposing a film trying to pass for straight. The very presences of heterosexual promiscuity and queer desire that surface in both book and film, albeit disparately plotted, coded, and valued, remain sufficient for some critics to mark the cultural value of both novel and author as fallen, to characterize the "dazzling artlessness" of the movie version as faithful to the "bad morals" of its literary source (Murf 1971, 18; Kitman 1971, B9). In its backlash toward the sexual revolution, the film adaptation of *The Love Machine* trumpets heteronormative morality, and as a "terrible" movie, reviewers parlayed the film's shortcomings to reinforce that sentiment of backlash through camp derision.

3

Wit Is Not Enough

Comedic Gossip, Camping Susann, and Women's Authorship

It was no secret in the late 1960s and 1970s that Jacqueline Susann's work was camp. Gloria Steinem first broke the news reviewing *Valley of the Dolls*, that camp was the key to appreciating—or tolerating—Susann's phenomenally popular work: "There are a few classic moments of the sort once deplored as embarrassing or inadvertently funny, and now exalted as Unconscious Low Camp" (Steinem 1966, 11). This camp key to Susann and her novels was disclosed in the cadences of gossip, apropos an author of romans à clef, and the disclosure was also supposed to be revealingly funny, two more trends that Steinem set: "*Literati* who thought the non-book world began with *The Carpetbaggers* are in for a surprise. Compared to Miss Susann, Harold Robbins writes like Proust" (Steinem 1966, 11). Even in the absence of the word "camp," reviewers framed their assessments through concepts recently popularized by Susan Sontag: art and people whose "passionate failures" and "failed seriousness" were humorous even though they did "not *mean* to be funny"; the "so-bad-it's-good," "exaggerated" and "androgynous"; and the "good taste of bad taste," a scale of value driven by the credo, "The new-style dandy, the lover of Camp, appreciates vulgarity" (Sontag 1966, 279–80, 282, 286–87, 289, 291; see also Larson 2003, 262–75, 305–12, 314–86).

Gossiping the secret that Jacqueline Susann was naive camp or unintentionally funny acknowledged the author's genuineness, but this view nonetheless bled all too easily into impressions of Susann as unselfconsciously robotic and inartistic, anathema to human and natural. The reception of *The Love Machine* especially showcased this dynamic. As the *New York Times'* Christopher Lehmann-Haupt pondered, for instance, the appeal of *The Love Machine* was in Susann's "sincerity, her complete ingenuousness" (1969, 45), yet according to Jonathan Baumbach's review for *The Nation*, Susann's novel "shares a common plastic reality with television commercials" among other "popular culture" (Baumbach 1969, 188–89). *Time* magazine pegged Susann with a pun on her book title, as "Jackie's Machine," churning out "a caricature of naturalism," marketing her novels with a "natural merchandiser's instinct," and promoting them through "absurdities, inconsistencies, generalities, banalities and wisecracks with calculated sincerity" (Anon. 1969b). The paradox of Susann's "calculated sincerity" fueled both critical ire and derision, contempt and camp, all of which sought to unmask the author as a creative automaton in the form of comedic gossip. Ridiculing the unwitting begetter of standardized, mass-produced trash, journalists abided by two of Henri Bergson's basic propositions about comedy: that it results from the incongruity of the human, natural being behaving like a machine, and that it elicits laughter that "corrects" such deviations from "nature" (Romanska and Ackerman 2016, 13, 185). Gossip similarly fulfills corrective and comedic functions, which rationalize the laughter of aggression and superiority (Spacks 1985, 49–51). Bergson postulates, *"The attitudes, gestures and movements of the human body are laughable in exact proportion as that body reminds us of a mere machine,"* and as Glenda Carpio adds, "Machines . . . are predictable" (Bergson 1928, 29 [emphasis in original]; Carpio 2008, 108–9).[1] Viewed as formulaic and "predictable," Susann embodied for journalists what Bergson encapsulates as the "automatism" of the "comic character," close cousin to the naively camp person, "comic in proportion to his ignorance of himself. The comic person is unconscious" (Bergson 1928, 16). Mocking Jacqueline Susann for her machine-made work and personality involved gossipy laughter that "intended to humiliate," to provide a "corrective" for social "manners," and a means by which "society avenges itself for the liberties taken with it" (Bergson 1928, 17, 197).

Jacqueline Susann certainly took liberties in the eyes of many scornful critics, with the definition of literature and attribution of cultural value. Laughter *at* Susann served as one corrective by figuring the author as the ultimate mass culture machine reaching a readymade audience, furnishing, as *The Nation* put it, "a shared inhuman cultural fantasy between author and readers" (Baumbach 1969, 189). *Time* extended this "inhuman" quality to the pervasive image of Susann, stamped on her book jackets and littered among random mass culture products, that "gazes down from between the Preparation H and mail-order-diploma ads" on drugstore shelves (Anon. 1969b). Talk show host Elaine Grand captured this last sentiment during a 1973 interview amid the debut of *Once Is Not Enough* in the UK, querying Susann, "Which is the product? You or the book?" Blurring producer with product, person and thing, critics justified their laughter as an antidote to a machine that stamped out "plastic" with "calculated sincerity," privileged vulgar style and predictable excesses over substance, and whose sole aim was to make a profit, not create "real literature."

Susann's rejection of modernist authors such as Henry James, Vladimir Nabokov, and James Joyce urged on the corrective, gossipy laughter at Susann as naive camp machine, and her slams on "egghead" and "double-dome" critics offered even more damning evidence of a lowbrow perspective.[2] Journalists replied with camp vocabulary that largely recycled modernist cultural constructions of women authors and audiences. Andreas Huyssen illuminates the "male mystique" of modernism born in the nineteenth century, how highbrow critics and artists envisioned themselves competing with women "knocking at the gate of a male-dominated culture," concurrent to facing the encroaching threat of mass culture; this position warranted demeaning women artists as the embodiment of mass culture and violators of high culture's governing philosophy, the "art-life dichotomy" (Huyssen 1986, 47, 50). High culture offered a male refuge from "mass culture and everyday life," Huyssen explains, liberation from feminized activities and dispositions such as domesticity, passive consumerism, and mechanical reproduction as well as a potent curative for the "lure of mass culture, . . . the threat of losing oneself in dreams and delusions and of merely consuming rather than producing" (Huyssen 1986, 47, 50, 54, 55). Alongside the melodramatic, existential threat of identity loss, this construct also lends itself to the image of the laughable automaton: female creators and consumers of mass culture as unselfconsciously ridiculous machines of reproduction and consumption, puppets whose strings are pulled by the culture industry. As Baumbach put it in the penultimate lines of his *Love Machine* review, "There is no discernible vision in the novel outside of popular culture's vision of itself . . . the novel is written in the very language of its world—a language wholly incapable of accounting for human experience, a language geared toward genocide" (Baumbach 1969, 188, 190). Hardly a laugh riot, this conception of Susann nevertheless fuels the "corrective" camp gossip making light of Susann. Such revelations solicited laughter to both explain and control the cultural event of "Jacqueline Susann," the personification of the modernist nightmare of female authorship, to resist and demystify her "lure."

Configuring Jacqueline Susann as unconscious kitsch machine involved conflating her with her works, a critical gambit that played off the author's signature genre, the roman à clef. The roman à clef always presented the risk of readers confusing the content with the author's personal life, which in Susann's case arose in direct conjunction with critics divulging the hysterical secret that she and her books as well as their movie versions—one and the same—were camp. Kevin Kelly exposed Susann to *Boston Globe* readers, for example, when analyzing how she responded to the question of her "literary worth": "Her words were vorpal, measured, no-fooling-with-me-palsie, like a typical Susann heroine in a moment of emotional explosion, one of her career girls named Neely O'Hara or Amanda O'Hara, Jennifer North or Judith South" (Kelly 1969, A22). Critics like Kelly, anxious over Susann's soaring popularity and what it meant for cultural and social standards, found it reassuring to condense the female author and her mass cultural creations, evidence of Susann's tasteless breach of the art-life dichotomy. The same highbrow aesthetic norms and misogynistic stereotypes applied as in the modernist nightmare—hysterical loss of control, lacking any critical distance from mass culture—now rendered comical.

The roman à clef that pinned Susann to her work was also a "roman à camp," to the delight of hostile critics, but also adoring readers. Reading the roman à clef in many regards approximated camp reception, and in Susann's case, the two converged. The roman à clef recycled gossip as well as spurred it, as Sean Latham illuminates, with the "powerful ability to transfer interpretive authority from writers to mass-mediated networks of reception" (Latham 2009, 47). Camp likewise reassigned "interpretive authority" from the creator to, as Philip Core proposes, "the eyes of the beholder" (Core 1984, 7). And similar to the gossip that the roman à clef spurred among its readers, the phrase "It's so camp" inspired, in Mark Finch's expression, "media gossip" (Finch 1999, 148;

Core 1984, 15). The camp subtext of *Batman*, for instance, functioned as a kind of media gossip, divulging the secret yet obvious homosexuality of these exemplars of "manliness" and "the American way" (Medhurst 2013, 240–41; Torres 1999, 338–40; Phillips and Pinedo 2018, 30). As a sensibility of disclosing secrets about art and people, then, camp sensibility thrived through gossip networks similar to the ones initiated by Susann's novels and "guessing game." To call someone or something "camp" or to read them in camp terms constituted, on top of that, not just gossip, but "badinage," witty gossip about camp people and things (Finch 1999, 148). The interpretive strategies and goals of camp, gossip, and the roman à clef finally converge in the activities of "finding in observed trivia material from which to manufacture entertainment," and, "identifying those seemingly innocuous textual details that can abruptly turn fiction into gossip" (Spacks 1985, 122, 136; Latham 2009, 56).

The interpretive strategies of camp and the roman à clef bore a singular symmetry in the reception of Jacqueline Susann in the 1960s and 1970s. Critics took voyeuristic and comedic pleasure in probing the "trivial" and "innocuous" details of Susann's life that exposed her machine-like ridiculousness as well as her likeness to her characters, exemplified by the *Boston Globe*'s Kelly just quoted. Scrutinizing the novelist's physical reaction to the question of her cultural value, Kelly evokes comic monstrousness and establishes his highbrow credentials by describing the author as "vorpal," Lewis Carroll's nonsense adjective for the beastly Jabberwocky in *Through the Looking Glass*. The reference to Susann's "no-fooling-with-me-palsie" follows, now employing the repetitive motion of a disability for comic effect.[3] Mocking references commence to equally "trivial" details that root Susann within her romans à clef, the names of her seemingly interchangeable characters, likewise comically indivisible from the author who speaks like them. Kelly might not use such keywords as "camp," "pop," or "kitsch," but he nonetheless exemplifies the posture of "camp oblige" when, Andrew Ross explains, "traditional intellectuals . . . go slumming" (Ross 1989, 136–37, 144). In the tone of badinage, and like so many of his journalist colleagues, Kelly reinstates his cultural power by packaging Susann as naive camp in a gossipy anecdote that exposes her unwitting ridiculousness.

The ascription of naive camp to Susann was widespread and imparted as gossip that largely denied the author any sense of self-conscious artistic agency, the loudest and most ostentatious example of which was delivered by Truman Capote in 1969. Calling Susann a "truckdriver in drag," Capote's line echoed throughout the media for years, with Capote repeating it on *Rowan & Martin's Laugh-In* in 1971, and it perpetually influenced Susann's reception. The overtly camp scrutiny of Susann's femininity followed Capote's quips in 1969, as if his gossipy disclosure outed a decisive, new, and terribly personal variable for assessing Susann according to the norms of taste and gender.

It would be inaccurate and unfair, though, to ignore Susann's defenders or suggest that the author was a mere victim. Fans like Carol Bjorkman, Rex Reed, Liz Smith, and John Alfred Avant framed their media gossip about the novelist through ironic identification with her sensibility, and moreover, jettisoned what Sontag calls "the seriousness . . . of high culture and of the high style of evaluating people" (Sontag 1966, 286–87). Sontag codifies this gesture toward the close of "Notes on 'Camp'": "Camp taste is a kind of love, love for human nature. It relishes, rather than judges, the little triumphs and awkward intensities of 'character.' . . . Camp taste identifies with what it is enjoying. People who share this sensibility are not laughing at the thing they label as 'a camp,' they're enjoying it. Camp is a tender feeling" (291–92). Inasmuch as Susann's comrades loved her as camp, they also recognized her *camping*, following Sontag's reasoning: responding to an audience that perceives her as camp, and, engaging in willful "self-parody" that also expresses her "self-love" (Sontag 1966, 282–83). Susann's advocates surely engaged in camp media gossip, as numerous *Women's Wear Daily* columns by Bjorkman demonstrated, but they adhered to what Matthew Tinkcom labels "the paradox of gossip," akin to Sedgwick's Glass Closet and the comedy of suggestion discussed in the prior chapter, the principal that "lowering the shades is always potentially (within the realm of fantasy) a way of raising them" (Tinkcom 1999, 282). Susann's camp performance, her supporters suggested, was the key to accessing her books as well as the key attraction of her authorship: the flamboyant gossip that manages secrets, her own and others, and ironically puts them on display in her best-selling romans à clef.

Susann also took measures to flag her ironic self-awareness and demonstrate her understanding of camp. Neely O'Hara refers to a dance among the patients during her "loony bin" stay as "a real camp" in *Valley of the Dolls*, and in *The Love Machine*, IBC TV executives occasionally refer to their programs as "high camp" (Susann 1997c, 393; 1997a: 439, 484). None of Susann's characters use the word "camp" in *Once Is Not Enough*, but Susann engages in it. Susann poises the pompous, sexist literary "man's man" Norman Mailer for parody, in addition to such vocal detractors as Steinem and Capote, in the spirit of such statements as, "When someone like Gloria Steinem pans me, I laugh," and, "now she just laughs at her assailants. Especially Truman Capote" (Kelly 1969, A19; Reed 1974, 243). Susann's posthumously published *Dolores* contains an even more protracted Capote parody in which the character's gossip reverberates with destructive results for the Jackie Onassis–inspired protagonist. Susann also integrated self-parody into her promotional appearances. On the television comedy programs *Rowan & Martin's Laugh-In* and *Love, American Style*, Susann played herself in vignettes and sketches that mocked her literary form yet attested to the power of her authorship.[4] All these examples spotlight the nexus of gossip, comedy, camp, and the roman à clef as well as how Susann engaged parody as an instrument for managing social gossip and the narratives defining her star persona. Susann's use of humor and allusions to camp reflect tactics to negotiate the comedy that surrounded her reception, a loud and boisterous conversation in which aesthetic evaluations remained as indistinguishable from gossip as Susann's novels.

Camping Susann, BC (Before Capote)

Gloria Steinem's 1966 *New York Tribune* review of *Valley of the Dolls* first put into print the idea of the camp Jacqueline Susann. Enlisting the highbrow perspective of "camp oblige," Steinem anticipates and appeases the concerns of mass culture critics as well as establishes the basis for her cultural distinction and camp wit. Intellectuals at the time, such as sociologist Bernard Rosenberg, were concerned that the criterion of "popular" would enable mass culture to subvert traditional aesthetic criteria and ascend as an equal to high culture: "To prefer Shakespeare to Spillane becomes mere eccentricity, and to publish *Valley of the Dolls* in contravention of one's own better taste becomes a form of philanthropy—a little self-interested, perhaps, but plainly benign" (Rosenberg 1971, 6).[5] Steinem leads her evaluation with the "surprise" disclosure that Susann made Robbins resemble high literary practitioners such as Proust (who also wrote romans à clef). Corroborating this declaration with evidence that numerous journalists would routinely cite, Steinem points to the crass, commercialized "merchandising game" devised by publisher Bernard Geis Associates to sell the book as well as the simplistic cautionary tale about drugs, sex, and career, drenched in Hollywood clichés and "bound to comfort, if not surprise, dime-store sales girls across the country" (Steinem 1966, 11). Having portrayed Susann and her publisher Bernard Geis as incarnations of the "cultural garbagemen" that made Rosenberg so anxious, Steinem proceeds to find a degree of pleasure in such mass culture detritus without jettisoning highbrow standards. As Sontag asserts, "Camp is the answer to the problem: how to be a dandy in the age of mass culture," and a few notes later explains that the new "new-style dandy, the lover of Camp . . . sniffs the stink and prides himself on his strong nerves" (Sontag 1966, 288–89). If highbrow camp helped sustain the taste distinctions that mass culture threatened to dissolve, it also answered similar challenges to cultural hierarchy presented by "Popism," the popular movement adjacent to camp associated with Andy Warhol and Roy Lichtenstein (among others), in which comic books and consumer graphics garnered the same aesthetic import as Monet or Picasso (Ross 1989, 152, 166–67; Torres 1999, 333–34). In Steinem's pithy 1965 *Life* magazine piece "A Vest-Pocket Guide to Camp," the critic responded to the crises faced by both the dandy and the traditionalist by stratifying camp with the same terminology as conventional coding—"High," "Middle," and "Low"—and distinguishing "Conscious" from "Unconscious" camp as well as discerning camp from pop (Steinem 1965, 84; also see Lynes 1949). Applying terminology from her "Vest-Pocket Guide" that directly reproduces highbrow criteria, Steinem locates in *Valley of the Dolls* "Unconscious Low Camp" and "inadvertently funny" dialogue, akin to examples in her *Life* magazine piece, "the biography of Johnny Weismuller [*sic*] by Narda Onyx and professional wrestling on television" (Steinem 1965, 84). Steinem's camp hierarchy and its foundations in conventional cultural codes combat the credo of cultural equivalence, instigated by mass culture, celebrated in pop art, and so feared by traditionalists.

Steinem ties these camp qualities of the "inadvertently funny" and "Unconscious Low Camp" to Susann's work and personhood, reproducing a chain of logic redolent of the aesthetic code that conflates mass

culture and the "feminine." "Most of the dialogue," Steinem continues, "is less classic-bad than television-bad, and authoress Jacqueline
Susann—a former TV actress—turns it out like a pro" (1966, 11). Having
linked "Unconscious Low Camp" to Susann's expertise in "television-
bad" dialogue as well as her appeal to women readers, Steinem then
stretches these ideas to her closing punchline, that Susann's first book
Every Night, Josephine! "was for many months the only book on display
at the Sixth Avenue Delicatessen in New York" (Steinem 1966, 11). Taking jabs at Susann's immersion in everyday culture coded as lowbrow,
domestic, and feminine—television, Hollywood, dimestores, and delicatessen dining—Steinem founds the camp discourse of Jackie Susann
in the bedrock of modernist taste codes.

Numerous comedic treatments of Susann undertake the same highbrow camp loophole, from reviews and feature articles about the author
to outright parody. Readers might have attributed camp to Thomas Meehan's "Portrait of a Babe," a 1967 parody of *Valley of the Dolls* for *Saturday
Evening Post*, because of his 1965 *New York Times* magazine story, "Not
Good Taste, Not Bad Taste—It's 'Camp.'" Meehan wields highbrow criteria as a satirical crusader and christens his parody with quotations of
Susann that expose her as an unconscious vulgarian, such as repudiating
the goal "to turn a phrase that critics will quote, like Henry James," and
affirming, "what matters to *me* is writing a *story* that involves people"
(Howard 1966, 69; Meehan 1967, 22). Meehan strikes back by imagining "Miss Jacqueline Susann, the authoress, tackling an updated version
of an old Jamesian plot," *Portrait of a Lady*. With James's heroine Isabel Archer uttering lines such as, "If I don't dig a fella, I don't dig him,"
the parody closes with Isabel's discovery that reading *Valley of the Dolls*
proves a more effective soporific than downing dolls (Meehan 1967, 22).
Although he satirizes both Susann and Bernard Geis Associates as cultural arrivistes—James's character Henrietta Stackpole writes a showbiz
roman à clef and sends it to Susann's publisher—Meehan's parodic and
satirical gambit nonetheless rests on an obvious high/low contradiction
akin to camp oblige. Meehan might don the mantle of highbrow taste
arbiter and assume the same attitudes in his readers, yet he captures
Susann's prose with expert precision, and in order to find such mimicry
funny, expects readers with equal knowledge of both *Valley of the Dolls*
and *Portrait of a Lady*.

MAD magazine's treatment of Jacqueline Susann, by contrast, eschewed both camp oblige and highbrow spoof by virtue of the diminutive, controversial cultural status of the publication that framed it. In the wake of the fabulously popular and notoriously bad 1967 movie version of *Valley of the Dolls*, Larry Siegel and Mort Drucker's "Valley of the Dollars" from September 1968 parodied the film as well as the book and singled out Susann. Self-directed humor ushers the reader into the *MAD* "satire," though, simultaneous to establishing its comedic targets: "YOU READ THE BOOK! YOU SAW THE MOVIE! NOW ENJOY THIS MAD SATIRE . . . IT'S ALMOST AS FUNNY" (Siegel and Drucker 1968, 4). By contrast to such bourgeois stalwarts as the *New York Herald* (Steinem) and *Saturday Evening Post* (Meehan), *MAD* emerged from the wreckage of the 1950s Senate hearings on the comic book industry and, in its incarnation as "magazine," parodied popular culture "from within popular culture," as Ethan Thompson explains (2011, 47, 52). Thompson ascribes both "sick" humor and camp sensibility to *MAD*, adding that "those who embraced *MAD* as trash, not art, were more in line with the magazine's own aestheticizing gestures" (46, 51, 68). A far cry from the superiority of Meehan's parody, and with shades of camp identification, Siegel and Drucker enact a power dynamic of trash trashing trash interwoven with a satire of blatant venality directed at Susann, the publishing industry, and the movie business. At the same time, the numerous accusations of "sick" content hurled at Susann, her novel, and the film signify more equitably, considering that the source of such insults—*MAD* magazine—was also "sick."

The signs of alliance first surface with the opening disclaimer, which submits that the movie is funnier than *MAD*'s satire of it. Following caricatured introductions of the film's main characters, the author "Jackpot Suzanne" appears, with oversized eyes and a Cheshire Cat grin. Gushing that her movie cameo pays "a fabulous fee," combined with all her other profits, Jackpot boasts, "I'd say I'm rolling in the—VALLEY OF THE DOLLARS" (Siegel and Drucker 1968, 4).[6] What might appear as a straightforward dig at avarice is qualified by two additional elements. First, a message in the bottom right of the frame reads "Bless Long John," an inside reference to New York's late-night radio host Long John Nebel, a mutual friend of both *MAD* and Susann (Bain 1974, 65–66, 222).[7] Second, the greed of everyone in the culture industry explodes throughout the parody. In a cameo at the end from "Mr. Jack Valencia" (a.k.a.

Jack Valenti), for instance, the newly hired MPAA chief initially seems to be chiding the movie's director and cast for filming "the most taste-less moment in the history of the motion picture," then continues, "but that's what SELLS movies nowadays . . . so keep up the great work!!" (Siegel and Drucker 1968, 8). Third, Siegel and Drucker ally themselves with Susann as "sick."

The news that *Valley of the Dolls* is "sick" pops up repeatedly, with respect to the film and novel, and just as inclusively as the parody's gro-tesque visual aesthetic, sickness implicates everyone involved. In an incestuous imbroglio involving "Juniper Nock" (Jennifer North), "Tony Dullard" (Tony Polar), and his sister "Mimi" (Miriam), Tony promises Juniper, "I'll explain it all to you later in a scene that's sicker than this one!" After "Leon Bunk" (Lyon Burke) proclaims his plans to "Write a SEX NOVEL!" he unpacks his reasoning: "Well, I'm semi-literate, I talk in clichés, and I'm sick" (Siegel and Drucker 1968, 6). Jackpot Suzanne finally calls the movie "sickening" in the closing line, a concluding gag that brilliantly magnifies both the camp attractions of the film and what Susann had in common with *MAD*. Parodying the notorious wig scene at the climax of *Valley of the Dolls*, the catfight between Neely O'Hara and Helen Lawson that culminates with Neely flushing Helen's wig down the toilet, "Ninny O'Horror" accidentally flushes Jackpot down the toi-let instead. A caricatured Patty Duke cries, "I—I flushed it! She's—She's GONE!" Thus incommoded (so to speak), Jackpot sends back a note, which director Mark Robson fishes from the toilet water and reads aloud: "if they think this movie was sickening, wait till they see the SEQUEL!" (Siegel and Drucker 1968, 9). Artist Mort Drucker pronounces the blatancy of such "sickening" and literal toilet humor as well as binds the sensibility of *MAD* to Susann: first, a frame of Robson kneeling over the toilet with an expression of utter confusion; next, a high-angle view of the toilet with Jackpot's note floating in the bowl like excrement; and last, Robson smiling, holding the note still dripping toilet water. Leon Bunk articulates the critiques hurled at Susann by many reviewers of the book *Valley of the Dolls*—as a "sex novel," "semi-literate," chock full of "clichés," and "sick"—but similar indictments could be tendered to the reputations of *MAD*, Siegel and Drucker, Twentieth-Century Fox, Mark Robson, Jack Valenti, and the MPAA. Although *MAD* reproduces the pattern of reducing Susann to venal kitsch peddler and collapses the author with her product, Siegel and Drucker sacrifice any signs of elitist detachment. The delight in "sick" humor is finally something that Siegel and Drucker appear to share with Susann, for whom *Valley of the Dolls* and its promised sequel prove to be a "sickening" joke, as well as with the readers of the novel and audiences of the film whom Siegel and Drucker address in the opening line. The egalitarianism and self-reflexivity of the *MAD* satire materialize a kind of camp identification that renders its faux gossip about Susann a simultaneous confession of the magazine's own sick sensibility.

The vocabulary of gossip and the pose of camp playfulness surface immediately in Lehmann-Haupt's *New York Times* review of *The Love Machine*, tellingly titled "Popcorn": "Doubtless you've heard through the well-fertilized grapevine the rumor that Jacqueline Susann's new novel, 'The Love Machine,' is based on the career of a ruthless power-hungry TV executive who gets canned when the public finds out about his hyperathletic sexual habits" (Lehmann-Haupt 1969, 45). Touching on *Love Machine*'s roman à clef formula, Lehmann-Haupt next scrambles hierarchical distinctions by situating Susann's novel next to high culture with seamy content and lowbrow literature with a highbrow setting: "you just know that Robin Stone is headed for trouble somewhere

From Jackpot Suzanne's opening introduction to the conclusion when she gets flushed down the toilet, the author gleefully confesses her venality in Mort Drucker and Larry Siegel's "Valley of the Dollars," a *MAD* parody that expresses ambivalent delight in Susann, the author's "sick" *Valley of the Dolls*, and the film adaptation. Note the "Bless Long John" button on the lower right of Jackpot Suzanne, referring to radio show host Long John Nebel, friend to Susann, and *MAD* illustrator Jack Davis.

in the next 500 pages, just as sure as you knew Oedipus was headed for his mother's bed and the phantom for the opera" (45). When the critic ponders how readers approach *Love Machine*—as "pop," "corn," or "popcorn"—Lehmann-Haupt finally abandons irony to pin down Susann and her novel. Although it looks like "pop," *Love Machine* lacks the conceptual questions about taste and culture posed by pop artists; the book remains a "sincere" amalgamation of "crashingly neutral clichés" drawn from "gossip columns," "trash literature," and "cocktail party psychoanalysis" (Lehmann-Haupt 1969, 45). Lehmann-Haupt credits Susann's "celebrity guessing game" for luring readers, but most of all her "complete ingenuousness," and he concludes that *Love Machine* is not "corn," which implies insincerity, but "popcorn": "It's salty (lots of four-letter words sprinkled into a morally square container). . . . It is the kernel of an idea, the seed of an inspiration, blown into bite-sized nothingness" (45). Lehmann-Haupt's shift from playful camp to bleak "nothingness" finally acts as an antidote to highbrow fears of the "Sontag Sensibility," which Paul Velde demystified in a 1966 *Commonweal* article as a "regressive" current in the arts and cultural criticism, in which sensuous form supersedes content and conditions the celebration of "junk" as an excuse for the "application of wit" (Velde 1966, 391, 392). If Lehmann-Haupt opened his review with camp badinage about *The Love Machine*, the closing revelation negated that delight and Susann's novel as insignificant, insubstantial, and worthless.

The C-Effect: Capote's Camp Gaze

Truman Capote contributed the most ostentatious, enduring as well as complicated camp gossip about Susann. Famous for delivering talk show banter, on July 23, 1969, Capote went after Susann on the *Tonight Show* amid her omnipresent promotion of *The Love Machine*. Applying a virtual checklist of camp criteria based on the evidence of both Susann's books and her ubiquitous promotional appearances, Capote knocked the novelist's "sleazy" fashion and hair, called her a "born transvestite" and "a truckdriver in drag" and recommended her as a prime candidate for casting as Myra Breckinridge, novelist Gore Vidal's eponymous transgender protagonist. Speaking to reporters the following day, Capote declared, "I don't consider I defamed her in any way," repeated what he said on the

Tonight Show, added "rotten, bad writer" to the list as well as, "She doesn't have a sense of humor, either" (Nizer 1980, 29–31; Anon. 1969c, B23; Pugh 2014). Capote's "truck driver in drag" line resounded throughout news and gossip columns, perhaps compounded by the threats of litigation from Susann, who enlisted famed libel attorney Louis Nizer (Haber 1970, C8). As Nizer understood it, Capote had wrongly outed Susann through "slanderous" "innuendo": "So, the innuendos to be ascribed . . . were many. One was that she was a lesbian of masculine inclinations, or that she was so unfeminine that she was more like a man who, because of perversity, dressed up as a woman, or that she was as ugly as an uncouth truck driver who aberrationally disguised himself in women's clothes—all clearly slanderous" (Nizer 1980, 29).[8] Nizer interpreted Capote's statements, not as gay camp humor, but as keys to possible truths about Jacqueline Susann that bespoke "lesbian," "unfeminine," "perversity," and "aberration," in addition to "ugly" and "uncouth." According to Nizer's perspective, Capote's camp kidding threatened to function as revelatory gossip about Jacqueline Susann, a hypothetical outing, and not a month after the Stonewall riots raged gay liberation into the headlines.

The disjunction between Capote's position—"I don't consider I defamed her in any way"—and Nizer's assessment of "clearly slanderous" is striking but not surprising and a clear indication of the strictness of social norms, the endurance of the closet, and the unspoken permission to punish coming out. Nizer's recollection of the feud suggests both his and Susann's inability to consider that, from Capote's position as camp, androgynous, and openly gay, calling a woman a drag queen or suggesting she was a lesbian did not constitute vilification even if it was scandalmongering. Biographer Tison Pugh enumerates the homophobic ribbing that Capote endured as a matter of course, about his voice and mannerisms, and in Nizer's recollection, Susann had apparently joined the ranks of Capote imitators prior to their quarrel. Nizer recounts Susann's impression of Capote during a TV interview in laughing prose that redoubles the homophobic sting at the same time as demonstrating that Susann was mocking Capote for being visibly, stereotypically gay, out whether he wanted to be or not:

> Whatever one might think of her writing, there was no doubt she was a great mimic. Capote lends himself to that art. He is very

short, pudgy, puffy, baldly blond and talks in a high-pitched, nasal, slow Southern drawl which outrageously exaggerates his homosexuality. He is like a cartoon of himself. . . . his rolling eyes, giggles, squeaky voice and feminine gestures provoke stifled laughter even from those most attentive to his views. Susann captured all this perfectly. Despite her large size and dark visage, she shrank to his gnome-like size, and her whining cadences, interrupted by stretched out "w-e-l-l-s," sent the audience into paroxysms of laughter. (Nizer 1980, 28–29)

Nizer's comments altogether attest to the closet mandate, which faults someone unable or unwilling to pass as straight, and its accompanying response, something akin to the film critic who ridiculed the failure of *The Love Machine* to pass as "a straight movie" (Resnik 1971, 178).[9] Nizer manifests this kind of homophobic camp response; Capote, who "outrageously exaggerates his homosexuality" and willingly fails to pass, provokes Nizer's laughter as a "queer" personification of "buffoonish masculinity," in Scott Balcerzak's terminology, or what Bergson refers to more broadly as "anything inert or stereotyped, or simply ready-made, on the surface of living society": a "machine" of queer traits incongruous to the heteronormative constructs of "human" and "natural" masculinity (Balcerzak 2013, 7, 10–12, 19; Bergson 1928, 44).

Nizer and Susann never openly consider what might have already occurred to readers of Susann's romans à clef, the slew of sly clues functional in promoting her books that cued both speculation and gossip about what the author might be confessing about herself. To date, *Valley of the Dolls* was Susann's only novel to represent lesbian love, the tender and sexually gratifying relationship between Jennifer and her school friend Maria, but *The Love Machine* brimmed with positive gay male characters, so much so that *New York Times* columnist Martin Kasindorf proclaimed in 1973, "her writing displays an unending tolerance toward homosexuality. . . . Sergio, who befriends Robin Stone in 'The Love Machine,' has done as much as Lance Loud to upgrade the gay image" (Kasindorf 1973, 86). Comparing the real-life Lance Loud from the cinema verité documentary series *An American Family* (PBS, 1970) to the fictional character Sergio, Kasindorf suggests the perception of Susann's realism, and based on the properties of the roman à clef, this could mean drawing from her lived experience knowing queer people and possibly being queer. The trans cabaret performer Brazillia in *The Love Machine* pushes the possibilities further in a compassionate sequence that qualifies Robin's condescension, after they have sex, with doubts about his own masculinity. Susann would continue to court speculation with her next novel *Once Is Not Enough*, in which the lesbian sex scenes between Dee and Karla proved the exception, one reviewer remarked, to "indescribably ugly" encounters among straight people, "an interesting contrast with Miss Susann's men, who are all absolutely bestial" (O'Reilly 1973, 6). In all of Susann's empathetic examples of queer sexuality, however, the responsibility of sustaining the closet endured for the characters, whose plotlines often revolved around the charades of passing and obfuscation.

Capote's gossip about Susann might have been motivated, therefore, by what he saw as her hypocrisy: Susann's compassionate accounts about a variety of queer people as well as dropping clues that she might be queer, meanwhile, affirming her marriage during book promotion, ambiguously moralizing about queer sexuality in her novels as well as mimicking Capote's queer performance to elicit "paroxysms of laughter." Susann personified what Michael Trask terms the "procedural liberalism" of Cold War–era culture, a kind of "camp slyness" in "a culture of command performances," which provided authors an instrument "for deflection in their public self-fashioning" (Trask 2013, 13–14). Trask cites the closeted queerness of authors Patricia Highsmith and Susan Sontag as well as the extreme divide between Mary McCarthy's public moralizing and private promiscuity, then concludes, "All these figures stood to benefit from camp's policy of cognitive dissonance" and represented "the alibi-ridden, impression-managed social space of a pre-Stonewall world that absorbs not only gay men but all comers in the logic of a closet culture" (14).[10] Capote disobeyed "the logic of the closet culture" with his own performance, and now he parodically "outed" Susann, not necessarily to expose her as a lesbian, a gay man in drag, or a trans woman but, paraphrasing Quinlan Miller, to unearth "the genderqueer within pop culture products assumed exclusively to be cis" (Miller 2019, 3).[11]

The real problem here consisted in what Capote left out: queer affiliation with Susann, in addition to any awareness of his own hegemonic advantage. Capote flaunted his disenfranchised queer status through camp discourse to devalue the capital considered so vital to Susann's image, her heterosexual femininity, but he also accomplished this by wielding his own cultural capital in addition to enlisting a misogynistic discourse of female authorship. Nowhere is this more obvious than in Capote's appearance on *Rowan & Martin's Laugh-In* on February 15, 1971, when the show altered its format in fawning deference to the author, and Capote repeated the "truckdriver" jab. Capote's visit was couched within the show's topical jokes and gags referencing vulgar queer antics, as Lynn Spigel avers, "burlesque depictions of queers as thrilling subjects of scandal" (Spigel 2008, 268). Several bits involved queeny cowboys using cast member Alan Sues, the resident "sissy" of the show, for the punchline; in another bit, a cop relates his experience raiding "a Gay Liberation riot" and arresting protestors for "assault with a deadly purse"; and during the news segment, a caption reads, "Liberace standing by in Alpine County," a reference to a widely reported gay liberation movement action in California that also functions to out the flamboyant pianist by association (Feil 2014, 99).

Laugh-In counterbalanced its gay baiting by tendering sycophantic attention to Capote and investing him with an authorial agency and stature that extended to creative control over the episode, privileges denied most of their celebrity guests, including Susann during her visit the prior season (Erickson 2000, 229–30). As the show had done for William F. Buckley Jr., the usually anarchic and rapid-fire program slowed its pace and altered its format, interrupting the usual barrage of brief sketches, musical numbers, and blackout bits with a talk show setting: "Ladies and gentleman," begins cohost Dan Rowan, "we are privileged to have one of the world's great men of letters with us tonight." Dick Martin continues, enumerating Capote's achievements: "Our guest has written award-winning short stories, novels, articles, screenplays, and plays for the Broadway stage . . . Mr. Truman Capote." Capotes smiles and, once the applause dies down, quips, "Imagine, to have done all that and ended up on *Laugh-In!*" Placing Capote in the ranks of Norman Mailer and Gore Vidal as well as addressing him as "one of the country's most brilliant authors" and "truly delightful raconteurs," the hosts present him with questions on a variety of public figures and ephemera that the writer greets with witty replies. The program's hosts also mock themselves as a means of democratizing the comedic dynamic; after Capote's initial joke about the career disappointment of appearing on *Laugh-In*, cohost Martin affirms, "That is a come down." Inasmuch as queer gags popped in on that episode, albeit none of them targeted at Capote as they had occasionally been (in his absence) on prior installments, the show's willingness to mock itself and venerate Capote sustained his authority and comedic agency.

Capote's repeat of the "truckdriver" line occurs early in the episode, prior to his sit-down with the hosts, promptly establishing his comedic prowess through gossip that had already sealed Capote's popular reputation as camp wit. Alternately directing his attention to cast member Ann Elder (standing alongside him) and the camera, Capote begins, "You know, I'd like to take this opportunity to apologize to calling Jacqueline Susann the way I did on television a truckdriver in drag," but when Ann says "that should make Miss Susann very happy," Capote corrects her misunderstanding: "I was apologizing to all the truckdrivers." Although Capote got another laugh at Susann's expense, he appeared now to distinguish Susann from truckdrivers, but as the bit continues, returns to the original gossipy proposition that Susann *was* a truckdriver in drag. After the backhanded apology, Ann scolds, "Well come on Truman. Now it was kind of a mean thing to say." Capote agrees, "Yes and I *am* sorry." "Because you hurt her feelings?" Ann asks, to which Capote replies, "No, because now she won't tell me all the good places to eat on Route 66."[12] Casting Susann as a connoisseur of highway cuisine, thus a truckdriver in drag, Capote reinstated ridicule of Susann on the same network as *The Tonight Show*, now for a prime-time audience on NBC's fifth most popular program, and buoyed by both a snickering cast member and a laugh track. Capote queered Susann's gender performance in the language of camp and in the mainstream setting of prime-time commercial television, but he performed this as voyeuristic gossip, devoid of queer identification. Rather than exposing "the logic of the closet culture" or the artifice of gender, Capote targeted Susann's agency of performance—gendered and authorial—as a woman of letters.

Well before *Laugh-In*, Capote established the comic frame for laughing at Susann as naive camp that numerous commentators implemented: the foundations for it, the merging of female failure with aesthetic failure; and the demonstration of it, Susann's inability to pull off her "drag"

Truman Capote repeated his quip about Susann to Ann Elder on
Rowan & Martin's Laugh-In, where the titular hosts exalted Capote as
"one of the world's great men of letters with us tonight."

as a woman and its correlation with her "rotten" writing. Sarah Davidson's article for *Harper's* magazine, appearing a few months after Capote's
Tonight Show appearance, enlisted this tactic of "outing" Susann's female
failure. Illustrated by Diane Arbus's photo of Susann and Irving Mansfield wearing bathing suits in their suite at the Beverly Hills Hotel, the
picture "frames the subject within her own freakishness," as Richard

Meyer characterizes another Arbus photo (1993, 371). Arbus's documentary evidence complements Davidson's opening remarks, about Susann's "mask of makeup," "black shoulder-length fall made of Korean hair," "body . . . covered with Pucci designs of yellow, purple, and pink," and her "baritone voice," comments that recall the "drag queen" comparison quipped by Capote, in addition to his remarks about her "sleazy" fashion (Davidson 1969, 65).[13] Davidson concludes the piece with what seems to be an homage to *MAD*'s scatological association between Susann and toilets, although here lacks any of *MAD*'s alliances with toilet humor. Referring to the *New York Times* Bestseller List "taped on the wall of their creamy bathroom in the Beverly Hills Hotel," Davidson then quotes Susann's rationale: "'It's great to watch when you're on the head. . . . It makes you relax. It's good for the soul.' Irving looks up from his copy of *Variety*. 'That's funny, isn't it?'" (Davidson 1969, 71). Davidson's concluding toilet tableau, like Arbus's photograph, "frames the subject within her own freakishness," and in accordance with the setting, her shit: mass cultural commercial novels and a grotesque femininity that blurs bodily waste with material opulence, creativity and "the soul." Finishing with Irving's question, "That's funny, isn't it?" and leaving it unanswered only reinstates the joke of Susann's agency. Davidson leaves the reader with an image of the author both denuded and undignified as well as content and unselfconscious, ridiculous according to hegemonic definitions of cultural decorum and feminine propriety.

Kelly's *Boston Globe* feature from August 1969 (just a couple weeks after Capote) opens with a view of Susann's apartment to coalesce the signs of her naive camp style, taste, and gender performance: "two of the living room lamps are nude female torsos"; on the cocktail table sits "Miss Susann's sulphorous [*sic*] new novel in the schlock tradition of 'Valley of the Dolls'"; and then Susann points to a "German promotion piece on female impersonators," giving credit to "one of the 'girls,' Daloa, as the model for a character in 'The Love Machine.' Studying the drag queen's make-up, she sat in a chair facing a wall with several sketches and paintings of female nudes" (Kelly 1969, A16). In the terms of the roman à clef, Capote, Davidson, Kelly, and Arbus disclosed a "key" to decoding Susann and her stories. In the terms of naive camp, this key threw open the closet door, or raised the shades, to reveal the "funny," unintended failure of both "tasteful" femininity and artistry.

Novelist Joseph Wambaugh provided a telling epilogue on a 1974 episode of NBC's *The Dean Martin Show* devoted to roasting Capote, finally and derisively uniting Susann and Capote in their mutual genderqueerness. Wambaugh turned Capote's jab at Susann back on Capote, now spotlighting both Capote's and Susann's gender nonconformity as a means of mocking Capote's authorial worth: "I respect Truman Capote. In my opinion, he's the greatest male literary figure since Jacqueline Susann" (quoted in Pugh 2014). Echoing the camp intonations of a manners comedy, Wambaugh divulges the gossipy open secret governing Capote's and Susann's camp performances, taking their perversity for granted yet also treating it as laughable.[14] Heteronormative closet logic positioned Susann and Capote alike for ridicule, a corrective laughter at both queers and women seeking access to "male-dominated culture."

The journalistic work of Jacqueline Susann's champions Carol Bjorkman and Rex Reed also bubbled with gossipy camp badinage, an expressed delight in Susann's style that established the author's camp agency and a sense of camp community among women and gay men.[15] Bjorkman and Reed's "Jacqueline Susann" courted an image wavering between sophistication and crudity, now the heroine of her own comedy of bad manners, and someone whose unlikely success story and controversial novels revalued feminine vulgarity as stylish. Bjorkman's 1966 interview with Susann in *Women's Wear Daily* celebrates Susann's camp agency as masquerader, adorned with photographs of Bjorkman and Susann sitting together in their haute couture outfits, hiding behind hardcover copies of *Valley of the Dolls*. As I explored in the introduction, Bjorkman renders Susann in the ensuing piece a playful exemplar of the success of female failure: a self-ironist who admits being ignored by "literary circles" and adored by "junkies," yet, in Bjorkman's eyes, someone with "vitality and female awareness," "modern" style, and "good looking legs."[16] An even spicier spirit of irony pervades Reed's 1973 piece on Susann and *Once Is Not Enough*.

Reed offered something of a counterbalance to Capote's gay camp objectification of Susann and evoked the novelist's admiring description of Sergio in *The Love Machine*, "exceptionally handsome, better-looking than any movie star. Definitely light on his feet but he didn't swish. . . . His manner was right—eager and enthusiastic, yet not subservient" (Susann 1997a, 270). The culture critic never officially came out but

Rex Reed defended Susann during the fallout from Capote, and in his piece on *Once Is Not Enough* (republished in *People Are Crazy Here*), Susann takes shape "like somebody in a Noel Coward play" whose flamboyant style and perverse sexual undertones mark her agency. (Jacket design by Loring Eutemy, photo by Victor Skrebneski.)

nevertheless touted his gay credentials in columns about queer theater and figures, from the gender-nonconforming drag group the Cockettes to Tennessee Williams, in addition to Bette Midler amid her success as a gay steam bath chanteuse (Reed 1974, 12–40, 41–46, 111–16). During the fallout from Capote, he also defended Susann, "not the new Flaubert, but she's a marvelous and good person," and referred to Capote as a "bitchy, jealous" author who should "shut up and write" (Quinn 1970, 19). Befitting the camping critic, Susann's agency takes shape in Reed's account by flaunting her style and the perverse sexual undertones underpinning her personality and work, but quite different from Capote's construction, Susann also materializes as someone who can "pass."

Reed traces Susann's victory in a cultural comedy of bad manners in which style and humor distinguish themselves by embracing the vulgar and forbidden as well as flamboyantly concealing them. Susann materializes in Reed's vision as the incongruous embodiment of "pretty and funny," applying Linda Mizejewski's formula, in this case to preserve the idea of "feminine" performance while incessantly deriving humor from its failure. "Her friends call her Jackie. Her enemies call her lots of other things," quips Reed, wasting no time citing one of Susann's loudest detractors. "When Truman Capote called her a 'truck driver in drag' on the *Tonight Show* she slapped him with a lawsuit. Now she's mellowed. Looking about as much like a truck driver as Raquel Welch, now she just laughs at her assailants. Especially Truman Capote" (Reed 1974, 243). Susann's power surfaces here as someone who weathers ridicule and "laughs at her assailants," in addition to resisting conventional femininity at the same time as embodying it.

No longer the oblivious target of camp gossip, Susann the deliberate performer emerges, someone whose style revolves around both entertaining failure and finding failure entertaining. In a reversal of Kelly's account and with echoes of Bjorkman's, Reed details entering Susann's "lemony-chiffon penthouse twenty-five floors above Central Park and the first thing I see is a giant pop-art book cover that says *Once Is Not Enough* in bright neon lights," after which "she flows in like somebody in a Noel Coward play, and we're off" (Reed 1974, 245). References to Noël Coward and pop art, to begin with, emphasize Susann's camp taste and style, following Sontag's categorization of both of them as deliberate camp (Sontag 1966, 282, 292). Lauding her latest novel *Once Is Not Enough*, Reed extends Susann's camp to the closet comedy of her roman à clef: "It has warmth, humor, wit, sharply defined characters, complex relationships, startling plot twists, a hypnotic story and enough thinly disguised public figures to keep cocktail parties guessing and every movie star in Hollywood fighting duels to get into the movie version for months to come" (Reed 1974, 244). Reed's initial nod to the book's "warmth, humor, wit" soon aligns with Susann's interplay of gossip, roman à clef, and guessing game when he references the "thinly disguised public figures" that "keep cocktail parties guessing." Reed's gossip about Susann is also funny, as he launches the penultimate paragraph of his feature with an additional, shocking bit of detail for the "thinly disguised" celebrities in the novel. Yielding a sense of Susann's self-aware game at the closet door, her shuttling between gossip and confession as well as truth and fiction, Reed begins, "Jackie's father, Robert Susann, was a famous portrait painter who lamented the fact that he had no sons to carry the family name. Her new novel about incest has a dedication: 'To Robert Susann, who would understand.' Raised eyebrows?" (Reed 1974, 248). Susann's playful perversity emboldens the camp agency established earlier in the piece through descriptions of the novelist and her apartment, but now it stretches to subverting feminine decorum.

Reed concludes with a gossipy sexual scene described by Susann that typifies the maintenance of her closet and celebrates its camp allure, the ironic amalgam of pretty/funny, tasteful/vulgar, and success/failure. Susann confesses to Reed, "'My secret wish is to spend one night with George C. Scott and . . . Mick Jagger. It doesn't have to be sex, but if we end up in bed Irving gives me his permission.' Like she says, once is not enough. And Jacqueline Susann is just the girl to prove it" (Reed 1974, 248). By way of repeating the title of her latest bestseller and recalling one of Neely O'Hara's campiest lines from the "lousy" film version of *Valley of the Dolls*—"Ted Casablanca is *not* a fag. And I'm the dame who can *prove* it."—Reed emboldens Susann's triumphant camp comedy through the happy failure of conventional manners, and related to that, the merry malfunctioning of confining constructions of gender, sexuality, and taste (Kingsley 1967, 62; Reed 1974, 247). Fallen woman and devoted wife, Susann announces her insatiable desire with the flimsiest facade of patriarchal license, that "Irving gives me his permission." When Reed affirms her as "just the girl to prove" that "once is not enough," he equates Susann's capacity for yielding both multiple bestsellers and sexual partners, which would normally signal failure in patriarchal terms, or as Susann had put it to *Life* in 1966, "Women who do that, of course, are weirdoes" (Howard 1966, 77). Reed attests to Susann's camp comedy of bad manners, and in the failure of traditional femininity, Susann's bright victory.

Susann Camps: The *Laugh-In* Machine

Appearing on *Rowan & Martin's Laugh-In*, in its third season and the highest-rated program on US network television, Susann performed in gags that played on the abundant sexual content of her latest bestseller, *The Love Machine*, and showcased the sense of humor that Capote had claimed she lacked (NBC, December 8, 1969).[17] Susann was a particularly good fit for the show, considering that the notoriety of *Laugh-In* partly stemmed from mediating the scandals of "the new sexual culture," as Elana Levine terms it, through a souped-up suggestiveness that pushed against self-censorship rules, and by featuring the antics of powerful, sexual women as well as flamboyant gay men (Levine 2007, 11, 170–73). *Laugh-In* was also a bastion of "Camp TV" in the late 1960s, characterized in its reception through period terminology such as "camp," "pop," "hip," "put-on," and the perception of the show's "borderline taste" (Feil 2014, 37–62; Phillips and Pinedo 2018, 20–22). Featuring a smorgasbord of topical social types ranging from counterculture to Establishment, *Laugh-In*'s psychedelic, rapid-fire associative editing further added to the program's camp irony by conferring suggestive meanings among the barrage of brief bits, if audiences watched closely enough (Marc 1998, 157; Bodroghkozy 2001, 66–75; Feil 2014, 4–7). Susann's inaugural bit, for instance, follows Henry Gibson as his recurring character of a Rod McKuen–type poet, who tonight wears an ankh around his neck, a piece of jewelry that features prominently in *The Love Machine* and adorns the book jacket, in addition to Susann's outfits for every appearance promoting the novel, including *Laugh-In*. The editing on *Laugh-In* also joined Susann in "conversation" with guest Phyllis Diller and cast member Jo Ann Worley, comedians who built their personas as sexually aggressive, unruly women. The primary celebrity guest that night, Diller's humor played on the era's popular camp sensibility: the "good taste of bad taste," "failed seriousness," and the "put-on" of celebrity.[18] In addition to Susann's onstage exchanges with ensemble members Ruth Buzzi and Alan Sues, these interactions punctuated the sexual themes of Susann's novels and the sexual agency of the author, her women characters, and both women and gay readers.

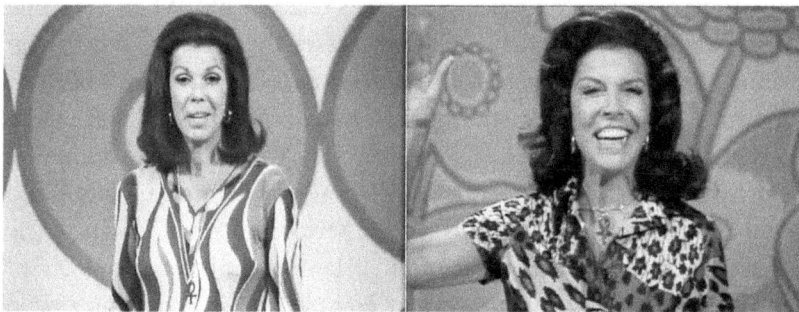

After first appearing on *Laugh-In* during season 3, Susann returned in season 5 with more self-parodic one-liners: "I'm Jackie Susann. I'm here on *Laugh-In*. That's 'Laugh': L-A-U-G-H. See! I *can* spell out five-letter words!"

Susann first appears alongside cast member Alan Sues, whose persona remained consistently tied to characters with gay connotations, such as Big Al the sportscaster, who in a sketch from the prior season announced, "Hockey, hockey, hockey. Today, the LA Kings were purchased by Steve McQueen. They will be known as McQueen's Kings. The poor gay blades can't make up their mind whether to wear helmets, crowns or tiaras. All I say is, God save McQueen. Is that dirty? Ta-ta!" (December 30, 1968; Feil 2014, 72, 107–9). Sues's routine with Susann initially plays off the roman à clef, as he queries, "Miss Susann, is it true that all the characters in your novels are based on real people?" "Yes, Alan, that's true." "I guess there's no doubt about it then," continues Sues snickering, "I'm the Love Machine." Susann looks him over, then simmers seductively, "Well, it looks to me like you need a . . . *body job*." She moves closer to buff his stomach suggestively, Sues utters "Gotcha!," and the scene cuts to Phyllis Diller. If Susann sounds a little like Mae West in her delivery of "*body job*," a pun on car maintenance and any number of euphemisms for sex acts, the exchange sexualizes her and her book with the adoring participation of a camp, closeted gay man. Imagining himself "the Love Machine," Sues indeed enlists Susann to play his "beard" as Sergio and Alfie do with Ethel in the book, and his final "Gotcha!" at the end might signal a revelation exposing the put-on of straightness they are both perpetrating; the rapid transition to Diller, however, leaves this to the imagination.

Susann's co-presence with Sues emphasizes their queer camp bond, but Susann and Diller's camp coupling must rely on the connotative operations of associative editing to forge a relationship. When the scene cuts from Susann and Sues, Diller addresses the camera: "*Boy*, if you wanna read some *dirty books*, just come over to my house! It's been so long since I've dusted the shelves even *Heidi* is *filthy*!"[19] Diller seems to be responding to Susann and Sues, implying that *The Love Machine* is a "dirty book"—although even wholesome *Heidi* could qualify—and complementing Susann's sultry camp performance with a spectacle of failed seriousness. Diller was, after all, famous for being a "put-on" of female stardom (Brackman 1967, 70). Her outlandish appearance (wild gray hair, psychedelic fashion), rhythmic cackle, and self-deprecating humor greeted the nation in the late 1960s through her commercial for Snowy Bleach: "This stuff is so good it can even get the yellow out of my birth certificate! A-ha-ha-ha-ha-haaaaaaa!" (quoted in Cohen, McWilliams, and Smith 1995, 152). Susann's next appearance on the show just a few minutes later draws an even more direct connection between her, Diller, and the comedy they derive from failed femininity. Susann faces the camera, wearing the same Pucci blouse and ankh necklace as before, and declares: "The University of Burbank is getting a lot out of my book *The Love Machine*. The English Department is trying to read it and the Engineering Department is trying to build it." Cut to Diller: "I was going to play the lead in a *nudie movie* till I found out it was called, 'I Am Curious *Wrinkled*.'"

The bits by Susann and Diller hinge on the categories of cultural value and erotic appeal, attributes emphasized by the temporal proximity of the sketches and their sexual content. Susann's account of curricular developments at the University of Burbank verifies both the broad reach and low brow of her sexy book's appeal, in addition to Susann's confident and self-deprecating wit. Her inclusion in the culture of Burbank was also important. References to "Burbank," the city where *Laugh-In* was produced, abounded on the show and always signified a vulgar culture populated by idiotic people. Susann's affiliation with *Laugh-In*, forged through a mutual reputation for vulgarity and soaring popularity, particularly in Burbank, invests her self-parody with camp authority. Diller's jests are also self-directed, and as in her famous TV commercial, address her age, which is now ambiguously connected to her desirability. The idea of Diller replacing the young protagonist of the sexy, Swedish art film blockbuster *I Am Curious (Yellow)* spurs a variety of images, presented here with a sense of camp incongruity regarding sexuality and the binaries of high and low, youth and old age, female and male, and desirable and undesirable.[20] If Susann is to be desired as sexy and successful while Diller is not—her casting choices are apparently limited as far as "nudie movies" are concerned—they share a connection to low culture as well as represent different emphases along Mizejewski's pretty/funny axis. Susann is "pretty" (if not young) and has cultural authority, but only in "Burbank," among the lowbrows, since her books are vulgar. Diller reminds us of the fact that she is neither young nor pretty, and she blurs the distinction between desirable and undesirable through her proposed appearance in *I Am Curious (Wrinkled)*. Although both bits with Susann erase the naive failure of femininity that Capote attributed, Diller takes this on with a cheerful eagerness that turns to boiling disappointment. By playing *off* rather than *with* each other, though, they elude a visible, reciprocal camp relationship that emerges when Susann and Sues perform for each other. Joined through editing but spatially separated and oblivious to each other, Susann and Diller's subversive community manifests through suggestion, but neither gets to deliver a "Gotcha!" that signifies their alliance in self-parodic performance.

Susann's third bit on *Laugh-In* with Ruth Buzzi fulfills the relationship between camp agency, identification, erotic appeal, and erotic desire, an anarchic formula the power of which the brief blackout sketch ascribes to Susann's novel. In this and the following sketches, moreover, exaggerated female masquerade and burlesque help to ironize and destabilize gender roles. Standing alone, Susann is approached by cast member Ruth Buzzi, famed for playing the repressed sourpuss Gladys Ormphby routinely trouncing her masher Tyrone F. Horneigh (Arte Johnson) with a lethal purse; Buzzi also occasionally played a gossip columnist modeled on Joyce Haber, one of Susann's frequent journalistic allies. Buzzi enters as herself and greets Susann, then calmly asks, "I understand that your book *The Love Machine* is about a man who makes love all the time, right?" Susann confirms this, then Buzzi inquires, "Where can I get one?" "Oh, a copy of the book?" queries Susann. Buzzi chuckles, then takes hold of Susann's hands: "No, you silly goose. A man who makes love all the time, get it? Sorry, Bill." Buzzi releases Susann, twirls, and dances away from a grinning Jackie. A brief bit follows in which Sues and movie star guest Romy Schneider muse on Otto Preminger's "pixie qualities," which cuts to another celebrity guest standing alone on stage, Roger Moore, the sexy young star of *The Saint* (NBC, 1967–69). The sounds of Jo Anne Worley chanting his name fill the air before she enters—"Oh, Roger . . . Roger . . . Roger . . ."—playing on the British euphemism for penis and coitus. The show's resident single woman, renowned for her sexual ardor and unashamed relations with a man named Boris, storms onstage. Enfolding Moore in her arms, Worley interrupts her fervent "Roger"-ing to turn to the audience and affirm, "I love that name!" with a grand giggle to follow. The sexualized pun of "Roger" finally grows concrete when Worley adds, "You know what, you're one of the nicest saints I've ever met! You know what, you could sit on my dashboard any old time!" Although her energy and flamboyance resemble a screwball heroine such as Rosalind Russell's Hildy in *His Girl Friday* (Hawks, 1940), Worley's height, shape, voluptuousness, and unrestrained sexuality liken her to Mae West, and her sexually suggestive lines recall any number of West's seductive wisecracks. Worley provides the exclamation point to Susann and Buzzi's encounter, even if at one remove in the sequence of bits, and now Worley embodies her own "love machine," Roger Moore perched (wishfully) on her "dashboard."

Laugh-In navigated Susann's meanings as a camp sexual icon quite differently when she was not a guest, such as in the "Sexy Sixties" musical number just a few weeks later (December 29, 1969) and Capote's appearance the following season. The lyrics to the "Sexy Sixties" treat Susann as a naive camp figure unaware of her own vulgarity, associating her not with other authors but with the fictional characters of two bestsellers notorious for their sexual perversity: Alexander Portnoy and Myra Breckinridge. Capote reinforced the camp perception of Susann as a ridiculous aberration of gender roles worthy of derisive gossip, and in an environment that conferred authority on his gossipy remarks, that venerated him as "one of the world's great men of letters." Although *Laugh-In* failed to host Susann with anywhere near the same fawning, Susann's appearance nevertheless pronounced her triumph as a bestselling novelist and what it signaled: the victory of scandalous, vulgar female sexuality over bourgeois taste and feminine propriety.

Once Is Not Enough: Susann Camps Again

Jacqueline Susann knew camp. Amid promotion and publicity for *Every Night, Josephine!*, as Letty Cottin Pogrebin recalled to Barbara Seaman, "Jackie would camp it up in a way that was sort of a secret code," particularly with gay bookstore clerks (Seaman 1996c, 278). By 1966, when Neely says, "It's a real camp," the word had already reached mainstream audiences via journalists and television. *The Love Machine* indeed exemplifies the absorption of camp into television production practices, in addition to the understanding of camp as a form of taste, one that can redeem commercial detritus and that operates among knowing audiences. Prior to mentioning camp, Susann makes sure to distinguish TV executive Robin Stone's "taste" from the "commercialism" of his boss, network CEO Gregory Austin, who believes that TV audiences just desire

"*Shit*" (Susann 1997a, 390). In a scene toward the end of the novel Robin wonders how to salvage a program starring Christie Lane, one of the network's star attractions: "It was so bad it was almost high camp; but unfortunately the girl playing opposite Christie was good enough to make it semiserious" (Susann 1997a, 438–39). Robin simply assumes that camp functions as an audience sensibility and shows a nuanced understanding that "semiserious" sharply differs from what Sontag calls "failed seriousness." Susann also implies but never explicates camp's contextual queerness, considering that the conversations about camp occur in close proximity to dialogue voicing suspicions about Robin's sexual orientation. Only a few pages follow Robin's thoughts about high camp when Christie refers to Robin as "Queersville" (Susann 1997a, 445). The second time "camp" is mentioned, the pattern intensifies. Network lawyer Cliff Dorne remarks to CEO Gregory Austin about Robin's "insane" programming choices, "two shows that *had* to flop and instead they came off as 'high camp' successes," then commences to comment on Robin a few lines later, "There are even rumors that he's queer" (Susann 1997a, 484).

Susann also exaggerated some of her characters into camp send-ups addressed to knowing readers of celebrity gossip. Judy Garland returns in *The Love Machine*, for instance, in the minor character Diana Williams, a "washed-up actress" making a "comeback." Susann renders Garland/ Diana both sympathetic and ridiculous, a camp survivor who arrives late in the novel at a lavish party, a "frail girl" who, "No matter how quietly she entered, Diana Williams *entered* a room. She stood there hesitant and alone, almost childlike" (1997a, 376). Diana ends up leaving the party with Robin for a sexual tryst that drives Maggie Stewart to sneak into Robin's apartment and light the bed on fire while the lovers cavort in the living room. Maggie takes pleasure in watching Diana and Robin among the tenants who evacuate due to the fire, "wrapped in his overcoat but she was she was barefoot, hopping up and down on one foot on the cold pavement" (1997a, 381). Published shortly before Garland's death, *The Love Machine* presents a brief and playful affirmation of the actress's determination to prevail, a sentiment that Susann had expressed two years earlier: "I think Judy will *always* come back."[21]

A brand of camp revenge in *Once Is Not Enough* is recognizable to anyone familiar with Susann's star persona and press coverage when a "plump little man who had written a best seller five years ago" turns up at a chic New York soirée and "smacked his lips in ecstasy and rolled his eye heavenward," spoke with a voice that "squeaked," and was "making a career out of going on talk shows and attending celebrity parties" (Susann 1997b, 242). Mocking Capote comprises outing him, parodying his infraction of closet politics through the camp characteristics that align with gay male stereotypes: flamboyant speech, high-pitched voice, feminine facial expressions, and referring to himself in feminine terms. The nameless "little capon," as competing writer and man's man Tom Colt mockingly refers to him, offers sycophantic praise and advice to Colt: "'My God, but I adore your work. But be careful about getting caught up in the rat race of television.' He giggled. 'Look what a whore it's made out of me'" (Susann 1997b, 242–43). Susann continues to travesty Capote in the posthumously published *Dolores*, now the dissolute artist Horatio Capon, friend to the title character's sister Nita (a Lee Radziwill stand-in) and "a professional gossip" whose loose lips lead to the public exposure in "the columns" of an affair between Dolores (Jacqueline Kennedy Onassis) and a married man (Susann 1976, 105–7). A number of gay men travel through *Once Is Not Enough* and *Dolores* without reproach, but they abide by the closet, discretion that improves their narrative reputations. This applies to a character Susann carried over from *The Love Machine*, Jerry Moss, a married ad executive in analysis over his obsession with Robin Stone. Promoted to president of the ad agency in *Once Is Not Enough*, Jerry also develops into "a closet queen" who, in love with a male model, recruits magazine editor Linda Riggs to be their "beard" (Susann 1997b, 181–82).

Susann establishes what appears to be a homophobic and heteronormative frame in *Once Is Not Enough* for her Capote parody, but also introduces ambiguity by depicting him through the hypermasculine point of view of rival author Tom Colt. The boozing and brawling Tom, a parody of Norman Mailer, one of the "brilliant authors" *Laugh-In* had ranked Capote alongside, is not the masculine ideal he presents so ostentatiously and publicly. When Tom gets involved with the book's protagonist January Wayne, the young woman learns the basis for his overblown masculine performance: "something inert lay between his legs. It was about the size of a man's thumb. She couldn't believe it. How could a man Tom Colt's size—a man as virile as Tom—have such a tiny penis? . . . Oh God, so this was the reason for all the prizefights . . . the scuba

diving ... the championship golf and tennis ... the barroom brawls. ...
Poor, poor Tom ... to have to write his sex fantasies because he couldn't
live them" (Susann 1997b, 306–7). The passage reads as if Susann was
dramatizing what *Time* magazine had said about Mailer in 1965: "Thus in
the tirelessly explicit writing of Norman Mailer, sex is a personal boast,
a mystique and an ideology—and, in all three capacities, solemn and
unconvincing" (Anon. 1965). Puncturing his "mystique" and exposing his
"ideology" as "unconvincing," Susann's scrutiny of Tom Colt's performance of masculinity and the physical reasons motivating it might have
also stemmed from Mailer's 1971 essay "Prisoner of Sex," an extended
attack on women's liberation and Kate Millett's *Sexual Politics*, first published in *Harper's* (Stumbo 1972, 8). Among Mailer's many condescending
jabs, one dig at Millett's writing style might have annoyed Susann in particular: "He read only a few lines, but it was enough to think she wrote
like a gossip columnist" (Mailer 1971, 45). Susann hinted at this possibility in a 1973 interview with the *Washington Post*, when she diminished
Mailer's "essayism" and granted ambivalent support for "women's lib,"
although never connecting the two (Illig 1973, BW2). Tom Colt serves
multiple social and ideological positions in Susann's parodies, as an
anchor for mocking Capote's queer affectations and a means of traves-
tying male chauvinism on behalf of liberated women.

Susann's creation of Linda Riggs, moreover, shores up the author's
mixed feelings about the women's movement, gay liberation, and the sexual revolution. Biographer Barbara Seaman lists Linda among Susann's
"tough ladies," "women who were unsentimental and frankly seeking
financial independence," clearly drawing parallels to Susann's personality
and experience (Seaman 1996c, 459). Susann's former press agent Abby
Hirsch describes the character differently, in terms of parody, "an aggressively successful editor of a women's magazine" whom Susann based on
Gloria Steinem as payback for excoriating *Valley of the Dolls* (Hirsch 1976,
6). Linda, the twenty-eight-year-old editor in chief of a women's lifestyle
magazine called *Gloss*, also forthrightly draws comparison to another
potential character model: "I'm not Helen Gurley Brown," Linda tells her
former schoolmate January, "But then *Gloss* is no *Cosmopolitan*. Give me
time" (Susann 1997b, 69). As Linda defines the difference between herself
and Helen Gurley Brown, she also hints at what differentiates the "single
girl" from the liberated sexual revolutionary: "And it all started from

Magazine editor Linda Riggs in *Once Is Not Enough* is a witty survivor and self-deprecating sexual revolutionary, a composite of Gloria Steinem (pictured here) and Helen Gurley Brown, both a parody and a tribute.

writing about how a single girl landed a divine husband. And the wild part is, no one gets married anymore . . . except older people" (Susann 1997b, 96). Susann fashions Linda as a sexual revolutionary and occasional bisexual, someone who publicly rejects the mandate of marriage on principal and embraces both her career and sexual freedom. Linda wavers privately, however, about the desire to get married and unabashedly expresses her insecurity over the male gaze, having lost weight and sought cosmetic surgery prior to inaugurating her career. Susann voiced some of the same mixed feelings to the *Washington Post* when promoting *Once Is Not Enough*: "As far as women's liberation goes, I am for it in certain ways. I've been women's lib from way back when I said to Irving before we got married, 'I'm not going to cook. I'm not going to run a house. . . . I love you more than anything in the world but my career is more important than marriage.' He never asked me to change it. I just did because he became more important than anything in the world" (Illig 1973, BW2). And similar to Susann, Linda's candor and sense of self-irony shine from the start, such as when Linda follows up the story about her physical transformation with, "I was kinky-looking—before it was 'in' to look kinky. Now that I've gone all through this, the uglies have come in. I swear, sometimes I wish I had my old nose back" (Susann 1997b, 95). The camp dimensions of Linda materialize further as she applies the terminology of Susann's friend Rex Reed, who had informed one journalist in 1970, "Ugly is in. . . . This is the age of freak, look at Tiny Tim and Barbra Streisand" (Quinn 1970, 18).

Linda's allusion to camp taste in the form of "kinky-looking" and "the uglies" is especially noteworthy because she applies it to herself. By rendering Linda a camp figure, someone who valorizes female independence yet satirizes feminism, Susann reconciles the apparent poles of gossipy parody and confessional self-parody. Linda Riggs invites the ambivalence of feminist camp: at once an "unsentimental" yet flawed feminist wit as well as a signal to some readers that Susann and her books "are cold to women's liberation," as Martin Kasindorf reasoned in the *New York Times* (1973, 88). Parallels can be drawn here to Wojcik's analysis of Mae West's feminist camp: "Functioning as an autonomous agent in the public entertainment sphere, West's character suggests the possibility of breaking free from prescribed roles for women in all spheres, especially in relation to sex and marriage" (Wojcik 1996, 45). Linda's career as women's magazine editor positions her squarely in the "public entertainment sphere," and she demonstrates "an ambivalent and transgressive attitude toward marriage and women's roles" (46). Far from being "autonomous," Linda lacks Mae West's seamless confidence and authority and consistently wavers as a feminist, yet she never fails to yield punchlines that signify her comedic agency in a variety of forms: as self-deprecating humorist and as joking satirist.

Linda displays her camp contradictions through vulgar wit, freedom from feminine decorum, in addition to intermingling her career with her sexuality, yet at the same time, practicing the feminine masquerade still demanded in a world largely controlled by men. Linda's speech to January about her breakup from a man nine years earlier conveys these contradictory, overlapping performances. In a layered nod to Jennifer North (and Tony Polar) in *Valley of the Dolls*, Linda admits to an attempted overdose and affirms, "Well, I survived. Both Tony and the pills"; her misery with men led her, she continues, to prioritize work, which also involves sexual intrigues such as escorting Jerry Moss's boyfriend to events so the married ad man can consort publicly with his lover (Susann 1997b, 181–82). If Linda's reliance on men's approval inspires masochistic self-sacrifice, such as in her unrequited love for the countercultural actor Keith, she nevertheless furnishes liberating and hilarious insights into masculine performance: "I love *Gloss*. It's been good to me. I can hold its sales growth in my hand better than a penis that goes limp on me. Oh, that's happened too. When they can't get it up and the guy just lies there with his limp cock and looks at you like *you're* the one who's made him impotent. He lies there and defies you to make him hard" (Susann 1997b, 182). Moments later when January recounts her recent, inaugural sexual experience and the pain it incurred, Linda's irreverence toward gendered double standards percolates through her profanity: "From what I hear those bastards come like crazy the first time. . . . *She* may not come . . . but goddam it . . . *they* come! And that's something Women's Liberation is never going to be able to change. . . . A virgin lady hurts when the glorious prick enters. And a virgin lady—whether you call her Ms., Miss, or Mrs.—rarely comes until she's properly stretched and oiled with passion. Thank God you're no longer a virgin lady" (Susann 1997b, 183). And when January adds that David (the chic socialite she had sex with) proposed to her, Linda blurts, "Then why are we sitting here having a wake for your lost hymen?" (Susann 1997b, 183).

Susann endows Linda with a grotesque sense of humor that serves as a survival mechanism and a means for fostering sisterhood with January. If Linda combines her sexuality and her work ethic and occasionally confuses self-empowerment with entrapment by the gaze, she also sees through the gaze, renders it limp, and, in front of her female audience—January and Susann's readers—testifies to the work of performing for it.[22] Linda's *work* translates to her wisecracks, sexual comedy, and camp humor that reflect, in Matthew Tinkcom's formulation of camp, "dissident sexual subjects who arrive at their own strategies for critique *and* pleasure" (Tinkcom 2002, 2, 4). Linda surely vacillates between dissident and conformist, or as she puts it, between "Establishment"—the label her countercultural boyfriend brands her with—and "not being part of a man, but being *the* Linda Riggs," as she articulates in her last scene in the novel (Susann 1997b, 123, 422). Linda's struggle nevertheless unveils the comedic hypocrisy of patriarchal logic, for instance, as she says of one liaison, "'Donald thinks Women's Lib is great, so maybe I'll join one of the groups.' She laughed. 'Except when he stays over he forgets all about Women's Lib and even expects me to wash out his underwear'" (Susann 1997b, 334). Perhaps a forerunner to the sexually boisterous best friend (female or gay) of postfeminist romantic comedies to come, Linda remains a wisecracking pessimist. January asks, "Linda, can't you ever find a nice available man?" And Linda replies, "No. Can you?" (Susann 1997b, 335). In *Once Is Not Enough*, such antiromantic rhetoric is not only funny but also nourishing and sustaining. Whereas January commits suicide, Susann implies, from grief over the death of her father, Linda endures as the victor in her own comedy of bad manners. Linda's sense of humor, talent, ambition, and intelligence coincide with her durability as well as her deep insecurities, indecisiveness about feminism, and occasional masochism. If Linda was a parody of Steinem, Susann nevertheless empowered her and endeared her to readers with a sense of humor as well as comic insight into male hypocrisy.

Susann Sontag: Camp Is Not Enough

Whether or not it was sweet coincidence, Jacqueline Susann finally joined a conversation with Susan Sontag, at least through the magic of editing. A 1974 *Cosmopolitan* feature, published just a few months before Susann passed away, positioned Susann and Sontag side by side. Although the article was not about camp, it involved a subject endemic to both camp generally and Susann's camp image in particular: the disadvantages aging women face. After quoting from Sontag's *Cosmopolitan* article, "The Double Standard of Aging," about the "shame" women endure, extensive quotations follow from *Once Is Not Enough* that represent Susann's impressions, including a bit of Linda's dialogue. Following her statement that "twenty-nine is over the hill," Linda (who is twenty-eight) commences, "*Gloss* is a swingy young magazine. I want shiny, beautiful young people in this office" (quoted in Greene 1974, 143). Showcasing Linda's camp self-irony, the quotation renders youthfulness in the disposable, consumerist imagery of pop art, as "shiny" and "swingy." Other women in *Once Is Not Enough* also remark on the indignities of aging, such as the lesbian duo Dee and Karla, as does Judith Austin throughout *The Love Machine*, all flags of Susann's trepidation. In this respect, Capote "camped up" Susann in the form of the "aging diva," characterized by Caryl Flinn as "the fleshy, excessive other to a more transcendent, cerebral masculinity" (Flinn 1999, 444). Susann likewise "camped up" Capote in terms that mockingly outed him, a far cry from her parody of Steinem in the character Linda, in which Susann expresses her own vitality, ambivalence, and irony, her struggles with femininity, sexuality, and style, through vulgar and funny dialogue.

Susann stopped short of publicly classifying herself or her work as camp, perhaps due to the "double standards of aging" for women and its built-in camp effect, which Mae West exemplified in the 1970s. Just a little more than a month before Capote's *Laugh-In* appearance, West wisecracked to *Playboy* magazine, "Camp is the kinda comedy where they imitate me" (quoted in Wojcik 1996, 24). Following the Capote incident, Susann might well indeed have wanted to avoid the kind of camp response West received, "revered in the 1970s merely as a burlesque of woman," Wojcik notes, "a grotesquerie, beloved for her ridiculous and narcissistic belief in her own sexual appeal," rendered "obsolete and outmoded" by the "camp effect" (Wojcik 1996, 26, 27). Susann clearly comprehended camp and embodied many of its classic precepts in her rejection of highbrow criteria for assessing her novels, but the author still held fast to certain elements that bespoke a "lower-middle" or "middlebrow" sensibility. She agreed with critic John Simon, for example, in denouncing the "loathsome," "camp" films of 1970, *Myra Breckinridge* and *Beyond the Valley of the Dolls* (Diffrient 2013, 70), despite the fact that Simon had attacked Susann on *The David Frost Show* and referred to *The Love Machine* as "trash." Susann did not openly consider the camp appeal of the movie versions of her novels, perhaps because critics conflated her novels with the film adaptations, nor did she directly associate the label *camp* with her novels, most likely due to the danger of being classified as, like one of Robin Stone's TV shows, "flops" that were bad enough to become "'high camp' successes."

Susann's gay readers nevertheless held fast, such as John Alfred Avant, book critic for *Gaysweek* and Brooklyn librarian, who paid praise to Susann's posthumously published *Dolores* in a 1976 column for *Library Journal*. A camp love letter to Susann, Avant invokes Oscar Wilde, The Factory, off-off-Broadway theater, and drag queens while rendering Capote's roman à clef *Answered Prayers* second rate. Acknowledging

"Susann's endearing sweetness and naïveté," Avant delights in *Dolores*, "a deliriously campy conceit . . . superior in every way to the Capote *roman à clef* excerpts in *Esquire* . . . and Susann devotees will relish the clichés, which come as quickly as the epigrams in *The Importance of Being Earnest*. Charles Ludlam's Ridiculous Theatrical Company should put *Dolores* on stage; if only Mario Montez were around to do the movie" (Avant 1976, 1660). Comparing Susann's clichés to Wilde's epigrams, Avant wittily and touchingly reconciles two different camp authors and their comedic repertoires as well as two polarized constructs of camp, naive and intentional. The same logic extends to the invocations of Ludlam and Montez as appropriate adapters of Susann's novel, in addition to contrasting Susann's roman à clef with Capote's. The fact that Avant finds *Dolores* "superior" to *Answered Prayers* both reaffirms Susann's authorship and further discombobulates the binary of naive and deliberate camp. This dynamic informed the enduring fandom for Susann and the percolating cult of *Valley of the Dolls*, in which the long travestied author would be resuscitated as a feminist and queer camp icon.

4

Dykes, Gays, and *Dolls*

From the Queer Cult Following to the Gay Susann Revival

Distressed over an awful movie review of *Valley of the Dolls* that trashed her novel all over again, Jacqueline Susann took a walk. Joined by husband Irving Mansfield, they strolled from their home at the Hotel Navarro on Fifty-Ninth and Sixth to the Criterion Theater at Broadway and Forty-Fifth where *Valley of the Dolls* had just opened. A line of prospective spectators busted the block, Susann later gushed to her friend Sherry Arden, a crowd with distinction: "Every hooker, every pimp, every pervert in New York was standing on that line, and I looked at Irving and I said, 'These are my people'" (Seaman 1996c, 350). Susann's jubilant recognition of her "people" jibed with what she had confessed to Carol Bjorkman in *Women's Wear Daily* the previous year—that the literary firmament was ignoring *Valley* but "junkies" were devotees—and anticipated what she would affirm to *Harper's* magazine in 1969, that "people reading *Valley* . . . have very good taste" (Bjorkman 1966a, 8; Davidson 1969, 71). More than quelling her distress over rotten reviews, Susann's fans redefined "good taste," and if their taste-making influence remained only marginally visible in her heyday, Jackie's "people" were just getting started.

Just a few weeks after Susann passed away in September 1974, an homage from one of Jackie's "people" hit movie theaters: John Waters's *Female Trouble*. Waters admitted to visually mimicking the iconic publicity shot from *Valley*, plastered on movie posters and album covers:

Anne Welles (Barbara Parkins), Jennifer North (Sharon Tate), and Neely O'Hara (Patty Duke) posed together on a bed, everything in white and pink, everyone with blank stares. In Waters's version, protagonist Dawn Davenport (Divine)—former juvenile delinquent, now felon and single mother—lounges on her bed, flanked by her girlfriends and partners-in-crime Chicklette (Susan Walsh) and Concetta (Cookie Mueller), all of them reveling in their misdeeds.[1] Waters's citation of *Valley* pushes further consideration of *Female Trouble* as a trash rehash of Susann, such as Dawn Davenport's resemblance to Susann's "single girl" heroines. Like Anne, Dawn flees from home desiring financial and sexual freedom with no inclination to return; and like Neely, she seeks celebrity, wisecracks with a vulgar vocabulary, and falls prey to drugs, promiscuity, and manipulative producers, still a diva, now homicidal. Spanning almost twenty years and divided into chapters, *Female Trouble* further compares to the epic *Valley* and follows the basic structure and themes of Susann's novel. Flaunting a "trash" aesthetic that far surpassed Susann's sleazy realism, Waters nevertheless had much in common with Susann, whose work was also called "dirty" and "shocking," and who likewise took "delight in disregarding customary notions of good taste" (Tinkcom 2002, 157; Cohan 2005, 8, 19). *Female Trouble* materialized something of what Lee Grant was envisioning when she mused many years later about *Valley of the Dolls*, the "disaster" she had appeared in as Miriam Polar: "Maybe if John Waters . . . had had a shot at it" (Grant 2014, 244, 246).[2] Waters continued to pay trash tribute to Susann's most famous work, now in a 1992 *New York Times* column, against the backdrop of a flourishing, underground queer cult following for Susann and *Valley*. At a chic, art-world party in Tribeca, a reporter caught Waters "looking out a window at a trash-filled alley. 'It's a pretty view,' he said. 'Sort of a valley of the dolls. A perfect view of the gutter'" (Morris 1992, 6).[3]

Amid the pressures of Reagan-Bush backlash and tragedies of the AIDS crisis, a new crop of Jackie Susann's "people" began again to assert their good taste. Queer cult interest in Jackie Susann and *Valley of the Dolls* surfaced throughout the 1980s and 1990s in drag performance, zines, and video art.[4] Many fans from this generation first encountered the film *Valley* through TV broadcasts, home video, and eventually drag performance, and their sensibilities brewed alongside AIDS activism, the political strategy of outing, "pro-sex" feminism, and a burgeoning "queer"

THE PYRAMID CLUB and John Epperson's Lucille Le Sewer Players present LYPSINKA! in the 3rd Annual Tribute to The World of Jacqueline Susann the author of Valley of the Dolls September 21

Her work, her loves, her tragedy and her fame.

For East Village audiences in the 1980s, John Epperson—a.k.a. Lypsinka—devised subcultural camp tributes to Jacqueline Susann at the Pyramid Club—a.k.a. "the Queeramid."

movement whose new *styles* of demonstration incorporated a radicalized revamping of camp. The 1985 theatrical parody *Ballet of the Dolls* by John Epperson committed to a drag parody of the film and Susann's novel that extended the sense of drag performance to all players, crossing gender or not.[5] The zine *Dead Jackie Susann Quarterly* (1992–96) bespoke the attitudes of its AIDS activist creators Sydney Pokorny and Liz Tracey, who engaged "Dead Jackie" as their engine for "lesbianizing the dominant culture" (Austin and Gregg 1993, 91). Leslie Singer's video short *Taking Back the Dolls* (1994) arrived at the popular apex of New Queer Cinema and playfully magnified as well as updated Susann's vision of queer scandalousness in celebrity culture.

Barbara Seaman's revelations in the 1987 biography *Lovely Me: The Life of Jacqueline Susann* surely had an influence on queer cult interest in the author and her work, most evident in the pages of *Dead Jackie Susann Quarterly*. With access to Susann's diaries, Seaman essentially outed her subject's bisexuality, in addition to Susann's liberal use of profanity and calculated, often angst-driven performance as herself. Although queer fans rejected the closet logic abided by Susann, they reveled in her closeted performance, Susann's inventive maneuvers to conceal and reveal herself, in addition to her legendary association with drag queens. Seaman also fashioned a kind of camp parable for gay men living with AIDS, in the depiction of Susann's fearless, fabulous persona, undeterred by her battle with breast cancer as well as a disguise to keep it a secret.

By fall 1997, Grove Press released new editions of *Valley of the Dolls*, *The Love Machine*, and *Once Is Not Enough*. The elaborate promotional strategy spearheaded by Grove Press editor in chief Ira Silverberg capitalized on the gay fandom for *Valley of the Dolls* and catalyzed what journalists began designating the "comeback" of Jacqueline Susann (Harris 1996, 44; Carvajal 1997, 23; see also Larson [2003, 314–86, in particular, 369–76]). Seaman had already begun reinforcing the narrative of gay male fandom for Susann to promote the 1996 reissue of *Lovely Me*. Appearing at lesbian-gay bookstores in the company of drag queens, Seaman prepared a new preface in which she recalled imagining Susann's life as a drag musical starring Van Johnson as Ethel Merman, and forthrightly thanked "all the smart, tasteful men in the gay community who, ahead of their time, saved this book from oblivion . . . by shelling out big bucks for second-hand copies of the first edition" (Seaman 1996c, 11–12). Grove Press's marketing campaign for the new editions of Susann's novels mingled genuine affection for Susann's work and careful research into her history and legacy, all with the purpose of drawing in potential readers and furnishing them with a gay camp "key" to unlock the pleasures of Susann and her romans à clef.

Concentrating on *Valley of the Dolls* and characterizing Susann as camp, feminist, and gay friendly before her time, Grove Press enlisted a range of representatives from gay male culture as well as some feminist spokespeople to reach what Ron Becker calls "cosmopolitan, gay-friendly Straight America," consumers whose sensitivity to feminist and queer concerns coincided with the aspiration "to be 'hip' and 'sophisticated'" (Becker 2006, 108–9).[6] Grove Press promotional events spanned both "high" and "low" as well as "gay" and "straight," in addition to east coast and west, and were cleverly timed with the thirtieth anniversary home video release of *Valley of the Dolls* as well as out pop singer k.d. lang's popular "camp" cover of the André and Dory Previn movie theme song.[7] At the New School for Social Research in October 1997, Silverberg organized an evening titled "The Other Jackie," with speeches by Silverberg and Seaman in addition to other colleagues and intimates of Susann, including author Rona Jaffe, columnist Rex Reed, poet David Trinidad, publisher Esther Margolis, and editor Michael Korda. A "Valley of the Dolls Weekend" in November at the Los Angeles County Museum of Art featured a revival of the hugely popular 1995/96 "Screen-to-Stage-Adaptation" of *Valley of the Dolls* by Theatre-a-Go-Go! as well as a screening of the film attended by Barbara Parkins, joined by numerous functions at queer bookstores and nightclubs (Anon. 1997a; Anon. 1997c; Anon. 1997d).[8] Perfectly consistent with the larger-than-life women as well as gay men peopling Jacqueline Susann's novels, and following in the footsteps of Seaman's strategy for *Lovely Me*, Grove Press promotional events regularly featured gay celebrity fans paying tribute, from gossip columnist Ted Casablanca (his nom de plume attesting adoration of the film) to drag queens Charles Busch and John Epperson/Lypsinka as well as Jackie Beat, who played Helen Lawson in the Theatre-a-Go-Go! hit.

The queering campaign to promote Jacqueline Susann's comeback was incomplete, though, due to the virtual exclusion of the lesbian fans whose cult interest in Susann had also contributed to the author's revival.[9] The commercialized camp construction of Jacqueline Susann and *Valley of the Dolls*, k.d. lang notwithstanding, obscured the presence of "dyke" fans as well as Susann's queer women characters in *Valley* and *Once Is Not Enough*, in addition to the camp comedy of sleazy realism that they all produced. Dimensions of Susann's sleazy realism surely surfaced in the Grove Press campaign, through the performance of drag and bitchy camp wit, citations of the word "fag" in Susann's work, and anecdotes about the author's flamboyant personality and sex life. Such disclosures paled in comparison, though, to the scandalous activities and erotic parody that Jackie's dyke fans attributed to the author's inspiration. The complex of camp, gossip, and confession especially applies to queer lesbian fans whose delight in the outed Susann was in perfect stride with the historical zeal for outing, the activist spirit of "new camp," and the rise of "pro-sex feminism."[10] Pokorny and Tracey's *Dead Jackie Susann Quarterly* as well as Singer's *Taking Back the Dolls* turned camp fandom into creative work that indulged Susann's sleazy realism and also served the function of taste-making, similar to gay fans like Epperson/Lypsinka. The promotional discourse of the Susann revival essentially defused the role of lesbian fans as tastemakers to influence the new, queer, feminist, and camp conception of Susann, and in turn, to design a queer camp key for "straight" consumers to unlock the delights of Susann's romans à clef.[11]

Biographical Gossip, Queer Outing, and Barbara Seaman's *Lovely Me*

Barbara Seaman's *Lovely Me* figures squarely in the queer reception history of Jacqueline Susann. Providing the first researched key to Susann's queer closet of celebrity secrets and female misbehavior, *Lovely Me* addressed Susann's bisexuality and intimate alliances with women as well as discussed the queer content of Susann's novels.[12] Framed through gossip among women about women, Seaman begins the original 1987 preface by recalling the genesis of the project, the stories told her by publisher Sherry Arden about Jacqueline Susann's "mental and physical indomitability" (1996c, 1). If gossip about Susann sparked the biographer's interest, Seaman also recognized the proximity between gossip and biography, a genre disparaged historically as an amalgamation of "pernicious gossip" (1996c, 16). Far from rescuing the reputation of her genre, Seaman doggedly demonstrates how biographical gossip presents a "resource of the subordinated," in Patricia Meyer Spacks's estimation, to criticize those in power or venerate the powerless, and "provides language for an alternative culture" (Spacks 1985, 46, 100, 103).[13] Seaman questions the dearth of biographies written about women by women authors and, by way of an explanation, brilliantly segues into the gossipy territory of her own work on Susann. Quoting a prolific woman biographer who concentrates on the lives of "truly great men" because "the valley of one's own condition will be forever greener," Seaman retorts with the example of a different, not-so-green "Valley of the Dolls," where the "lives of women worthy of biographies . . . are not often pretty," proof of "the exorbitant price women pay for their success" (Seaman 1996c, 16–17).

Seaman's blurring of gossip with biography compares in many regards to Kenneth Anger's *Hollywood Babylon*, which Matthew Tinkcom explains, "refuses to isolate gossip as a lesser feature of star lore, and perversely reads Hollywood backward through its gossip," not to humiliate stars but in many cases to glory in their transgressive secrets (Tinkcom 1999, 277–78, 280–82). Anger produces, furthermore, "a fan's history of film colony gossip and scandal," generated "from Anger's camp sensibilities and his intense love of Hollywood cinema" (Tinkcom 1999, 272, 277). Seaman vitally discloses her affection for Susann and her scandalous life in identifiably camp terms; "I love her," Seaman announces in the preface: "Loyal to her friends, malicious to her enemies, Jackie was outrageous, original, and brave. Her enemies thought her an outright liar; her friends understood that she deals in illusion and flimflam—card tricks, as it were, or sleight of hand. What you seem to be might be what you become, as indeed Jackie did" (Seaman 1996c, 15). And in the epilogue, Seaman avers that "Jackie Susann's life was a story of appearances," an idea that touchingly and hilariously reflected the performative "sleight of hand" Seaman had earlier attributed to Susann. "Jackie Susann was not an artist but she mastered the art of living," Seaman proclaims in her closing lines, a final invocation (whether intentional or not) of Sontag's famous proposal that camp "sees everything in quotation marks . . . Being-as-Playing-a-Role. It is the farthest extension, in sensibility, of the metaphor of life as theater" (Seaman 1996c, 15, 458, 460; Sontag 1966, 280).

Seaman revels in Susann's "life as theater," and every gossipy detail of Jackie's "not often pretty" behavior contributes to the perception of her as a camp hero in the face of enormous tribulation, even death, ready to appear glamorous, cuss, and fight like her characters Judith Austin, Helen Lawson, Neely O'Hara, Ethel Evans, Linda Riggs, and Maggie Stewart. Seaman conveys comedic delight in Susann's theatrical life and personality, particularly noticeable in the running gag that develops throughout *Lovely Me* regarding Susann's virtually bare refrigerator and its eccentric contents. A side-splitting symbol of Susann's alienation from domesticity and convention, different friends and family open the fridge throughout Susann's life to variously discover a lonely bottle of cocktail olives, prescription drugs, dog food, or soporific suppositories (Seaman 1996c, 11, 131, 404, 428). Seaman also relishes Susann's performances with other camp women, such as the author's circle of girlfriends dubbed "the Hockey Club," the name purportedly drawn from a Yiddish expression that combines metaphors for both "fucking" and "gossip" (Seaman 1996c, 218). Speaking with Susann's compatriot Ruth Batchelor, for instance, Seaman learns about "Jackie's love of vulgar language," "the words 'pussy' and 'coose.' . . . She loved to toss casual references to 'blow jobs,' 'hard-ons,' and 'cock sucking' into conversations" (Seaman 1996c, 420). While always respectful to her subject, Seaman nonetheless reveals Susann's performances from behind the mask, backstage, closet open. Migrating from farcical, flamboyant gender performances, such as challenging publisher Bernard Geis to a "peeing contest" and clocking a critic, to the bleaker dimensions of artifice, namely, concealing her cancer and autistic son yet writing about them, Seaman enumerates Susann's disguises related to sexuality, career, religion, health, marriage, and motherhood (1996c, 334, 458–59).

Riffing on the idea of Susann's life as "a story of appearances," Seaman enumerates Jackie's closets and performances: "She appeared to be a man's woman. . . . In fact, although many men passed through her life, her books suggest that her strongest allegiances were to her own sex. . . . And she could be almost grotesquely macho, swearing like a sailor and even slugging men" (Seaman 1996c, 458). Seaman's archive of interview transcripts and correspondence evidence the biographer's initial hypothesis that Susann was a closeted lesbian. The biographer declared to Kathy Brady, a former colleague of Carol Bjorkman's at *Women's Wear Daily*, "Oh my god. Jackie was gay," then explained, "one of the reasons this book is taking me so long is that . . . this is a lesbian story. And yet. She lived a heterosexual life" (Seaman 1984, 1). Seaman's announcement came after Brady's unprompted disclosure, "I hate to tell you there was also a rumour [*sic*] that Carol was gay" (Seaman 1984, 1). Although Seaman never confirmed if "they really made it together," *Lovely Me* details Susann's passionate relationship with Carole Landis as well as dalliances with Coco Chanel. With particular camp pleasure, moreover,

Seaman details Susann's "'star-crush' infatuation with Ethel Merman," which included Susann teaching Merman how to bump-and-grind for her role in the musical *Gypsy*: "It was a highly erotic performance, and whether it taught Ethel how to strip or not, it certainly turned Jackie on" (Seaman 1996c, 244, 246). Investigating the pair as "the subject of much gossip," Seaman turns to Susann's buddy Anna Sosenko for an account of a drunken Broadway party where Susann and Merman "lay down on a couch and they just made out in front of everyone" (Seaman 1996c, 246–47).

Even in Susann's struggle against cancer, biographical gossip traces the author's theatricality as well her humor as signs of camp fortitude. In the midst of arrangements for her Christmas Day biopsy in 1962, for example, Susann sacrificed all holy decorum in a plea to Saint Andrew at Saint Patrick's Cathedral: "Do one thing for me before I die. . . . Make me important enough to get a bed in a fucking hospital!" (Seaman 1996c, 22). When Susann participated in the anticensorship movement following the Supreme Court's 1973 obscenity ruling, despite her rapidly declining health, Seaman pays tribute to Susann's "witty if often earthy" commentary among literary "heavyweights" on talk shows and panels, imparting uproarious pearls such as, "Think of how many girls in the Ozarks went wrong without any books or movies at all. With only Uncle Clem to misguide them" (Seaman 1996c, 443). Seaman amplifies the comedy and the camp describing the appearance Susann tailored for these events, her sacrifice of "jazzy costumes," "her wigs and makeup subdued and quietly elegant," then provides a coda pronouncing Susann's theatricality all over again: "for a time at least" (1996c, 443–44). Seaman's accounts of Susann's last days veer sharply from comedy to tragedy. Underscoring Susann's fondness for sick and absurd humor, Seaman recounts the author's ambulance ride on the morning of her fifty-sixth birthday, just a month before passing away, when Susann saw out the ambulance window her and Irving's car being driven by a stranger, clandestinely rented out by their garage attendants. Touching testimony from friends likewise eulogizes Susann in the terms of theatricality and vulgarity: Esther Margolis's rendering of Susann's "fabulous" and "truly radiant" appearance the night Jackie confided about her impending death; and Joanna Carson's recollection that Jackie was "a great lady—the last of the sweet, swinging broads. She loved to be called that. She lived and enjoyed celebrity life to the hilt. She was laughing, generous, earthy. When she got those first two bestsellers, back to back, she bragged to me that she 'had life by the short hairs'" (Seaman 1996c, 452, 454–55).

After engaging the camp dimensions of gossip to explore Jacqueline Susann's life, Seaman's closing sentences dignify the author in the terms of camp, masquerade, and human endurance: "Perhaps what her life was about was told best at the end. In the face of great adversity and sorrow, she 'showed them all.' She was, in a word, indomitable. Jackie Susann was not an artist, but in dying she mastered the art of living, if that means making most of a bad hand that was dealt" (Seaman 1996c, 460). As Seaman unearths the sleazy realism of Susann's life and personality, a writer who thrived on gossip, confession, and dissimulation, she magnifies Susann's complexity, her camp nobility, magnetism, and hilariousness.

In preparing the 1996 reissue, Seaman grew convinced of Susann's appeal to gay male culture in the era of AIDS. The lesbian fandom for Susann, however, did not seem relevant to her, based on interviews, promotional statements, and letters. The self-professed "dyke" zine *Dead Jackie Susann Quarterly* openly drew from the revelations of *Lovely Me*, though, such as in "The Many Girl Loves of Jackie Susann" from issue 3, and in the final issue plugged Seaman's new edition of the biography

Gossip about Susann sparked feminist writer Barbara Seaman's interest and generated *Lovely Me: The Life of Jacqueline Susann*.

(Pokorny and Tracey 1995; Pokorny 1996).[14] Even as Seaman outed Susann's feminist camp masquerade with an accent on her love for women, the biographer nevertheless overlooked the novelist's queer, feminist, and camp appeal to lesbian fans.

Setting the Scene: The "New Camp," Gender Trouble, and Queer Fandom

Fashion writer and drag queen Glenn Belverio (a.k.a. Glennda Orgasm) suggested a concrete narrative of gay male camp engagement in the film *Valley of the Dolls* directly associated with drag performance, beginning in the 1980s with the taste-making influence of East Village drag artist John Epperson. Epperson created the 1985 parody *Ballet of the Dolls*, in which men in drag played female characters alongside female-to-female and male-to-male drag performers, consistent with the East Village performance space and bar where *Ballet* played, the Pyramid Club. Dubbed "the Queeramid," according to the writer and AIDS activist Sarah Schulman, it was home to the burgeoning drag careers of Lypsinka (Epperson), RuPaul, and Lady Bunny, and one of the few spaces where queers of all genders socialized (Chermayeff, David, and Richardson 1995, 81; Schulman 1994, 84; Feil 2013, 144–45). The movie *Valley of the Dolls* remains central to *Ballet*, with incidental music that quotes from Previn's *Valley* theme and character monikers that cite the film's stars, such as the protagonist Barbara Parkavenue and her nemesis Susan Wayward. The backstage showbiz story mimics the film and evokes particular scenes, such as Tony Polar's singing seduction of Jennifer North and Anne Welles's Gillian Girl cosmetics commercial. The overtly stylized dialogue, acting, and costumes playfully call attention to themselves, and so does the low-tech production style. In Epperson's camp translation of Helen Lawson's production number "I'll Plant My Tree," for instance, the pendulous, psychedelic, and mammoth mobile that hangs over the stage as Hayward's Helen belts turns into a diminutive mobile hanging from a stick planted in Susan Wayward's wig. Subtle references to the novel also appear, with Susan Wayward's resemblance evoking Ethel Merman, lines such as "Send in that fag for rewrites," and a song lyric that refers to *Hit the Sky*, the show that plays such a pivotal role in the novel.[15] A "Tribute to the World of Jacqueline Susann" followed in 1987, presented by the

Pyramid Club and John Epperson's Lucille Le Sewer Players.[16] For the 1988 revival of *Ballet of the Dolls*, the production moved to La Mama, an off-off Broadway institution, and as the *New York Times* reported, Epperson appeared as "Miss Susann" (Holden 1988b, C6).

Belverio recalled, in the midst of the mainstream Jackie Susann revival in 1997, the centrality of *Valley of the Dolls* in the East Village drag community as well as Epperson's role as tastemaker:

> Then in 1989 I got to know the drag queen, Endive, who was best friends with Lypsinka. So we went over to Lypsinka's apartment one day. I'm in combat boots; everything's for the gay cause, for AIDS, etc., and Lypsinka sits me down and makes me watch "Valley of the Dolls." Lypsinka and Endive are laughing and carrying on, and I'm going, "I don't get it." Then all of a sudden it seeped in. And it was shortly after I saw the film that I began doing drag. So you could say I had a conversion experience—"Valley of the Dolls" allowed me to rediscover my camp roots. (Paglia and Belverio 1997)

Belverio's recollection confirms the gestating cult of *Valley of the Dolls* in the late 1980s East Village and posits a causality between seeing the movie (thanks to Epperson's home video collection) and doing drag that solidifies *Valley* in the history of gay male camp.

This narrative of cultural "conversion" forgets, though, how *Valley of the Dolls* appealed to the camp perspectives of queer women who delighted in subverting gender.[17] Another 1989 East Village conversion story about drag, by way of example, came in the pages of *OutWeek*, a New York periodical dubbed the *Pravda* of the AIDS activist group, ACT UP New York.[18] In Sydney Pokorny's "Confessions of a Lesbo Drag Hag," the future co-creator of the zine *Dead Jackie Susann Quarterly* wittily staked a space for lesbian participation and pleasure in gay male drag, and by extension, camp. "It is a cruel act of God," posits Pokorny, "that the drag queen Taboo! can perform *The History of the Platform Shoe*, while many women I know are only interested in building a platform bed" (Pokorny 1989, 52). Pokorny deflates lesbian stereotypes through thoughtful praise for gay drag, debunks feminist critiques of drag as misogynistic mimicry, and engages in an ambivalent critique of pop culture that Pokorny claims drag activates. Pokorny's appropriation of gay male drag further-more confronts the restrictions of both lesbian culture and patriarchal mass culture.[19] "If I were a good lesbian," the journalist playfully taunts, "I would suppress my frivolity and give up worshiping Brigitte Bardot, but part of the fun of being a dyke is being a bad girl" (Pokorny 1989, 52). After positing "that drag glamour strays from dominant constructions," Pokorny substantiates drag's applications to feminist critiques of mass culture: "Rather than replicating fashion and entertainment industry images, they mock all their sources. . . . Femininity becomes a mask to be worn and we laugh (and marvel) at the masquerade of femininity once removed. Drag also trashes masculinity, making mincemeat of machismo" (Pokorny 1989, 53).[20] As a dyke fan of gay male camp, Pokorny turns into a performer of feminist, female-as-female drag whose pleasure in "worshiping Brigitte Bardot" reconciles "being a dyke" with "being a bad girl."

The historical specificity and uniqueness of this moment of les-bian camp also matters and ties directly to the genesis of Pokorny and Tracey's zine. In their 1990 overview of AIDS activist art, Douglas Crimp and Adam Rolston emphasize the functions of camp humor for survival, political endurance, and community, and in his 1993 *Out* magazine arti-cle "Old Camp, New Camp," gossip columnist and AIDS activist Michael Musto also verified these claims (Crimp and Rolston 1990, 21–22).[21] Musto connects participation in AIDS and queer activism to a "new camp" that bespeaks "rising queer consciousness in the face of disaster," yet, "is not as innately tragic and self-pitying as the old camp, because the last thing anyone needs right now is a maudlin torch song" (1993, 34–35). Along-side the optimism of new camp, however, "we've learned to purge our darkest impulses through black humor," which includes the "plague-era 'zine, *Diseased Pariah News*," and as Musto mentions a few pages on, *Dead Jackie Susann Quarterly* (34, 38). Identifying *Dead Jackie*'s "irreverent" humor, along with the rise of the Drag Kings, Musto declares that "camp is now officially unisex," effectively binding together *two* vital political applications of the new camp: AIDS activism and feminism (38). Musto closes with reflections about the drag queens RuPaul and Lypsinka, that they "can successfully make fun of showbiz clichés while emphatically embracing them" (39), sentiments that apply equally to the dyke camp of *Dead Jackie* and the queer video parody *Taking Back the Dolls*.

Lesbian Avengers of the Dolls: Camping Susann in the *Valley* and Beyond

Inspired by Susann and her sleazy realism, and according to the new camp sensibility of irreverence, morbidity, and ambivalence toward dominant culture, *Dead Jackie Susann Quarterly* and *Taking Back the Dolls* both invoke "showbiz clichés" and skewer them through gossip, scandal, and pop culture parody. Andrew James Patterson offers an effective and funny summation of *Taking Back the Dolls* that also speaks to the project of *Dead Jackie*: "*The Valley of the Dolls* is flamboyantly reclaimed and then injected. The chemical cocktails that queers and other camp-enthusiasts knew were on the sets, but still not within the frames of Hollywood psycho-dramas and melodramas, are now deliriously highlighted and fetishized" (Patterson 2000, 81). Patterson overlooks, however, the lesbian plotline in Susann's novel "not within the frames" of the original camp classic that *Taking Back the Dolls* fervently "highlighted and fetishized." *Taking Back the Dolls* indeed concretized a historic moment of queer women appropriating camp. If the ability to identify camp comprises an act akin to gossip (Finch 1999, 148), part of this kinship relates to the power of gossip as a form of taste-making, and for queer campers, outing. *Taking Back the Dolls* and *Dead Jackie* both *out* Jackie Susann's work as not just camp but queer *lesbian* camp.

The erotic parodies of *Dead Jackie* and *Taking Back the Dolls*, fueled by pro-sex feminism, further politicized their camp retreads of Susann and her sensibility by infusing them with an overtly scandalous, explicit, and sapphic sleazy realism. Both *Dead Jackie* and *Taking Back the Dolls* delight in what Caryl Flinn calls the "voluptuousness" of "female-as-female drag," the erotics of mocking "the clichés of heterosexual femininity" (Flinn 1999, 454), all central to the "new" lesbian camp exploding in zines and the New Queer Cinema. Female-as-female drag presents the most consistent, perhaps essential, activity in *Dead Jackie* and *Taking Back the Dolls*, one that motivates their sleazy realism, the camp performance of outrageous activities by queer women making havoc of gender roles and Hollywood tropes. Regarding dyke zines born out of the AIDS activist and queer movements, S. Bryn Austin and Pam Gregg emphasize the project "to retaliate against the sexphobic and virulently homophobic climate of censorship" in both right-wing politics and "anti-porn" feminism

So You Want to Be a

LESBIAN?

How to Study for—and Pass—Your LATs (Lesbian Aptitude Test)	GYNADDICTION: Women Who Love Women *WAY* Too Much
Breaking Up—Without Going into the Witness Protection Program	Lesbian Cuisine—Beyond Granola and Back Again
Kinky Sex Made Simple	Trucker Wallets, Tattoos, Baseball Caps, and Other Important Accessories
Lesbian Bed Death: The Real Story	
The Great Lesbian Haircut Conspiracy	LIZ TRACEY and SYDNEY POKORNY

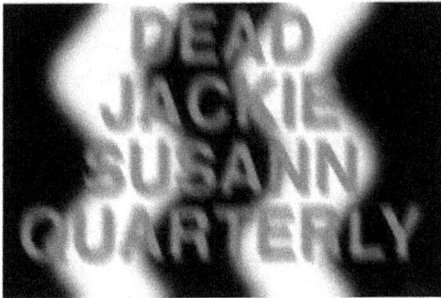

Can we get you a cocktail?

Liz Tracey and Sydney Pokorny's zine and website *Dead Jackie Susann Quarterly* championed Susann, particularly *Valley of the Dolls*. Their 1996 satirical self-help book *So You Want to Be a Lesbian?* continued to pay tribute, now distinguishing *Once Is Not Enough*.

(1993, 86). Cherry Smyth offers a similar motivation for the unashamed sexuality of "queer dyke cinema" within the larger New Queer Cinema of the early 1990s. Observing that "dykes have reacted fiercely against the anti-sex prescriptiveness of certain strands of feminism," Smyth exemplifies director Alison Murray's reflections on her latest video shorts: "Some people call it pornographic, which I take as a compliment—it is and it's meant to be" (Smyth 1992, 39). The dyke reception of Jacqueline Susann revised sleazy realism through pro-sex feminism, an expression of camp fandom whose joy sprung from celebrating the failure of the closet and the vulgar victory of queered femininity.

Tracey and Pokorny, ACT UP activists and co-writers of the *Out-Week* column "Out on the Town with Liz and Sydney," enlightened *Dead Jackie Susann Quarterly* readers in their third edition,

You may be asking why Jackie Susann? She's camp, she's glam, she's frivolous, she typed her manuscript pages on pink paper, she understood the appeal of modern celebrity better than anyone else (except maybe Warhol), she loved melodrama, and on top of it all, her heroines were always powerful, independent women who were not afraid of going after what they wanted. . . . how can you help but love someone who kept nothing but dog food, nembutal suppositories, a bottle of cocktail capers, and Dom Perignon in her refrigerator? How can you help but worship someone for whom the concept of "practical" seemed totally alien?

Dead Jackie fulfilled the promise of both feminist camp and lesbian zine production of the era: expressing a "taste for the outrageous," appropriating sexuality as well as popular culture, and satirizing identity politics as well as mainstream norms (Austin and Gregg 1993, 82, 85–86, 91–92). By the time the Susann revival got cracking in 1996/97, *Dead Jackie* had garnered a kind of mainstream attention unusual for a zine, with four mentions in the *New York Times* as *the* Susann source as well as praise for its pop culture parody (Herring 1993, F2; Carvajal 1997, 23; Lohr 1993, A1; Anon. 1993, 3). As Pokorny and Tracey detailed the novelist's countercultural significance and inspiration of camp fun, *Dead Jackie* indeed helped resurrect Susann.[22]

The vitality and visibility of *Dead Jackie Susann Quarterly* exemplify women's contributions to the queer camp cult of Jacqueline Susann, but the relative disappearance of *DJSQ* from the narrative of Susann's fandom once the revival was underway also reflects what Katrin Horn refers to as the problem of "seeing lesbians" in the context of camp (Horn 2017, 24–26).[23] In the 1992 article "The New Queer Cinema," Horn points out, queer feminist critic B. Ruby Rich initially doubted the prevalence of lesbian camp at the same time as coining the term "New Queer Cinema," but two years later, Rich concluded in a review of *Go Fish* (Troche, 1994), "lesbian camp does exist and even has a lineage," beginning with Jan Oxenberg's 1975 film *Comedy in Six Unnatural Acts* (Rich 1992, 33; Rich 1994, 15; Horn 2017, 46–47).[24] Rich does not consider fandom as a form of camp practice, however, and as a result, misses the connection between camp spectatorship and media gossip in addition to their combined impact on camp creative production. In another classic piece that Rich contributed to, the introduction to *Jump Cut*'s 1981 issue on "Lesbians and film," the authors consider that "Gossip provides the official unrecorded history of lesbian participation in film," and, "feeds into audience expectation and interpretation" (Becker et al. 1981). These insights pertain directly to Susann, whose camp reputation rests on gossip about her sexuality as well as the gossip about sexuality that her novels inspired, all of which fueled the lesbian camp appropriation of Susann and nourished the creative work of *Dead Jackie*.

Tracey and Pokorny published *Dead Jackie* together from 1992 to 1995, the last installment in 1996 produced solo by Pokorny. Written with punk zeal and fueled by a marked sense of silliness, infuriation, and joy that illuminated their queer activist sensibility, *Dead Jackie* espoused the Susann sensibility through sexually explicit political and pop culture satire, usually spun in the form of gossip narratives. Their first issue in 1992 contains, by way of illustration, the satirical, erotic, and gossipy "Lame Ducks in Lust or Scenes from a Rightwing Love Story," which imagines the Republican second lady Marilyn Quayle carrying on an illicit affair with the closeted, homophobic head of the National Endowment of the Arts, Anne-Imelda Radice (Pokorny and Tracey 1992). The second issue's "Fear and Loathing the Brady Way" fantasizes about the drug-fueled and depraved adventures of *The Brady Bunch* in Las Vegas, which include Jan Brady's sadomasochistic union with singer Peggy Lee (Pokorny and Tracey 1993).

The idea of "Dead Jackie" originated as an abstract camp concept, a sensibility related to disclosing dyke subjectivity, sexuality, and taste in the form of carnivalesque gossip and confession. Sexual fantasies, cultural critique, and even keywords were furnished by "Dead Jackie," as the first issue declares: "Cybersluts. Slackerdykes. Butch Bikerchicks. Femme Tops. Muffdiving Channel Surfers. Bitch Barharlots from Hell" (Pokorny and Tracey 1992). And in the second issue: "So for those sisters of Sappho out there asking, 'Why Jackie?' I give the following translations into lesbianese for the title of our twisted zine"; a list of silly and suggestive words ensue redolent of Seaman's rendering of a profanity-loving Jackie, beginning with "Boobs-a-gogo," ending with "Pussy," and topped off by the rhetorical rejoinder, "any questions?" (Pokorny and Tracey 1993). Reviews of books, music, and films neighbor the satirical pieces and complement them, as in the second issue that delves into both lesbian history titles and erotica.

Leslie Singer's video short *Taking Back the Dolls* employs a drag and camp sensibility, as the title promises, to "take back" *Valley of the Dolls* from both a censorious Hollywood, which deleted the dyke content and references from the book, and the gay camp cult that claimed ownership of the film. Shot in stylized black-and-white video with the boxed-in and blurry appearance of Pixelvision, alternately segueing into color, *Taking Back the Dolls* has much in common with the earlier avant-garde video *Grapefruit* (1989) by Cecilia Dougherty, a frequent creative collaborator with Singer who also happens to play Jennifer in *Taking Back the Dolls*. Liz Kotz submits that Dougherty's video "is not explicitly 'lesbian' in terms of realist representation or content. Instead, it functions more analogously to a form of 'camp,' working with impersonation and quasi-parodic imitation to reappropriate mass cultural figures and reinvest them with lesbian fantasies and desires" (Kotz 1993, 94). *Taking Back the Dolls* trumpets its camp investment in "impersonation and quasi-parodic imitation" less than a minute into its running time when Dougherty's character, model Jennifer North, mutters in the flattest, most deadpan monotone possible, "But I'm not getting into acting. If I tried to . . . *act*, I'd probably stink." No one in the film *tries* to act, realistically at least, an aesthetic choice that underscores the theme of drag historically associated with *Valley of the Dolls'* gay male camp reception, now reconfigured through queer lesbian camp. Patterson alludes to Kotz's conception of camp when placing *Taking Back the Dolls* in the tradition of underground cinema such as Jack Smith's *Flaming Creatures* (1963), a film abounding in a variety of male drag, trans, and genderqueer performance. Similar to Smith's queer retinue, Singer's performers appear to be "simultaneously acting (with their extreme disdain for naturalism) and not acting (because of their utter disdain for verité or believability)" (Patterson 2000, 81).

Acting unnaturally and not acting believably define the drag aesthetic of *Taking Back the Dolls*, in turn complemented by additional gestures that, as Kotz puts it, "destabilize realism": "cross-gender and cross-race casting"; "mix-and-match music, costumes and performance styles" (Kotz 1993, 93–94). Singer interrupts the taken-for-granted whiteness pervading Susann's oeuvre as well as her gay camp following by reconfiguring Neely O'Hara as Neely Shannon Chen (Valerie Soe). And in a gesture reminiscent of Pokorny's penchant for drag, Singer turns the sexually aggressive nightclub singer Tony Polar into the woman "torch singer" Tony Polaris (Monique Nobo). The fact that Jennifer and Anne Welles (Leslie Singer) wear obvious blond wigs provides another signal of the female-as-female-drag on display, which ultimately comes to a head (so to speak). Quoting one of the favorite scenes for camp fans of *Valley of the Dolls*, Neely and Helen Lawson's powder room brawl, Neely in *Taking Back the Dolls* rips off Anne's wig and screams, "You're a phony," laughs at her friend for being "as bald as a Nazi skinhead," vows to "shit right on your wig," and then flushes the hairpiece down the toilet.

Although *Taking Back the Dolls* resists prescriptive didacticism with irony, a moral theme endemic to camp finally surfaces when Neely screams at Anne "You're a phony!" In a most camp way *Taking Back the Dolls* maneuvers the "phony"—mannered and stilted acting, pop culture references, and "women" very apparently *playing* "women"—to communicate an authentic queer perspective.

As a queer feminist camp creation, *Taking Back the Dolls* interweaves both the novel and film version of *Valley of the Dolls* with the attitudes of AIDS and queer activism, in addition to the historical threats of right-wing "family values" rhetoric and "anti-sex feminism." Employing a genderqueer erotic gaze in two relatively explicit sex sequences, Singer parlays the sexual themes of the novel into undermining anti-sex feminism as well as the constrictions of gender: Tony and Jennifer's dalliance with s/m, which reinscribes both Susann's lesbian scenes and what Nora Ephron had referred to as the "masochism" of Susann's women characters; and in an acknowledgment of gay fan wish fulfillment, a "sex on ecstasy" interlude between two het male characters from the novel and film, Lyon Burke (Cliff Hengst) and cosmetics executive Kevin Gillian (Kevin Killian). As Singer revises Susann, the director quotes directly from *Valley* to accentuate the queer appropriation of the proto-feminist novel, such as when Dougherty's Jennifer flatly explains about appearing in art movies, "Oh, I don't mean dirty pictures—I mean movies with a real plot. Only when you take a bath in a scene, they photograph it" (Susann 1997c, 244). Singer's sexualized parody of *Valley of the Dolls* compares to Tracey and Pokorny's work in *Dead Jackie*—for instance, the satirical ad in their second edition for "The Jackie Susann Card," endorsed by Neely O'Hara who would "never leave the Valley of the Dolls without it!!!" A line toward the end refers to "hobnobbing on 'The Love Machine,' or simply dropping acid with 30 of your closest friends and having group sex" (Pokorny and Tracey 1993). In all these ways, Singer as well as Pokorny and Tracey *take back* the *Dolls* from Hollywood, and from a gay male culture that was politically queer yet often oblivious to the cultural impact and validity of queer dyke sensibilities.

Taking Back the Dolls frames its queer scandal through more pressing recent history with the additional character of Gia Caravaggio, a drug-addicted model and friend to Jennifer.[25] Singer is clearly citing lesbian supermodel Gia Carangi, who rose to front-page celebrity through her stunning beauty and wild behavior among the Studio 54 set before succumbing to AIDS in 1986. An outspoken, sexually liberated, and unruly woman, moralistically blamed for the tragic results of her own exploitation, Gia emerges in Singer's video as an ironically reflexive reference, both politically and culturally. Gia signals the AIDS crisis, Religious Right, and anti-sex feminism as an impetus for recent queer, feminist political organizing, and her presence in *Taking Back the Dolls* flags the applicability of *Valley of the Dolls* as a harbinger of the celebrity culture that Gia emblematized. In this regard *Taking Back the Dolls* predicts what Pokorny and Tracey would state in their 1995 edition of *Dead Jackie*:

> Almost daily it seems like pages of *Valley of the Dolls* spring to life in numerous sound bytes and headlines made by a coterie of suicide obsessed, professionally unhappy grunge(TM) rock millionaires. One week's study of MTVs buzz bin yields enough heartache and perversion (and I'm only counting one Alanis video) to prove dead Jackie was blessed with Cassandra-like gifts of foresight. Forget Warhol, McLuhan, Baudrillard, and Jackie Collins, Jackie Susann is the one and only grandpooba of pop, the true prophetess of fin de sicle [*sic*] mass media. (Pokorny and Tracey 1995a)

Similar to *Dead Jackie*'s favorite poster child of the Susann sensibility, Courtney Love, Gia exemplifies in *Taking Back the Dolls* what Susann recognized as, in Tinkcom's terminology, a "star-scandal system" where "scandalous sexualities" remain the forbidden and integral object of the public's imagination and the culture industry's publicity machine (Tinkcom 1999, 277). As Pokorny and Tracey knew well, *OutWeek* and the outing campaigns it engaged with celebrities and politicians arose out of awareness in the gossip and publicity industries about closeted figures with immense power whose neglect, and sometimes outright homophobic bigotry, exacerbated the AIDS crisis and the rising public backlash against queer people (Signorile 1994, 71–93). Singer's addition of Gia in *Taking Back the Dolls* subtly coalesces gossip, scandal, celebrity, lesbian queerness, the AIDS crisis, and drug addiction, on top of the fact that both Gia Carangi and Jacqueline Susann were natives of Philadelphia transplanted to New York.

The emphasis on *Valley of the Dolls* in these dyke appropriations of Susann nonetheless iterated one of the oversights of the mainstream Susann revival: the involved lesbian plotline of *Once Is Not Enough*. Tracey and Pokorny's brief entry on Jacqueline Susann in their 1996 satirical lifestyle manual *So You Want to Be a Lesbian?* alludes to the hegemony of the *Dolls*: "In *Once Is Not Enough*, the thinly veiled Garbo character [Karla] has an affair with another woman. While Jackie certainly wasn't a poster-child for lesbian fiction, she was at least getting it out there and into the faces of millions of readers" (Tracey and Pokorny 1996, 133). Susann actually confirmed the wide appeal of the bisexual character Karla when she objected to director Guy Green's film adaptation. As Green informed *Variety*, Susann "told me her fan mail indicated Karla was readers' favorite character, and she was irked at the way we changed her for the film" (Anon. 1974, 4).[26] In the 2004 anthology *Small-Town Gay*, writer Traci Lynn testifies as one of those readers, recalling her coming-of-age as a closeted high school girl in 1976 Texas. Faced with the dearth of lesbian literature available, works such as *The Children's Hour* where "the guilt-ridden one kills herself," Lynn remembers, "that wasn't an option for me, so I turned instead to the book *Once Is Not Enough*" (Lynn 2004, 35). Ignoring the fact that *Once* also ends tragically for the lesbian couple—after vowing to make their relationship exclusive, Karla's lover Dee dies in a plane crash—Lynn relishes the considerable scenes of passion that the closeted lovers share: "Now that was a relationship I could get into! The secretive, sexy meetings between the two older women sent me reeling" (35). Lynn proceeds to account for "the fantasies I would conjure up" involving women she knew in proportion to her waning desire for boys, which leads to the conclusion: "I had to explore" (35). A vivid sense of causality materializes here, from Lynn locating affirming and hot lesbian love in *Once* to the uses of fantasy for exploring her desires, and finally to seeking relationships. Dee, Karla, and their lesbian partnering in *Once Is Not Enough* might be camp in a number of ways, beginning with the portrait of Garbo that Susann presents in Karla, and Susann denies them a happy ending with potentially moralistic connotations, but for readers such as Lynn, Susann's affirmative representation of their passion and love mattered.

A comedic tone also creeps into Lynn's sincere story. Her joyful admission, "Now that was a relationship I could get into!" puns on the meaning of "get into," collapsing a reader's immersion in the novel with Lynn's personal desire to be in a lesbian relationship. Lynn takes gossipy glee in the characters' scandalously "secretive, sexy meetings," a humorous interruption in an otherwise sober account. More than that, Lynn's line abounds with sexual *suggestion* at the same time as championing erotic liberty, a feature of camp humor and some forms of gossip. Akin to sleazy realism, the scene of furtive sexual pleasure Lynn evokes arrives as a revelatory confession that barges in unexpectedly, just after the reference to tragedy in *The Children's Hour*, which in turn had followed a bleak overview of her family life. The affinity among camp, gossip, and confession surfaces momentarily in Lynn's innocent, delighted, yet controlled disclosure.[27] In Lynn's testimony, gossip no longer serves as a replacement for sexual pleasure, what Spacks calls "meta-sex" (Spacks 1985, 136), but turns into a vehicle for sexual discovery, which in turn provides the substance for Lynn's confessional.[28]

Tracey and Pokorny seem to have sensed a pattern forming at the outset of the Jacqueline Susann revival, the hardening of the interpretive key to Susann in the form of gay male camp. In *So You Want to Be a Lesbian?*, the authors opine, "*Valley of the Dolls*, a masterpiece of blockbuster fiction, was more than just camp. It was also an exploitation of lesbian desire (that part didn't make it into the movie)" (Tracey and Pokorny 1996, 133). The blunt minimizing of camp and indication of what the movie censored strike as a marked departure from their zine, in whose third issue Pokorny and Tracey finally give a "straight" reply to the question, "Why Jackie?" Defining their Susann sensibility directly in the opening editorial, camp led the way in their reasoning: "You may be asking why Jackie Susann? She's camp, she's glam, she's frivolous" (Pokorny and Tracey 1995a). Their subsequent comments in *So You Want to Be a Lesbian?* that *Valley of the Dolls* "was more than just camp" now beg a new question, not "Why Jackie?" but Why not "camp" Jackie? The gay camp reception key to Susann, by reveling in gay male drag and honing in on the film *Valley of the Dolls*, overshadowed the signs of lesbian camp fandom, the power of lesbian taste-making, and Susann's location in the history of lesbian culture.

The Susann Revival

Barbara Seaman identified *Lovely Me*'s "cult following among gay men" in a 1996 fax to her publisher Dan Simon, how an "LA gay activist TV producer / businessman informed me recently that he's noticed 'it's on the bookshelf of every home' he visits" (Seaman 1996b). Seaman's biographical gossip appealed to gay camp sensibility, but not just with private details about a larger-than-life female cultural icon of the 1960s. As Seaman saw it, illuminating Susann's flamboyant performance in the face of terminal disease spoke to a camp disposition particular to the AIDS crisis. Seaman suggested these dual elements of Susann's camp appeal in 1997 to gossip columnist Liz Smith, a friend of Susann's, in an invitation for a *Lovely Me* promotional event in New York at the LGBTQ bookstore A Different Light: "Women like Jackie, who are variously called 'loveable grotesques' or 'glorious monsters' seem to be more kindly regarded now, and even recognized as one kind of role model for today's harsh world. . . . But, LOVELY ME has been kept alive through becoming a cult book in the AIDS-stricken communities (perhaps more on the West Coast than the East) due, I am told, to Jackie's example of 'leaving her mark,' despite—and because of—her cancer" (Seaman 1997a).

When again pontificating to her publisher, Seaman suggested how the convergence of drag, camp, and Jacqueline Susann could at once address the gay "cult" as well as cross over from subculture to dominant culture.[29] Seaman recognized the compatibility of gay camp and drag sensibility with other reasons for rising interest in Susann, such as the retro taste of the 1960s revival taking place, as well as altered attitudes about breast cancer, autism, and powerful, successful, "offbeat" businesswomen. As for gay male drag culture, which was surging into the mainstream, Seaman speculated, "Maybe she's graduated from a minor transvestite role-model to the top tier. (If so this may have been due to LOVELY ME)" (1997c). The reference here to "top tier" drag (notwithstanding the misapplication of "transvestite") alludes to both the drag contingency among the biography's fans and the rising notoriety of gay male drag in a range of cultural contexts. Lypsinka had already made it to off-Broadway, and in 1996 *The RuPaul Show* began airing on the cable channel VH1, two clear progressions from East Village queer subculture to the mainstream. It was no surprise then that Epperson, in the drag guise of Jacqueline Susann or Lypsinka, frequently surfaced during the revival: as the author of a glossy promotional piece about the novelist in *Interview* magazine, pictured in an accompanying photo spread; appearing at Different Light during the promotion of *Lovely Me* and *Valley of the Dolls*, and attending the premiere of the 1998 TV biopic *Scandalous Me*, adapted from Seaman's biography.

Promoting Susann and her most famous work, *Valley of the Dolls*, through gay male camp and drag offered readers and film audiences outside the cult a ready-made reception key, a means to decode and enjoy Susann's roman à clef. On the high heels of the *Valley* book release in fall 1997, Lypsinka's piece for *Interview* magazine offered a Jackie Susann primer alongside an elaborate pictorial spread of the drag artist in various Jackie poses. And for the New York nightlife magazine *Paper*, East Village drag queen Lurleen fashioned a key to Susann and *Valley* for curious clubbers. Lurleen and Lypsinka each honored the gay camp history of Susann, including her association with drag and frequent use of the word "fag," as well as provided a camp spectatorial guide to *Valley of the Dolls*. Lurleen opens, for instance, by pointedly framing the discussion through Susann's relationships with bitchy gay men. "Jacqueline Susann was trashed by every famous fag of her day," the piece begins, accumulating the expected example from Truman Capote, and (according to legend) Gore Vidal, yet also speciously referencing Rex Reed, one of Susann's consistent champions.[30] Lurleen follows such fabled and fabricated acrimony with the rejoinder, "Yet it's the gays—along with the drag queens and other camp-a-holics—who kept the flame burning for Jackie since her untimely demise in 1974" (Lurleen 1997).

Lypsinka likewise uses the word "fag" as a playful, ambivalent connection to a recurrent term in the novel *Valley of the Dolls*, applied affectionately and as a dysphemism, and whose derogatory utterance in the film remains central and legendary to gay camp engagement: Jennifer's (Sharon Tate) line, "You know how bitchy fags can be"; Neely's (Patty Duke) proclamation, "Ted Casablanca is *not* a fag!"; and as Neely tells Helen (Susan Hayward) about the elder star's date, prior to their legendary contretemps, "Well, that's a change from the fags you're usually stuck with." As the poet David Trinidad explained in his speech for the Grove Press event "The Other Jackie" at the New School, "A few weeks ago as I reread *Valley of the Dolls*, I kept stopping at each reference—and they are numerous—to 'fags' and 'faggots' and 'queers.' . . . But Susann's fags and faggots and queers sang and danced and directed plays, designed costumes, escorted aging Broadway actresses to openings. They may have been stereotypes, but they actually functioned in the world. And more importantly, they had sex with each other. . . . No wonder my gratitude to Jacqueline Susann refuses to wane" (Trinidad 1997, 7–8). In Lypsinka's "interview" with the ghost of Susann, Jackie mentions that she might have been "the first lady novelist to pen the words *shit, fuck* and *goddam*." "And faggot," adds Lypsinka; "Yeah, one of my faves," affirms Jackie. After Susann rationalizes her use of the word, Lypsinka starts to broach the subject of Capote, but Susann snaps, "That faggot! He called me a truck-driver in drag on the *Tonight Show*" (Lypsinka 1997, 141).

Treading similar territory, Lurleen and Lypsinka define a playfully rancorous, camp relationship between gay men and Jackie Susann that underpins drag queens' historical affinity for her. Lypsinka reinforces the sense of Jackie as drag queen by repeating the famous Capote line as well as hearing "the husky voice of Jacqueline Susann" by way of introduction, attributes that combine with all her other witty and outrageous banter to exemplify what Lurleen refers to as "the sheer force of her dynamic persona" (Lypsinka 1997, 139; Lurleen 1997). Both writers also suggest the camp play of high and low, a locus of ironic and shifting value analogous to the irony of being gay in a heteronormative society, and which also characterizes one gay relationship to Susann. Lurleen refers to an event at Different Light where "downtown drag queens will read their favorite excerpts from *Valley of the Dolls*," by contrast to the New School evening of "The Other Jackie," "highbrow attention she so craved." Lypsinka politicizes the play of high and low surrounding Susann, telling the author's ghost, "Some critics dismiss your work as pulp trash, and others defend it as the work of a pop-culture feminist" (141). Lurleen alludes to Susann's feminist appeal, too, in a description that merges Susann's drag queen persona with her bisexuality and struggle with illness, "the tough babe in a wig with a pampered poodle and a gutter mouth, relentlessly promoting her books and herself . . . chasing Jewish comics (and Ethel Merman!), all while secretly dying of cancer. Now *that's* a star, baby!"

Lurleen tops this camp portrait of Susann by appreciating the novelist's closeted performance at the same time as outing her.[31]

Apart from the smooch with Merman, though, where is the lesbian gossip about Jackie, and where are her lesbian fans? The conflation of the book *Valley of the Dolls* with the movie only exacerbates the deletion of lesbian visibility and desire from the camp key furnished for the Susann revival, as Tracey and Pokorny point out, as does the absence of *Once Is Not Enough*. Epperson's piece for *Interview* never acknowledges the book's lesbian love and the film's excision of it when Susann's phantom compares the novel *Valley of the Dolls* to the film: "The movie version was more liberated, with Anne ditching Lyon Burke for a walk in the New England woods" (Lypsinka 1997, 141). Susann famously loathed the movie version of *Valley of the Dolls*, however, as Seaman documents and both Barbara Parkins and Patty Duke confirmed (Duke and Turan 1987, 180; Seaman 1985, 3–4, 9; Seaman 1996c, 348–49). Besides the ending, the film undoubtedly cut out a deeply personal aspect for Susann: her affair with performer Carole Landis that inspired Jennifer North's lesbian backstory, and who, like Landis, commits suicide from an overdose of pills.[32] In all these respects Tracey and Pokorny's proposition that *Valley* was "more than camp" emerges as a call to take Susann and her novels seriously as well as to reassess camp, a call to question how liberatory and inclusive a sensibility it was.

The *New York Times* also provided an omen for this lesbian lacuna in its story reporting the "new Jacqueline Susann zeitgeist." With one fleeting mention of "lesbian sex" in *Valley of the Dolls*, the journalist neither takes notice of the popular lesbian storyline in *Once Is Not Enough* nor makes any links to biographical details about Susann, outed by Seaman and crucial to her lesbian fans. The *Times* writer quotes heavily from Sydney Pokorny and *Dead Jackie Susann Quarterly* at the top of the article, but never identifies Pokorny or *DJSQ* as lesbian, despite the zine's routine use of the word "dyke" and humorous, queerly sexual stories. The writer additionally fails to mention Pokorny's coauthorship with Tracey of *So You Want to Be a Lesbian?* in which they discuss Susann. And apart from one phrase about "gay men and lesbians" viewing Susann as a "diva of fiction," the narrative of Susann's fan-following traced in the article never forges ties between queer women fans such as Pokorny with other fans identified: the many men exemplifying "core gay fans," whose testimonies and images fill the piece; and feminist fans such as poet Lynn Crosbie, who valorize Susann for "'saying something serious about women's lives'" (Carvajal 1997, 23–24). The promotional discourse for the Jackie Susann revival parlayed the gay male camp reception of Susann into the interpretive key for mainstream readers to access Susann's *Valley of the Dolls*, a gay camp *clef* that virtually erased lesbian readers and pleasures from view. The reception of Jacqueline Susann and her work—from early devotees such as Carol Bjorkman and Liz Smith to Sydney Pokorny, Liz Tracey, Leslie Singer, and Traci Lynn—indeed illuminated the path toward what Horn (2017) terms "seeing lesbians" in the history of camp, even if the official Susann revival failed to see the light.

5

The Laugh Machine

Telling the Jacqueline Susann Story

The Jacqueline Susann revival of the late 1990s was as much about tell-ing the novelist's life story as it was about reinstalling her novels—*Valley of the Dolls* in particular—in popular culture. Camp delight in Susann's work trumpeted by queer tastemakers entwined with the revelation of Susann's own personal history and its subversion of the typical star biography, which Mary Desjardins illuminates, "is offered for consump-tion as a success story to be imitated with a celebration of capitalist culture" (Desjardins 2015, 233). Susann surely presented herself as a role model for female success in the 1960s and early 1970s, a self-made, pros-perous, and glamorous career woman as well as a font of advice on sex, marriage, and show business. Despite a succession of record-breaking bestsellers, though, Susann remained for many the personification of vulgarity and unruly femininity, disqualified from cultural legitimacy let alone being a subject for historical appreciation. Biographer Barbara Seaman testified to "the frequency with which I was required to defend my choice of a subject. . . . Jackie was still held in derision by a significant portion of the American public. . . . I had selected a topic which proved unerringly controversial" (Seaman 1996c, 11). Although the Susann revival replaced such contemptuous perceptions with camp celebration, the stream of biographical dramatizations incited by the author's come-back still had to negotiate the challenges of Susann's "success story," the author's provocation "to be imitated," and her complicated relationship to "capitalist culture." Throughout the Susann revival, the repetition of gossipy nuggets about the author congealed into what Steven Cohan calls a "bio-persona" (2017, 532), one particularly resistant to the typical

star story of success, redemption, and legacy, and evident in every dramatization of Susann's life: the made-for-TV adaptation of Seaman's
biography, *Scandalous Me: The Jacqueline Susann Story* (USA, December 9,
1998); the Hollywood biopic *Isn't She Great* (Bergman, 2000); and the
theatrical bio-plays *Paper Doll* (Mark Hampton and Barbara Zitwer, 2001)
and *See How Beautiful I Am* (Paul Minx, 2001).

Susann's bio-persona coincided with some of the terms of the celebrity "success story," such as the rise to fame, scandal-fueled downfall
for heightened "authenticity," recovery and triumphant comeback, but
inevitably chafed on the assumed conditions founding traditional star
biographies: the celebrity's "raw," "natural" talent; beautiful or at least
functional body; and the star's ability to orchestrate these according to
social norms (Desjardins 2015, 191–92, 217). Michael DeAngelis adds "legacy" to this formula, the requirement "that the influence of the figure
extends into the future . . . across time and beyond death," an enduring
value that enables "redemption" and justifies the audience's identification (DeAngelis 2017, 582–83). Exposing Susann's private, closeted transgressions might have made the novelist more authentic, but the signs
of her success, including Jackie's camp personality, scandalous experiences, and gossipy novels, all undermined the normative arcs of redemption and legacy that rendered the fallen star deserving of renewed "mass
love."[1] The features of Susann's bio-persona simply failed to redeem her
according to conventional standards: the voracious desire for fame,
the litany of feuds with celebrities, drug use, profanity, illness, familial
dysfunction, closeted queerness and Jewishness, flamboyant wigs and
fashion choices, outrageous book promotion strategies, undeterred promiscuity; and perhaps, that refrigerator containing nothing but champagne, dog food, capers, and sedative suppositories. Susann's legacy, in
turn, warranted little by customary criteria to justify her redemption
and the public's identification: leaving a mark on postmodern feminism,
drag culture, camp film cults, the culture of celebrity scandal, the gossipy
roman à clef, and the commercial promotion of popular fiction.

Susann's life and work had no consistency outside of the reflexive
interplay of camp, gossip, and scandal, beginning with romans à clef that
divulged the outrageous behavior of celebrities, novels enjoyed as gossip
and that invited speculation about the author's sources and forbidden
forays. Susann's tales incessantly tempted the punitive threats of gossip

in both form—as "trash" literature—and content, as "true" stories about her own experiences. The confinement of the closet fueled a comedy of bad manners in the 1960s and 1970s, although it was only partially recognizable, but the retrospective view in the 1990s during Susann's revival reveled in Susann's closeted play through the biographical gossip that outed her. Seaman's *Lovely Me* shaped Susann's life as an ambiguously triumphant tragicomedy of bad manners in which the assertion of style served as a means of expression and concealment, the components of an elaborate masquerade in which Susann traded in telling and selling scandalous stories. As Seaman put it, "she 'showed them all,'" a statement of ironic triumph that also signifies, equally ironically, in terms of the "sleight-of-hand" Susann played with gossip and scandal (Seaman 1996c, 15, 460). Jackie Susann *did* show them all in her record-breaking "tell-all" bestsellers, but her genre provided an alibi, a disclaimer, lest the repercussions for her divulgences surfaced. She could relate her background as a prim Philadelphia girl who went to New York for a showbiz career when promoting *Valley of the Dolls*, about a prim New England girl who flees to New York for a showbiz career. She could also secretly draw from her own exploits to describe the sexual adventures of single girls like Ethel Evans in *The Love Machine*, and then give cautionary advice in interviews about the woman who "says yes" two nights in a row (Adams 1969, 90). And she could dedicate *Once Is Not Enough* to her father and then promote it as a book about "mental incest." And on top of all that, she could compare her writing to Flaubert, Hemingway, Fitzgerald, and Zola, repudiate "boring" modernist authors such as Nabokov and their "double-dome" critical apologists, and altogether assert the "good taste" of her writing.[2]

The creators of Susann biopics and plays had to negotiate the tension between star biography conventions and Susann's scandalous, newly popularized feminist and queer camp bio-persona. Susann's bio-persona proved for some "too much" in the classic terminology of camp, too deviant a challenge to the norms of celebrity biography across a range of media, in addition to the norms of gender, sexuality, and taste expected of "great" figures worthy of biography. The reflexivity of Susann's bio-persona, in turn, rendered her in camp "quotation marks," borrowing Sontag's expression, firmly, and comedically fixed in an echo chamber of gossip, scandal, and performance. The signs of all these obstacles soon surfaced, along with portents of limited marketability. The made-for-TV *Scandalous Me* relocated from CBS to the lesser-viewed basic cable network USA, followed by the resounding flop of *Isn't She Great* in movie theaters and the fate of Hampton and Zitwer's Broadway-bound *Paper Doll*, which never made it. The diminutive scale of Paul Minx's one-woman, one-act monologue *See How Beautiful I Am*, which originated at the 2001 Edinburgh Fringe Festival starring Debora Weston as Susann, signaled a narrower but enduring appeal in a critically acclaimed run in London, but the 2008 revival at the New York International Fringe Festival met with critical disfavor that reflected dwindling interest in Susann.

Susann's feminist camp, compounded by her queerly scandalous life, vulgarity, and success as a writer of gossipy romans à clef, confounded conventional knowledge about talent and literature, in addition to exacerbating what Cohan observes as a common thread in films about Marilyn Monroe, "an underlying anxiety about female agency that motivates the constant retelling of Monroe's story—and our culture's obsession with it—and that still informs the complexity and currency of her bio-persona" (Cohan 2017, 532). That treatments of Monroe's life and other women celebrities such as Jean Harlow concealed their ability to perform comedy signaled both a struggle over women's agency and the determinants of narrative economy, the turn to tragic melodramatic tropes of manipulation and victimization (Cohan 2017, 534). Susann's bio-persona arrived, however, with a built-in resistance to such controls. The 1990s revival narratives had already turned Susann's life into a self-conscious comedy about taste, gender, and sexuality that revolved around gossip, scandal, masquerade, and concealment; a comedy in which Susann's agency, the signs of her success, and reasons for both her redemption and legacy remained fixed in ambiguity and ambivalence, an excess that the Susann biographies wrangled with to contain.

The repetition of Susann's bio-persona throughout two films and two plays bears many consistencies, yet each star bio devises a different stylistic solution to the "problem" Susann poses as a biographical subject. "Divergent renderings of a human life," Patricia Meyer Spacks informs, "may each contain its own truth. The truth they contain, however, like that of gossip, belongs partly to the creating sensibility" (1985, 120). Signs of the "creating sensibility" in each Susann biography surface through the interplay among camp and the comedy of bad manners, the tenets of star biography, and the power relationships of gossip. The "attitude" that each Susann story takes to the author arises in how these plays and films negotiate Susann's ornery resistance to the celebrity biography's normative conceptions of success, legacy, redemption, and identification.[3] The basic cable TV movie *Scandalous Me* sneakily insinuates camp cues into an otherwise dramatic story about Jackie, her relationships to Irving and her girlfriends, particularly Bea Cole, in addition to her perpetual sorrow over her son Guy, unresolved feelings for her father, and struggle with breast cancer. The film finally establishes Susann's legacy in terms of her feminist and queer significance as well as her impact on the publishing industry. Universal Studios' glossy star vehicle *Isn't She Great* develops a comedy of manners about show business centered on Jackie's desire for "mass love," Irving's adoration of her, and their ensuing intrusion into the literary establishment. The one-woman play *See How Beautiful I Am* consists of Jackie's spirit, out of the closet and clad in Pucci, reviewing her life with unrestrained candor in an extended cocktail party confession staged in her room at Doctor's Hospital, alongside her bedridden, still body drifting into death. Directly addressing the audience, Jackie also acts out scenes from her life and fantasies, between her and a host of entities from Ethel Merman to God. The two-act comedy *Paper Doll* reimagines Jackie's final days as she pens a fictional fourth novel and centers on larger-than-life Jackie and Irving, their outsized personalities and devoted yet pragmatic and polyamorous relationship. Similar to *See How Beautiful I Am*, the main couple break the fourth wall to strike an intimate and self-aware relationship with the audience.

According to the conventional criteria of star biography, Susann remained a failure: as naturally talented, conventionally beautiful, intrinsically deserving, or appropriately contrite. In a life constructed through gossip and scandal, partial truths, numerous disguises and some facial work, cut short by addiction and disease, together with an unlikely, ambiguous triumph as the record-breaking, best-selling author of "dirty" books—drawn from her own experiences, no less—Susann's stardom shined through, as drag queen Lurleen put it in 1997, "sheer force." Susann's scandal-ridden life was ripe with story material that provided a rich source for camp comedy, but she presented an improbable, irrepressible subject for star biography.

Queasy Realism: Comedy, Bad Manners, and Narrativizing the Susann Bio-Persona

At the conclusion of Paul Minx's *See How Beautiful I Am*, after a Pucci-clad Jackie has divulged her deepest secrets, imparted a plethora of dirty one-liners, and haggled with God for a place in Heaven and a Pulitzer Prize for her final book *Dolores*, she lets loose a stream of sick jokes: "'80% of a good death is just showing up.' [pause] 'After you die your fingernails keep growing. It's the phone calls that taper off.' [pause] 'Death is the biggest kick of all. That's why they save it for the end.' Sorry, I couldn't resist." Suddenly discovering a party next door, she asks the audience, referring to her makeup, "What do you think? Too much?" After a pause, Jackie bids the room goodbye with an appeal to her legacy: "Don't forget me!" (Minx 2018, 31–32).[4] Minx's play both incorporates the conventional terms of star biography and subverts them, cutting to the heart of what is at stake—Jackie's legacy—without pandering to the usual conditions for such longevity: repentance, abject suffering, recovery, and natural talent. In the terms of the comedy of bad manners, of course, Jackie's assertion of style—to the literal end of her life and the play—makes her the winner. She cannot beat death, however, so she meets her demise looking fabulous and cocked for celebration. Insulated by ironic camp humor, Susann's last words posit an admission of vulnerability, that her legacy is in the audience's hands now, and although she maintains her agency in the form of style, she must depart to attend another soiree. Minx's Jackie is surely memorable for her unrestrained vulgarity and the sleazy realism that she injects into the star bio formula, qualities that in the play's view justify her endurance as a fabulous failure. *See How Beautiful I Am* is a play about coping with multiple kinds of failure through performance, but when the vehicle for performing—the body—falters, a hopelessness arises that can only be compensated for by fantasy and laughter: Jackie's animated performance next to her virtually lifeless body.

Minx turns star biography inside out in *See How Beautiful I Am*, the most extreme of the Susann bios in its jarring, tragicomic swerves, and by far the bleakest portrayal of the four discussed here in terms of refusing to straightforwardly ennoble Susann or sentimentalize her life. Enlisting camp parody as a deconstructive tool, Minx's Jackie collapses biography with gossip and conflates subjectivity with style. Casting Susann as the

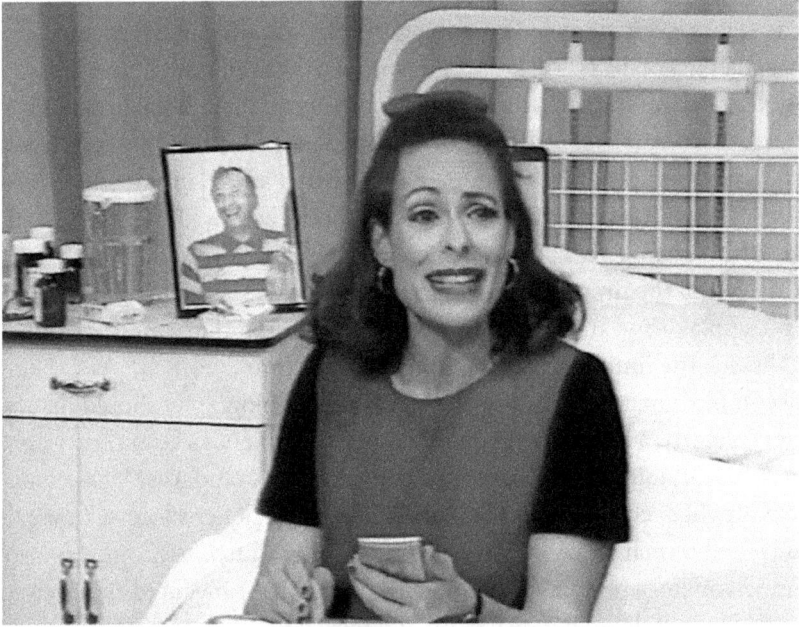

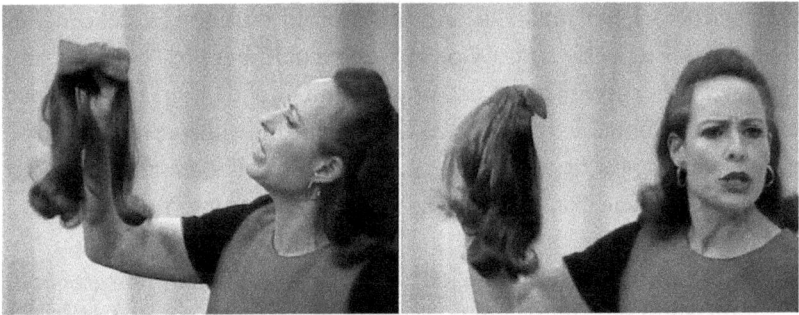

Alone in her hospital room next to her near-lifeless body, Paul Minx's Jackie
Susann (Debora Weston, in the 2001 Tambar production) spills the beans on
her messy life, and among her many routines, enlists her hairpiece to replay
the restroom showdown between Helen and Neely in *Valley of the Dolls*.

flamboyant gossip of her own life, her divulgences persistently test the
tenets of star biography, such as when Jackie spills the beans about Merman: "But Ethel was my first real taste of the only thing worth having in
life: fame. . . . I really loved her for it. And I'm not talking about the way
you love your pet poodle. I'm talking real love. The kind of love straight
men fantasize about. Pussy-eating dykes" (Minx 2018, 6). Minx raises

the stakes, even more, by organizing the play around Susann facing "the inevitability of death," in DeAngelis's words, the event that in star biography challenges the construction of a compelling, unpredictable narrative (DeAngelis 2017, 582). Minx confronts the narrative fact of death from the start, positing fantasy, comedy, vulgarity, and glamor as the only recourses. Susann the historical subject faces death with humor, whose power to change reality presents concrete limits. "The best thing about cancer's all the drugs you get to take," Jackie jokes at her first reference in the play to years of coping with illness, a line that simultaneously calls out the limitations of humor and dolls (Minx 2018, 4). As for her accomplishments—which in the terms of star biography should justify her celebrity, a biography about her, and the audience's attention—they remain dubious at best based on conventional standards. Jackie enumerates her achievements throughout the play, but her successes appear unseemly, such as when she informs Johnny Carson (whom she also impersonates), "I created the modern best seller. I invented the housewife who put down her dish cloth and picked up a vibrator" (Minx 2018, 23). Just before her final exit and the morbid outburst of death jokes that precede it, Jackie voices God's assessment of her life: "Let's see. You slept with over 500 men, an unknown number of women and . . . Coco Chanel. You bought the chopped liver then told the guests you made it. [pause] But you tipped the garbage men at Christmas. You gave your mother a fur coat. You made Irving's life have meaning. You swallowed. But what really tips the scales is . . . you made an effort with your lipstick" (Minx 2018, 30). Jackie's God, of course, recodes her transgressions through camp sensibility and Jewish humor, treating moral seriousness and mortality as child's play, such as Freud's example of the death-row inmate who, on the Monday of his execution, comments, "Well, this is a good beginning to the week" (Freud 1963, 263).

Illness, the precursor to death, offers no platform for Minx's Jackie to redeem herself with nobility, self-sacrifice, or creating "great" art, which further disputes the legitimacy of her legacy in the typical terms of star biography. When Jackie explains the relationship between illness, image, and success, what might be an inspiring epiphany or a dramatic turning point in a traditional bio turns into vulgar wisecracking, self-promotion, and sick humor that manifest cynicism and egoism rather than enlightenment:

Fame and sickness don't mix. . . . Don't you get it? Friends are to
drink cocktails with, not stand sobbing around a hospital bed. I
wasn't put on this planet to make mascara run. Life should be a
party. Laughs and champagne. Vomit and cancer, yeah it exists.
Who cares? The truth, fine, but only if it's beautiful. The world
should remember Jackie Susann as the famous writer always got
the extra turn on the merry-go-round. Not as some sad loser with
one tit who has a retard for a son and a husband with zero sex
appeal. There are winners and losers in this life. And I am definitely
one of the winners. Losers scare me. They always have. I don't
want them around. (Minx 2018, 25)

In pronouncing her credo about "winners," "losers," and "beauty," and
speaking in the language of so many of Susann's characters, Minx's Jackie
simultaneously resists the star biography's oppressive mandate for success and yet also adheres to its corrupt value system.

Each of the biographical dramatizations touches on Susann's insight
into performing herself as the "beautiful" "winner" through the concealment of illness, all as a means of selling her "sexy" romans à clef, but as
Desjardins explains, "focus on the failed body" in star biography further
undermines the normative demand for successful "subjecthood" (Desjardins 2015, 192, 233). The Jackie of *Isn't She Great*, for instance, tells one
character who discovers her secreted cancer, "I am not sick! Sick people
are *losers*! Sick people get *nothing*! Do you think anyone is going to buy
a sexy book written by someone with cancer?" (Rudnick 1998, 71). The
bifurcation of Jackie Susann into "sick loser" and "healthy winner" also
follows in the pattern of "doubling" that Cohan locates in Hollywood
"backstudio" films about troubled movie stars, a device that emphasizes
"the fractured psyches created by the Hollywood machine" and often
serves as a device for structuring these narratives (Cohan 2017, 528,
536–37).

Hampton and Zitwer's *Paper Doll* determinedly reconstitutes the
doubled "Jacqueline Susann" as fabulous performer, consistent with
the bio-persona concretized during the late 1990s Susann revival, a
strategy that serves to unify the fragmented Jackie into a coherent and
able-bodied biographical subject. The Jackie of *Paper Doll* initially defines
the double, not in terms of concealing illness but in distinguishing her

celebrity self. Breaking the fourth wall, Jackie explains to the audience: "I've been Jackie Susann and I've been 'Jacqueline Susann' and honey—if they only knew. . . . The fabulousness of fame is a very well-kept secret" (Hampton and Zitwer 2001, II-6). After gossip leaks about her cancer, a fictional event fabricated by the playwrights, Jackie reconfigures her doubling in terms of healthy versus sick; before people knew about her illness, she confides to Irving, they "looked at me the way they look at *Jacqueline Susann*. That's what kept her alive," but due to public awareness of her cancer, "Jacqueline Susann is dead," and as she subsequently declares, continuing to speak about herself in the third person, "You're talking about Jacqueline Susann. Irving, I can't be her anymore" (Hampton and Zitwer 2001, II-10, II-24). Less isolated than Minx's Jackie, who is physically alone on stage (apart from her silent, bedridden body) as well as self-exiled from both Irving and her son Guy by her code of "winners" and "losers," the Jackie of *Paper Doll* receives encouragement from Irving, her young lover Jesús, and a woman fan, and through dramatic fantasy, an extension. After a newspaper reports her death, the play flashes back to 1969 amid the exhilarating hoopla over *The Love Machine*. Jackie transforms back into the flamboyant, "healthy" *Jacqueline Susann*, planning the book release party—to which she and Irving invite the audience—and the promotional tour with the pink "Love Machine" plane, finally blurting out exuberantly to the audience, "Are we great, or what?" (Hampton and Zitwer 2001, II-31).

Paper Doll additionally maneuvers Jackie's sleazy realism toward an escapist, comedic function rather than the disruptive force it produces in *See How Beautiful I Am*. Jackie flaunts her sleazy realism as the defining characteristic of her persona from the first line of *Paper Doll*, spoken directly to the audience in the midst of hitting writer's block: "Okay. I'll give anybody a blowjob who can give me an ending. I'd offer to make you breakfast but I don't cook" (Hampton and Zitwer 2001, I-3). All the excitement about *The Love Machine* at the conclusion of the play spurs Jackie to tell Irving a dirty joke that she attributes to the Jewish comedian Belle Barth, and which helps draw the piece to closure. The joke, about a man attending a Rita Hayworth movie with a peckish chicken in his pants and two women with popcorn sitting next to him, turns into vaudeville shtick when Irving joins in, having heard it scores of times before. Following the phallic punchline, Jackie blurts out (ostensibly to the audience), "Do I embarrass you? Please tell your friends!" The two set off for a party and the play ends (Hampton and Zitwer 2001, 11-33).[5] Minx likewise milks Susann's sleazy realism to the end, but to underscore Jackie's doubling as well as subvert the normative celebrity biography treatment.

Both *See How Beautiful I Am* and *Paper Doll* close with tasteless jokes that confirm the continuity of Jackie Susann—her vulgarity—as well as the doubling of Jackie Susann, based on the division of the healthy celebrity and sick civilian. Each play also concludes with Jackie asking spectators if they approve of her vulgarity—"Too much?" questions Minx's Jackie, "Do I embarrass you?" inquires Jackie in *Paper Doll*; and each Jackie next engages in self-promotion—"Don't forget me!" and "Please tell your friends!"; finally, Jackie departs in both plays for a celebration. Minx's glamorous Jackie leaves behind her corpse with her legacy, a lifelessness that punctuates her doubleness and flamboyant exit, as Minx describes in the stage directions following Jackie's departure to the party: "The hospital overheads dim, leaving only the body illuminated. This light eventually goes out too" (Minx 2018, 32). Hampton and Zitwer sustain the fantasy of "Jacqueline Susann," by contrast, resorting to a flashback that seals the ideality, permanence, and seamlessness of Jackie's performance as "Jacqueline" in addition to her camaraderie with Irving as friend and business partner. And where illness and death cast their shadow over all of Jackie's antic confessions and bawdy blue humor in *See How Beautiful I Am*, *Paper Doll* delays airing the reality of Jackie's illness until Act II, which enables the fun and fortune of the fantasy "Jacqueline Susann" to endure unimpeded for most of the play's action. Vulgarity, flamboyance, death, and the desire for "mass love" motivate Minx's Jackie, for whom a fatalistic sleazy realism is the norm, but they fail to contain her ambiguities or heal her fragmentation. In *Paper Doll*, vulgarity and flamboyance provide a refuge from death for Jackie and the audience for more than half the play. Both plays end ambiguously, but the ambivalence about performance and doubling in *See How Beautiful I Am* persists in a way that will not displace or obscure the sick body, nor will it define Susann's life as a comedy or a tragedy. The comedy of bad manners subsists in *Paper Doll* and, following Jackie's dirty joke, provides a happy ending preserving the fantasy construct of the healthy, glamorous, and performative "Jacqueline Susann."

Michele Gallery organizes the teleplay for *Scandalous Me*, adapted
from Seaman's *Lovely Me*, around the doubled Jacqueline Susann and the
secrets that enforce this fragmentation: her sickness, in addition to her
autistic son and feelings about her father. Vulgarity permeates Jackie, as in
the other three star bios, although in *Scandalous Me* this aligns with conventional TV biopic melodrama and a relatively restrained, realistic performance by Michele Lee as Jackie. *Scandalous Me* presents itself, though, as
a doubled star biography in which camp serves to ironize the conservative
conventions of the TV biopic, through citations of the movie version of
Valley of the Dolls interspersed throughout the film as well as other reflexive, intertextual cues. The opening sequence establishes this doubling
of tones and selves with a suggestion of sleazy realism. As Tom Jones's
"She's a Lady" charges the soundtrack, a close-up reveals Jackie's red high
heels strutting along the swimming pool at (we soon learn) the Beverly
Hills Hotel circa 1974, sexy onlookers craning their necks and returning
stares of admiration and desire. A medium shot in the classic tradition
of the male gaze captures Jackie's long, thin legs with her poodle Josephine in a red bow trotting alongside her.[6] Jackie's voiceover commences,
establishing her "place in history" alongside Cleopatra, Mata Hari, and
Marilyn Monroe as one of the "women who understood the power of
sex." She wittily links this, first to her identity and then to her ambiguous
success: "Scandalous me: I am Jacqueline Susann. . . . The critics don't
appreciate me, but I've sold so many books, I'm running a close second
to the Bible. Can you believe it? Me and God on the same best-seller list!"
The sequence eventually transitions to Susann's bungalow, where in the
privacy of her room she addresses the accusations of being "vulgar" and
"untalented" as well as identifies the means of her "survival": keeping a
diary, as her mother advised, to house her "secrets" without telling anyone. The camera ultimately captures a number of wig heads followed by
a shot of Jackie in front of the bathroom mirror, staring at herself, as she
removes her wig to reveal her bald head: "That's one secret," her voiceover divulges, and thrusting the film forward she informs us, "There are
more." Speaking directly to the viewer through voiceover during her silent
unmasking establishes intimacy and, in addition to citing the source of all
of the gossip to follow—Susann's diaries, which Seaman had access to for
her research—establishes the structure of the forthcoming narrative and
its affective contours: the funny, beautiful, flamboyant, and successful

Jackie in public; and in private, the serious, dramatic image of "failure," as terminally ill, mother of an autistic son, daughter with unresolved oedipal trauma, unfaithful wife, and drug addict.

Not surprisingly for a TV movie, *Scandalous Me* hews closely to biopic conventions at the same time as offering, in Desjardins's words, "a sympathetic look at female gender roles in flux" (Desjardins 2015, 219). Women indeed fill many creative roles on the film, with Michele Lee not only starring but also executive producing, future coauthor of *Paper Doll* Barbara Zitwer as coexecutive producer, in addition to Michele Gallery's teleplay (Gallery had written for the sitcom Rhoda [CBS 1974–78], surely a kindred Jewish "single girl" to Susann). It is in that sympathy for Jackie's defiance of gender norms that the film comes closest to incorporating feminist camp and sleazy realism as well as further dramatizing Susann's doubling. The opening sequence, for instance, cites camp cues immediately with the retro strains of Tom Jones, a figure of the 1990s sixties revival, accompanying Jackie's initial procession.[7] Jackie's camp personality further shines, in her strut by the pool and, before returning to her bungalow, when she and Josie sit in the swanky Polo Lounge, the hotel dining room; Jackie hollers to the maître d'hôtel, "Henry, it's colder than the Tin Man's ass in here! Turn the damn air conditioning off!"[8] These comedic moments of flamboyance are soon countered in Jackie's bathroom when she removes her wig, a shock that also unavoidably recalls one of the iconic, camp scenes from *Valley of the Dolls*, Neely's removal of Helen's wig during their restroom wrangling. Numerous references to the film *Valley of the Dolls* follow, including Ethel Merman's line, redolent of Helen Lawson, amid one of Jackie's rowdy ruckuses: "Too much booze and dope don't cut it with me, Jackie. . . . Irving, get your crazy dyke wife offa me." As Helen tells Neely in the infamous powder-room scene from *Valley*, leading up to their brawl, "They drummed you out of Hollywood, so you came crawling back to Broadway. Well, Broadway doesn't go for booze and dope. Now get out of my way. I got a guy waiting for me." To which Neely replies, "Well, that's a change from the fags you're usually stuck with!" (Kingsley 1967, 114). Barbara Parkins, who played Anne Welles in *Valley of the Dolls*, appears in *Scandalous Me* as Susann's literary agent Annie Laurie Williams, a casting choice that culminates when Annie Laurie joins Jackie for a visit to the movie set of *Valley of the Dolls*; about to shoot the wig scene, Annie Laurie inquires, "Where is Barbara Parkins?"

Lest these appear as mere in-jokes, *Scandalous Me* inserts references to the film *Valley of the Dolls* at key dramatic points, such as Jackie's own startling revelation in the opening sequence, that italicize their significance simultaneous to undercutting the clichés of TV movies and biopics. The "Theme from *Valley of the Dolls*" underscores central plot turns, such as when Jackie first discovers the desire to write her freshman book *Every Night, Josephine!* on a visit to her mother in Philadelphia, and when she gets the inspiration to create *Valley of the Dolls*. *Scandalous Me* emphasizes the importance of the Philadelphia scene additionally by costuming Jackie in an outfit almost identical to the beige Travilla ensemble worn by Anne/Parkins in her initial New York scenes in *Valley*. As the sequence continues, after her mother gives Jackie the impetus to write *Josephine!* and with the *Valley* theme still playing, Jackie contemplatively strolls down a quaint Philadelphia block holding a stick and letting it knock against the white picket fence, her actions mimicking Anne/Parkins in the last scene of *Valley of the Dolls* that Jacqueline Susann despised but the film's cult fans adored. Although the camp effect of *Scandalous Me* could be viewed as undermining the authority of these scenes, as reviewers David Bianculi (1998) of the *New York Daily News* and Ray Richmond (1998) of *Variety* complained, promotional pieces indicated that the citations of *Valley of the Dolls* were deliberately and meaningfully ironic. Michele Lee's commentary on Susann's "pre-feminist" strength complemented her comparison of Jackie to postmodern feminist icon Madonna, and Lee revealed her sense of self-reflexive humor in the casting of Barbara Parkins and securing Lypsinka's attendance at the movie premiere in full Susann drag (Bark 1998; Werts 1998, B31; Lubenski 1998; Smith 1998).

Alongside its camp cues legible to knowing fans of Susann and *Valley of the Dolls*, *Scandalous Me* remains entrenched in conventional biopic conventions, fashioning a recovery arc of sorts enabling Jackie to redeem herself as wife, daughter, friend, and mother, followed by not one but two speeches establishing Jacqueline Susann's legacy. Adherence to social and genre conventions surely guide the film toward redeeming Susann, rendering her sympathetic, and clarifying her legacy, but both the recovery arc and the legacy statements coincide with the film's own doubling as conventional made-for-TV movie and camp-cult tribute. In the recovery/redemption arc, Jackie atones for her selfishly one-sided

The spirit of camp framed the premier of Michele Lee's *Scandalous Me: The Jacqueline Susann Story*. Guests included Susann's friends Liz Smith, Rex Reed, and Helen Gurley Brown, and as Smith noted, "the fabulous cross-dresser Lypsinka, who arrived in full Jackie S. drag," and who "laughed when somebody commented to him, 'Jackie would be so happy to see you . . . she finally looks feminine!'"

Before she wrote *Valley of the Dolls*,

Jacqueline Susann
lived it.

MICHELE LEE in
"SCANDALOUS ME:
THE JACQUELINE SUSANN STORY"

USA
NETWORK

Wed, December 9 at 9PM/8C

relationship with her closest girlfriend Bea Cole (Sherry Miller), musters the courage to face her unresolved father issues and guilt over her son Guy, and supports her endlessly self-sacrificing husband Irving (Peter Riegert). These redemptive acts occur in the last ten minutes of the film to ingrain Susann's worthiness of celebrity as well as rationalize the TV audience's attention, and further, to provide motivation for her legacy statements. First, amid an argument with Irving instigated by Jackie, she initially blames him for thinking, "there's something wrong with me inside" that caused Guy's autism, and then she realizes, "I wanted him to love me, I wanted him to be proud. I wanted my father to be proud." The next sequence delivers the news that, as Jackie puts it, "Time's up"; her cancer has spread, but Jackie remains determined to aid Bea for her charity event by appearing as the guest of honor, because "Bea's been there for me since day one." Just before Jackie makes her entrance at the fancy fundraiser, Bea informs Jackie that they raised $300,000, and Jackie's mother Rose (Goldie Semple) observes that her daughter is wearing the pin Jackie's late father gave her. Introducing Jackie at Bea's charity function, Rex Reed (Ben Bass) delivers the first legacy speech by putting a humorous spin on Gloria Steinem's scathing review of *Valley of the Dolls*, which had asserted, "Compared to Miss Susann, Harold Robbins writes like Proust" (Steinem 1966, 11). Reed remarks that "all she did was write her books, and they weren't *Remembrances of Things Past* by Proust. . . . Her voice resonated with all people, no matter their social station, sexual preference or walk of life." Building on the allusion to Steinem's review, Reed proceeds: "Jacqueline Susann was going to change the publishing world and Gloria Steinem was the first one to see it." Mentioning that Steinem would have delivered a speech that night "but we couldn't guarantee her safety," Reed grins mischievously over to Jackie. The last dramatic sequence shows Jackie soberly facing the truth of her impending death, communicating this to Irving, and paying Guy one last visit before she dies. When next Jackie goes to see her girlfriends, the Hockey Club, for the final time, Irving's voiceover delivers another legacy statement, virtually verbatim from Seaman's epilogue: "Jackie changed the face of book publishing, taking power from the critics and giving it to authors," and, "Jackie explored the emerging themes of the 1960s—the drug culture, the acceptance of homosexuality, the changing aspirations of women" (Seaman 1996c, 459).

Causality and structure here are noteworthy, with a steady continuity from redemption to legacy: confronting her unresolved relationships as daughter and mother, facing her responsibilities as girlfriend and wife, and finally braving death with fortitude, forgiving, and a sense of self-sacrifice, all of which justify the final statements about Jacqueline Susann's accomplishments and contributions. Jackie's redemption could easily be viewed as affirming the need to be a better mother, wife, and daughter, with her husband Irving enlisted for a closing endorsement of Jacqueline Susann's significance. Far from the camp tragicomedy of Minx's Jackie, whose value the audience must assess based on the evidence of her outrageous confession, or the charming camp fantasy about Jackie and Irving that Hampton and Zitwer concoct, Lee and company's Jackie ascends as a figure worthy of star biography, although the justification for honoring Susann heralds accomplishments most appreciable according to the historical and cultural criteria of feminists and queer people. Reed's and Irving's declarations might stem from the generic and conventionally patriarchal norms of biopics but they iterate Jackie's queer and feminist legacy, despite the fact that Bea Cole might have been a better symbolic choice than Irving to voice the words of Susann's feminist biographer Barbara Seaman.

If *Scandalous Me* revolves around a doubled protagonist whose play between personas provides the substance of the story, the film itself endeavors to engage a form of doubling: as conventional TV movie biopic, centered on women, confirming family values; and also as closeted camp biography, slyly addressed to cult fans, feminists, and queers. The legacy statements bring out this last dimension and frame the feminist "creating sensibility" of *Scandalous Me* by explicating Susann's appeal to "all people, no matter their social station, sexual preference, or walk of life," and with respect to her books' themes, "the acceptance of homosexuality, the changing aspirations of women," ironically emphasized by referencing Susann's early detractor, the future feminist icon Gloria Steinem. *Scandalous Me* offers itself as camp, but unlike *Paper Doll* and *See How Beautiful I Am*, takes no chances with the slippage between "important" and "frivolous" that camp might engender. Jackie Susann is important to women and queers, constituencies the film validates, in addition to influencing the publishing industry. If Minx's Jackie must remind us, "Don't forget me," and Jackie in *Paper Doll* coaxes the audience to "Please tell your friends," Lee and Gallery's Jackie emerges, doubled by both her secrets and the layering of camp and TV biopic, as an established historical figure, remembered and researched.

Isn't She Great remains entrenched in a conflicted "creating sensibility" regarding the queer and feminist construction of Jackie Susann, complicated to begin with by the creators' limited access to biographical material based on the source optioned for adaptation (Feil 2017, 556–57). Desjardins speaks to the conditions that inform a creator's access to the biographical subject, everything from opportunities for examining personal documents to legal issues such as threats of litigation and copyrights on a celebrity's creative property, all of which impose limits on how the star biography depicts its subject (Desjardins 2015, 220). Desjardins's example of two Karen Carpenter biopics centers on the repressive relationship between granting rights to creative material and the social, political, and cultural perspectives guiding the treatment of Karen Carpenter's life, especially the reasons behind her illness and the Carpenter family's relationships (Desjardins 2015, 220–30). In the case of *Isn't She Great*, the choice to option Michael Korda's diminutive 1995 *New Yorker* article "Wasn't She Great?" rather than Barbara Seaman's extensive tome *Lovely Me* necessitated reducing Susann's life to a situational comedy of manners and effacing her queer experiences. From Seaman's perspective, bypassing her biography for Korda's involved an "operational old boys network" taking advantage of a "feminist" writer, especially when the screenplay for *Isn't She Great* smuggled a potpourri of details about Jackie and Irving from *Lovely Me* (Seaman 2000; Rudnick 1998).[9] If *Isn't She Great* swiped from Seaman's biography, one conspicuous absence was queer subject matter. Seaman remains the sole biographical source for these claims, which she developed through her access to Susann's diaries and letters as well as interviews with Susann's friends and colleagues, and which constituted one of her driving research hypotheses. The producers of *Isn't She Great* might have stinted Seaman, but they also barred themselves from access to material integral to Susann's personal life, relationships, creative work, and economically speaking, a component of her bio-persona dear to Susann's contemporary fanbase.[10] Squeezing out Seaman the feminist also meant eliminating Susann the polyamorous bisexual.

Isn't She Great consequently pales in depicting the queerness of Jacqueline Susann, despite its R rating, by contrast to all of the other bio treatments. *Scandalous Me* navigated the institutional self-censorship of made-for-TV movies by suggesting Jackie's bisexuality through dialogue as well as a sultry kiss she shares with a television actress during Susann's days of pitching for Schiffli Lace. The unpublished 2001 script for *Paper Doll* contains one queer reference that relies heavily on coded camp suggestion when Jackie recounts, "*I was in love*. With Ethel Merman." Jackie's dialogue commences to queer her infatuation with Merman by way of quoting the premiere camp line in *The Wizard of Oz*: "Jackie, you're not in Philadelphia anymore" (Hampton and Zitwer 2001, I-53). A review for a 2003 production of *Paper Doll* suggests that the play added a queer interlude, referring to a scene in which a female fan kisses Jackie (Taylor 2003, 35). And in *See How Beautiful I Am*, Minx illuminates Susann's bisexuality through explicit lines such as her disclosures about Merman and Coco Chanel in addition to, "I'd go out with my Irving . . . and my boyfriends . . . and all the gals. When you're bi, the world is your sexual oyster. I had a revolving door on my bedroom and a hat check in the hall" (Minx 2018, 15). Consistent with Jackie's camp bio-persona, such dialogue redeems Susann's queer legacy at the same time as undercutting the traditional terms of star biography.

Isn't She Great strikes a particularly cautious attitude in the portrayal of Susann's bio-persona, in particular the use of the doubling trope and depiction of her failed body with respect to gender and sexuality, vulgarity and illness. Rudnick constructs *Isn't She Great* as a romantic comedy of manners organized around four areas: Jackie (Bette Midler) lusting for fame and asserting her sense of entitlement; her vulgarity, chutzpah, and lack of talent; her relationship with "prissy" Michael Hastings (David Hyde Peirce), editor for *Valley of the Dolls* and Jackie's most resistant reader; and her relationship with Irving Mansfield (Nathan Lane), which transpires as a business deal between star and manager and a marriage between husband and wife. The film redeems Jackie as a figure for identification and establishes her legacy by transforming the characteristics of "loser" and talentless vulgarian into a winning, irresistible style. Allowing glimpses of her tragic struggles with their son Guy and bout with cancer, as well as a quick reveal of Jackie's seamy affair—*prior* to marrying Irving—with a comedian named Maury (John Larroquette), the film bypasses gossip about the mistress of gossip narratives. The film instead establishes the contrast between Jackie's real life and the books she writes, rather than the continuity between them portrayed in the other star bios. This also results in reducing Jackie's doubling to a plot device for winning over her loudest detractor, book editor Hastings. The weight and burden of secrets conveyed in the three other Jackie bios, particularly *Scandalous Me* and *See How Beautiful I Am*, remain barely visible in *Isn't She Great*, so the need to hide the truth, the activity that doubles Jackie overall in the other bios, never really transpires.

Courting Jackie with a lovely dinner at Lindy's, a location central to the musical *Guys and Dolls* (an adaptation of two Damon Runyon stories), Irving's rose-tinted view comically clashes with Jackie's brassy demeanor and profane vocabulary, such as when Irving insists that she was "Too classy" for Maury the comic, Jackie's ex-lover and Irving's former client (Rudnick 1998, 9). Jackie nevertheless despairs over her stalled career and, during a timid attempt at suicide in a Central Park pond, mentions among her reasons a failed acting career and the fact that "Maury didn't want me." Irving pleads with her, "I want you. . . . As a woman . . . and a client"; Jackie then explains that what she wants "is what everybody wants . . . to be famous. World famous." Moments later, Irving woos her with the promise, "I want—I want to make you *so famous*" (Rudnick 1998, 12–13). Rudnick takes this one step further, casting Irving as the force inciting Jackie's authorial career, the only star bio treatment of Susann to credit Mansfield for motivating Susann's writing. Depressed over institutionalizing Guy on top of her failure as an actress, Jackie tells Irving and her actress friend Florence (Stockard Channing) that their love is not enough, that she requires "mass love"—a key term in *Valley of the Dolls*—whereupon Flo attempts to encourage her with the reassuring advice, and the film's tagline, "Talent isn't everything" (Rudnick 1998, 30; Susann 1997c, 114, 268, 269).

When she finally pens *Valley of the Dolls*, the Jackie of *Isn't She Great* assumes the mantle of the outwardly directed gossip rather than the confessional gossip, a compromise that cleanses Jackie's persona without sacrificing her vulgarity. When Irving urges Jackie to become a "world famous writer" by drawing from her experience, the speech that follows seals Susann as the gossipy author of *Valley of the Dolls* in addition to drawing a line between what she "knows about" and what she does: "All I know about is show business. All I know about are people fucking their way into the movies, popping pills and ending up in the gutter.

Similar to Mark Hampton and Barbara Zitwer's portrayal of Susann in *Paper Doll*, Paul Rudnick renders Jackie (Bette Midler) a Runyonesque Auntie Mame whose doubling as sick and healthy is healed through lowbrow love—Irving (Nathan Lane) and her friend Flo (Stockard Channing)—and highbrow, her editor Michael Hastings (David Hyde Pierce).

All I know about are aging stars, hopeful whores and cheap studs. All I know about are tits, ass and the truth. And nobody writes books about that" (Rudnick 1998, 33). The line that follows from Florence flags Jackie's role as observer rather than participant: "You wouldn't—use real names, would you?" (Rudnick 1998, 33A). Only Florence implicates herself in the showbiz debauchery Jackie lists, and the biopic gives little reason to assume that Jackie lived the experiences of her characters. If, as Seaman accounted, "Jackie had always used the casting couch to further her thwarted ambitions and to 'stay in the game,' as she put it" (Seaman 1996c, 14), the sordid affair in *Isn't She Great* with Maury the comedian—clearly based on Jackie's affairs with Eddie Cantor and Joe E. Lewis—sends the crestfallen Jackie into isolation, not further fornication, a career tailspin and not "fucking [her] way into the movies, popping pills and ending up in the gutter." In the montage that follows of Jackie writing *Valley of the Dolls* and seeking Irving's feedback, she therefore maintains a safe remove from the litany of dirty activities she catalogs, including when Irving asks her what she means by an "unspeakable sexual act"; "Up the butt," she replies amid typing (Rudnick 1998, 35).

To achieve the ultimate victory of taste and style as the hero of this comedy of manners, Jackie must win over other fans besides Irving and Flo to demonstrate that her deviance is unthreatening, and to redeem her. Recruiting highbrow book editor Michael Hastings to her side marks a crucial victory of taste that, narratively speaking, justifies the "mass love" to come. Michael is presented as the stand-in for the author of the film's source, Michael Korda, whose *New Yorker* piece relates his experience at Simon and Schuster editing *The Love Machine* with Susann. Rudnick's Hastings more closely resembles, however, the editor from Bernard Geis Associates assigned to *Valley of the Dolls*, Don Preston, his key role in Susann's career described in great detail in *Lovely Me* (Seaman 2000; Seaman 1996c, 287–90, 296–99). Michael provides the concrete foil of traditional taste in Jackie's comedy of bad manners, alternately evoking highbrow detractors such as Bernard Rosenberg and John Simon: "prissy," "traditional," "Ivy League," someone who views "pop culture" as "vulgar and dangerous" and who considers himself "a guardian of fine literature and old world values" (Rudnick 1998, 42). Offended by Jackie's "illiterate garbage" and unable to overhaul *Valley of the Dolls* with her amid the ballyhoo of Jackie's Broadway enclave, Michael sequesters Jackie at his Connecticut family home with Irving and Josie accompanying her, Michael's parents and grandma Mimsy their hosts. The culture clash is immediate, from the austere colonial decor of the Hastings home to Jackie's first sight of Michael's patrician mother: "She gave birth?" (Rudnick 1998, 59–62). The sequence proceeds with Michael's family siding with Jackie in the view of the world she exposes in *Valley*, signaling the normality of scandalous behavior and dispelling any shame in Jackie's vulgarity. Michael first insists on cutting Jennifer's backstory about her boarding school relationship with Maria—"Right. The dyke," interjects Jackie. Claiming that it is implausible, Michael's critique withers when Jackie appeals to, not her own experiences but those of grandma Mimsy and Michael's Aunt Abigail, who wax nostalgic about their erotic girls school crushes (Rudnick 1998, 65–66). In the next scene, Mimsy verifies another plot detail that Michael objects to as preposterous: Jennifer's willingness to have sex with Tony because of his looks and lovemaking prowess and despite his dull-wittedness. Michael's father then announces, after devouring the manuscript, his own approval of Jackie's "immoral brazen journey into the unspeakable hell of modern show business . . . I *am* Lyon Burke" (Rudnick 1998, 67).

Winning Michael over finally requires, not his cultural approval but his realization of Jackie's cancer and agreement to keep her illness a secret, the event that closes the Connecticut sequence. As Michael fetches bags from the empty guest room for the drive back to New York, Irving and Josie waiting outside at the car, Jackie's makeup case unfastens to reveal not cosmetics but numerous bottles of prescription drugs that betray her illness. Upon discovering Michael, Jackie pleads (quoted in full earlier), "Do you think anyone is going to buy a sexy book written by someone with cancer?" Establishing they are "friends," and that "friends *don't tell*," Michael agrees to keep mum, and when Irving honks the car horn, Jackie seals their alliance with a racy joke about fornication: "We're coming! We're having sex!" (Rudnick 1998, 71). The "prissy," "Ivy League" Michael now unites with Jackie, repairing the doubling—that is, reconciling the parts of Jackie cleaved by her secrets—that the other biographies depict as agonizing. At the conclusion of the film, Jackie on her death bed, Michael visits her in the hospital; reading her a telegram from the British publishers of *Once Is Not Enough*, who demand to cut the word "fuck," Jackie replies, "Dear England, Fuck you. Love, Jackie Susann" (Rudnick 1998, 121). Michael smiles warmly, clutches Jackie's hand, and the image freezes, leading to Irving's closing voiceover and final confirmation, "Wasn't she great?" (124).[11] Apart from Irving's idealized affirmation, though, Michael's approval practically assures Jackie's ultimate victory: in the comedy of manners, as a tastemaker whose success encompasses the triumph of her style; and in the biopic, as an unthreatening subject. That Rudnick's doubled Jackie is "only" concealing her illness and son Guy, as opposed to—as Minx's Jackie, playing God, puts it—sleeping "with over 500 men an unknown number of women and . . . Coco Chanel," the Jackie of *Isn't She Great* embodies a kind of tasteful, palatable vulgarity; she is also innocent, loveable, and vulnerable, signified by the prissy highbrow Michael turning into friend, confidant, and champion.

It is worth saying that portrayals of Susann's experiences editing *Valley of the Dolls* in *Scandalous Me* and *See How Beautiful I Am* are not quite so quaint as in *Isn't She Great*, although they do function to underscore Jackie's virtues as a hard worker and thick-skinned showbiz veteran. In *Scandalous Me*, editor Don Preston calls *Valley* "unpublishable trash," but he grows to respect Jackie's work ethic ("You never quit, do you?") as well as betrays his curiosity about the real-world models for Jackie's characters ("Is Helen Lawson Ethel Merman?"). Although *Scandalous Me* voices cultural approval for Jackie through the figure of culture critic Rex Reed, the film never endeavors to reconcile high and low so directly and completely as in *Isn't She Great*, whose mission remains to render Jackie ultimately adorable and easily assimilable in the effort to redeem her worthiness of celebrity, identification, and cultural immortality. Minx portrays Don Preston most severely, as a cruelly pompous taskmaster; of course, the portrayal remains biased because Jackie impersonates Preston, who calls her "a thoroughly amateurish writer. . . . It must be comforting to be so completely talent free" (Minx 2018, 20–21). When she tells him that "God must be punishing me for something," Preston replies, "He is. Crimes against literature. I sentence you to another rewrite" (Minx 2018, 21).[12] And when Jackie confides to Preston her existential motives for becoming a famous writer—"So I don't disappear. If I'm not famous, I'm invisible"—Preston replies, "If you want to be famous so bad, do something else. Go kill someone. I'm sure you've got enough enemies. Bang! You'll be famous and I'll be free" (Minx 2018, 22). And where the sequence in *Isn't She Great* at Michael's family home justifies Jackie's cultural inclusion through the approval of his WASPy, upper-class and accepting family, Minx's Jackie must resort to self-promoting herself to the audience: "People used to say Don Preston made that book, but it was me. All me. . . . *Every Night, Josephine! Valley of the Dolls. The Love Machine. Once Is Not Enough.* Words are something society values. Those books are in libraries. Right alongside Shakespeare. Dickens. They were the soap-opera kings of their day. Who does the world remember? Don Preston or me?" (Minx 2018, 22). By contrast to Rudnick's Jackie, who breezily charms characters such as Michael and his family into embracing her vulgarity, Minx's Jackie remains a pugilistic raconteur who punches out stories to prevent being "invisible" and to manage her secrets, someone striving to finally assure the audience of her cultural value and repair her fragmentation. She wins the contest of style by ascending to celebrity but never receives the approval, let alone loving friendship, of highbrows such as Preston, nor does she achieve the magical reconciliation of high and low that Michael's affection suggests in *Isn't She Great*. Jackie must make the postmodern push on her own according to Minx, by referring to Shakespeare and Dickens as "the soap-opera kings of their day," a line paraphrased from Susann's interview with *Harper's* magazine (Davidson 1969, 70).

Isn't She Great doubles Jackie through her closeted sickness, but Rudnick's portrayal stresses her unity through being adorably vulgar and untalented, compensating for and perhaps cancelling out her deception and secrecy. Although Michael redeems Jackie for her cultural reception, Irving ultimately redeems Jackie's heteronormativity, through his adoration and their heterosexual romance, no matter how qualified it might be by the artist/manager dynamic. Their marriage lacks any hint of the reputed nonmonogamy of their real-life counterparts, which normalizes Jackie without the interference of scandal that would dispute this image. When Irving asks at the end of the film, "Wasn't she great?" he *seems* to be putting the question of Jackie Susann's legacy in the audience's hands, similar to the conclusions of *Paper Doll* and *See How Beautiful I Am*; however, this time it is a purely rhetorical question. *Isn't She Great* strives to concretize and valorize Jackie's loveable unruliness so many times that, when Irving utters the last line it arrives as an affirmation. Repeating the film's title at the end, and in the past tense, seals Jackie's legacy by conveying Irving's enduring love. This extends to heterosexualizing the recovery/redemption motif; Jackie's suffering over her autistic son Guy and her cancer redeem her humanity, but only when her marriage falters does the narrative require a grand gesture from Jackie. After Irving leaves Jackie, feeling eclipsed by her fame, Jackie renews her business relationship with him as well as their matrimonial vows in a replay of the earlier scene in Central Park: "Irving," she asks, "will you—will you be my agent?" (Rudnick 1998, 108). The agony Jackie experiences in *Scandalous Me* and which, in *See How Beautiful I Am*, she conveys through dirty jokes, monstrous confessions and salty repartee—about her parents, son, Irving, disease, love affairs, and addiction—disappears for the most part in *Isn't She Great*, along with the scandalous behavior associated with it. Rudnick's is a happy Jackie, untainted by anything "sordid," as Nathan Lane described Seaman's treatment of Susann in *Lovely Me* amid promotion for *Isn't She Great* (*Charlie Rose*).

Although Barbara Seaman optimistically proclaimed in 1996, "The culture is catching up with a woman who was frankly and fiercely ambitious, often 'kitsch,' and sometimes tacky, a woman who had attitude" (1996c, 11), it would appear by virtue of the fate of Susann's dramatized biographies that the author still remained a few stretches ahead. *Isn't She Great* tanked at the box office and received lukewarm to hostile reviews, including accusing the filmmakers of cribbing from Seaman and erasing Susann's bisexuality (Jacobs 1998; Bartell 2000, 17; Covington 2000; Durbin 2000, 1, 28; Judell 2000). *Paper Doll* never reached Broadway, and *Scandalous Me* fell off the pop culture radar. *See How Beautiful I Am* fared well in its intimate venue at London's Bush Theatre, ranked one of "The Five Best Plays in London" by the *Independent* in 2001, "as uplifting as it is hilarious" (Taylor 2003; Koenig 2001). Its New York reception seven years later met a cooler response, the *New York Times* classifying it as "lounge-act vulgar" with an "unlikable" depiction of Susann, sentiments concurred by the *Village Voice* (Gates 2008: E6; Soloski 2008, 38).

Jacqueline Susann persists as a resistant subject for star biography. Irreparably doubled, confoundingly performative, and fixed in an echo chamber of gossip and scandal, her undeniable success runs alongside a host of failures not the least of which continues to be her messy personification of "womanhood" and culture. While *Scandalous Me* impresses Susann's legacy according to TV-biopic conventions, camp irony unsettles those conventions as much as the queer evidence of Susann's success challenges the typical terms for cultural legacy. *See How Beautiful I Am* demystifies star biography and celebrity in toto: first, by portraying Jackie as the antihero of a tragicomedy of bad manners in which flamboyantly vulgar style signals an ambiguous victory; and at last, by requiring spectators to adjudicate on Susann's legacy based on the proof of Jackie's messy, performative testimony. Alternately funny, sick, and tragic, Lee and Gallery's *Scandalous Me* and Minx's *See How Beautiful I Am* convey Jacqueline Susann's feminist and queer unruliness, albeit quite differently, as social subject and the stuff of celebrity biography. Their portrayals of the author's failures—vulgarity, sleazy realism, bad manners, and camp humor—mark her style, found her redemption, and charge the subversiveness of Jackie's "success" story.

Conclusion

Sleazy Summaries and Camp Positions

Lee Daniels, Carrie Fisher, and the Legacy of the Susann Sensibility

Dead Jackie Susann Quarterly once proclaimed their namesake "the true prophetess of fin de sicle [*sic*] mass media," whose "Cassandra-like gifts of foresight" predicted the centrality of gossip and scandal to celebrity culture and popular storytelling, particularly for narrating the lives of women and queers (Pokorny and Tracey 1995a). Susann understood the appeal of celebrity and scandal, and even more, how the protective, playful closet of fiction maximized that appeal. Maneuvering the roman à clef made it possible for Susann to tell scandalous stories through a sleazy realism that subverted aesthetic norms and challenged social conventions, and it enlivened a gossipy guessing game requiring readers' involvement, not just to recognize which celebrities were being portrayed but also which Hollywood films were being recycled, revised, and parodied. Susann surely portrays the lives of women and queer people as scandal stories that invoked the voyeuristic, moralistic dimensions of both gossip and social melodrama; however, the ironies driving Susann's project run rampant: intermingling gossip and confession; dismantling the closet in story content yet reconstructing it through narrative logic; humanizing and making fun of unruly women, homosexuals, and gender nonconformists; pinpointing the painful, patriarchal conditions of women's experience as well as enabling women to laugh at them. These ironies charge Susann's commandeering of the roman à clef and fuel her sleazy realism; they pertain to the pleasures as well as the limitations of Susann's work in her own era, and they contribute to the new camp pleasures brimming in Susann's work.

Since the camp reception of *Valley of the Dolls* and the 1990s revival, the "Susann sensibility" has materialized through what the *Washington Post* called in 2001 the author's literary "triumph of trash over taste," in addition to Susann's flamboyant female performance expressive of drag (Stuever 2001, C2).[1] And consistent with the 1990s revival, taste-makers visibly asserting the Susann sensibility tended to reflect two groups, straight white women and white gay men. The gay camp aesthetic of *Pee-wee's Playhouse* (CBS, 1986–90) included, for instance, the titular "sissy boy" awakening in one episode to the exhortation, "Sparkle, Pee-wee, sparkle!" (November 3, 1990).[2] During the initial wave of the Susann revival, the author's most salient fan constituencies converged with Darren Star and Michael Patrick King's television sitcom adaptation of Candace Bushnell's *Sex and the City*, a gossipy, confessional comic novel about single career women in New York City exploring sex, money, and Manhattan. As Deborah Jermyn points out, "critics . . . were quick to ponder whether Star and King's sexuality (both men are gay) was also responsible for imparting a particularly queer sensibility on the show" (2009, 25). This is especially evident in the show's homages to Jacqueline Susann. An early season-one episode titled "Valley of the Twenty-Something Guys" (June 28, 1998) likens sex with younger men to drug use, but it is "The Baby Shower" (August 9, 1998) that concretizes the thematic allusions to Susann. A former star of the downtown party scene, Laney (Dana Wheeler-Nicholson), now miserably married and pregnant, admonishes her single, career-minded girlfriends Carrie (Sarah Jessica Parker), Miranda (Cynthia Nixon), Charlotte (Kristin Davis), and Samantha (Kim Cattrall): "At some point you have to get serious and settle down. I mean, life is not a Jacqueline Susann novel. Four friends looking for life and love in the big city." Laney's tone of superiority and the envy that oozes underneath confirm the Susann-ian design for living she diminishes—women's professional advancement, sex, fashion, partying—and which structures the sitcom.[3]

Amenable to outright comedy, camp allusion, and the pleasures of melodrama, the Susann sensibility surfaces most apparently in contemporary adaptations of Susann's work: Rae Lawrence's 2001 "swimming pool novel" *Jacqueline Susann's Shadow of the Dolls*, the official sequel spun from Susann's notes; and Ryan Field's 2010 gay erotic parody, *Valley of the Dudes*. Each author relates a sincere story inspired by Susann's urtext sprinkled with reflexive camp references to their source novel. Rae Lawrence (a pseudonym for Ruth Liebmann) underplayed camp to the *Washington Post*, commenting, "There's too much to say about the idea of camp, and I don't feel like even looking at it that way." . . . "Camp is a bubble. If you breathe on it or look at it too hard, it explodes. It's four-inch, orange, cork-soled platform sandals: I don't want to think about them, I just want to have them" (Stuever 2001, C2). Lawrence nevertheless plants reflexive camp nods to the original novel and film as well as Susann's persona: an offhanded observation about "a drag queen in Los Angeles who makes a pretty good living out of imitating Jennifer North," and a mention of Anne's favorite lipstick color, "Barely Pink" (Lawrence 2001, 235, 299). Most elaborately, Lawrence concludes the sequel with a clever variation on Susann's original ending, in which Anne downs dolls having just spied her husband Lyon's philandering in their bedroom. *Shadow of the Dolls* likewise closes on Anne in bed taking dolls, but with one modification: "Nothing bothered her anymore. She felt as calm as a sleeping animal. She had gotten what she wanted: peace of mind. Two baby dolls a day was all it took. Terry was a big man, he needed three. They took them together, just before bed" (Lawrence 2001, 305). Lawrence's ironic twist on Susann's conclusion returns Anne to the marital bedroom setting equally opiated, now alongside her husband, in addition to mimicking Susann's vocabulary and phrasing. The line, "She felt as calm as a sleeping animal" reworks Susann's opening to *Valley of the Dolls*, following the famous prose poem prologue, in which the author describes New York during a heat wave as "an angry concrete animal" (Susann 1997c, 5). By contrast to Lawrence, Field forthrightly considers *Valley of the Dudes* "a gay erotic romance parody," signified by repeating key camp moments such as the Neely-Helen wig scene, here played between two rival male stars fighting over a toupee (Field 2010, 2, 209–13). Field nonetheless pays tribute to Susann's import in the history of the sexual revolution and the gay liberation movement as well as expresses the need to give his gay characters the "happy ending" usually denied them (Field 2010, 1–3).

When celebrities such as Candace Bushnell, Kathy Griffin, and Andy Cohen cite Susann or *Valley of the Dolls*, they clearly mean to illuminate their taste through camp sensibility and style. Citing Susann can legitimate and confer coherence on a creative sensibility, such as when Bushnell reflected to *New York* magazine in 2003 on the genesis of her novel *Sex and the City* (1997): "When I was eight years old, I said, 'I will live in New York and be one of those women like Jackie Susann and Helen Gurley Brown' . . . I knew my fate. I'm like a character in one of my books" (Ginsberg 2003, 16). Bushnell wraps herself in a "single girl" literary tradition now ironized in postmodern feminist camp as a component of her creative vision, whereas Griffin and Cohen engage the forthrightly queer, feminist camp dimensions of Susann and *Valley of the Dolls*. The Bravo network television producer and talk show host Cohen approximates a latter-day Rex Reed through his role as camp cultural commentator and clearly asserts a gay camp gaze in his diaries of celebrity ephemera, overtly inspired by Andy Warhol. One entry observes, for instance, that Sarah Jessica Parker "appeared looking very Jackie Susann in a Mary Katrantzou dress," and another refers to Lee Daniels's TV drama *Empire* (Fox, 2015–20) as "an updated *Valley of the Dolls*" (Cohen 2016, 17, 146). The first citation of Susann draws attention to the similarity between Mary Katrantzou and Pucci as much as it reflects Parker's star image, forged playing Bushnell's fabulously dressed alter ego on *Sex and the City*. Comparing Daniels's *Empire* to *Valley of the Dolls* draws attention to the gay sensibility shared by Daniels and Cohen in addition to the tropes of Susann's novels that reverberate in *Empire*. Cohen's references to Susann and *Valley* furthermore reveal influences on the producer's *Real Housewives* reality show franchise, from the focus on independent, aging women comparable to Judith Austin in *The Love Machine* and Dee Granger in *Once Is Not Enough* to shocking scenes of female misbehavior reminiscent of Neely and Helen in *Valley of the Dolls*.

"D-List" comedian Kathy Griffin likewise conjures *Valley of the Dolls* in her memoirs, now specifically to illuminate her particular comedic sensibility of gossip and female failure. Mizejewski deliberates over the link between pretty/funny and success/failure as well as tasteful/vulgar in the comedy of Griffin and evokes a kindred spirit to Jacqueline Susann. Griffin's demystification of celebrity and glamour involves gossip, which nourishes the comedian's cocktail of ridicule and self-deprecation regarding "gender failure," "failure at mainstream stardom" and "heterosexuality itself," garnished by the knowledge that all these forms of failure are "funnier and more interesting than success" (Mizejewski 2014, 31). Mizejewski extends this chain of failure to Griffin's "vulgar language," "camp," "queer politics," and star "gossip" (35, 52, 55–56). A logic emerges shared by Griffin and Susann in which vulgar femininity remains a sign of failure worthy of gossip and a cue for women to embrace "gender failure," appropriate vulgarity, defy (and defile) "pretty," and wield the creative power of "funny."

Recounting a "celebrity run-in" with Barbara Walters in "the bathroom at *The View*," Griffin confesses, "When I replay this scene in my head, it's eerily similar to the bathroom scene in *Valley of the Dolls*. (I admit I do go back and forth on which of us gets to be Neely O'Hara and Helen Lawson. Please submit your answers to www.KathyGriffin.com.)" (Griffin 2016, 261–62). Griffin's badinage echoes in the annals of female camp and comedy, invoking not only Neely and Helen in *Valley* but also Joan Rivers's classic jest, "I'd love to put Barbara Walters and Jacqueline Susann in the same room and see which one came out alive," a joke that Walters admits in a 1971 *Cosmopolitan* article led to her friendship with Rivers. As Walters put it in the language of failure for her female readers, "You're only human, though, and there are times when it's a strain to be civilized" (Walters 1971, 126). Griffin's play on this "strain to be civilized," especially for women in show business, reaches pitch-perfect clarity by conjuring Helen and Neely's brawl in *Valley of the Dolls*. Griffin's comedy blurs the line with gossip just as Susann muddied gossip and fiction, but the *Valley* reference flags her feminist camp awareness, addresses her loyal gay fans, and embraces what Susann deflected, the likeness to drag queens.

The rest of this chapter focuses on two more media artists who tapped into *Valley of the Dolls* to surpass as well as refashion the Susann sensibility. Carrie Fisher's screenplays for *Postcards from the Edge* (1990) and *These Old Broads* (2001), and Lee Daniels's TV drama *Star* (Fox, 2016–19) invoke gay, white, male camp traditions through homages to *Valley of the Dolls*, but each revises the commercial camp formula that hardened during the Susann revival.[4] Fisher's and Daniels's camp applications of *Valley* furthermore validate and reward groups of fans not usually commended or illuminated in either popular culture or white, gay male camp. Fisher's *films à clef* revise the camp of *Valley of the Dolls* by inscribing space for elderly women as camp practitioners and agents to perform their sexuality and gender both ridiculously and fabulously, and, to perform for each other as well as gay male audiences. Fisher adheres to the format and generic tone of the comedy of bad manners, which now includes the incorporation of her family's messy experiences, and presents elderly celebrity divas as victors whose vulgar style vanquishes all obstacles.[5]

Daniels enlists *Valley of the Dolls* to challenge the presumed divide between "serious" art and camp in addition to the imagined border between gay camp and Black popular cultural practices. Daniels establishes an intertextual chain of camp texts connected to *Valley of the Dolls* that prioritizes the performance of gender and sexuality but, to paraphrase Racquel J. Gates, also "highlights the specifically racialized nature of these dynamics" (Gates 2018, 18). In the face of what Gates refers to as "respectability politics on network television" (2018, 34), *Star* spotlights Black female and gender-nonconforming performativity, centralizes the cultural impact of "negative" Black texts such as *The Real Housewives of Atlanta* within the narrative fabric of *Star*, and blends the sacred space of the Black church with the secular, sometimes profane spaces of Black popular culture. Daniels remains committed to an approach consistent with Susann's novels, though, in which sleazy realism bursts out unexpectedly and incongruously amid dramas fueled by both contemporary social problems such as racism and transphobia and the melodramatic conventions of backstage, showbiz narratives. Daniels's investment in African American, queer, and trans social politics as well as cultural politics, moreover, raises the stakes on his melodramatic narratives and uses of camp. Camp style bursts forth, motivated by Daniels's citation of *Valley of the Dolls* in his promotion of *Star* and through occasional references to the film on the show, imbued with the importance of both "hope" and "escape" as well as the intersectional goal to reconcile conflicting factions of Black cultural taste and identity.

Postcards from the Valley of the Broads

Carrie Fisher punctuated the film adaptation of her autobiographical novel *Postcards from the Edge* (Nichols, 1990) with a movie reference that conferred a camp modus operandi on her story of addiction and celebrity.[6] Toward the conclusion, Fisher's alter ego Suzanne Vale (Meryl Streep), a young movie star fresh out of rehab and making a comeback, locks horns with her mother Doris (Shirley MacLaine), a former Hollywood movie star. Their climactic argument airs a blend of familial and professional history that echoes Fisher's, her upbringing by mother Debbie Reynolds and the fallout from father Eddie Fisher's affair with Elizabeth Taylor. Following their quarrel, Suzanne nearly breaches her sobriety and Doris gets into a drunken car accident. In her mother's hospital room, paparazzi swarming down the hall with their cameras cocked and ready, Suzanne makes up with Doris—frail, her forehead bandaged and head bare, deprived of her wig and cosmetics—simultaneous to helping Doris reapply her makeup and restore her glamor. In a revision of Neely and Helen's powder room scene in *Valley of the Dolls*, Doris wraps her head in a scarf—as Helen does in *Valley* after losing her wig—dons her fur, and meets the press, followed by Suzanne. Marveling in her mother's rebound, Suzanne runs into the same doctor who just weeks before had pumped her stomach and sent her get well flowers, and who now asks the actress out on a movie date. Suzanne kids, "Okay. We could go see *Valley of the Dolls*," an homage that reveals the punning proximity between "Suzanne Vale" and Susann's *Valley*.

Fisher positions herself here in the late author's legacy as innovator of the roman à clef—now film à clef—its comedy of gossip, and its alluring play with truth and fiction. Commentators have traced Jacqueline Susann's legacy to novelist Jackie Collins, who drew from scandalous Hollywood figures and escapades, and Collins extended that lineage to Carrie Fisher when she hailed the novel *Postcards from the Edge* as "a sharply irreverent, deliciously witty trip through Hollywood-land," a recommendation emblazoned on ads and the paperback.[7] A *New York Times* article about the upcoming film version characterized the novel according to the low reputation of the celebrity roman à clef and its formula, calling *Postcards* "a kind of literate trash novel" and an "at least-autobiographical book [that] charted the chemical, sexual and emotional obsessions of a frantic, wisecracking 30-year old Hollywood actress" (Linfield 1990, H15). Fisher forthrightly drew from her experience of Hollywood stardom, drug addiction, and institutionalization, and the first part of her novel echoes with Susann's scenes of Neely O'Hara in rehab, but Fisher largely bypassed the "guessing game" for the rest of the characters. Just briefly revealing Suzanne's movie star mother Doris, other celebrities and industry *machers* circulating in the novel only signify as vaguely recognizable composites of Tinseltown denizens (Fisher 1987, 176–77). Fisher embraced the conventions of the roman à clef for the film adaptation, though, which sharpened the clarity of her real-life models and, in the spirit of the guessing game, overtly teased audiences to speculate about "who's who."

Magnifying the role of Suzanne's aging celebrity mother in the film adaptation and crafting tight causality among plotlines about Suzanne's recovery, professional comeback, and rocky relationship with Doris, Fisher defined *Postcards* as a film à clef about her Hollywood family, and, a comedy of manners about navigating Hollywood society. Although Fisher voiced concerns to the *New York Times* about audiences making assumptions that could embarrass her family (Linfield 1990, H15), this could only fan the fire of speculation. As Roger Ebert confirmed in his review, Fisher's adaptation "turns into a comedy of manners," "a domestic show-biz comedy that plays up the mother-daughter rivalry," and a movie "preoccupied with gossip; we're encouraged to wonder how many parallels there are between the Streep and MacLaine characters and their originals, Fisher and Debbie Reynolds" (Ebert 1990). If *Postcards* is "preoccupied with gossip," it also marvels in the art and style of concealment consistent with the comedy of manners; when Suzanne witnesses Doris's ability to face the reporters in the hospital scene, she concludes with admiration, "We're designed more for public than for private."[8]

Fisher amplified these tactics a decade later for the TV movie she cowrote with Elaine Pope as a gift to her mother, Shirley MacLaine, and Elizabeth Taylor, *These Old Broads* (Diamond, ABC, February 12, 2001). A comedy about three aged movie stars making a comeback on TV, Fisher enlists the materials of the Susann-styled celebrity roman à clef—star gossip and personal confession—to configure her elder divas through feminist camp, drag humor, and the comedy of bad manners, as well as the camp genres of "woman's film" and "backstudio picture" crystallized in *Valley of the Dolls*. The TV movie involves the efforts of filmmaker Wesley Westbourne (Jonathan Silverman) to reunite the aging stars of a recently rediscovered Hollywood musical, *Boy Crazy*, for a network TV special. Despite the scandalous secrets and rancor among the divas, who include Wesley's adopted mother Kate Westbourne (MacLaine), Piper Grayson (Reynolds), and Addie Holden (Joan Collins), their longtime agent Beryl Mason (Taylor) finally leverages a deal. In the course of the harried production, catfights ensue generated by age-old rivalries over men and career, in addition to airing their scandalous secrets, such as prim Piper's disclosure that she had a clandestine affair with the director whom Addie and Kate were competing over, and Kate's earthshaking revelation to her son and costars that she secretly bore Wesley as a single mother and then sustained the charade that she adopted him for the sake of her movie career.

Fisher's version of the Susann guessing game, bad manners comedy, and camp self-parody remain central attractions of *These Old Broads*. A piece in the *New York Times* opens, for instance, describing a scene involving Reynolds's and Taylor's characters discussing what sounds like the home-breaking affair between Taylor and Eddie Fisher, Reynolds's then-husband and Carrie Fisher's father. "It's fact. It's fiction. It's 'These Old Broads,'" the article announces, a film that "makes every effort to blur fact and fiction" (Weinraub 2000, E1, E5). Soon after, Joan Collins articulates the intersection of film à clef with self-parodic comedy: "We all send each other up. This is a camp pastiche. Very naughty, very close to the mark" (Weinraub 2000, E1).[9] The *Los Angeles Times* hints at the comedy of bad manners unifying all these elements: "Tonight's reunion of these living legends is made even more remarkable by the jokes Taylor's and Reynolds' characters swap about a man named 'Freddie Hunter' who had come between them years earlier. Where it gets just a little strange is that the jokes—some referring to Freddie's sexual prowess (or lack thereof) were penned by screenwriter Carrie Fisher. . . . Though Carrie Fisher, now 44, admits the amount of sex she included in her movie leaves her 'sort of mortified,' she couldn't resist the opportunity to exploit her family's rich history for laughs" (Keck 2001, F1). Contributing to the manners comedy as well as retrenching the film's camp address, Fisher fashions Wesley, her stand-in adult-child-of-a-celebrity, as a gay man, a detail that reviewers and columnists leave out.[10] Although Wesley's outing serves as a sensational plot point, this revelation pales in comparison to Kate's airing of her dreadful, scandalous secret.

The presence of gay culture and characters in the film prompts the amplification of camp and coincides with allusions to *Valley of the Dolls*. The climactic revelation of scandalous secrets explodes in the studio backlot, first propelled by Addie, who outs Wesley to Kate. When the oblivious Kate verifies this news with Wesley, she blurts out to her son that Wesley is her biological child. The sparks finally combust when Piper confesses to her affair with the same director over whom Addie and Kate have maintained a decades-long feud and who, Kate ultimately divulges, also happens to be Wesley's father. Addie tears off Piper's wig, Kate grabs the hairpiece and whips the two women with it, all of which begets an all-out brawl that closes down production on the TV special and only intensifies Wesley's alienation. The three divas consequently bury the hatchet, chiefly by bonding over their shared need for what Susann refers to as "love on a mass scale" in *Valley of the Dolls*: "We can't be ourselves unless we're in front of an audience!"

Their camp revelation of theatricality and performative identity propels the rest of the plot and explodes the tragic themes and misogynistic causality of backstudio pictures such as *Valley of the Dolls*. The protagonists and plots of these films, Steven Cohan explains, include "narcissistic, self-indulgent, has-been female stars crashing in a Hollywood that first created and now callously abandoned them," in storylines that "tended to vilify the studio system's female victim for her driving ambition, which is, in turn, portrayed as unhealthy and excessive, hence 'monstrous', female desiring" (2017, 529, 530). For the *Old Broads*, what was formerly coded as "narcissistic," "monstrous," "female desiring" for "mass love" now leads to the renewed determination of the divas to reunite Kate with Wesley as well as make their big comeback. They track down Wesley to a gay dance club where Kate and her son reconcile as Piper and Addie entertain an ecstatic audience with a rendition of "Get Happy."[11] The film establishes Addie, Piper, and Kate as self-aware of their camp value, as agents of their own self-parody, and when the women perform Judy Garland's signature "camp star turn" (Cohan 2005, 120–21), their gay fans' adoration confirms it, punctuated with one spectator cheering, "I dressed like you for Halloween!" The reference to Garland coalesces numerous themes and cultural citations, from her impact on the backstudio genre and role as camp icon to her connection with *Valley of the Dolls* (Cohan 2005, 285; Cohan 2017, 529–30). Recycling her own life story, family dramas, and Hollywood scandal, Fisher's film à clef combines with what cast member Joan Collins calls "camp pastiche" as well as the comedy of bad manners to satirize a cluster of sexual norms, gender roles, and conventions of motherhood alongside the particulars of celebrity, Hollywood, and its treatment of women.

Fisher's films à clef echo the movie version of *Valley of the Dolls* in their replays of feuding, malfunctioning female celebrities, along with other tropes of "failure" such as elder divas reliant on gay male admirers, and of course, the excessive style of glamorous femininity. Closer to Susann's novel, though, Fisher cues identification with the failure of pretty and routinely invests it with value: elder women appropriating vulgarity as a means of acquiring power and fomenting community. Although E. Ann Kaplan detects in *Postcards from the Edge* "constructs of sad, aging stars, forced to take a back seat" (Kaplan 2003, 240), something akin to Flinn's "'aging diva' phenomenon" in the context of camp (Flinn 1999, 444), Fisher's version of this trope nevertheless underscores the empowering irony of female failure, and in *These Old Broads*, positions the elderly stars center stage and laughing. At the film's finale, their television performance, as Piper, Kate, and Addie belt about their "crazy, wacky, loony, tacky . . . fabulous life," the primary gaze of joy that greets them belongs to their agent Beryl, the fourth "old broad" played by Elizabeth Taylor, cackling in the studio audience. "Failure loves company," ponders Halberstam, company in which "all our failures combined might just be enough, if we practice them well, to bring down the winner" (Halberstam 2011, 120). Debbie Reynolds understood this when she gave Shirley MacLaine her blessing to portray her in *Postcards*: "The main thing about playing me is just to be funny" (Linfield 1990, H15). MacLaine echoed the sentiment a decade later when she gave Fisher license to parody her in *Broads*: "Look, if you want to make fun of all my New Age beliefs, then go right ahead—as long as they're funny jokes" (Keck 2001, F1). Through her comedic, camp lens, Fisher practices failure and foments a community of failure in *These Old Broads* that invokes identification with the "loser" as a means of redefining "winning." The "failures" of age, taste, gender, sexuality, and scandal transform, through the reflexive theatrics of gossip and self-parody, into a form of success that contradicts patriarchal Hollywood hegemony. Marshalling star gossip and genre reflexivity as well as reworking the camp tropes of the aging diva, Fisher embraces the camp dimensions of *Valley of the Dolls* and the film à clef to devise a comedy of bad manners celebrating the empowering irony of female failure, that funny far surpasses pretty in lifespan, style, and value.[12]

In *These Old Broads*, Fisher draws from personal history and Hollywood gossip to sculpt her three aging divas Piper (Debbie Reynolds), Kate (Shirley MacLaine), and Addie (Joan Collins), who brawl more furiously over a wig than Helen and Neely and perform the Garland number "Get Happy" at a gay club.

"Oh, you better quote *Valley of the Dolls*, bitch": Lee Daniels's *Star*

Although Lee Daniels could not secure the rights to produce a television adaptation of *Valley of the Dolls*, the media mogul nonetheless developed his Fox drama series *Star* with Susann's novel and the 1967 film version closely in mind (Gardner 2012). For the *Rotten Tomatoes* article titled "Lee Daniels on How *Star* Began as *Valley of the Dolls*," Daniels explained, "Because it lived in me a little bit about women and their struggles for fame in Hollywood. For me, it was about women and fame and people taking advantage of them, and also what these three girls would do to get to the top" (Topel 2016). *Star* traces the struggles faced by three aspiring girl group performers: the eponymous Star Davis (Jude Demorest), streetwise and blond, fleeing foster care and hell-bent on musical superstardom; her half sister Simone Davis Rivera (Brittany O'Grady), a recent escapee from an abusive foster home; and Star's friend Alexandra Crane Jones (Ryan Destiny), multitalented scion to music industry royalty (Naomi Campbell and Lenny Kravitz) determined to forge an independent music career. Equipped with peerless pipes and single-mindedness, they drive to Atlanta to seek the guidance of Carlotta Brown (Queen Latifah), an aging music business veteran who once performed with Star and Simone's deceased mother, now deeply religious and proprietor of the hair salon God's Blessings, which Carlotta runs with her trans daughter Cotton (Amiyah Scott) and gender-nonconforming stylist Miss Bruce (Miss Lawrence).

Debuting amid the fiftieth anniversary of *Valley of the Dolls* when the novel was being "Pitched to a New Generation," *Star* figured into an extensive *New York Times* article that included Daniels as one of the tastemakers maintaining the novel's legacy. The sole Black gay man among the elder gay aficionados whose views open the *Times* story, Daniels characterizes *Star* as "a little 'Valley of the Dolls,' a little 'Dreamgirls,' a little Supremes, a little bit of TLC and a little bit of me"; the article follows Daniels's statement with the quote, "'Valley' hits on all levels," attributed to Jonathan Adler, a gay interior designer and creator of the "Dolls" pillbox. Acknowledging the wide appeal of *Valley of the Dolls* yet also reproducing the implicit whiteness of gay culture, Adler proceeds to explain, "Canonical gay things tend to have tragic heroines, check; outré hair, check; glamour, check. And most importantly, that ineffable thing: camp" (Meltzer 2016). This celebration of *Valley*'s diverse camp appeal, that "'Valley' hits on all levels," ultimately enfolds Daniels's perceptions into the context of "canonical gay things," a "camp" aesthetic framework whose color-blind contents of "tragic heroines," "outré hair" and "glamour" reveals, to paraphrase Pamela Robertson Wojcik, "the degree to which camp is assumed to be white" (1996, 20). Andy Cohen conjures this power dynamic as well when encapsulating Daniels's *Empire* as "an updated *Valley of the Dolls*" (Cohen 2016, 146). These acts of liberal inclusion into the camp community via *Valley of the Dolls* nevertheless whitewash Daniels's appropriation of *Valley* and gay camp. Daniels engages in what David Gerstner observes in the work of Black queer male artists such as Bruce Nugent, James Baldwin, and Marlon Riggs: revising "the white aesthetics that purportedly infuse the terms for Black-queer cultural identity," and engaging in a "queer-pollination" of racialized and sexualized cultural territories, "resisting a fixation on concrete identities and desires" (Gerstner 2011, 5–6). Daniels's unofficial adaptation of *Valley of the Dolls* and quotations from the film upset the implicit whiteness in

Susann's novel and gay fanbase as well as the camp canon in which *Valley of the Dolls* resides. Daniels conveys a camp intertextual framework that diverges from and intersects with white gay culture, and simultaneously, spotlights alternate means of interpreting, enjoying, and creatively applying *Valley of the Dolls*.

Daniels also reconfigures television narrative norms, the conventional narrative patterns and realist styles of both comedy and drama, as far as they relate to Black queer and trans representation. Daniels first undermines what Alfred L. Martin Jr. refers to as the "generic closet" by never marginalizing Black queerness in finite story arcs structured around "detection," "discovery," and "discarding" (2021, 15). Although Martin concentrates on sitcoms whereas *Star* is a drama series, the significance of Daniels's camp approach pertains to Martin's assertion that "white gayness and black gayness create distinct possibilities for stories and jokes," and, in turn, "the belief system that Black homosexuality is absurd within the narrative universe" (Martin 2018, 223; Martin 2021, 107). Daniels incorporates a comedic camp aesthetic on *Star* usually associated with white gay TV comedy characters, as on *Will & Grace* and *Glee*, as well as white-cast TV dramas like *Dynasty*. Camp complements all the characters' tribulations on *Star*, enables humor, and functions variously to ironize the action, deflate stereotypes, punctuate the drama, and offer wish fulfillment. Camp occasionally provides comic relief in a narrative universe that juggles a variety of melodramatic absurdities, but it also resides in the show's stories about social struggle to enable bonds among the characters and nourish liberatory perspectives.

Daniels enlists the camp, trashy reputation of *Valley of the Dolls* among other movies, television, and music groups to make *Star* a "negative" text, applying Gates's term. "Negative texts" are positioned at a "distance from normative, white hegemonic standards of quality," and they "signify on white hegemonic as well as black hegemonic norms . . . in a mode that is markedly different from their positive counterparts, one that is often embedded with troublesome performances and politics that obscure the more subversive work in which they are engaged" (Gates 2018, 17, 20). *Star* signifies on Daniels's own celebrated TV drama *Empire*, which Gates assesses as "a positive text masquerading as a negative one," "a show that gets to play at being ratchet because of the buffering effects of 'quality,' as opposed to the ratchet reality shows [that

Empire draws from] whose negativity is simply taken as a given" (Gates 2018, 185, 186). Daniels revises *Empire*'s exclusions and pretenses in *Star* through the central intertextual alliance with the "negative" reality show *The Real Housewives of Atlanta*, which also contributes to Black gay, trans, and genderqueer revisions of *Valley of the Dolls* and the numerous other works referenced on the show that inspired Daniels's aesthetic.[13]

Daniels forges concrete links to *Real Housewives of Atlanta*, a negative text famous and controversial for its "larger-than-life" representations of Black women (Gates 2013, 141). It is also worth noting how the *Real Housewives* franchise as a whole is founded on a formula of gossip, confession, scandal, and unruly, upper-middle-class women very much akin to Susann's novels.[14] Setting *Star* in Atlanta, Daniels cast gender-nonconforming hair stylist Miss Lawrence, a frequent figure on *RHoA* in 2012–13, in addition to a cameo from Porsha Williams as well as appearances from *Love & Hip Hop: Atlanta* alumni Joseline Hernandez and Mimi Faust. Gates helps identify the tropes of Black female performance on *The Real Housewives of Atlanta* that overlap with Daniels's camp interest in *Valley of the Dolls*, *Dreamgirls*, *Paris Is Burning*, and the Supremes, "the women's femininity, speech patterns, and mannerisms" (Gates 2013, 142). The women of *RHoA* delight some audiences according to a gay camp lens, as Gates's quotation of *RHoA* producer Andy Cohen attests: "Gays love these shows for the same reason gays love drag queens. They're an exaggerated portrayal of women, what gay guys want women to be in their twisted fantasy lives" (Gates 2013, 141–42). Gates suggests the risks involved when camp remains blind to race, however, that the exaggerated, purportedly funny traits of camp performance on *RHoA* also comprise "sites where preconceived notions of 'upper class,' 'successful,' and 'housewife' (historically underscored by an implicit vision of whiteness) did not match the image that the Black Atlanta housewives projected" (Gates 2013, 142). Considering that Gates illustrates how such racist incongruity fuels comedic reactions to *RHoA* as well as generates a sense of the show's "authenticity," Cohen's variation of color-blind camp demonstrates not only the default whiteness of gay camp but also how "the tropes of blackness operate in much white camp as an authenticating discourse that enables the performance of sex and gender roles" (Gates 2013, 142; Wojcik 1996, 20). Camp in this dynamic easily fuses with racial and gender difference, implicating some audiences while permitting risk-free pleasures for others. As Gates informs, "It is, in fact, a *privilege* to be able to ignore the ways that racialized images have operated throughout history, one that African Americans have not traditionally been able to afford" (Gates 2013, 154).

Gates nevertheless makes the case for "alternative or negotiated readings of these shows" that embrace the "'unruly' women" on reality shows because they "subvert the conventions of race and gender" and "can choose to privilege their version of reality over those of the institutions that attempt to control them," then opines, "we as viewers can similarly *choose* to read their realities as dominant" (Gates 2013, 143, 153, 154).[15] Gates ultimately argues about reality shows that their "melodramatic conventions enable the nonnormative identity performances of the cast members and their legibility to viewers, while the conventions of the reality TV genre simultaneously work to naturalize and hide the labor that undergirds these performances" (Gates 2018, 150). Gates adds, furthermore, that the subversive labor of reality shows' Black women is further obscured by a "double negative" of cultural disreputability, the resemblance of reality TV to soap operas (Gates 2018, 151).

The critical failure of *Star* can be traced to the program's immersion in negative texts and cultural influences. The disparaging response to the show hinges on comparing *Star* to *Empire*, exemplified in Joshua K. Wright's assertion that *Star* "has failed to live up to the lofty expectations of its predecessor. The media unanimously bashed the pilot episode" (Wright 2018, 171). As explored in greater detail at the end of the chapter, reviewers estimated the failure of Daniels's "girls' show with music and a little bit of edge" through the perception of unintentional camp in "bad" dialogue, plotting, and acting (Moore 2016; Ryan 2016, 185; Butler 2016; Hale 2016, C4). The "quality" "buffers" of *Empire* that Gates examines—the program's renowned auteur Daniels, a cast led by Oscar-nominated actors Taraji P. Henson and Terrence Howard, and a marked distance from the reality TV shows whose women provided role models for *Empire*'s most celebrated character, Henson's Cookie Lyon—enabled critics to appreciate that show as deliberately exaggerated as well as having a "positive" social impact (Gates 2018, 183–85). *Star* might still have been insulated by the signs of "quality," considering the celebrated, Oscar-nominated vitas of Daniels and Queen Latifah, but camp negativity pushes *Star* into cultural territory proximate to the movie *Valley of the Dolls*: flaunting an aesthetic of failure in the eyes of critics that drew a cult following of devoted fans attuned to Daniels's sensibility.

Daniels enlists camp negativity to resituate the power dynamics underpinning the "privileges" of pleasure and identification. *Star* turns the entitlements of camp pleasure into a force for challenging numerous normative constructs of race, gender, sexuality, and class as well as providing ironic escapism. For the *Rotten Tomatoes* piece, the creator-producer stressed the balance of social commentary and escapism when designing his new show in the wake of Donald Trump's election: "We need to escape from the pain that we are all in. You see a shift as you see the series progress into a place of, not denial, but hope." Daniels wittily elaborates on this later after discussing some of the social issues he plans to expose: "You can still have fun with it. Look, Sharon Tate committed suicide in *Valley of the Dolls*, and it was still a party" (Topel 2016). Daniels's camp negativity additionally strives for Black queer and trans visibility, or to paraphrase Charles I. Nero, work that "validates our lives as black and gay" as well as "signifies repeatedly on racial stereotypes and on middle-class culture" (1991, 246, 247). This mission further embraces what Quinlan Miller terms "trans gender queer camp," which occasions audiences to challenge "racist norms of perception, identity, and attraction enacted through binary gender" (Miller 2019, 15).[16] These combine with the program's central theme of religion, including what Jeffrey Q. McCune Jr. calls "transformance," the incorporation of gospel performance in Black queer culture, particularly drag (2004, 154, 161–62). Queen Latifah's Carlotta exemplifies the queer contradictions of the Black church, a "(dys)functional and (de)mobilizing" space (McCune 2004, 159). In her array of fabulous wigs and quotations from *Valley of the Dolls*, Carlotta bespeaks female-as-female drag, yet as a churchgoing woman also shows fierce trans- and homophobia toward her daughter Cotton who, just like her mother, also quotes from *Valley of the Dolls*.[17]

A key moment of episode 7 in the first season, "Black Wherever I Go" (February 8, 2017), exemplifies the camp "place of hope" that materializes on *Star* alongside occasioning what Cael M. Keegan refers to as "a trans point of reception for popular media" (2016, 28). Addressing painful and persistent issues related to police violence, the Atlanta community of the show faces the wrongful death of beloved neighbor Danielle Jackson (Jasmine Burke) by a white policeman, a tragedy that sparks a Black Lives

Matter rally. Amid this social, political struggle, and as everyone awaits breaking news on the legal action involving the murder, Miss Bruce closes up God's Blessings when Carlotta's daughter Cotton descends the stairs. "Where you think you going, Miss Thing?" asks Miss Bruce. On her way to a date, Cotton marches by with the flourish of a diva and utters, "Get out of my way. I got a man waiting for me," the same line that Helen Lawson blurts just before the legendary skirmish with Neely O'Hara. Miss Bruce's reply first appears as a smiling recognition of Cotton's homage. "Oh, you better quote *Valley of the Dolls*, bitch," snaps Miss Bruce, but the camp tone of the *Valley* citation immediately shifts back to realistic social drama, interrupted by the TV news. After the chief of police makes the obligatory, tragically clichéd statement to "extend my sympathies" to the family and community of the deceased, Miss Bruce retorts, voice breaking, "Extension denied." The news segment then closes with the announcement of the suspect policeman's official exoneration. The reference to *Valley of the Dolls* furnishes camp humor and genderqueer reflexivity, but this is jarringly joined with the bleakly real presence of racist police brutality, the two opposites bridged by the quare characters whose intersectional experiences figure centrally in *Star*. Miss Bruce and Cotton persist as quare participants in the show's community, far from the closet plotlines and punchlines that have historically determined and contained Black gay characters in television, and Miss Bruce emerges as a bitterly witty commentator on the absurdity of racism and transphobia.

The very next episode offers another reference to *Valley of the Dolls*, again adjacent to the ongoing plotline about the racist criminal justice system, now revealing the wit that empowers and unifies the girl group at the heart of the show (February 15, 2017). Preparing for a benefit performance to help a wrongly arrested member of Black Lives Matter, Star, Simone, and Alex reflect on the pettiness of their personal dramas. As Simone and Star lean on the end of their bed, Alex joins them to form a three-shot that mimics the iconic promotional still for *Valley of the Dolls* with the three protagonists posed on a bed.[18] Alex—Daniels's answer to Anne Welles, proper and upper middle class—asks, "Weren't we just supposed to start a girl group? Now look at us. I just got arrested. Star's a frigging WAG. Somebody killed Otis." Simone chimes in, sounding a little like Neely O'Hara, "You forgot the whole loony-bin part," in reference to her suicide attempt and brief institutionalization.

Simone then queries, "Do you think Destiny's Child ever went through something like this?" Alex replies, "Nah. Now TLC? They for sure did." The three women laugh, then rise to continue preparing for the show. Inviting comparisons to *Valley of the Dolls* through visual cues and dialogue pokes fun at the "whiteness" of the original, quite literally illustrated in the 1967 publicity shot of the women—three white women, one dressed in pink, the other two in white, perched on a white bed with a white background—and more figuratively, upends the film's fantasy world through the social and political realities conveyed on *Star*. Although the young women do not verbalize their likeness to Neely, Anne, and Jennifer, or indeed those characters' likenesses to the real stars Susann based them on, they identify their similarities to Black girl groups, and with a sense of self-irony that unifies them. At the same time, by citing the legendary dramas experienced by Destiny's Child and TLC, Daniels embeds *Valley of the Dolls* in an alternative intertextual chain of camp divas as well as a different constellation of star gossip, both now directly applicable to African American culture.

When in the first season finale Simone jokingly sings "Dreamgirls" back stage awaiting their climactic performance—the success of which will decide if they receive a recording contract—Daniels develops the intertextual motif of back-stage stories about aspiring female stars, their particular significance among young Black women, and the function of reflexive wit to unify and empower the women (March 15, 2017). As the *New York Times* had informed, "The idea of using desperate, wily young women . . . grew out of Mr. Daniels's childhood love of 'Dreamgirls,' which he said taught him that 'we're from the 'hood and we can still be fabulous.' Other influences included 'Valley of the Dolls' and 'Paris Is Burning,' both of which Mr. Daniels had considered remaking" (Coscarelli 2016). Just before Simone sings, Alex reflects on her journey with Star and Simone to Atlanta as they prepare back stage in their dressing room: "I walked away from the Upper East Side of New York, darling." "Like a crazy person," interjects Star, as Alex continues: "Got in a stolen car . . . That smelled like weed. And came all the way here to ATL. Because I believed in you. I believed in us and what we could become. . . . Look at how far we've come." "By ourselves," adds Star, which inspires Simone: "Yo, 'cause, 'We're your Dreamgirls / Boys we'll make you happy!'" The reference inspires all three women to laugh, scoff, and briefly sing along, which unifies the group, nourishes their readiness to perform, and embodies Daniels's sentiment, "from the 'hood and we can still be fabulous."

When Carlotta quotes from *Valley of the Dolls*, the rigidly religious single mother and entrepreneur flaunts her pragmatism and her fabulousness in the face of looming threats, conflicts that combine sensational melodrama and social realism (February 22, 2017). Speaking with Latifah about her character for a *Los Angeles Times* interview, Daniels suggests Carlotta's significance as a force of playful camp escape and social realism at the intersection of Black and gay culture. Once again citing the inspirations of *Dreamgirls*, *Valley of the Dolls*, and *Paris Is Burning*, Daniels adds, "I really wanted to bring people back into the church in an honest and cool way," then identifies the model for Carlotta, "a woman that is a relative. Just that 9-to-5 working woman that occasionally has problems paying her bills. That has probably had a kid that's been in jail. That may have a husband that left her, but is a devout Christian. That's what keeps her alive. That's what makes her real. And I told her we were going to have fun with it. That she was going to be rockin' some magical wigs" (Villareal 2016, E1). Carlotta indeed sports a "magical wig" when she quotes from *Valley of the Dolls* in an environment that bespeaks camp, drag, and divas: the Atlanta Hair Show, where the girl group is dressed in Gladys Knight drag for a tribute to the singer. Simone's sexually abusive foster father, who has since been stalking her, winds up murdered, and Carlotta runs damage control. Carlotta advises the traumatized trio, "There's a lot of people out there, there's cameras everywhere. You'll need to get up on that stage. It's called an alibi. And we don't talk about this, you understand? Not ever. *Now . . .*" The camera angle changes to a medium shot of Carlotta, wearing a silver gray wig, who intensifies her last words before sending the young women on stage: "Sparkle, Neely, sparkle," she stage whispers, flicking her hands, nodding her head, and grinning mysteriously. Quoting the great camp catch phrase from *Valley of the Dolls*, Carlotta simultaneously impresses the power of performance, underscored by the group's Gladys Knight costumes and Carlotta's wig.

Carlotta's quotation of "Sparkle, Neely, Sparkle" gains special meaningfulness as a line that echoes throughout gay crossover culture, repeated on *RuPaul's Drag Race* since its early days on the LGBTQ network Logo. Daniels fulfills numerous goals here, especially by assigning a line immensely popular among drag queens to a churchgoing

Valley of the Dolls
CONDUCTED BY JOHNNY WILLIAMS · SONGS BY DORY AND ANDRE PREVIN

20th CENTURY FOX RECORDS

THE MOTION PICTURE "VALLEY OF THE DOLLS" IS BASED
ON A BOOK BY JACQUELINE SUSANN

Lee Daniels's *Star* quotes lines and visuals from *Valley of the Dolls*, such as posing pop singers Star (Jude Demorest), Simone (Brittany O'Grady), and Alex (Ryan Destiny) similar to the record cover of the original film soundtrack, and Carlotta's (Queen Latifah) advice to the girl group, "Sparkle, Neely, sparkle."

fundamentalist. Daniels performs a tele-dramatic variation of what McCune calls "transformance," "what is at work in the spaces where drag queens perform gospel. The gay club space . . . transitions into the 'church' scene while it sustains characteristics of the club . . . The drag performance of gospel transforms the club space into a hybrid place, where the church and the club can meet" (McCune 2004, 161–62). In Daniels's example the transformance materializes in reverse, an example of camp negativity that casts the bewigged, respectable church lady to perform like a drag queen. These elements come to a dramatic head in episode 8 (February 15, 2017) when Carlotta cajoles Cotton into a conversion ritual with Pastor Harris (Tyrese Gibson). Witnessing Cotton's agony as the pastor forces her to repeat "I am a man," Carlotta suddenly envisions a fantasy version of her hair salon in which Miss Bruce in drag shrieks, "Let your hair down!": "If you got on a wig / Like some people think I got on a wig / But this is my own beautiful hair / What to do with it fellas? Take it off!" This soon turns into a production number headed by Carlotta in a song about queer acceptance and personal authenticity: "Stay true to myself. So, who are you to judge? / Worry 'bout you. Why does it matter who I love?" As Carlotta leads a chorus of dancing women, Miss Bruce gyrating and chanting "Get down," Carlotta blatantly refutes the kind of rhetoric she has hurled at her daughter: "We all got a path, they say I ain't living right / But life ain't worth living if you've got to live a lie." Carlotta also raps a reference to *A Star Is Born* in the number, a backstudio picture and camp predecessor to *Valley of the Dolls*. Although the lyric's reference to "a star's born" flies quickly by, the additional link to another camp classic similar to *Valley of the Dolls* and *Dreamgirls* further frames the action and format of *Star* in a quare reinscription of Black popular culture (sacred and profane) as well as the tacitly white gay camp canon. When horrible reality overcomes the fantasy production number, Carlotta returns to the scene of Cotton's conversion and knows the terrible impact of her actions on her child. Daniels's transformation of televisual space combines drag, music video, and club music with religious themes, rituals, and characters to motivate Carlotta's acceptance of Cotton, Miss Bruce again present as a camp commentator.

For Daniels, camp negativity remains integral to delivering a positive message at the same time as ironizing the aesthetics of quality that *Empire* rested on. What Gates speculates could happen with *Empire* indeed befalls *Star*, that it might "push too hard against the politics of respectability, become too excessive, too dramatic, too black, in its subsequent seasons" (Gates 2018, 190). The *New York Times* TV critic Mike Hale encapsulated this process, in a deracinated manner, in one of the many adverse mainstream reviews of *Star*. Comparing *Star* to *Empire*, Hale considers,

> where "Empire," while overheated, is fairly consistent stylistically, at least nodding toward naturalism, "Star" is all over the place—adventurous or nuts, depending on your point of view. The fanciful story is shot in a gritty, pseudo-documentary style, but with breaks for incongruous music-video production numbers . . . It's sobering to think that "Empire" may have been too conventional for Mr. Daniels. The real difference between the shows is a simple matter of quality, though. (Hale 2016, C4)

In light of Gates's critique of *Empire* for its strategically won position on a "lofty perch as the media darling du jour," a critique driven by a studied respect for "the gutter of negative representations" (Gates 2018, 186, 190), Hale's rebuke of *Star* could not be more complimentary. Daniels's camp negativity flowers in the flight from "the conventional" "naturalism" of *Empire* to the "all over the place" style of *Star*. If this seemed "a simple matter of quality" to Hale, according to Gates's criteria as well as Nero's, Daniels's flight from "naturalism" to "nuts" signified on the "quality" of *Empire* to validate a range of Black, trans, and queer identities, representations that disrupt respectability politics and coincide with Daniels's "negative" affection for *Valley of the Dolls*.

"throwing it back": Jacqueline Susann's Fearless Failure

Jacqueline Susann continues to gel with fans and media artists—and even some "double-dome" critics the likes of whom the author once lambasted—through the vehicle of the roman à clef and the components of gossip, confession, and Hollywood pastiche. Susann's depictions of powerful show business women through the style of sleazy realism, combined with her spotlight on a range of "deviant" people and pursuits, once provided the vulgar proof of the author's venal ambitions, lowbrow sensibility, and kitsch cultural threat, but these same features now signify as subversive signs of a uniquely feminist, queer vision. Taking Jackie Susann seriously, however, has consistently led to overlooking the centrality of her camp creative vision and the comedy of bad manners she generated in her novels and publicity appearances. Theatrical tributes to Susann, biographical treatments, and media homages nevertheless consistently and eagerly draw from Susann's diverse comedic repertoire in addition to the author's larger-than-life persona: the seasoned showbiz veteran who flaunted her brassy taste, ribald cant, and relaxed moral code, eager to spill the beans with the protective alibi of writing fiction. Overlooking humor in Jackie Susann's work negates the core of her queer, feminist agency and the complicated delights her bestsellers furnished.

Susann's sleazy realism and command of the roman à clef communicated queer irony, the closeted play at being *both* queer *and* mainstream. The mass-market magnetism and superficial moralizing of Susann's romans à clef camouflaged an address to marginal readers living within the shadows of heteronormative society, failures from the perspective of

bourgeois common sense: "single girls" seeking careers and sexual satisfaction (lesbian, bisexual, and straight), as well as gay men and gender-
nonconformists among an array of outcasts. Through her fictionalized
celebrity characters, Susann performed a variation on the comedy of
manners in which gossip, confession, and disguise merged as the vehicles
to showcase heteronormative failure. Susann's queer irony renders *Valley of the Dolls* and *Once Is Not Enough* antiromantic tragicomedies that
test a central narrative feature and ideological function of popular love
stories, what Halberstam terms "the hetero-logic of futurity" (2011, 120).
When heterosexual romance malfunctions, Susann challenges heteronormative narrative causality: the equation between success, marriage,
the promise of reproduction, and the happy ending. *Once Is Not Enough*
brings every romantic union to ruin, from Dee and Karla's seemingly
ideal affair about to burst out of the closet, to the heterosexual romances
of the heiress heroine January Wayne, who disappears in the midst of a
drug trip but whose incestuous desire for her father doomed a heterosexual happy ending to begin with. Although *The Love Machine* provides
significant exceptions in its happy ending of heterosexual fulfillment,
a queer causality intersects all the major characters' plotlines with the
secondary plotline about the closeted gay couple Sergio and Alfie and
pins their prosperity to the ambiguous welfare of the straight couples.
Ethel Evans resorts to both motherhood and her friendships with the gay
men rather than her husband for fulfillment, and Judith Austin replaces
marital bliss with the scandal involving the gay men that restores her
social standing and her sexiness, while Sergio and Alfie remain coupled,
closeted, and in the background, central and marginal.

It is in the margins of her novels where Susann plants her most
subversive material, in the subplots overlooked by most critics, and in
incidental dialogue where Susann's witty philosophers of antiromance
find voice: Linda Riggs in *Once Is Not Enough* and Ethel Evans in *The Love
Machine*, and in *Valley of the Dolls*, Hellen Lawson and Neely O'Hara in
addition to the beautiful, bisexual Jennifer North. Jennifer bemoans her
unsuccessful relationships with men to best friend Anne Welles, kidding,
"It's a pity we're not queer—we'd make a marvelous team," and she even
implants humor into her suicide letter, redoubling the heartache of her
loss: "Anne—No embalmer could make me up as well as I do myself.
Thank God for the dolls. Sorry I couldn't stick around for your wedding.

I love you. Jen" (Susann 1997c, 317, 336). Ironized by her emphasis on style and frivolity, Jennifer's tragicomic camp also emerges in her other letter to the senator, a veiled critique of her fiancé's fetishism. Folding the queer margins back onto the straight social melodrama, any concrete and simplistic moral reading requires tunnel vision, as Susann the storyteller concludes *Valley of the Dolls* with a joke in which heteronormative failure serves a queer object lesson. Susann posited queer insights that her readers could detect in conjunction with the fun of finding the keys to her novel's characters, such as in *The Love Machine* when the William S. Paley character—IBC network CEO Gregory Austin—blurts to Robin Stone, "You know what the public wants. *Shit*—that's what it wants" (Susann 1997a, 390). If the patriarchs running the culture industry felt this way, Susann exposed them with the language of queer failure, sleazy realism and the comedy of bad manners.

The queer failure emblematized by Jackie Susann and her characters inspired in her aficionados, not "nihilism and negation," paraphrasing Halberstam, but "generative models of failure" that "remind us that there is something powerful in being wrong, in losing, in failing" (Halberstam 2011, 120–21). Susann's fans relish the signs of "trash" that critics mistook her work for: her sleazy realism, and the hilarious transpositions that unpretentiously unseated bourgeois taste and heteronormative futurity, that transformed defeat into delight. "Failure loves company," Halberstam illuminates, an audience, and so do camping and the comedy of bad manners. A central facet of that company remains the laughter shared among failure's fan club on the funny victory of vulgarity. In the case of Jacqueline Susann's legacy, the fans of failure often seem inspired to join in and perform in return. Susann's fashionable champion Carol Bjorkman perhaps articulated this sentiment best at the conclusion of her adoring piece on Jackie for *Women's Wear Daily*: "jump into the 'Valley of the Dolls.' You won't be sorry!" (Seaman 1984a; Bjorkman 1966a, 8). Matching this invitation to the photos of Bjorkman and Susann, stylishly dressed, coiffed, and sitting next to each other, smiling and making faces behind hardcover copies of *Valley of the Dolls*, one can hear the laughter echoing in that valley, closeted though it may have been, and shared by more of Jackie's champions, Rex Reed and Liz Smith among them.

The considerable creative work of Susann fans provides further models of failure to generate further queer visions: Lee Daniels's *Star*,

Carrie Fisher's *films à clef*, Barbara Seaman's *Lovely Me*, Lypsinka's *Ballet of the Dolls*, Sydney Pokorny and Liz Tracey's *Dead Jackie Susann Quarterly*, Leslie Singer's *Taking Back the Dolls*, and the biographical depictions of Susann by Paul Minx, Michele Lee, and Michele Gallery. "I am a feminist, you know," says Jackie to Johnny Carson in *See How Beautiful I Am*, "I believe in equal orgasms and equal pay. I also believe in makeup, waxing and plastic surgery" (Minx 2018, 23). Her admirers have variously shined light on Jacqueline Susann's legacy of vulgar victory, which in Minx's play God encapsulates to Jackie: "Listen, you're a great kid, Jacks. I threw a lot of shit at you. More than most. But you kept throwing it back. That's all I ask" (Minx 2018, 31). The "fearless vulgarity" of Jacqueline Susann really crystallized around her moments of "throwing it back," in the form of gossipy revelations, shocking confessions, and vibrant, funny, and queer performances. Some of the recipients of Susann's "shit" grimaced and mocked, but for connoisseurs of failure—Susann's "heirs"—Jackie's life and work generated laughing communities delighted by her sleazy realism and the victory of style in her comedies of bad manners.

Notes

Introduction

1 Latham launches his discussion of the roman à clef by emphasizing the genre's low reputation (Latham 2009, 4–5).

2 Seaman leaves out the struggle for racial equity among the "emerging themes of the 1960s," an absence that reflects Susann's own oversight. Apart from the subplot in *The Love Machine* involving Rose and Amanda, her novels fail to include developed BIPOC (Black, Indigenous, and people of color) characters or storylines that include racism among the social challenges that beset her characters. This lacuna coincides with Susann's own closeted Jewish identity, passing for gentile throughout most of her celebrity, and such plotlines as the white model Amanda's secreted Black foster mother Rose in *The Love Machine*, and in *Once Is Not Enough*, the Polish movie star Karla's clandestine past as a Catholic victim of Nazi atrocities.

3 The question of which stars inspired Susann's characters continues to press readers, especially considering *Valley of the Dolls*, even after Susann's initial revelations in 1966–67 as well as Barbara Seaman's dogged research on the matter for *Lovely Me*. As one informed reader suggested to me, the TV celebrity Betty Furness might have provided the basis for Anne Welles. Furness was enormously popular, synonymous with Betty Crocker in the industry of domestic products geared to women consumers, as Janet L. Wolff clarified in the 1958 study *What Makes Women Buy* (49). Although I was unable to locate evidence of Susann's intentions to make Furness the basis for Anne, I found a book reviewer making this connection, Anne De Saint Phalle writing in 1967 for the *Harvard Crimson*: "Anne Welles, a small-town

girl and frigid Radcliffe graduate, escapes her destiny of 'shrivelling [*sic*] into another New England old maid' by coming to The Big City. In New York she melts into the arms of a handsome English writer and becomes a TV commercial star a la Betty Furness."

4 Hirsch refers to this legendary event in Susann's career (1976, 6). Seaman gives an extended account (1996c, 389–90).

5 My prior approaches to Jacqueline Susann displace questions of authorship with attention to camp reception and star biography conventions, never adequately exploring how Jacqueline Susann's complicated agency and star persona materialize through the imbrication of her literary and bodily performances, the comedic relationship between text and paratext: her novels and publicity performances, inextricably bound in her reception, the framework for her camp reception from the 1960s to the 2000s (Feil 2013; Feil 2017).

6 Gelder furthermore dismisses queer theories of camp, in which camp "failure" remains a privileged means to undercut heteronormative, bourgeois definitions of "success" (Halberstam 2011, 109–10; Muñoz 2019, 149; Tinkcom 2002; Cohan 2005; Miller 2019). Gelder emphasizes the prevalence of failure in Susann's work, yet by assuming Susann's ignorance of camp, never investigates Susann's feminist and queer comedic agency, nor her feminist and queer fandom. In addition, *The Love Machine* is a "success" narrative in which romance endures for both straight and gay characters through a queer revision of classical Hollywood romantic comedy tropes that would otherwise negate the very same characters or doom them to funny failure.

7 According to both Seaman's and Mansfield's accounts, Amsterdam's show was initially titled *The Golden Goose Café*, and ran first on CBS from 1948 to 1949, then on the DuMont network.

8 George S. Kaufman and Moss Hart were, according to Seaman, Susann and Cole's playwrighting role models (Seaman 1996c, 155).

9 Besides Seaman's discussions (1996c, 213–14), see the reviews of *Lovely Me* (Atkinson 1946, 30; Anon. 1946, 49).

10 Susann makes these comments in the promotional documentary, *Jacqueline Susann and the Valley of the Dolls*.

11 The roman à clef actually constitutes both a genre and a mode. Nora Ephron demonstrates the popular understanding of the term meaning genre by situating Susann's *Valley of the Dolls* and *The Love Machine*

in the "sub-category of popularly-written *romans à clef*," a view that Susann's editor Don Preston verified: "Show-biz *romans à clef* are virtually a category, like Westerns or science fiction" (Ephron 1969, 12; Preston 1969, 39). Scholarly assessments waver, from Latham's and McCoy's arguments that it is a "vital" but elusive genre to Judson's final determination that "it is a literary mode which highlights the instability of genre demarcations among different kinds of prose narrative" (Latham 2009, 12; McCoy 2014, 129; Judson 2000, 159).

12 See Eisner for the discussion of camp reception and *Myra Breckinridge*; see Brackman for assessments of *Candy* as a "put-on" novel (1967, 44), and the emergence of Phyllis Diller as a "put-on" of celebrity coterminous with "manufactured Camp" (69, 70).

13 See Frontain for a discussion of the gay significance of the comedy of manners (161–62).

14 That Coward played opposite his old friends, the acting couple Lynn Fontanne and Alfred Lunt, also gave cause to wonder about the truth to their relationship.

15 Of particular note, see Susann's comments to Howard (1966, 74, 77); McLendon (1966, B5); and Smith (1969, 4). See also Ephron (1969, 3).

16 Seaman investigated whether Carol Bjorkman was bisexual and if she and Susann had an affair (Seaman 1984, 1).

17 I am alluding here to a few of Sontag's ideas about camp, as well as examples, that ensuing chapters will explore (Sontag 1966, 279–80, 283, 286–87, 289, 291).

18 I am adapting Judith Mayne's paradigm of lesbian, feminist irony in the films of Hollywood director Dorothy Arzner. Susann's irony approximates Arzner's, which theatricalizes women and their relationships in a manner that both appeases the heterosexual male gaze and "exerts a pressure against the supposed 'natural' laws of heterosexual romance" (Mayne 1991, 118).

19 Epperson's parody musical *Dial "M" for Model* also reflected traces of *Valley of the Dolls* and *The Love Machine* in its backstage, high-fashion setting.

Chapter 1. Sleazy Realism and the Single Girl

1 The roman à clef intensified the charge of Susann's sleazy realism by furnishing what Lauren McCoy encapsulates as "the blending

of the novel and gossip" and by affording the generic heterogeneity
implied in Whelehan's film examples (discussed later in the chapter),
what Barbara Judson elucidates as "a literary mode which highlights
the instability of genre demarcations among different kinds of prose
narrative (romance, novel, history, memoir, biography) in the early
nineteenth century and even today . . . shifty with respect to form,
malicious with respect to a content richly attentive to the intrigues of
those in the public eye" (McCoy 2014, 128, 131; Judson 2000, 159–60).

2 It is also worth considering how Susann's dramatization of the television, stage, and film industries likens her to fellow bestseller writer
Arthur Hailey, who writes about "institutions"; Cawelti nevertheless
differentiates the novelists and pegs Susann as a writer who focuses
on sex and seduction (Cawelti 1991, 44).

3 This is also the case in Susann's third novel, *Once Is Not Enough*, and
her fourth, posthumously published novella *Dolores*.

4 Susann incorporates what Barbara Judson spies in Lady Caroline
Lamb's 1816 roman à clef *Glenarvon*, "the disclosure of other people's
secrets" and "the revelation of the writer's own history" (Judson
2000, 159).

5 Similar to Susann's women, each of Jaffe's women characters "represents a different category of single girl," Wojcik explains, "and each
meets a different degree of success and failure"; Jaffe's inclusion of an
elder "spinster" figure also prefigured Susann's Helen Lawson (Wojcik
2010, 159, 161). Stephen Rebello also mentions the "three girls genre"
shared by *Valley* and *Best of Everything* (2020, 45, 65).

6 This argument resonates with Ken Gelder's premise that *Valley of
the Dolls* distinguishes itself as "the first great anti-romance novel"
(2004, 132), although Gelder's assertion is debatable, considering the
decidedly unromantic conclusion of *Valley*'s predecessor, *The Best of
Everything* (1958).

7 Seaman discusses the friendship between Runyon and Susann,
although she does not explore his literary influence on her (1996c,
151–52).

8 Also noteworthy, characters that roam *Every Night, Josephine!* with
names such as Last-One Hershkowitz and Portland Hoffa recall the
colorfully monikered denizens of popular Runyon stories and their
movie adaptations: Sorrowful Jones in "Little Miss Marker" (adapted

in 1934, 1949, and 1962), Nicely-Nicely Johnson in "Lonely Heart" and "A Piece of Pie" (adapted with other stories into *Guys and Dolls* in 1955), and Dave the Dude in "Madame La Gimp" (adapted twice, most recently in *Pocketful of Miracles*, 1959).

9 Jane M. Greene points to wife characters in Classical Hollywood sophisticated comedies of the early 1930s for another inheritor of the Truewit (2011, 240–42).

10 The carnivalesque dimensions of "animalizing" characters are notable here (see Eco 2018, 26).

11 Mrs. Addison's questions for Jackie and attitude toward TV suggest Cold War–era positions about "low" mass culture that were embedded with anti-Semitic conspiracy theories about Jewish kitsch peddlers responsible for mass produced Stalinism (see Ross 1989, 29–31, 44–45).

12 Susann's sick humor is akin to Runyonesque "comic violence," as discussed by Szuberla (1993, 71, 77–78).

13 Following Mizejewski's discussion of Sarah Silverman, the derogatory association between Jewishness and animals also haunts *Josephine!*, from the dog breeder's implications of anti-Semitism to Susann's own collapsing of human and dog (2014, 105, 111–12)

14 For examples, see Susann (2004, 21, 25, 167, 199, 223, 237). See also Seaman (1996c, 218, 220).

15 For extensive demonstrations of these patterns, see Robbins (1961, 242, 248–53, 257).

16 Explaining his writing style to the *New Yorker* in 1996, Robbins elucidated his voyeuristic strategies in the form of a Freudian "tendentious" joke, cracked among men, objectifying women and meant to embarrass the women who listen to it. Asked why he employs both first- and third-person narration, "Robbins said, in the mock-sleazeball voice he also uses with his wife, 'Well, sometimes I like a little pussy and sometimes I just like to talk about it'" (Parker 1996). Robbins's quip personalizes his creative choices through a male gaze defined by distance, omniscience, separation, and sexual practice. See Mulvey (2000), in addition to feminist analyses of Freud's jokes/wit theory that apply Mulvey: Mizejewski (2014, 17); Fischer (1996, 112–13).

17 In this respect Robbins remains consistent with the modernist, masculinist perspective on feminized mass culture that I discuss in chapter 3,

despite the fact that he is also a producer of kitsch. See Huyssen (1986, 47, 50, 55).

18 Disclosing someone else's secrets can ensnare the gossiper and intersect with confession. This "serious" gossip is "private," Spacks clarifies, shared among only a few people who "talk about others to reflect about themselves, to express wonder and uncertainty and locate certainties, to enlarge their knowledge of one another" (Spacks 1985, 5).

19 Herbert Gans identifies Jacqueline Susann, Harold Robbins, and *Cosmopolitan* editor Helen Gurley Brown as the "progressive" variants within the taste groupings of "lower-middle" culture of the early 1970s. One could say that Susann, in her moralistic pose as gossip, appeased "conservatives," but her confessional tone spoke to the progressives, "the constituency for the sexual frankness that appears today in Cosmopolitan, the Susann and Robbins novels" (Gans 1999, 112–14). This polarity corresponds to Susann's novels, in addition to her promotional appearances that oscillate between the kind of moralizing she dished to numerous journalists and the kind of confessional interviews she conducted with Carol Bjorkman and Rex Reed.

20 Brown and Susann shared the publisher Bernard Geis, and both collaborated with director of publicity and future feminist lifestyle writer Letty Cottin Pogrebin on historic book promotion campaigns (Reed 1966, 97, 99; Seaman 1996c, 81–284; Trask 2013, 186–87).

21 The fiftieth anniversary edition of *Sex and the Single Girl* (2003) reproduces the original 1962 edition published by Bernard Geis.

22 See Kaufman and Hart, *The Man Who Came to Dinner*, Act 1, scene 2 (1939, 243).

23 See Dyer (1986), Staiger (1992), Tinkcom (2002), and Cohan (2005) for lasting scholarship on Garland, camp, and gay fans.

24 Michael Trask tracks the "relentless hypothetical queerness" and closet logic that pervade *Valley of the Dolls* (2013, 182). Susann acknowledges the ubiquity of queerness among women as well as the lingering stigma. Neely speculates about Helen to Anne, for example, "Maybe the old war horse is turning queer in her old age. . . . It happens. Listen, some of those big stars—especially broads like Helen who like sex—they get so fed up with the cold shoulder from men that they turn to women for their kicks" (Susann 1997c, 89). As usual,

Anne disputes such unseemly implications despite her flight from the repressive manners of her upbringing: "Neely, Helen is absolutely normal!" (Susann 1997c, 7, 89). Anne eventually alters her impressions of "normal," however, through her friendship with Jennifer.

25 Susann encourages a redefinition of her social melodrama's "moral occult," the system dictating good/evil and right/wrong, which both propels the narrative and is reflected in the plot causality (Brooks 1976, 5).

26 Jennifer's "mechanism" juxtaposes human and machine with a sense of comic incongruity germane to Bergson's theory of laughter (Romanska and Ackerman 2016, 188; Bergson 1928, 29).

27 Susann's subtle and shocking depiction of Jennifer's sexual assault compares to the "understated brutality" and "comic violence" (Szuberla 1993, 71, 75) of Runyon's stories. For example, see the aptly titled "Sense of Humor" (Runyon 1944, 629–30).

28 Staiger notes the patriarchal safety valve employed in narratives about fallen men, thereby "distancing the threat implied to all men" (2010, 47). This is applicable to rationalizing Tony's misogynistic abuse as the result of a genetic disease.

29 Cawelti, remember, reads Valley as a "parable of regeneration" that casts "promiscuity" as "the primrose path to unhappiness" and sometimes death (Cawelti 1991, 44, 46–47).

30 For more on Ann Bannon's Beebo Brinker books, see Keller (1999, 2–3, 17); Grier (1966); and Michele Aina Barale, "When Jack Blinks: Si(gh)ting Gay Desire in Ann Bannon's Beebo Brinker," in Abelove, Barale, and Halperin (1993, 604–15).

31 Keller adapts Kobena Mercer's theory of ambivalent reading, pertaining to Black gay spectatorship of Robert Mapplethorpe's photography. See Mercer, "Looking for Trouble" (1993, 350–59).

32 See Wojcik for a discussion of Sex and the Single Girl (2010, 176–78). The film bridges the sex comedy, in which the priority remains to render the two sexually dysfunctional protagonists as marriageable, with the screwball comedy of remarriage. See also Glitre (2006, 35, 149); and Neale and Krutnik (1990, 170–71).

33 Geoffrey Shurlock of the Production Code Administration—in its last gasp prior to turning into the Classification and Rating Administration—never objected to the gay epithets or allusions,

which makes sense considering the increasing allowances the PCA was making throughout the 1960s; strangely enough, though, Shurlock nevertheless raised questions about such innocuous vocabulary as "boobies," "damn," and "Geez," all of which stayed in the film (Shurlock 1967a; Shurlock 1967b; Bart 1965, 37).

34 Published after I completed my manuscript, Rebello's *Dolls! Dolls! Dolls!* offers an engaging and well-researched account of *Valley of the Dolls*, particularly the production of the film. Although our research overlaps, Rebello's book primarily focuses on the film and largely bypasses cultural studies approaches.

35 This is consistent with some of the backstudio pictures of the same period. Cohan notes that two backstudio biopics from 1965 about Jean Harlow, in addition to the adaptation of Robbins's *The Carpetbaggers* with its Harlow-inspired Rina Marlow, efface Harlow's "genuine comedic talent" and reduce the actor's appeal to the "currency" of her body (Cohan 2017, 534).

36 See Jerome Edwards's (1967) telegram (from the Fox legal department) to Richard Zanuck regarding the need for a prominent disclaimer, in addition to Zanuck's (1967) memo to Barbara "Bobbie" McLean iterating the need for a blatant disclaimer.

37 The Head most obviously is inspired by Louis B. Mayer of MGM, given the connection of Neely to Judy Garland, but Daryl F. Zanuck might also have been the model. Susann based Jennifer North, who eventually works for the Head, partly on Carole Landis, who had been a Fox contract player.

38 Downplaying the exposé of the entertainment industry additionally eliminated Susann's clever insight into television's impact on sexuality in the movies, something reflected in the casting of Barbara Parkins as Anne: from the fallen woman role of Betty Anderson that Parkins played on ABC's *Peyton Place* to the virginal yet much more sexually explicit role of Anne in *Valley*.

39 The presold dimension of the film, its ad campaign and theme song all anticipated "high concept" filmmaking of the 1970s and the 1980s. See Wyatt (1994).

40 See Carr's (1999) reception history of *Bonnie and Clyde*.

41 For a remarkable dissection of camp in *Valley of the Dolls*, see Richard Henke's "Imitation of Life" (1994).

42 Retrofitting Susann's plot and characters to the formula of Hollywood social melodrama only exacerbates the undermining of heterosexual closure. See Feil (2017, 555–56) for an earlier discussion of this narrative contradiction.

Chapter 2. The Roman à Closet

1 Regarding the Cold War discourses that collapse television and consumerism with femininity, see Joyrich (1988, 130, 135), Spigel (2008, 39), and Cohan (1997, 266).

2 Although Seaman does not contemplate the influence of *Lady in the Dark* on *The Love Machine*, the biographer notes the impact of *Lady in the Dark* on Susann's aspirations as an actress, in addition to discussing Susann's close comrades, Joyce Matthews (wife of theatrical producer Billy Rose, who knew the creators of *Lady in the Dark*) and the chanteuse Hildegarde, who famously recorded songs from *Lady in the Dark* (1996c, 123, 148–49). Besides the enduring popularity of the show's Kurt Weil–Ira Gershwin standards, the popular appeal of *Lady in the Dark* and its currency as an intertext for *The Love Machine* might also have been helped by NBC's live production with Anne Southern (September 24, 1954).

3 Considering the Amanda-Rose plotline, both as a symptom of Susann's closeted Jewishness and a recycling of *Imitation of Life*, the cross-racial casting of Susan Kohner—a Jewish, Mexican American actor—as Sarah Jane might have borne some added significance for Susann.

4 Jewishness always hides in plain sight in Susann's novels, in any number of tertiary Jewish characters such as Henry Bellamy and Mel Harris (Neely's first love) in *Valley of the Dolls*, and in *Love Machine*, Amanda's Jewish-Irish boyfriend Ike (who drops Yiddish-isms), Maggie's lover Adam Bergman as well as her agent, Hy Mandel.

5 Particularly influential in my reasoning here are the arguments of Martin (2018, 223–25) and Joyrich (2001, 454).

6 Mayne hones in on the climactic sequence of *Dance, Girl, Dance*: protagonist Judy interrupts her burlesque performance to rebuke a (mostly) male audience for their puerile prurience, receives a standing ovation led by a female spectator, then engages in a public,

knock-down brawl with her erstwhile friend, burlesque queen
Bubbles, the once chastened audience now erupting again in hoots
and hollers. The famed scene from Arzner's film begs comparison to
the analogous climactic confrontation in *Valley of the Dolls* between
Helen Lawson and Neely O'Hara, for whom the stage is "an extension
of their conflicted friendship, not an alienated site of performance"
(Mayne 1991, 116).

7 Susann forges unexpected connections to misogynistic male characters in *The Love Machine*. For example, Christie Lane's loathsome-
ness is first established amid his racist, sexist to rant to Amanda
(quoted in the chapter), and next when he explains to Ethel, after
her appeal for a marriage proposal from him, "If and when I get
married, I want a decent girl. Your cooze is like the Lincoln Tunnel,
everyone's been through it" (Susann 1997a, 209). Susann nevertheless confers an extremely intimate experience of hers on the TV
comedy star; during a phase when Susann flirted with Catholicism
while also living with cancer, she would converse with the statue of
Saint Andrew at Saint Patrick's Cathedral, chosen for the humorously self-deprecatory reason that he was "the least popular saint
there, who she hoped 'might have more time to heed the prayers of
a Jewish girl'" (Seaman 1996c, 232). In one of Christie's few sympathetic scenes in *The Love Machine*, Susann milks character comedy
from the comedian's flight to Saint Patrick's Cathedral after agree-
ing to marry Ethel, where he confesses his ambivalence to Saint
Andrew, "the only saint in the place who wasn't doing any business"
(Susann 1997a, 311, 313). In addition to endowing the villainous Danton Miller with an activity Susann famously engaged in, bargaining
with God by promising to give up smoking, Susann shares her
birthday with the hero of *The Love Machine* Robin Stone (Seaman
1996c, 458).

8 Susann also bears similarities to Liza Elliot in terms of oedipal
issues with her father that she replicates in Robin's traumatic relationship with his birth mother, and as a professional woman whose
power is constantly undermined by those who question her femininity (Seaman 1996c, 53; McClung 2007, 269, 292). Susann evokes *Lady
in the Dark* more subtly in *Once Is Not Enough* through the protagonist January's father-fixated oedipal narrative.

9 Seaman describes Sergio as "the most likable character in the book" (1996c, 381).

10 Susann's expressed political beliefs included legalizing sex work and protecting sex workers, as she explained to the *New York Times*: "Legalize prostitution, and then there'd be no venereal disease, no stabbings, no pimps" (Anon. 1973, 39).

11 As Nora Ephron observed in 1969, this plotline comes right out of Hitchcock's *Marnie* (12). Susann once again aligns Robin with a woman protagonist whose narrative conflict, like Liza in *Lady in the Dark*, revolves around overcoming her oedipal trauma and sexual repression.

12 Fleeting signs of Elizabeth Taylor emerge in Maggie Stewart, through her looks as a full-figured brunette, her marriage to an abusive scion redolent of Nicky Hilton, and eventual ascendance as a free-spirited movie star known for her gay friends and extramarital affairs.

13 As Trask argues, *Valley of the Dolls* showcases the normative gaze of gossip that stigmatized women's sexuality, "from the repressed woman who withholds sex entirely to the nymphomaniac," or "the queer": "In the book's reckoning, there are ultimately no exceptional women—only women who think they can pass as such. Susann suggests, moreover, that such delusion is a liability that no woman can escape . . . stigma can come at any juncture" (2013, 182–83, 189).

14 Ethel also evidences numerous evocations of the young Susann, according to biographer Barbara Seaman, including keeping a list of her sex partners with commentary (1996c, 120, 122, 126, 137–44, 200, 381).

15 The suggestion that Christie could be gay might be Susann's veiled reference to comedian Joe E. Lewis, with whom she maintained a decades-long affair that turned platonic when he told her to address him with a woman's name during sex (Seaman 1996c, 219). Although Seaman informs readers that Susann modeled Christie primarily after Eddie Cantor, Christie nevertheless utters one of Lewis's most famous punch lines, "Once is enough" (Susann 1997c, 206).

16 Both Wojcik and Doty explore the power dynamics of the "fag-hag" relationship (Wojcik 1996, 8; Doty 1993, 86–89). This remains an ongoing theme, as well, in Susann's reception (Indiana 2008, 216).

17 Mayne eschews the closet as an element of Arzner's irony (Mayne 1991, 137–38). This indicates significant material differences between

Susann and Arzner, the extent to which Susann's romans à clef and her promotional tactics revolved around the irony and inner comedy of the glass closet in a manner that Arzner's genderqueer production stills—posed with her close-cropped hair in any number of suits—were never meant to. Susann's irony included the masquerade of femininity to pass as straight while delivering queer signals in her books and statements, the detection of which was part of the pleasure of being both a fan and a detractor.

18 As Seaman chronicles, Susann and Batchelor were close friends. Batchelor also wrote and composed the title song for the 1967 promotional documentary *Jacqueline Susann and the Valley of the Dolls*.

Chapter 3. Wit Is Not Enough

1 Glenda Carpio points to the racialized dimension of Bergson's paradigm through the example of Bergson's discussion of blackface, which Bergson explains as funny because it can be perceived as a "disguise" "that surprises us." Bergson reinstates the norm of whiteness, its constructed naturalness, but never pursues the racist implications related to laughter's corrective function. See Carpio (2008, 109); and Bergson (1928, 40–41).

2 Susann's comments are quoted in numerous pieces about her—for example, Meehan 1967, 22; Howard 1966, 69; Anon. 1969b; Davidson 1969, 70; Kelly 1969, A20.

3 Bergson's theory supplies explanations for many forms of exclusionary ridicule based on normative definitions of "natural" and "human," including bodily motion, physical ability, and, as mentioned previously, race (Bergson 1928, 22–24).

4 Launched by a phone chat between Jackie Susann and gossip columnist Joyce Haber, the *Love, American Style* vignette "Love and the Hidden Meaning" features Susann portraying herself during promotion for *Once Is Not Enough*. Martha Raye plays a hysterical fan whose husband she suspects of having an affair with Jackie, deluded into thinking that he inspired one of Jackie's amorous characters. Jackie assures the distraught reader that it is fiction, emphasizing her happy marriage to Irving Mansfield whose portrait she keeps at her side (ABC, November 30, 1973).

5   In *Hollywood Highbrow*, Shyon Baumann refers to Rosenberg's concern about the loss of cultural hierarchies in light of the soaring popularity of mass culture works such as *Valley of the Dolls* and *The Beverly Hillbillies* (2007, 48–49).

6   This might be the first carnivalized evocation of Susann, predating the descriptions of her by Capote and subsequent journalists, in addition to Diane Arbus's photo of Jackie and Irving accompanying Sarah Davidson's *Harper's* article.

7   Long John Nebel, a popular late night radio host broadcast from New York from the 1950s to the late 1970s, and he frequently hosted Jacqueline Susann (and Irving Mansfield on occasion). Susann refers to Nebel in both *The Love Machine* (1997a, 294, 295) and in *Once Is Not Enough* (1997b, 41) in tributes to the radio host as a beloved fixture of New York, and Seaman's biography of Susann regularly mentions him. Susann is also a recurrent figure in Donald Bain's 1974 biography, *Long John Nebel: Radio Talk King, Master Salesman, Magnificent Charlatan*.

8   Seaman also provides an account of the Capote incident (1996c, 390–91).

9   For Capote, this also involved highbrow hostility toward what Eve Sedgwick calls "the empty secret," literary discourse that devalues signs of an author's queerness as corrupting artistic form with "content," a violation of the art-life dichotomy that turns the work into "kitsch" (Sedgwick 1990, 156, 165–66).

10   Michael Trask subsequently reads Capote's cracks about Susann as "fiendish delight in seeing through her makeup to its unprepossessing foundation" (Trask 2013, 181), however, Trask provides in his previous discussion of "procedural liberalism" a plausible subtext for Capote's maneuvers.

11   Capote might also have been resentful that Susann beat him to the punch in her portrayal of Judith Austin, stand-in for Babe Paley, in *The Love Machine*. Capote would later render his close friend Paley in his own roman à clef, *Answered Prayers*, although the publication of excerpts in a 1975 edition of *Esquire* ended his and Paley's relationship. See Kashner (2012).

12   Capote might also be making a reference to gay West Hollywood, its main strip located along route 66.

13 Trask (2013, 181) also compares Davidson's comments to Capote's in his analysis of gender and sexual performativity in *Valley of the Dolls*.

14 Capote eventually wrote his own roman à clef, *Answered Prayers*, first published in 1975 in *Esquire*, which had its own problems with litigation. The *Esquire* story exposed the antics of his rich friends Babe Paley and Lee Radziwill, among others. When Gore Vidal sued Capote in 1975 for libel over gossip about Vidal's drunken antics at the White House, Radziwill refused to affirm her firsthand knowledge of the event (she had gossiped the story to Capote in the first place). See Kashner (2012), and Roshan (2015).

15 This is a manifestation of what Wojcik identifies as "the crucial role women have played as producers and consumers of both gay and feminist camp" (1996, 19).

16 Even when subsequent columns by Bjorkman simply included Susann as a fashionable celebrity-about-town, she spotlighted the novelist's playfulness alongside her glamorous desirability and literary triumph, such as at one fashion show when Bjorkman enthusiastically identifies "THAT GOOD-LOOKING brunette," boasts her bestselling *Valley of the Dolls*, and comments, "Jacqueline took some time out from work on her new book . . . to join the biggest game going today!—the fashion game!" (Bjorkman 1966b, 12). Bjorkman also exhibited her own playfulness when alluding to Susann's scandalous side, such as when she spotted Susann at the same party as Ethel Merman. Mischievously enclosing the following line in parentheses, Bjorkman confides, "No, Jacqueline and Ethel certainly did not sit down and chat" (1966c, 8).

17 Susann appeared again on *Laugh-In* during the fifth season (October 4, 1971). Paired with Johnny Brown, Alan Sues, Ruth Buzzi, and Lily Tomlin, as well as delivering a one-liner solo, Susann performed in even more bits that called attention to the sex in her books and singled out Robin Stone in *The Love Machine*, the movie version having just opened at the end of August.

18 Phyllis Diller factors in to a variety of historical currents in comedy of the late 1960s. As Mizejewski observes, "Failure at domesticity has been a theme of women's comedy since Phyllis Diller" (2014, 31), and as Quinlan Miller informs, according to anecdotal accounts, Diller honed her comic persona through working with drag queens (2019, 183).

19 Shecky Greene, who played Christie Lane in the 1971 movie version of *The Love Machine*, cracked a similar one-liner as Diller's when he joked about *The Love Machine*, "It's the first book I read after *Heidi*" (Seaman 1996c, 412).

20 Theories of gay camp centralize the binaries of high and low, youth and old age, female and male, as well as desirable and undesirable (Babuscio 1999, 119; Cohan 2005, 10–11).

21 Susann makes these statements in the 1967 promotional film, *Jacqueline Susann and the Valley of the Dolls*.

22 A testament to the "theatricalizing of female friendship" central to Mayne's conception of "lesbian irony" (1991, 116–17), Linda's performances for January anchor their relationship in ambivalent back talk to the male gaze.

Chapter 4. Dykes, Gays, and *Dolls*

1 Waters refers to his "parody of the *Valley of the Dolls* shot" in the commentary track for *Female Trouble* (19:30). Carol Burnett had re-created the same popular visual for her 1968 parody of the film, in which the actors stay frozen in their poses for the whole bit, and Lee Daniels would create an homage fifty years hence on his TV drama *Star*.

2 Grant states that these thoughts were inspired by seeing a "foot-stompingly funny" gay male stage production of *Valley of the Dolls* (2014, 246).

3 This article was among the clippings in Grove Press editor in chief Ira Silverberg's research prior to the new 1997 edition of *Valley of the Dolls*. Ira Silverberg Papers.

4 My research for this chapter began several years back for an essay I contributed to Pamela Demory and Christopher Pullens's collection *Queer Love in Film and Television*. Other areas of this chapter's research and analysis correspond to my essay for Mary Desjardins and Michael DeAngelis's special issue on star biography for *Celebrity Studies*. I remain grateful in both cases to the editors' insightful feedback as well as the anonymous readers' feedback, which helped considerably to refine my arguments.

5 In some respects *Ballet of the Dolls* also resembled the drag artist's later, better-known work as Lypsinka, nostalgic cultural pastiche that

expressed a "yearning for the 'simplicity' of life before AIDS" (Román 1993, 215).

6 Susann's Jewishness did not figure into her renewed appreciation, quite unlike the popular "rediscovery" of Mel Brooks that transpired just a few years later, inspired by the Broadway hit musical *The Producers*.

7 Holden (1997) refers to lang's cover as "campy" (H32).

8 In the 1995 Theatre-a-Go-Go! production of *Valley of the Dolls*, actors performed in drag across the gender spectrum, similar to Epperson's strategy for *Ballet of the Dolls*, including Kate Flannery as Neely O'Hara, drag queens Benjamin Zook and Jackie Beat as Helen Lawson, and Illeana Douglas playing Jacqueline Susann in the author's cameo from the film.

9 The conclusion of this book delves into the white and middle-class norms of the gay camp cult of *Valley of the Dolls*, to the extent that Black queer fan activity is only recently garnering representation. In appropriating and appreciating *Valley of the Dolls*, RuPaul's many quotations on *RuPaul's Drag Race*, Lee Daniels's *Star*, Steven Canals's *Pose*, and Laverne Cox's statements about *Valley of the Dolls* when promoting the audio book simultaneously revise the camp canon as well as establish further space and presence for Black queer and trans fans.

10 The sensibility for being out as well as pride in nonheteronormative sexuality was emblematized in the slogans of Queer Nation and ACT UP t-shirts, posters, and stickers, such as "I am out therefore I am," "I CAN SEE QUEERLY NOW," and "PROMOTE LESBIANISM." See Crimp and Rolston (1990, 21–22).

11 The recent BluRay edition of *Valley of the Dolls* strikes a compromise between gay fandom and straight female fandom, mining the commentary track from the 2006 edition with gay gossip columnist Ted Casablanca in conversation with star Barbara Parkins, combined with a video essay by Amy Fine Collins and another by film critic Kim Morgan. Just as in the 2006 edition, lesbian fandom still remains unaccounted for.

12 Irving Mansfield's 1983 memoir *Life with Jackie* also contributed to Susann's queer reception, as evidenced in the pages of *Dead Jackie Susann Quarterly*, but Mansfield's romanticized depiction of his

beloved partner softens the harder edges of Susann's personality and their relationship, and includes no indication of Susann's bisexuality.

13 Linda Mizejewski's discussion of Spacks's argument in the context of Kathy Griffin's comedy proved highly influential in the development of my arguments here. See Mizejewski (2014, 55–56).

14 As I discuss in prior research, an acrimonious relationship developed between *Dead Jackie* (*DJSQ*) and Barbara Seaman over the rights to discussing the details of Susann's life: "In August 1996, two of Seaman's legal representatives sent letters to the zine regarding its uncredited use of material from *Lovely Me*; the first missive threatened legal action, and the second requested the zine cite *Lovely Me* and plug the upcoming new edition (Altman 1996; Salem 1996). *DJSQ* responded by email in October to Seaman's legal representatives. Conciliatory and combative, the zine apologized for their prior oversight and assured their compliance with Seaman's wishes. The *DJSQ* writers nevertheless demanded that Seaman give them some credit for helping to revive the interest in Susann that motivated the reprint of *Lovely Me*: 'you owe us just as much as we owe you' (Dead-Jackie 1996). . . . The sadly rancorous exchange between Seaman and *DJSQ*, however, revolved around the power of tastemaking, a struggle over cultural capital between two generations of feminists, Jacqueline Susann fans, and cultural producers" (Feil 2017, 556).

15 The video fragment of the 1985 production is the basis for my analysis here; see Lypsinka's *Ballet of the Dolls*.

16 Epperson's name for the ensemble "Lucille Le Sewer Players" puns on Joan Crawford's birth name, Lucille LeSueur. Epperson's reference to Crawford might also be hinting at Susann's caustic comments about the Hollywood star quoted by Seaman: "Ethel Merman is a lady and philanthropist compared to Joan . . . If I had known Joan when I was writing *Valley of the Dolls*, Helen Lawson would have been a monster" (1996c, 440).

17 To the extent that queer women and a range of genderqueer fans are excluded from the origin story of this camp cult, this narrative also forecloses on the dynamic gender fluidity among the emerging "queer" generation that arose out of challenges to traditional identity politics.

18 Schulman compares *OutWeek* to *Pravda* in an interview with Michelangelo Signorile about the origins and impact of ACT UP (2003, 37, 41).

19 Pokorny performs a virtual checklist of Pamela Robertson Wojcik's framework for feminist camp and "represents oppositional modes of performance and reception" in addition to expressing a sensibility that comprises "a female form of aestheticism, related to female masquerade . . . that articulates and subverts the 'image- and culture-making processes' to which women have traditionally been given access" (Wojcik 1996, 5–6, 9–19).

20 Pokorny exemplifies what Wojcik calls for, "viewing the exchange between women and gay men as a two-way street" (Wojcik 1996, 7). Pokorny employs camp, for instance, as "a means of negotiating subject positions," and through camp, "negotiates between different levels of cultural practice" (Wojcik 1996, 18). Pokorny's assertion of style through an analysis of drag performance finally enacts "masquerade as both a performative strategy and a mode of reception," interpreting gay male drag in the context of feminist critique, and then translating gay drag into a "dyke" sensibility (Wojcik 1996, 18).

21 Writing on the changes in camp of the 1990s, Wojcik and Flinn note the politicization of camp due to the AIDS crisis and queer activism (Wojcik 1996, 119; Flinn 1999, 454)

22 When in 1993 the *New York Times* reported on the publishing stunt of *Just This Once*, a novel Scott French generated by a computer programmed "to turn out a trashy page-turner—the sort of steamy fiction that Jacqueline Susann, author of 'Valley of the Dolls,' used to crank out," the paper deferred to *Dead Jackie Susann Quarterly*, "a New York publication that writes about Ms. Susann with equal measures of enthusiasm and irreverence. 'She would be proud,' its review declared. 'Lots of money, sleaze, disease, death, oral sex, tragedy and the good girl gone bad'" (Lohr 1993, A1). Conspicuously absenting the "dyke" dimensions of *Dead Jackie* while emphasizing its camp sensibility, the *Times* closeted the zine again a month later with gleeful news about the home video edition of *Valley of the Dolls*, "this summer's rage among camp-loving couch potatoes," alongside the paper's recommendation of *Dead Jackie*, "satirical fluff about the late author and other celebrities" (Anon. 1993, V3).

The digital dimension of *Dead Jackie Susann Quarterly* is also noteworthy. By 1995 and its third issue, *Dead Jackie* was accepting emails and had a digital edition, which is still preserved online.

This might have appealed to what Becker discusses as "the Creative Class," a lucrative cultural and consumer "social class" emerging in the 1990s and related to the "Bourgeois Bohemian" phenomenon (2006, 111).

23 Joanne Hollows alludes to some of these problems of inclusion and classification in her critique of the masculinized norms of cult movie culture; indicating "the power relations that sustain certain definitions" of what is and is not "cult," she points to elision of both gay and female viewers, offering as alternatives to the usual sex and gore films of the cult canon "other more feminized films such as *Valley of the Dolls*" (2003, 39). Ironically, similar power relations have functioned to efface queer women's participation in the *Valley* cult, in addition to Black queer fans.

24 The visible emergence of lesbian camp in the 1990s (if not necessarily in name) coincided with a growing presence of straight feminist camp, emblematized by pop star Madonna (Wojcik 1996, 123–38).

25 Paraphrasing Kotz's comments on *Grapefruit*, *Taking Back the Dolls* "aggressively opens itself up to different, intersecting cultural histories," which in this case pertains to AIDS, celebrity culture, Susann's novel and the Hollywood film version, and the queer feminist culture blooming in the 1990s (Kotz 1993, 93).

26 Julius J. Epstein's screenplay for *Once Is Not Enough* initially included considerably more screen time for Karla, evident in the draft from March 19, 1974, which I viewed in the Renata Vanni script collection at UCLA's Charles E. Young Research Library. This earlier draft includes more development of Dee and Karla's romance, Karla's backstory as a Polish war refugee, and reflection about her disabled daughter in addition to an alternate ending that pairs Karla and January as friends mourning the loss of Mike and Dee, who have died in a plane crash.

The finished film, however, excised all of Karla's backstory and offered only one substantial love scene between Karla and Dee. This might have reflected the director Guy Green's continual resistance to including *any* of the lesbian material from the novel. As he informed the British film critic Margaret Hinxman in a private letter, "if I had had my way, the lesbian scene . . . would never have been in the film" (Green 1975).

27 Lynn's memoir bespeaks what Spacks refers to as the "intimate involve-ment between gossip and sexuality" (Spacks 1985, 135–36).

28 Such logic extends to the operations of the campier and more explicit *Dead Jackie Susann Quarterly* and *Taking Back the Dolls*. The gossipy revelations that their sexual displays engender implicate the teller/performer and are meant to solicit contact from and among the audi-ence, queer erotic community.

29 This speaks to Gans's conception of "part-timers" consuming the counterculture (Gans 1999, 123), and especially to Becker's discussions of the crossover marketing of queer culture in the 1990s (Becker 2006, 108–9).

30 Among numerous examples of Reed's support for Susann, see Reed's interview with Quinn (1966, 19), in addition, Seaman's discussion (1996c, 391).

31 Strangely, Lypsinka bypasses any reference to Susann's sexuality, or any disclosures unique to Seaman's work for that matter.

32 See Seaman (1996c, 153–54, 293–95). Susann also has one character define Carole Landis as a beauty ideal, and later, names one of Neely's fellow patients Carole in the mental institution sequence (Susann 1997c, 6, 369).

Chapter 5. The Laugh Machine

This chapter is based on a paper that originated in Mary Desjardins and Michael DeAngelis's special edition of *Celebrity Studies* on star biography (Feil 2017). I am grateful to the editors as well as the anony-mous readers for their invaluable feedback.

1 In *Valley of the Dolls*, Neely avows her craving for "mass love" (Susann 1997c, 268–69).

2 See Susann's comments to *Life* (Howard 1966, 69), the *Boston Globe* (Kelly 1969, A16), and *Harper's* magazine (Davidson 1969. 66, 69, 71), quotations from her publicity interviews in *Time* magazine (Anon. 1969a), and testimonies in the promotional film, *Jacqueline Susann and the Valley of the Dolls*.

3 The discussion here is especially influenced by Desjardins (2015, 192–93), DeAngelis (2017, 583), and Spacks (1985, 118).

4 I am grateful to Robert Silman at Tambar Arts and author Paul Minx for their generosity and kindness, supplying reviews, video, and the script for *See How Beautiful I Am*.

5 The stage direction in *Paper Doll*, "To audience," usually signals when characters break the fourth wall, however, there is no such direction for the final line of the play. It seems more plausible, especially considering the frequency of her direct addresses, that Jackie tells the audience "Please tell your friends!" rather than saying this to Irving.

6 None of the dramatized Susann bios address the death of Josephine in 1970, a devastating event for Susann that both Seaman and Korda discuss. (Following Josie's passing, she was given the poodle Joseph Ian: Seaman 1996c, 400–401.) This central event provides another challenge to Susann's star biography, considering the kitsch clichés associated with ailing pets in melodramas as well as the amount of tragic setbacks already confronting Susann.

7 Tom Jones had just made something of a comeback in Tim Burton's Ed Wood–inspired sci-fi epic *Mars Attacks!* (1996), another sign of the nostalgic camp recirculated in the 1990s, along with the novels of Jacqueline Susann.

8 For a humorous account of Susann's stays at the Beverly Hills Hotel, see *The Pink Palace Revisited: Behind the Doors at the Beverly Hills Hotel* (Stuart and Prince 1993, 108–9).

9 As I discuss in prior work on Susann, Seaman, and *Isn't She Great*, Paul Rudnick's screenplay officially adapted Korda yet the material of the film clearly draws from Seaman's *Lovely Me*. As Seaman claimed, her literary agent (the son of a "longtime intimate associate, and friend" of Korda's) rushed her into selling the option rights for her book as a made-for-TV movie so that Korda's article would be the only source on Susann available for the more lucrative film rights (Feil 2017, 556; Seaman 2000). Seaman informed a friend that she learned (through hearsay) that Rudnick preferred to adapt her rich biography rather than the slim Korda article, and the screenplay for *Isn't She Great* surely reflects that, particularly the 1998 version that Seaman perused and annotated in consideration of a lawsuit (Seaman 2000; Rudnick 1998).

10 See Larson's discussion of this in the context of the Susann revival (2003, 382–85).

11   The finished film punctuates Michael's narrative function as redeemer
     by eliding an intimate scene that Rudnick had written between Jackie
     and Irving during her final moments of life (Rudnick 1998, 121–22).
     Although Irving's narration closes the film, Michael's approval of
     Jackie increases in importance because his contact with her is the last
     of her interactions the film shows.

12   Minx (and Rudnick) might also be drawing from Preston's stinging
     1969 letter to the *New York Times Book Review* rebuking Nora Eph-
     ron's contention that Morton Cooper and Henry Sutton, authors of
     romans à clef published by Bernard Geis, were "sloppy imitators of
     Susann's style": "As executive editor at Bernard Geis Associates, I have
     had first-hand experience with all three writers. Having spent weeks
     struggling with Miss Susann's fractured version of our native tongue,
     I could testify that one thing no one could ever accuse her of perpe-
     trating was style. There simply isn't any, good or bad . . . Therefore,
     it is difficult to see how anyone could be accused of imitating it. . . .
     The last thing I would have considered at that time was to encourage
     anyone to emulate Miss Susann." Preston closes by affirming that the
     success of *The Love Machine* rested on readers "who have never read
     a book before and therefore do not know what they are getting, or
     missing" (1969, 39).

Conclusion. Sleazy Summaries and Camp Positions

I am indebted to Alfred L. Martin Jr. for his generous and invaluable
feedback on this chapter.

1   Jacqueline Susann's science-fiction novel *Yargo* (written in the early
    1950s and published posthumously in 1979) deserves some attention
    for its fusion of romance fiction tropes, including female homoerot-
    icism, with what Susan Sontag called "the imagination of disaster"
    (Seaman 1996c, 154; Sontag 1966, 209–25).

2   Doty refers to Pee-wee as a "sissy boy" in his analysis of gay camp on
    Pee-wee's Playhouse. See Doty (1993), 81–95.

3   Even in the big-budget 1999 horror film *The Haunting*, references
    to Susann arrived with a queer, feminist camp tinge; "I think I see a
    little . . . Jackie Susann in Theo," one character wryly remarks, swiftly

defining the drug use, bisexuality, sophistication, and high-fashion style of Catherine Zeta-Jones's character.

4 Halberstam characterizes conventional camp as a "repertoire of formalized and often formulaic responses" (Halberstam 2011, 110).

5 See Mizejewski (2021).

6 A longer version of the Carrie Fisher discussion appears in Linda Mizejewski and Tanya D. Zuk's collection *Our Blessed Rebel Queen*. I first developed these ideas for their Carrie Fisher panel at the 2018 Society for Cinema and Media Studies conference, and I remain grateful to both Linda and Tanya for their smart as well as supportive feedback on various drafts of my chapter; it was a joy to work with them.

7 Novelist Jackie Collins, famed for penning romans à clef such as *Hollywood Wives* and *The Bitch* about celebrity scandal in Hollywood and London, was clearly a successor to Susann; see Whelehan (2005, 41) and Gelder (2004, 130–33). The new documentary *Lady Boss: The Jackie Collins Story* (Fairrie 2021) surprisingly contains no mention of Susann, giving credit to Collins for many of Susann's innovations, such as turning the author into a brand as well as writing about sexually active women.

8 I am again drawing from David L. Hirst's (1979) discussion of manners comedy.

9 Mark Finch's (1999) analysis of the popular 1980s TV drama *Dynasty* identifies Collins's camp agency and its impact on the program's gay reception. The presence of Collins in *These Old Broads* surely draws on her camp persona forged through *Dynasty*, but also invokes her sister Jackie's Hollywood exposés.

10 Carrie Fisher clearly identifies with a gay man as her stand-in for a celebrity child, but in the novel *Postcards from the Edge*, she appears uncomfortable about being associated with lesbian desire. During Suzanne's sleepover with her friend Lucy, for instance, the narration makes sure to supply the detail that they "slept in different rooms" (Fisher 1987, 185). Fisher's cameo in *These Old Broads* nevertheless has lesbian overtones; she plays a sex worker in a holding cell, dressed suggestively and lying with her head in the lap of another sex worker.

11 This scene could also be an allusion to Fisher's reconciliation with "ex-stepmother" Elizabeth Taylor when they both attended a lesbian-gay awards show in the 1990s (Keck 2001, F1).

12 I am alluding here to Mizejewski's (2021) pretty/funny dynamic.

13 Daniels also signifies on the exclusions of both white gay camp and Black popular culture through what Charles I. Nero refers to as, in his application of Gates's theory of signifyin(g), "capping": "a figure of speech which revises an original statement by adding new terms" (Nero 1991, 235, 237). Daniels adds new terms to (white) gay camp that democratize the camp cannon and whom it addresses and represents.

14 The formula of the *Real Housewives* franchise consists of upper-middle-class women acquaintances who gather and gossip about each other as well as confess and gossip "privately" in segments interjected among the scenes, all of which motivates social events in which women become unruly and engage in scandalous behavior.

15 Gates explains the confluence of textual and reception practices in the operation of negativity by way of exemplifying "the racially and culturally specific [practice of] 'signifyin(g),'" drawn from the groundbreaking work of Henry Louis Gates Jr., as well as "alternative reading strategies, such as camp" (Gates 2018, 20). Daniels effectively intersects these proximate sensibilities into camp negativity, signifying on white gay camp and Black respectability culture.

16 I understand the historically specific dimension of Miller's argument, that "trans gender queer" pertains to a period of TV comedy (roughly late 1940s to 1970) before popular culture identified queer and trans identities. The space for trans gender queer camp viewing and performance still exists in contemporary television, however, tied to now salient trans and gender-nonconforming artistic sensibilities, as a means for challenging the racialized normativity of binary gender performance.

17 Star Davis compares to many characters in *Valley of the Dolls*, most obviously Neely O'Hara, but also Jennifer (in the novel, not the film version). Star's sexual sophistication compares to Jennifer's, as does her blond hair, and the sexual abuse she endures from her boyfriend and then quells approximates Jennifer's relationship to Tony Polar. Apart from the *Valley* references, Star's blonde hair and proximity to African American culture also compare closely to Amanda in *Love Machine*. Star's upbringing and cultural sensibility are African American, her half sister Simone is biracial, and when Star and Simone seek

refuge, their only living "family" consists of Carlotta Brown, their deceased mother's best friend and bandmate.

18 John Waters's parody of this in a shot from *Female Trouble* (1974) might also be an influence, considering that Daniels also refers to *Female Trouble* as influencing *Star*. It is also likely that the actors were aware of these cultural references, as Coscarelli (2016) of the *New York Times* informs: "Ms. Demorest [who plays Star] also said that he [Lee Daniels] told her to watch 'Sweet Charity' and 'Female Trouble' during the audition process."

References

Abelove, Henry, Michèle Aina Barale, and David M. Halperin. 1993. *The Lesbian and Gay Studies Reader*. New York: Routledge.

Adams, Cindy. 1969. "Do Hollywood Men Make Wrecks of Their Women?" *Photoplay* 76, no. 2: 38–39, 90–91. Margaret Herrick Library, Academy of Motion Picture Arts and Sciences.

Adams, Marjory. 1966. "Author Susann Has 'Em Guessing on 'Dolls' Stars." *Boston Globe*, May 10: 21.

———. 1967. "Judy Stops Gossipers, Signs 'Dolls' Contract." *Boston Globe*, March 15: 32.

Additional Papers of Barbara Seaman, 1933–2008. Arthur and Elizabeth Schlesinger Library, Radcliffe Institute for Advanced Study, Harvard University, Cambridge, MA.

Altman, Dennis. 1982. *The Homosexualization of America, the Americanization of the Homosexual*. New York: St. Martin's Press.

Altman, Richard A. 1996. Letter to *Dead Jackie Susann Quarterly*. August 14. Additional Papers of Barbara Seaman.

Anon. 1946. "Lovely Me." *Women's Wear Daily*, December 26: 49.

Anon. 1962. "The Garbagepickers." *Time*, October 26: 105.

Anon. 1965. "The New Pornography." *Time*, April 16. Time.com. https://content.time.com/time/subscriber/article/0,33009,841826,00.html.

Anon. 1966a. "Best Dressed?" *Washington Post*, June 15: C1.

Anon. 1966b. "No 'Dolls' Rinsing, But in Good Taste." *Film Daily*, September 1: 1, 8.

Anon. 1966c. "'Valley of Dolls' as Dialog Dilly in Screen Form." *Variety*, September 7: 5.

Anon. 1967a. Advertisement. *New York Times*, March 13: 38.

Anon. 1967b. "Homo Theme Pix Rated A-III and B; NCOMP Hits 'Dolls.'" *Variety*, November 22: 4.

Anon. 1967c. "Independent Trade Reviews: Valley of the Dolls." *Independent Film Journal*, December 23: 24.

Anon. 1978d. Pressbook: *Valley of the Dolls*. 20th Century Fox. Ira Silverberg Papers.

Anon. 1967e. "The Shock of Freedom in Films." *Time*, December 8.

Anon. 1967f. "Showbiz Sickies." *Time*, December 22: 88.

Anon. 1967g. "Two 'Dolls' Contests Tie In Exhibitors." *Boxoffice*, November 13: a2.

Anon. 1967h "Valley of the Dolls." Advertisement. *Variety*, December 20: 19.

Anon. 1967i. "Valley of the Dolls." *New York Times*, March 13: 38.

Anon. 1967j. "Valley of the Dolls." *Variety*, December 20: 6.

Anon. 1968. "Pictures: Catholics Pass Nude 'Stranger'; Can't Rap Camus." *Variety*, January 24: 3, 20.

Anon. 1969a "Cosmo Reads the New Books." *Cosmopolitan*, June: 8.

Anon. 1969b. "Jackie's Machine." *Time*, June 20: 104. Academic Search Premier.

Anon. 1969c. "Jacqueline Susann to Sue NBC, Capote." *Chicago Tribune*, July 25: B23.

Anon. 1969d. *Literary Guild Newsletter*. April 28. Literary Guild of America. Additional Papers of Barbara Seaman.

Anon. 1969e. "WWD'S Chutzpah Ratings." *Women's Wear Daily*, April 14: 4–5.

Anon. 1973. "For City's Next Mayor, Words of Advice, Wisdom, and Warning." *New York Times*, November 6: 39.

Anon. 1974. "Is 'Once Enough' for Guy Green?" *Variety*, July 10: 4, 13.

Anon. 1993. "Surfacing: Revival." *New York Times*, August 15: V3.

Anon. 1994. "Frameline Presents: Eighteenth San Francisco International Lesbian and Gay Film Festival." Festival Program.

Anon. 1997a. Grove Press Promotional Flyer: "The Other Jackie." October 21. Ira Silverberg Papers.

Anon. 1997b. Press Release: *Valley of the Dolls*. Grove Press. Fall. Ira Silverberg Papers.

Anon. 1997c. Promotional Flyer: Blur, *Valley of the Dolls Screening*. December 10. Ira Silverberg Papers.

Anon. 1997d. "Theatre-A-Go-Go! Presents Jacqueline Susann's Valley of the Dolls: A Screen-To-Stage Adaptation." Playbill. Los Angeles. Ira Silverberg Papers.

Atkinson, Brooks. 1946. "Not So Attractive." *New York Times*, December 26: 30.

Austin, S. Bryn, and Pam Gregg. 1993. "A Freak among Freaks: The 'Zine Scene." In *Sisters, Sexperts, Queers*, edited by Arlene Stein, 81–95. New York: Plume.

Avant, John Alfred. 1976. "Jacqueline Susann's Dolores." *Library Journal*, August 1960.

Babuscio, Jack. 1999. "The Cinema of Camp." In Cleto, 117–35.

Bain, Donald. 1974. *Long John Nebel: Radio Talk King, Master Salesman, Magnificent Charlatan*. New York: Macmillan.

Bakhtin, Mikhail. 1984. *Rabelais and His World*. Bloomington: Indiana University Press.

Balcerzak, Scott. 2013. *Buffoon Men*. Detroit: Wayne State University Press.

Bark, Ed. 1998. "Michele Lee Plays the Other Jackie." *Chicago Tribune*, December 9: NP. Additional Papers of Barbara Seaman.

Barnes, Clive. 1969. "'Oh, Calcutta!' a Most Innocent Dirty Show." *New York Times*, June 18: 33.

Bart, Peter. 1965. "Hollywood's Morality Code Undergoing First Major Revisions in 35 Years." *New York Times*, April 7: 37.

Bartell, Gerald. 2000. "Drag Queen's Dream." *New York Blade News*, January 28: 17. Additional Papers of Barbara Seaman.

Baumbach, Jonathan. 1969. "The Stupid Machine." *The Nation*, September 1: 188–90.

Baumann, Shyon. 2007. *Hollywood Highbrow: From Entertainment to Art*. Princeton, NJ: Princeton University Press.

Becker, Edith, Michelle Citron, Julia Lesage, and B. Ruby Rich. 1981. "Introduction to Special Section Lesbians and Film." *Jump Cut*, nos. 24–25, March 17–21.

Becker, Ron. 2006. *Gay TV and Straight America*. New Brunswick, NJ: Rutgers University Press.

Bergson, Henri. 1928. *Laughter: An Essay on the Meaning of the Comic*. Trans. Cloudesley Brereton. New York: Macmillan.

Bianculli, David. 1998. "Susann—the valley of the dreadful." *New York Daily News*, December 9: 92. John Epperson Collection.

Bisbort, Alan. 2008. *Media Scandals*. Westport, CT: Greenwood Press. ProQuest Ebook Central.

Bishop, Lisa. 1997. Fax to Ira Silverberg. October 14. Ira Silverberg Papers.

Bjorkman, Carol. 1966a. "Features: Carol." *Women's Wear Daily*, March 28: 8.

———. 1966b. "Features: Carol." *Women's Wear Daily*, May 25: 12.

——. 1966c. "Features: Carol." *Women's Wear Daily*, December 5: 8.

Bodroghkozy, Aniko. 2001. *Groove Tube: Sixties Television and the Youth Rebellion*. Durham, NC: Duke University Press.

Boyde, Melissa J. 2009. "The Modernist *roman à clef* and Cultural Secrets; or, I Know That You Know That I Know That You Know." *Australian Literary Studies* 24, nos. 3–4: 155–66.

Boyum, Joy Gould. 2015. "Columbia's Screwball Comedies: Wine, Women, and Wisecracks." In *Columbia Pictures: Portrait of a Studio*, edited by Bernard F. Dick. Lexington: University Press of Kentucky.

Brackman, Jacob. 1967. "The Put-On." *New Yorker*, June 24: 34–73.

Bronski, Michael. 1984. *Culture Clash: The Making of Gay Sensibility*. Boston: South End Press.

——. 1998. *The Pleasure Principle: Culture, Backlash, and the Struggle for Gay Freedom*. New York: St. Martin's Press.

Brooks, Peter. 1976. *The Melodramatic Imagination: Balzac, Henry James, Melodrama, and the Mode of Excess*. New Haven, CT: Yale University Press.

Brown, Helen Gurley. 2003. *Sex and the Single Girl*. New Jersey: Barricade.

Butler, Bethonie. 2016. "'Star' Isn't Even the Good Kind of Bad: Lee Daniels's New Fox Drama Is Just Bad." Weblog post. *Washington Post*, December 14.

Butler, Judith. 1990. "Lana's 'Imitation': Melodramatic Repetition and the Gender Performative." *Genders*, no. 9, fall: 1–18.

Cameron, Ardis. 2015. *Unbuttoning America: A Biography of Peyton Place*. Ithaca, NY: Cornell University Press.

Carpio, Glenda. 2008. *Laughing Fit to Kill: Black Humor in the Fictions of Slavery*. New York: Oxford University Press.

Carr, Steven Alan. 1999. "From 'Fucking Cops!' to 'Fucking Media': *Bonnie and Clyde* for a Sixties America." In *Arthur Penn's* Bonnie and Clyde, edited by Lester D. Friedman, 71–100. Cambridge: Cambridge University Press.

Carvajal, Doreen. 1997. "Pink Trash: The Return of the Dolls." *New York Times*, July 27: 23–24.

Cawelti, John. 1991. "The Evolution of Social Melodrama." In *Imitation of Life*, edited by Marcia Landy. Detroit: Wayne State University Press.

Chermayeff, Catherine, Jonathan David, and Nan Richardson. 1995. *Drag Diaries*. San Francisco: Umbra.

Cleto, Fabio, ed. 1999. *Camp: Queer Aesthetics and the Performing Subject*. Ann Arbor: University of Michigan Press.

Cocks, Jay. 1975. "Cinema: Father Lusts Best." *Time*, July 21.

Cohan, Steven. 1997. *Masked Men: Masculinity and the Movies in the Fifties*. Bloomington: Indiana University Press.

———. 2005. *Incongruous Entertainment: Camp, Cultural Value, and the MGM Musical*. Durham, NC: Duke University Press.

———. 2017. "'This Industry Lives on Gossip and Scandal': Female Star Narratives and the Marilyn Monroe Biopic." *Celebrity Studies*, December: 527–43.

———. 2019. *Hollywood by Hollywood: The Backstudio Picture and the Mystique of Making Movies*. New York: Oxford University Press.

Cohen, Andy. 2016. *Superficial: More Adventures from the Andy Cohen Diaries*. New York: Henry Holt.

Cohen, Jaffe, Danny McWilliams, and Bos Smith. 1995. *Growing Up Gay*. New York: Hyperion.

Collins, Amy Fine. 2000. "Once Was Never Enough." *Vanity Fair*. http://www .vanityfair.com/culture/2000/01/jacqueline-susann-valley-of-the-dolls -books. Accessed April 15, 2017.

Core, Philip. 1984. *Camp: The Lie that Tells the Truth*. New York: Delilah Books.

Coscarelli, Joe. 2016. "With 'Star,' Lee Daniels Tries to Expand an Empire." *New York Times*. ProQuest US Major Dailies.

Covington, Richard. 2000. "Jackie's Peaks and Valleys." *Los Angeles Times*, January 27. ProQuest Central.

Crimp, Douglas, and Adam Rolston. 1990. *AIDS Demo Graphics*. Seattle: Bay Press.

Crowther, Bosley. 1967. "The Screen: 'Valley of the Dolls' Opens." *New York Times*, December 16: 51.

Cunningham, Mark D. 2012. "Nigger, Coon, Boy, Punk, Homo, Faggot, Black Man: Reconsidering Established Interpretations of Masculinity, Race, and Sexuality through *Noah's Arc*." In Smith-Shomade, 172–86.

Dallos, Robert E. 1968. "TV's Quiet Revolution: Censors Giving In." *New York Times*, April 29: 86.

Davidson, Sara. 1969. "Jacqueline Susann: The Writing Machine." *Harper's* magazine, October 1: 65–71.

DeadJackie. 1996. Email. October 11. Additional Papers of Barbara Seaman.

DeAngelis, Michael. 2001. *Gay Fandom and Crossover Stardom: James Dean, Mel Gibson, and Keanu Reeves*. Durham, NC: Duke University Press.

———. 2014. "Queerness and Futurity in *Superbad*." In *Reading the Bromance*, edited by Michael DeAngelis. Detroit: Wayne State University Press.

———. 2017. "There and 'Not There': Todd Haynes and the Queering of Genre." *Celebrity Studies*, December: 578–92.

Demory, Pamela, and Christopher Pullen, eds. 2013. *Queer Love in Film and Television*. London: Palgrave Macmillan.

De Saint Phalle, Anne. 1967. "A Secretary's Schmaltz." *Harvard Crimson*, August 22. www.thecrimson.com/article/1967/8/22/a-secretarys-schmaltz-priding-the-subways/. Accessed March 27, 2021.

Desjardins, Mary R. 2015. *Recycled Stars: Female Film Stardom in the Age of Television and Video*. Durham, NC: Duke University Press.

Deutsch, Helen. 1966. *Valley of the Dolls*. First draft. November 3. Mark Robson Papers.

Diffrient, David Scott. 2013. "'Hard to Handle': Camp Criticism, Trash-Film Reception, and the Transgressive Pleasures of Myra Breckinridge." *Cinema Journal* 52, no. 2: 46–70.

Doty, Alexander. 1993. *Making Things Perfectly Queer*. Minneapolis: University of Minnesota Press.

Douglas, Illeana. 2015. *I Blame Dennis Hopper*. New York: Flatiron Books.

Dresner, Lisa M. 2010. "Love's Labor's Lost? Early 1980s Representations of Girls' Sexual Decision Making in Fast Times at Ridgemont High and Little Darlings." In *Virgin Territory: Representing Sexual Inexperience in Film*, edited by Tamar Jeffers McDonald. Detroit: Wayne State University Press.

Duke, Patty, and Kenneth Turan. 1987. *Call Me Anna*. New York: Bantam.

Duralde, Alonso. 2005. *101 Must-See Movies for Gay Men*. New York: Advocate Books.

Durbin, Karen. 2000. "A Princess of Pulp Returns to Even the Score." *New York Times*, January 16: 1, 28.

Dyer, Richard. 1986. *Heavenly Bodies*. New York: St. Martin's Press.

Ebert, Roger. 1990. "Postcards from the Edge." September 12. www.rogerebert.com/reviews/postcards-from-the-edge-1990. Accessed January 2, 2019.

Eco, Umberto. 2018. "The Frames of Comic 'Freedom.'" In Marx and Sienkiewicz: 25–33.

Edwards, Jerome. 1967. Telegram to Richard Zanuck. Mark Robson Papers.

Eisner, Douglas. 1999. "*Myra Breckinridge* and the Pathology of Heterosexuality." In Smith, 255–70.

Ellis, Samantha. 2001. "Sextacular!" *The Guardian*, August 7. www.theguardian.com/culture/2001/aug/07/edinburghfestival2001.fiction. Accessed December 23, 2017.

Ephron, Nora. 1969. "The Love Machine." *New York Times Book Review*, May 11: 3, 12.

———. 2007. *Wallflower at the Orgy*. New York: Penguin.

Epperson, John. 1986. *"Dial 'M' for Model."* Unpublished manuscript. John Epperson Collection.

Epstein, Julius J. 1974. *Once Is Not Enough*. March 19. Renata Vanni scripts, 1955–88. Charles E. Young Research Library, University of California, Los Angeles.

Erickson, Hal. 2000. *"From Beautiful Downtown Burbank": A Critical History of Rowan and Martin's Laugh-In, 1968–1973*. Jefferson, NC: McFarland.

Farfan, Penny. 2005. "Noel Coward and Sexual Modernism: Private Lives as Queer Comedy." *Modern Drama* 48, no. 4: 677–88.

Feil, Ken. 2005. *Dying for a Laugh: Disaster Movies and the Camp Imagination*. Middletown, CT: Wesleyan University Press.

———. 2013. "'Fearless Vulgarity': Camp Love as Queer Love for Jackie Susann and *Valley of the Dolls*." In Demory and Pullen, 141–51.

———. 2014. *Rowan and Martin's Laugh-In*. Detroit: Wayne State University Press.

———. 2017. "Scandal, Critical Gossip, and Queer Failure: Jacqueline Susann, *Valley of the Dolls*, and Star Biography." *Celebrity Studies*, December: 544–60.

———. 2021. "Postcards from the Valley of the Broads: Carrie Fisher, Jacqueline Susann, and Feminist Camp Authorship." In Mizejewski and Zuk, 149–173.

Ferguson, Frank H. 1967. Letter to R. Zanuck et al. October 11. Mark Robson Papers.

Field, Ryan. 2010. *Valley of the Dudes*. Riverdale, NY: Riverdale Avenue Books.

Finch, Mark. 1999. "Sex and Address in *Dynasty*." In Cleto, 143–59.

Fischer, Lucy. 1996. *Cinematernity: Film, Motherhood, Genre*. Princeton, NJ: Princeton University Press.

Fisher, Carrie. 1987. *Postcards from the Edge*. New York: Simon and Schuster.

Flicker, Seth. 2000. "Return to the Valley of the Dolls." *Genre*, February: 40–45, 83–88. Additional Papers of Barbara Seaman.

Flinn, Caryl. 1999. "The Deaths of Camp." In Cleto, 433–57.

———. 2009. *Brass Diva*. Oakland: University of California Press.

Floreani, Tracy. 2013. *Fifties Ethnicities: The Ethnic Novel and Mass Culture at Midcentury*. Albany: State University of New York Press.

Freedman, Jonathan. 2009. *Klezmer America: Jewishness, Ethnicity, Modernity*. New York: Columbia University Press.

Freud, Sigmund. 1963. *Character and Culture*. Edited by Philip Rieff. New York: Collier Books.

Frontain, Raymond-Jean. "Comedy of Manners." *Gay and Lesbian Literary Heritage*, edited by Claude J. Summers. Taylor and Francis, 2002. ProQuest Ebook Central.

Gans, Herbert. 1999. *Popular Culture and High Culture*. New York: Basic Books.

Gardner, Eriq. 2012. "Lawsuit Threatens Lee Daniels' 'Valley of the Dolls' TV Series." *Hollywood Reporter*, March 16. www.hollywoodreporter.com/thr-esq/valley-of-the-dolls-tv-series-lee-daniels-301111. Accessed March 23, 2018.

Gates, Anita. 2008. "The Human Condition." *New York Times*, August 20: E6.

Gates, Racquel J. 2013. "Keepin' It Reality Television." In Smith-Shomade, 141–56.

———. 2018. *Double Negative: The Black Image and Popular Culture*. Durham, NC: Duke University Press.

Gelder, Ken. 2004. *Popular Fiction: The Logics and Practices of a Literary Field*. New York: Routledge.

Gerharter, Rick. 1993. Untitled photo: *Valley of the Dolls. Frontiers*, November 19: 67. Ira Silverberg Papers.

Gerstner, David A. 2004. "The Practices of Authorship." In *Authorship and Film*, edited by David A. Gerstner and Janet Staiger, 3–25. New York: Routledge.

———. 2011. *Queer Pollen*. Urbana: University of Illinois Press.

Ginsberg, Merle. 2003. "Blonde Ambition." *New York*, June 3: 16.

Girelli, Elisabetta. 2013. *Montgomery Clift, Queer Star*. Detroit: Wayne State University Press.

Glitre, Kathrina. 2006. *Hollywood Romantic Comedy: States of the Union, 1934–1965*. Manchester: Manchester University Press.

Grant, Lee. 2014. *I Said Yes to Everything*. New York: Blue Rider Press.

Green, Guy. 1975. Letter to Margaret Hinxman. Guy Green Papers, Margaret Herrick Library, Academy of Motion Picture Arts and Sciences.

Greene, Alexis. 1992. "The New Comedy of Manners." *Theater* 23, no. 3: 79–83.

Greene, Gael. 1974. "The Crisis at 30!" *Cosmopolitan*, March: 142–45, 180.

Greene, Jane M. 2011. "Manners before Morals: Sophisticated Comedy and the Production Code, 1930–1934." *Quarterly Review of Film and Video* 28, no. 3: 239–56.

Grier, Barbara, writing as Gene Damon. 1966. "The Lesbian Paperback" *Tangents, June-July*. www.tangentgroup.org/lesbian-paperback/. Accessed January 3, 2020.

Griffin, Kathy. 2016. *Kathy Griffin's Celebrity Run-Ins: My A–Z Index*. New York: Flatiron Books.

Gunn, Drewey Wayne, and Jaime Harker. 2013. Introduction to *1960s Gay Pulp Fiction: The Misplaced Heritage*, edited by Drewey Wayne Gunn and Jaime Harker. Amherst: University of Massachusetts Press.

Haber, Joyce. 1969. "Beautiful People Love Jacqueline Susann." *Los Angeles Times*, June 29: R19.

———. 1970. "Brickbats Fly Early in the 70s." *Los Angeles Times*, January 6: C8.

———. 1971. "Jackie Susann Huddling with Garbo." *Los Angeles Times*, December 29: F12.

Halberstam, Jack. 2011. *The Queer Art of Failure*. Durham, NC: Duke University Press.

Hale, Mike. 2016. "Wishing upon a Fairy Tale." *New York Times*, December 15: C4.

Hampton, Mark, and Barbara J. Zitwer. 2001. *Paper Doll*. Unpublished manuscript. Additional Papers of Barbara Seaman.

Harris, Daniel. 1996. "Queen of Camp." *Bay Area Reporter*, November 21: 44–45. Ira Silverberg Papers.

Henke, Richard. 1994. "Imitation of Life." *Jump Cut* 39, June 7, 2011. www.ejumpcut.org/archive/onlinessays/JC39folder/imitationLife.html.

Hennessy, Chris. 2009. "Princess Leia: Leia's Kiss." In *My Diva: 65 Gay Men on the Women Who Inspire Them*, edited by Michael Montlack, 285–88. Madison: University of Wisconsin Press.

Herring, Hubert B. 1993. "Business Diary: He Caressed the Modem . . ." *New York Times*, July 4: F2.

Heung, Marina. 1987. "'What's the Matter with Sara Jane?': Daughters and Mothers in Douglas Sirk's *Imitation of Life*." *Cinema Journal* (Spring): 21–41.

Hicks, Jessica. 2013. "Can I Get an Amen? Marginalized Communities and Self-Love on *RuPaul's Drag Race*." In Demory and Pullen, 153–59.

Hirsch, Abby. 1976. "Dolores." *New York Times Book Review*, July 11: 6.

Hirst, David L. 1979. *Comedy of Manners*. London: Methuen.

Holden, Stephen. 1988a. "A Campy Showgirl," *New York Times*, December 4: 95.

———. 1988b. "For Melodies from Weill to Webb, Come to the Cabaret." *New York Times*, January 8: C1, C6.

———. 1997. "A Torch-Song Anthology about Dangerous Pleasures." *New York Times*, June 8: H32.

Hollows, Joanne. 2003. "The Masculinity of Cult." In *Defining Cult Movies*, edited by Mark Jancovich et al., 35–53. Manchester: Manchester University Press.

Horn, Katrin. 2017. *Women, Camp, and Popular Culture*. New York: Palgrave Macmillan.

Howard, Jane. 1966. "Happiness Is Being Number 1." *Life*, August 19: 69–78.

Hutcheon, Linda, with Siobhan O'Flynn. 2013. *A Theory of Adaptation*, second edition. London: Routledge.

Huyssen, Andreas. 1986. *After the Great Divide: Modernism, Mass Culture, Post-modernism*. Bloomington: Indiana University Press.

Illig, Joyce. 1973. "'Everybody' Was a Virgin Once." *Washington Post*, April 8: BW2.

Indiana, Gary. 2008. *Utopia's Debris*. New York: Basic Books.

Ira Silverberg Papers. 1980–2007. Fales Library and Special Collections, Elmer Holmes Bobst Library, New York University.

Jacobs, Alexandra. 1998. "Once Is Not Enough! Hollywood Brawls Over the Life of Jacqueline Susann." *New York Observer*, December 7: 19. Newyorkobserver.com, May 24, 2000. Additional Papers of Barbara Seaman.

———. 2000. "The Eight-Day Week." *New York Observer*, February 21, n.p. Additional Papers of Barbara Seaman.

Jaffe, Rona. 2005. *The Best of Everything*. New York: Penguin.

J. C. 1971. "Valley of the Dregs." *Time*, August 30: 60.

Jeffreys, Joe E. 2008. "The Soundplay's the Thing: A Formal Analysis of John (aka Lypsinka) Epperson's Queer Performance Text." In *"We Will Be Citizens": New Essays on Gay and Lesbian Theatre*, edited by James Fisher, 174–84. Jefferson, NC: McFarland.

Jermyn, Deborah. 2009. *Sex and the City*. Detroit: Wayne State University Press.

John Epperson Collection of Lypsinka Ephemera. 1994–2005. New York Public Library for the Performing Arts, Dorothy and Lewis B. Cullman Center, Billy Rose Theatre Division, New York.

Joyrich, Lynne. 2001. "Epistemology of the Console." *Critical Inquiry* (Spring): 439–67.

Judell, Brandon. 2000. "Lovely Jackie!: A Bisexual Icon Goes Straight." *Popcorn Q*, January 27. PlanetOut.com. October 15, 2001. Additional Papers of Barbara Seaman.

Judson, Barbara. 2000. "Roman à Clef and the Dynamics of Betrayal: The Case of Glenarvon." *Genre* 33, no. 2: 151–70.

Kaplan, E. Ann. 2003. "Wicked Old Ladies from Europe: Jeanne Moreau and Marlene Dietrich on the Screen and Live." In *Bad: Infamy, Darkness, Evil, and Slime on Screen*, edited by Murray Pomerance, 239–53. Albany: State University of New York Press.

Kashner, Sam. 2012. "Capote's Swan Dive." December, *Vanity Fair*, www .vanityfair.com/culture/2012/12/truman-capote-answered-prayers. Accessed March 8, 2019.

Kasindorf, Martin. 1973. "Jackie Susann Picks Up the Marbles." *New York Times*, August 12: 11, 85–89.

Kaufman, George S., and Moss Hart. 1939. *The Man Who Came to Dinner.* In *Three Plays by Kaufman and Hart*, 207–307. New York: Grove, 1980.

Keck, William. 2001. "Scandal's History for 'These Old Broads.'" *Los Angeles Times*, February 12: F1.

Keegan, Cael M. 2016. "Revisitation: A trans phenomenology of the media image." *MedieKultur* 61, 26-41.

Keller, Yvonne. 1999. "Pulp Politics: Strategies of Vision in Pro-Lesbian Novels, 1955–1965." In Smith, 1-25.

Kelly, Kevin. 1969. "The Love Machinery." *Boston Globe*, August 3: A16-A23.

Kessel, Looi van. 2016. "Digital Drag: Queer Potentiality in the Age of Digital Television." In *Queer TV in the 21st Century: Essays on Broadcasting from Taboo to Acceptance*, edited by Kylo-Patrick R. Hart, 111–27. Jefferson, NC: McFarland.

Kingsley, Dorothy. 1967. *Valley of the Dolls.* Final Screenplay: January 6 (last revised April 18). Mark Robson Papers.

Kitman, Marvin. 1971. "The 'Love Machine' as a Documentary." *Washington Post*, September 6: B9.

Klinger, Barbara. 1994. *Melodrama and Meaning: History, Culture, and the Films of Douglas Sirk.* Bloomington: Indiana University Press.

Knowles, Claire. 2016. "Working Girls: Femininity and Entrapment in Peyton Place and Valley of the Dolls." *Women: A Cultural Review* 27, no. 1: 62–78.

Koenig, Rhoda. 2001. "Life in Lipstick." *The Independent.* September 17: NP.

Korda, Michael. 1995. "Wasn't She Great?" *New Yorker*, August 14: 66–72.

Kotz, Liz. 1993. "An Unrequited Desire for the Sublime." In *Queer Looks: Perspectives on Lesbian and Gay Film*, edited by Martha Gever, John Greyson, and Pratibha Parma, 86-102. New York: Routledge.

Krefting, Rebecca. 2014. *All Joking Aside: American Humor and Its Discontents.* Baltimore: Johns Hopkins University Press.

Larson, Allen Robert. 2003. "Alienated Affections: Stardom, Work, and Identity in United States 20th Century Culture." PhD diss., University of Pittsburgh.

The Last Word: Liz Smith. 2017. Produced by Erik Olsen, Patrick Flynn, Joyce Purnick. November 12. www.nytimes.com/video/obituaries/1247467924075/last-word-liz-smith-obituary.html.

Latham, Sean. 2009. *The Art of Scandal: Modernism, Libel Law, and the Roman à Clef.* New York: Oxford University Press.

Lawrence, Rae. 2001. *Jacqueline Susann's Shadow of the Dolls.* New York: Crown.

Lehmann-Haupt, Christopher. 1969. "Popcorn." *New York Times,* May 9: 45.

Levine, Elana. 2007. *Wallowing in Sex: The New Sexual Culture of 1970s American Television.* Durham, NC: Duke University Press.

Lewis, Paul. 2006. *Cracking Up: American Humor in a Time of Conflict.* Chicago: University of Chicago Press.

Linfield, Susan. 1990. "First It Was Drugs, and Now It's Mother." *New York Times,* September 2: H15.

liz@gate.net. 2001. Email to Barbara Seaman. March 15. Additional Papers of Barbara Seaman.

Lohr, Steve. 1993. "Potboiler Springs from Computer's Loins." *New York Times,* July 2: A1.

Lubenski, Cathy. 1998. "Best Remembered as One of the 'Dolls.'" *New York Now,* December 6: n.p. Additional Papers of Barbara Seaman.

Lurleen. 1997. "Valley Girl." *Paper.* October, n.p. Ira Silverberg Papers.

Lynes, Russel. 1949. "Highbrow, Lowbrow, Middlebrow." *Harper's* magazine, February, 19–28.

Lynn, Traci. 2004. "The Long Ride Home." In *Small-Town Gay: Essays on Family life beyond the Big City,* edited by Elizabeth Newman, 33–48. Memphis: Kerlak Publishing.

Lypsinka. 1997. "Valley Girl." *Interview,* October: 138–41.

Mailer, Norman. 1971. "Prisoner of Sex." *Harper's Magazine,* March 1: 41–92.

Manners, Dorothy. 1966. "No Types in 'Dolls.'" *The Washington Post,* October 10: C10; ProQuest Historical Newspapers.

Manning, Scott. 1997. Fax to Ira Silverberg, July 10. Ira Silverberg Papers.

Mansfield, Irving, with Jean Libman Block. 1983. *Life with Jackie.* New York: Bantam.

Manville, W. H. 1967. "So You Want to Be a Writer?" *Cosmopolitan,* January: 76–81.

Marc, David. 1998. *Comic Visions: Television Comedy and American Culture.* Malden, MA: Blackwell.

Mark Robson Papers, 1943–79. Charles E. Young Research Library, University of California, Los Angeles.

Martin, Alfred L., Jr. 2018. "Generic Closets: Sitcoms, Audiences, and Black Male Gayness." In Marx and Sienkiewicz, 222–37.

———. 2021. *The Generic Closet: Sitcoms, Audiences, and Black Gayness and the Black-Cast Sitcom.* Bloomington: Indiana University Press.

Marx, Nick, and Matt Sienkiewicz, eds. 2018. *The Comedy Studies Reader.* Austin: University of Texas Press.

Matthews, Peter. 1988. "Garbo and Phallic Motherhood: A 'Homosexual' Visual Economy." *Screen* 29 (Summer): 14–39.

Mayne, Judith. 1991. "Lesbian Looks: Dorothy Arzner and Female Authorship." In *How Do I Look?: Queer Film and Video*, edited by Bad Object Choices, 103–35. Seattle: Bay Press.

———. 1994. *Directed by Dorothy Arzner.* Bloomington: Indiana University Press.

McClung, Bruce D. 2007. *Lady in the Dark: Biography of a Musical.* New York: Oxford University Press.

McCoy, Lauren. 2014. "Literary Gossip and the Roman à Clef." *Eighteenth-Century Fiction* 27, no. 1: 127–50.

McCune, Jeffrey Q., Jr. 2004. "Transformance: Reading the Gospel in Drag." In *The Drag Queen Anthology: The Absolutely Fabulous but Flawlessly Customary World of Female Impersonators*, edited by Lisa Underwood, 151–67. New York: Taylor and Francis.

McLendon, Winzola. 1966. "Behind the Glamor of Show Business." *Washington Post*, February 22: B5.

Medhurst, Andy. 2013. "Batman, Deviance, and Camp." In *The Superhero Reader*, edited by Charles Hatfield, Jeet Heer, and Kent Worcester, 237–51. Jackson: University Press of Mississippi.

Meehan, Thomas. 1965. "Not Good Taste, Not Bad Taste—It's 'Camp.'" *New York Times Sunday Magazine*, March 21: 30, 113–14.

———. 1967. "Portrait of a Babe." *Saturday Evening Post*, March 25: 22.

Meltzer, Marisa. 2016. "'Valley of the Dolls,' Pitched to a New Generation." *New York Times* (online), March 12. www.nytimes.com/2016/03/13/fashion/valley-of-the-dolls-jacqueline-susann-lena-dunham.html.

Mercer, Kobena. 1993. "Looking for Trouble." In Abelove, Barale, and Halperin, 350–59.

Meyer, Richard. 1993. "Robert Mapplethorpe and the Discipline of Photography." In Abelove, Barale, and Halperin, 360–80.

Meyers, Helene. 2011. *Identity Papers: Contemporary Narratives of American Jewishness.* Albany: State University of New York Press.

Miller, Quinlan. 2019. *Camp TV: Trans Gender Queer.* Durham, NC: Duke University Press.

Millstein, Gilbert. 1958. "Books of the Times." *New York Times,* September 9: 33.

Minx, Paul. 2018. See How Beautiful I Am. Final Bush script. Unpublished manuscript, December 17.

Mizejewski, Linda. 2014. *Pretty/Funny: Women Comedians and Body Politics.* Austin: University of Texas Press.

———. 2021. "Comedy from the Edge: Carrie Fisher's Autobiographical Writing." In Mizejewski and Zuk, 129-148.

Mizejewski, Linda, and Tanya D. Zuk, eds. *Our Blessed Rebel Queen: Essays on Carrie Fisher.* Detroit: Wayne State University Press.

Moore, Frazier. 2016. "Cue the Music, Cue the Drama! Lee Daniels Introduces 'Star.'" *Precinct Reporter,* December 15: A5.

Morris, Bob. 1992. "Tone Worship." *New York Times,* September 20: 6-7.

Mulvey, Laura. 2000. "Visual Pleasure and Narrative Cinema." In *The Film Studies Reader,* edited by Joanne Hollows, Peter Hutchings, and Mark Jancovich, 238-48. London: Arnold.

Muñoz, José Esteban. 2019. *Cruising Utopia, 10th Anniversary Edition: The Then and There of Queer Futurity.* New York: New York University Press.

Murf. 1971. "The Love Machine." *Variety,* August 4: 18.

Murray, Susan. 2002. "Ethnic Masculinity and Early Television's Vaudeo Star." *Cinema Journal* 42, no. 1: 97-119.

Musto, Michael. 1993. "Old Camp New Camp." *Out,* April/May: 32-39.

Neale, Steve. 1986. "Melodrama and Tears." *Screen,* November/December: 6-22.

Neale, Steve, and Frank Krutnik. 1990. *Popular Film and Television Comedy.* New York: Routledge.

Nero, Charles I. 1991. "Toward a Black Gay Aesthetic: Signifying in Contemporary Black Gay Literature." In *Brother to Brother: New Writings by Black Gay Men,* edited by Essex Hemphill, conceived by Joseph Fairchild Beam, managed by Dorothy Beam, 229-51. Boston: Alyson Publications.

Nizer, Louis. 1980. "He Who Steals My Name." *Saturday Evening Post,* July/August: 26-31.

O'Reilly, Jane. 1973. "Once Is Not Enough." *New York Times,* April 1, Book Review 6.

Paglia, Camille, and Glenn Belverio. 1997. "All Hail the Bitch Goddess!" *Salon*, December 19. Accessed July 2, 2011.

Palmer, Jerry. 1994. *Taking Humour Seriously*. New York: Routledge.

———. 2018. "The Logic of the Absurd." In Marx and Sienkiewicz, 51–54.

Parker, Ian. 1996. "Making Advances." *New Yorker*, April 1. Retrieved September 3, 2018. https://www.newyorker.com/magazine/1996/04/01/making -advances.

Parnes, Uzi. 1985. "Pop Performance in East Village Clubs." *Drama Review* 29, no. 1: 5–16.

Patterson, Andrew James. 2000. "Performative Impulses." In *Lux: A Decade of Artists' Film and Video*, edited by Steve Reinke and Tom Taylor. Toronto: YYZ Books/Pleasure Dome.

Phillips, W. D., and Isabel Pinedo. 2018. "Gilligan and Captain Kirk Have More in Common Than You Think: 1960s Camp TV as an Alternative Genealogy for Cult TV." *Journal of Popular Television* 6, no. 1: 19–40.

Pierson, David. 2005. "American Situation Comedies and the Modern Comedy of Manners." In *The Sitcom Reader*, first edition, edited by Mary M. Dalton and Laura R. Linder, 35–46. Albany: State University of New York Press,.

Pogrebin, Letty Cottin. 1966. "Pill Publicity Gimmick." Letter from Bernard Geis Assoc. to Edwin Harper, Cassell and Co. August 18. Ira Silverberg Papers.

Pokorny, Sydney. 1989. "Confessions of a Lesbo Drag Hag." *OutWeek*, October 29: 52–53. Accessed February 10, 2011. http://www.stardustlanes.com/ oott/.

———. 1996. "Blah, Blah, Blah . . . The Editorial Windbag Page." *Dead Jackie Susann Quarterly* 4. Accessed February 10, 2011. www.stardustlanes.com/ deadjackie/blah4.html.

Pokorny, Sydney, and Liz Tracey. 1992. *Dead Jackie Susann Quarterly* 1. Accessed February 10, 2011. www.stardustlanes.com/deadjackie/djsq1.html.

———. 1993. *Dead Jackie Susann Quarterly* 2. Accessed February 10, 2011. www .stardustlanes.com/deadjackie/djsq93.html.

———. 1995a. "Blah, Blah, Blah—The Editorial Windbag Page." *Dead Jackie Susann Quarterly* 3. Accessed February 10, 2011. www.stardustlanes.com/ deadjackie/blah.html.

———. 1995b. "Dead or Dead Jackie." *Dead Jackie Susann Quarterly* 3. Accessed February 10, 2011. www.stardustlanes.com/deadjackie/dordj.html.

Preston, Don. 1969. "The Love Machine." *New York Times Book Review*, June 15: 39.

Pugh, Tison. 2014. *Truman Capote*. Athens: University of Georgia Press. ProQuest EBooks.

Quinn, Sally. 1970. "Rex Reed, Writing Scourge of the Famous." *Boston Globe*, July 1: 18–19.

Radner, Hilary. 1999. "Introduction: Queering the Girl." In *Swinging Single: Representing Sexuality in the 1960s*, edited by Hilary Radner and Moya Luckett, 1–35. Minneapolis: University of Minnesota Press.

Rebello, Stephen. 2020. *Dolls! Dolls! Dolls! Deep Inside Valley of the Dolls, the Most Beloved Bad Book and Movie of All Time*. New York: Penguin.

Reed, Rex. 1966. "Girls in the Publishing Business." *Cosmopolitan*, November: 96–100.

———. 1974. *People Are Crazy Here*. New York: Delacorte Press.

Reign, Eva. 2018. "Miss Lawrence Won't Change for Anyone—He's a STAR." *Them*, September 27. www.them.us/story/miss-lawrence-star.

Resnik, Muriel. 1971. "People Are Talking About: Movies; How to Love That Machine." *Vogue*, October 1: 178, 179.

Rich, B. Ruby. 1992. "The New Queer Cinema." *Sight and Sound*, September: 30–34.

———. 1994. "Goings and Comings." *Sight and Sound*, July: 14–16.

Richmond, Ray. 1998. *Variety*, December 9: n.p. Ira Silverberg Papers.

Robbins, Harold. 1961. *The Carpetbaggers*. New York: Simon and Schuster.

Robins, Cynthia. 1995. "Best Stuff, Best City." *San Francisco Examiner*, December 31: n.p. Ira Silverberg Papers.

Román, David. 1993. "'It's My Party and I'll Die if I Want To!': Gay Men, AIDS, and the Circulation of Camp in U.S. Theater." In *Camp Grounds: Style and Homosexuality*, edited by David Bergman, 206–33. Amherst: University of Massachusetts Press.

Romanska, Magda, and Alan Ackerman, eds. 2016. *Reader in Comedy*. New York: Bloomsbury.

Rosenberg, Bernard. 1971. "Mass Culture Revisited." In *Mass Culture Revisited*, edited by Bernard Rosenberg and David Manning White, 3–21. New York: Van Nostrand Reinhold.

Roshan, Maer. 2015. "At 92, Liz Smith Reveals How Rupert Murdoch Fired Her, What It Felt Like to Be Outed." April 8. www.hollywoodreporter.com/news/general-news/at-92-liz-smith-reveals-787004/.

Ross, Andrew. 1989. *No Respect: Intellectuals and Popular Culture*. New York: Routledge.

Rowe, Kathryn. 1995. *The Unruly Woman*. Austin: University of Texas Press.

Rudnick, Paul. 1998. *Isn't She Great*. Unpublished screenplay. Additional Papers of Barbara Seaman.

Rudnick, Paul, and Kurt Anderson. 1989. "The Irony Epidemic." *Spy*, March: 93–98.

Runyon, Damon. 1944. *A Damon Runyon Omnibus*. Project Gutenberg Australia, https://gutenberg.net.au/ebooks11/1100651h.html. Accessed September 30, 2018.

Ryan, Maureen. 2016. "TV Review: Star." Variety.com. December 14.

Salem, Jon. 1996. Letter to *Dead Jackie Susann Quarterly*, August 20. Additional Papers of Barbara Seaman.

———. 1998. Letter to Barbara Seaman. July 3. Additional Papers of Barbara Seaman.

Sampey, Kathleen. "It's Hard to Get Beyond 'Valley of the Dolls.'" AdFreak, June 14, 2006. February 11, 2011. http://adweek.blogs.com/adfreak/2006/06/you_dont_have_t.html.

San Filippo, Maria. 2013. *The B Word: Bisexuality in Contemporary Film and Television*. Bloomington: Indiana University Press.

Sarris, Andrew. 1993. Foreword to *Screening the Sexes: Homosexuality in the Movies* by Tyler Parker, ix–xiv. New York: Da Capo.

Schmidt, Randy L., ed. 2014. *Judy Garland on Judy Garland*. Chicago: Chicago Review Press.

Schulman, Sarah. 1994. *My American History*. New York: Routledge.

———. 2003. *Interview with Michelangelo Signorile*. ACT UP Oral History Project. Accessed June 30, 2011. https://actuporalhistory.org/numerical-interviews/029-michelangelo-signorile.

Seaman, Barbara. 1984. Kathy Brody [*sic*] on Carol Bjorkman. Additional Papers of Barbara Seaman.

———. 1985. Interview with Barbara Parkins. Additional Papers of Barbara Seaman.

———. 1996a. Fax to Dan Simon. February 25. Additional Papers of Barbara Seaman.

———. 1996b. Fax to Dan Simon. February 26. Additional Papers of Barbara Seaman.

———. 1996c. *Lovely Me: The Life of Jacqueline Susann*. New York: Seven Stories Press.

———. 1997. Letter to Liz Smith. January 12. Additional Papers of Barbara Seaman.

———. 1998. Letter to Fifi Oscard. September 14. Additional Papers of Barbara Seaman.

———. 2000. Email to liz@gate.net. July 17. Additional Papers of Barbara Seaman.

Sedgwick, Eve Kosofsky. 1990. *Epistemology of the Closet*. Berkeley: University of California Press.

Shurlock, Geoffrey. 1967a. Letter to Frank Ferguson. February 16. Mark Robson Papers.

———. 1967b. Letter to Frank Ferguson. February 23. Mark Robson Papers.

Siegel, Larry (writer) and Mort Drucker (artist). 1968. "Valley of the Dollars." *MAD*, September: 4–9.

Signorile, Michelangelo. 1994. *Queer in America*. New York: Anchor.

Sikov, Ed. 1996. *Laughing Hysterically*. New York. Columbia University Press.

Smith, Liz. 1969. "The Boy in the Penthouse Next Door." *Washington Post*, May 25: 4.

———. 1995. "Midler as Susann? Poifict!" *Los Angeles Times*, September 21: F2.

———. 1998. "Salute to Susann." *New York Post*, November 30: NP. John Epperson Collection.

Smith, Patricia Juliana, ed. 1999. *The Queer Sixties*. New York: Routledge.

Smith-Shomade, Beretta E., ed. 2013. *Watching While Black: Centering the Television of Black Audiences*. New Brunswick, NJ: Rutgers University Press.

Smyth, Cherry. 1992. "Trash Femme Cocktail." *Sight and Sound*, September: 39.

Soloski, Alexis. 2008. "Theater." *Village Voice*, August 20–26: 38.

Sontag, Susan. 1966. *Against Interpretation and Other Essays*. New York: Farrar, Straus and Giroux.

Spacks, Patricia Meyer. 1985. *Gossip*. New York: Knopf.

Spigel, Lynn. 2008. *TV by Design: Modern Art and the Rise of Network Television*. Chicago: University of Chicago Press.

Stacey, Jackie. 1987. "Desperately Seeking Difference." *Screen*, January: 48–61.

Staiger, Janet. 1992. *Interpreting Films*. Princeton, NJ: Princeton University Press.

———. 2000. *Perverse Spectators: The Practices of Film Reception*. New York: New York University Press.

———. 2010. "*Les Belles Dames sans Merci*, Femmes Fatales, Vampires, Vamps, and Gold Diggers: The Transformation and Narrative Value of Aggressive Fallen Women." In *Reclaiming the Archive: Feminism and Film History*, edited by Vicki Callahan, 32–57. Detroit: Wayne State University Press.

Steinem, Gloria. 1965. "The Ins and Outs of Pop Culture." *Life*, August 20: 73, 76, 79–89.

———. 1966. "A Massive Overdose." *New York Herald Tribune Book Week*, April 24: 11.

Stern, Jane, and Michael Stern. 1992. *Jane and Michael Stern's Encyclopedia of Pop Culture*. New York: HarperPerennial.

Stillinger, Jack. 1991. *Multiple Authorship and the Myth of Solitary Genius*. New York: Oxford University Press.

Stuart, Sandra Lee, and John Prince. 1993. *The Pink Palace Revisited: Behind the Doors at the Beverly Hills Hotel*. Fort Lee, NJ: Barricade Books.

Stuever, Hank. 2001. "The Feel-Good Story of the Summer." *Washington Post*, June 26: C1–C2.

Stumbo, Bella. 1972. "Kate Millett Speaks Out: Giving Us Some of Her Lib." *Los Angeles Times*, May 8: F1, F8–9.

Susann, Jacqueline. 1976. *Dolores*. New York: William Morrow.

———. 1979. *Yargo*. New York: Bantam Books.

———. 1997a. *The Love Machine*. New York: Grove.

———. 1997b. *Once Is Not Enough*. New York: Grove.

———. 1997c. *Valley of the Dolls*. New York: Grove.

———. 2004. *Every Night, Josephine!*. New York: Penguin.

———. 2016. *Valley of the Dolls*. New York: Grove.

Szuberla, Guy. 1993. "Damon Runyon at the Movies." *Literature Film Quarterly* 21, no. 1: 71–79.

Taylor, Markland. 2003. "Paper Doll." *Variety*, March 24–March 30: 34–35.

Taylor, Paul. 2001. "The Five Best Plays in London." *The Independent*, October 6–12: n.p.

Thompson, Ethan. 2011. *Parody and Taste in Postwar American Television Culture*. New York: Routledge.

Tinkcom, Matthew. 1999. "Scandalous! Kenneth Anger and the Prohibitions of Hollywood History." In *Out Takes: Essays on Queer Theory and Film*, edited by Ellis Hanson, 271–87. Durham, NC: Duke University Press.

———. 2002. *Working Like a Homosexual: Camp, Capital, Cinema*. Durham, NC: Duke University Press.

Topel, Fred. 2016. "Lee Daniels on How *Star* Began as Valley of the Dolls." *Rotten Tomatoes*, December 13. https://editorial.rottentomatoes.com/author/fred-topel/. March 23, 2018.

Torres, Sasha. 1999. "'The Caped Crusader of Camp': Camp, Pop, and the *Batman* Television Series." In Cleto 330–43.

Tracey, Liz, and Sydney Pokorny. 1990. "Out on the Town with Liz and Sydney." *OutWeek* September 19: 48, 55.

———. 1996. *So You Want to Be a Lesbian?* New York: St. Martin's Griffin.

Trask, Michael. 2013. *Camp Sites: Sex, Politics, and Academic Style in Postwar America*. Stanford, CA: Stanford University Press.

Trinidad, David. 1997. "The Big Valley." The Other Jackie. October 21. Additional Papers of Barbara Seaman.

Vallittu, Marjo. 2018. "Context in Film Adaptations." In *Reading Today*, edited by Arnoldo Hax and Lionel Olavarría. London: UCL Press.

Vatter, Walter. 1997. Fax to Ira Silverberg. October 7. Ira Silverberg Papers.

Velde, Paul. 1966. "The Sontag Sensibility." *Commonweal*, June 24: 390–92.

Villarreal, Yvonne. 2016. "'Star' Connections: Lee Daniels Hits Chord with Queen Latifah." *Los Angeles Times*, December 14: E1.

Vils, Ursuala. 1967. "Success Spoils Her Routine." *Los Angeles Times*, April 30: 10.

Walters, Barbara. 1971. "How to Talk to Difficult People." *Cosmopolitan*, March, 118–26.

Warga, Wayne. 1969 "Author of Genre Novel: A Beautiful Person Looks at Beautiful People." *Los Angeles Times*, July 22: C1, C11.

Watkins, Mel. 1968. "In the Ghettos." *New York Times Book Review*, February 25: A24.

Weinraub, Bernard. 2000. "For 4 Superstars, Art Is Now Imitating Life." *New York Times*, October 12: E1, E5.

Weinstock, Matt. 1969. "It's Hard to Take Rock That Early." *Los Angeles Times*, June 9: E4.

Weiss, Andrea. 1991. "'A Queer Feeling When I Look at You': Hollywood Stars and Lesbian Spectatorship in the 1930s." In *Stardom*, edited by Christine Gledhill, 283–99. London: Routledge.

Werba, Hank. 1967. "Sexy Novel Tops the Magellan Bit: 'Dolls' Rolls Home." *Variety*, November 29: 5.

Werts, Diane. 1998. "'Scandalous' Susann." *Newsday*, December 9: B31. John Epperson Collection.

Whelehan, Imelda. 2005. *The Feminist Bestseller: From Sex and the Single Girl to Sex and the City*. New York: Palgrave Macmillan.

White, Patricia. 1991. "Female Spectator, Lesbian Specter: *The Haunting*." In *Inside/Out: Lesbian Theories, Gay Theories*, edited by Diana Fuss, 142–72. New York: Routledge.

Wilson, Andrew. 2007. *Harold Robbins: The Man Who Invented Sex*. New York: Bloomsbury.

Wojcik, Pamela Robertson. 1996. *Guilty Pleasures: Feminist Camp from Mae West to Madonna*. Durham, NC: Duke University Press.

———. 2010. *The Apartment Plot: Urban Living in American Film and Popular Culture, 1945 to 1975*. Durham, NC: Duke University Press.

Wolff, Janet L. 1958. *What Makes Women Buy: A Guide to Understanding and Influencing the New Woman of Today*. New York: McGraw Hill.

Wright, Joshua K. 2018. *Empire and Black Images in Popular Culture*. Jefferson, NC: McFarland.

Wright, Robert A. 1973. "Broad Spectrum of Writers Attacks Obscenity Ruling." *New York Times*, August 21: 38.

Wyatt, Justin. 1994. *High Concept: Movies and Marketing in Hollywood*. Austin: University of Texas Press.

Yockey, Matt. 2014. *Batman*. Detroit: Wayne State University Press.

Zanuck, Richard. 1967. Memo to Bobbie McLean. October 16. Mark Robson Papers.

Film and Television

Best of Everything, The. 1959. Twentieth Century-Fox. Dir. Jean Negulesco. Starring Hope Lange, Suzy Parker, Diane Baker, Joan Crawford. Fox, 2005.

Bitch, The. 1979. Brent Walker Film. Dir. Gerry O'Hara. Starring Joan Collins, Michael Coby, Sue Lloyd. Kino Lorber, 2017.

Carol Burnett Show, The. 1968. CBS. January 29. Time-Life, 2014.

Charlie Rose. 2000. PBS Network. February 3. Charlie Rose, Inc. 2006.

Comedy Tonight. 1970. CBS. August 16. Paley Center for Media, New York.

David Frost Show, The. 1969. Syndicated. July 16. Paley Center for the Media, New York.

Design for Living. 1933. Paramount. Dir. Ernst Lubitsch. Starring Miriam Hopkins, Gary Cooper, and Fredric March. Criterion, 2011.

Divine Ms. Susann, The. 2006. DVD Special Feature, *Valley of the Dolls*, Fox.

Female Trouble. 1974. Dir. John Waters. Starring Divine, Cookie Mueller, Edith Massey. Criterion, 2018.

Good Afternoon!. 1973. Elaine Grand, host. Thames Television, September 25. YouTube, ThamesTv, May 5, 2018.

Hollywood Backstories: Valley of the Dolls. 2001. In *Valley of the Dolls*, Fox, 2006.

Hollywood Wives. 1985. ABC. February 17–19. Dir. Robert Day. Starring Angie Dickinson, Candice Bergen, Stephanie Powers. Vei, 2015.

Isn't She Great. 2000. Universal Pictures. Dir. Andrew Bergman. Starring Bette Midler, Nathan Lane, Stockard Channing, David Hyde Pierce. Universal Studios, 2000.

Jacqueline Susann and the Valley of the Dolls. 1967. Dir. Alan Foshko. Prod. Sherry W. Arden, David B. Fein. In *Valley of the Dolls*, Fox, 2006.

Jacqueline Susann: The Writing Machine. 2000. *Biography*. A&E Network, January 18. YouTube, Mustafa Torphy, December 16, 2017.

Lady in the Dark. 1954. Dir. Max Liebman. Starring Anne Southern, Carleton Carpenter, Luella Gear. NBC, September 24. Video Artists International, 2016.

Long John Nebel Show, The. 1966. WMCA-AM. December 18. Paley Center for the Media, New York.

Love, American Style. 1973. ABC. November 30.

Love Machine, The. 1971. Columbia Pictures. Dir. Jack Haley Jr. Starring John Phillip Law, Dyan Cannon, David Hemmings, Maureen Arthur, Jodi Wexler. Sony, 2011.

Lypsinka's Ballet of the Dolls (Excerpts). 1985. Dir. Andy Rees. Pyramid Club. Starring John Epperson, John Kelly, Michael Berube, Meryl Goodfader, Stephen Pell, Mark Oates, Dan Taylor, Marleen Menard, Joey Smith, Billy Basinski. YouTube, TheLypsinkaı, April 26, 2012.

Man Who Came to Dinner, The. 1942. Warner Bros. Dir. William Keighley. Starring Bette Davis, Monty Woolley, Mary Wickes. Warner Bros., 2006.

Once Is Not Enough. 1975. Paramount. Dir. Guy Green. Starring Kirk Douglas, Melina Mercouri, Brenda Vaccaro. Olive Films, 2011.

Peyton Place. 1957. Twentieth Century-Fox. Dir. Mark Robson. Starring Lana Turner, Hope Lange, Diane Varsi, Russ Tamblyn. Fox, 2004.

Postcards from the Edge. 1990. Columbia Pictures. Dir. Mike Nichols. Starring Meryl Streep, Shirley MacLaine, Mary Wickes. Columbia Pictures, 2017.

Rowan & Martin's Laugh-In. 1969. NBC. December 8. Time Life, 2018.

Rowan & Martin's Laugh-In. 1971. NBC. February 15. Time Life, 2018.

Rowan & Martin's Laugh-In. 1971. NBC. October 4. Time Life, 2018.

Scandalous Me: The Jacqueline Susann Story. 1998. Dir. Bruce McDonald. Teleplay by Michele Gallery. Starring Michele Lee, Peter Riegert, Barbara Parkins, James Farentino, Sherry Miller, Kenneth Welsh. USA Network, December 9. Paley Center for the Media. New York.

See How Beautiful I Am. 2001. Playwright Paul Minx. Dir. Sarah Esdaile. Starring Debora Weston. Video excerpt of live performance, October 5, 2001, Bush Theatre, London. Robert Silman, Tambar Arts.

Sex and the Single Girl. 1964. Warner Bros. Dir. Richard Quine. Starring Natalie Wood, Lauren Bacall, Tony Curtis, Henry Fonda. Warner Home Video, 2009.

Star. 2017. Fox. February 8. Twentieth Century Fox, 2018.

Star. 2017. Fox. February 15. Twentieth Century Fox, 2018.

Star. 2017. Fox. February 22. Twentieth Century Fox, 2018.

Stud, The. 1978. Brent Walker Film. Dir. Quentin Masters. Starring Joan Collins, Oliver Tobias, Sue Lloyd. Kino Lorber, 2017.

Taking Back the Dolls. 1994. Dir. Leslie Singer. Starring Leslie Singer, Valerie Soe, Cecilia Dougherty. Outfest Collection, Archive Research and Study Center, University of California, Los Angeles.

These Old Broads. 2001. Dir. Matthew Diamond. Starring Debbie Reynolds, Shirley MacLaine, Joan Collins, Elizabeth Taylor. Sony Pictures, 2009.

Tonight Show, The. 1973. NBC. May 2. Paley Center for the Media, Beverly Hills, CA.

Valley of the Dolls. 1967. Twentieth Century-Fox. Dir. Mark Robson. Starring Barbara Parkins, Patty Duke, Sharon Tate, Susan Hayward, and Jacqueline Susann. Fox, 2006.

Index

Pucci, 1, 140, 147, 191, 192, 218
Pyramid Club, 33, 161, 169, 170

Queen Latifah (Dana Elaine Owens), 36,
    228, 231, 232, 235, 236, 237
queer irony, 239–40. See also *Love
    Machine, The*

Radziwill, Lee, 151, 256n14
Razor's Edge, The, 41
Real Housewives of Atlanta, The, 220,
    230–31
Rebello, Stephen, 246n5, 250n34
Reed, Rex, 12, 17, 101, 154, 218, 248n19,
    262n30; camp appreciation for
    Susann, 126, 141, 143–44, 241; and
    Scandalous Me, 201, 202–3, 210; and
    Susann revival, 163, 182. *See also*
    comedy of bad manners
religion. *See* humor: Jewish; *Love Machine,
    The*: and Jewishness; *Once Is Not
    Enough*: and Susann's Jewishness;
    Star; Susann, Jacqueline: Jewish
    identity of; transformance
Resnik, Muriel, 113, 117, 119–20
Reynolds, Debbie: fictionalized in Fisher's
    screenplays, 35, 221, 222, 223, 225;
    self-parodic, 225; in *These Old Broads*,
    221–24, 227
Rich, B. Ruby, 174
Ridiculous Theatrical Company, 158
Riggs, Marlon, 228
Rivers, Joan, 219
Robbins, Harold, 2, 31, 39, 42, 49–50, 69;
    compared to Susann, 121, 127, 247n15;
    as lower-middle taste, 248n19. See
    also *Carpetbaggers, The*
Robson, Mark, 70, 72, 73, 77, 79, 131
roman à clef, 2, 4, 15, 215–16, 239, 244n11,
    246n4; and camp sensibility, 18–19,
    29–30, 121, 124–26, 127, 140, 157–58,
    162, 164, 182, 216; and celebrity
    scandal, 19, 31, 188; and closet
    comedy, 11–12, 24, 27, 29, 69–70,
    91–92, 143, 146, 254n17; and comedy
    of bad manners, 5–6, 11, 19, 20, 24–27;
    and duplicity, 15; feminist history
    of, 19; and Fisher's work, 35, 221–22;
    gossip and confession in, 9, 18–19,
    50, 72, 143, 190; guessing game, 16–17,
    19, 23, 26, 92, 133, 143, 215; and *Lady

in the Dark, 93; as low culture, 15,
    19, 127–28, 189; and masquerade,
    15; and parody, 33, 129, 132, 156, 157,
    215; queer authorship, 19, 20, 69–70,
    135–36; and sleazy realism, 4, 11; and
    voyeuristic gossip, 31, 49–50. *See also*
    Capote, Truman; Collins, Jackie;
    Jaffe, Rona; Judson, Barbara; Latham,
    Sean; McCoy, Lauren; Preston, Don;
    Robbins, Harold; Susann, Jacqueline
Rose, Billy, 48, 93, 251n2
Rowan & Martin's Laugh-In: and 1960s
    sexual culture, 144–45, 146–47,
    148–49; aging women, 147–48; as
    camp, 145, 146, 147, 148; Capote's
    appearance, 126, 137–39; demeaning
    Susann's authorship, 17–18, 149; gay
    liberation jokes, 137; gay men, 146,
    148; highbrow perspective, 137–38;
    pretty/funny, 147–48; sexually
    active women, 144–45, 146, 148–49;
    Susann referenced on, 1; Susann's
    appearances, 144–49; Susann's self-
    parody, 145, 147, 148
Royal Family, The, 13
Runyon, Damon, 15, 35, 45–46, 48, 206–7,
    246n7
RuPaul: and camp, 169, 171; and *The
    RuPaul Show*, 182
RuPaul's Drag Race, 8, 235, 258n9

*Scandalous Me: The Jacqueline Susann
    Story*, 8, 34–35, 182, 188, 190, 191,
    198–204, 205, 206, 210, 212–13. See
    also *Lovely Me*; star biography
Schiffli Lace, 13
School for Scandal, 21
Schulman, Sarah, 169, 259n18
Scott, Amiyah, 36, 228
Seaman, Barbara: affection for Susann,
    165; AIDS, 181; drag, 162, 181–82;
    feminism, 203, 204; gay readership
    observed, 162, 168, 181–82;
    overlooking lesbian fans, 163, 169;
    participation in Susann revival, 163.
    See also *Lovely Me*
See How Beautiful I Am, 8, 34–35, 188, 190,
    192–95, 197, 203, 205, 210–11, 213, 242,
    263n4, 264n12. *See also* star biography
Sex and the City: novel, 218; TV series, 216
Sex and the Single Girl (film), 70

CPSIA information can be obtained
at www.ICGtesting.com
Printed in the USA
LVHW020349290423
745604LV00001B/48

9 780814 346044